CULTIVATING DIFFER

Cultivating Differences

SYMBOLIC BOUNDARIES

Differences

AND THE MAKING

OF INEQUALITY

EDITED BY

Michèle Lamont and
Marcel Fournier

THE UNIVERSITY OF CHICAGO PRESS
CHICAGO AND LONDON

The University of Chicago Press, Chicago 60637
The University of Chicago Press, Ltd., London
© 1992 by The University of Chicago
All rights reserved. Published 1992
Printed in the United States of America

01 00 99 98 97 96 95   5 4 3 2

ISBN (cloth): 0-226-46813-5
ISBN (paper): 0-226-46814-3

Library of Congress Cataloging-in-Publication Data

Cultivating differences : symbolic boundaries and the making of
  inequality / edited by Michèle Lamont and Marcel Fournier.
      p.   cm.
    Includes bibliographical references and index.
    1. Culture.   2. Social structure.   3. Equality.   4. Social status.
  5. Symbolic interactionism.   I. Lamont, Michèle, 1957–
  II. Fournier, Marcel, 1945–
  HM101.C83   1992
  305—dc20   92-15204
                                                    CIP

Excerpts in Chapter 9 are from Randall Collins, "Women and Men
in the Class Structure," *Journal of Family Issues* 9 (1988): 27–50.
Reprinted with permission from Sage Publications, Inc. Excerpts
in Chapter 10 are from Cynthia Fuchs Epstein, "Workplace
Boundaries: Conceptions and Creations," *Social Research* 56,
no. 3 (1989). Reprinted with permission from *Social Research*.

CONTENTS

PREFACE

Herbert J. Gans

I

This is a book about culture, class, gender, and boundaries, four complicated concepts that social scientists and humanists use to try to understand even more complicated social arrangements. A single preface cannot pretend to summarize a very broad book, but at least I can write a little about what I learned from it and how I was stimulated by it. A preface writer is, among other things, an initial stand-in for the readers of a book, and if I am at all representative of later readers, I can promise that they will come away from *Cultivating Differences* with a great deal of learning and stimulation.[1]

Several disciplines use *culture* as a basic concept, and of course they mean different things by the same word. I shall not review these conceptual differences; suffice it to say that many American sociologists currently favor Ann Swidler's notion of culture as a kit of tools and action strategies for coping with social life. Swidler's tool-kit metaphor is graphic and useful, for it tells us at once that different people have access to tool kits of different costs and completeness.

This is only to state in another way what I consider to be one basic theme of this book: that culture is shaped above all by class and thus particularly by economic and related inequalities. True, culture is also shaped by gender, among other things, but as a late section of the book reminds us, gender is itself fundamentally affected by class. While working-class women may have their differences with working-class men, they also have sharp differences with upper-middle-class women. The feminist movement, like the civil rights movement and other political movements, has suffered from the inability to understand how much gender, race, and other statuses are influenced, and split, by class.

II

In this book, *culture* is used mainly in two ways. A number of authors write first about the media and popular culture, that is, what the tool kit provides for entertainment or diversion, and second about culture in its translation from the German *Kultur,* that is, what the tool kit offers for intellectual-aesthetic experience. In past generations, European intellectuals, mainly of the Right but also of the Left, complained about the culture of the masses, decrying what they conceived to be the mass desire for entertainment rather than intellectual-aesthetic experience. Rightly or wrongly, they assumed that, as intellectuals, they sought mainly the latter and shunned the former while for the masses it was the other way around. Intellectuals of the Left thought that the masses could be mobilized to give up entertainment for more intellectual-aesthetic experience—and during the same process in which they would be converted to socialism. Conversely, intellectuals of the Right believed that the masses were too stupid and vulgar to give up mass culture.

In America, this debate was reframed as the choice between high culture and popular culture, with some taking up the European argument that everyone should really be choosing high culture. However, others, myself included, argued that it was unfair to expect workers to behave like upper-middle-class professionals as long as they could not obtain access to the time, money, learning, and other opportunities of the professional strata. Besides, in an individualistic society, people have the right to the culture of their choice, provided that choice cannot be proved to harm anyone.

This debate eventually ended, at least for the present, sometime during the late 1970s or early 1980s, in part because of the inability of the two "sides" to say anything new. However, at about that time, the distinction between high and popular culture also became fuzzy. A new generation of professionals, managers, and technicians appeared who decided that they did not have to imitate the tastes of their elders and that they could be, to use a current phrase in a different sense, multicultural. That is, people could choose from both popular and high culture, from museum and poster art, from classical music and jazz and rock—and without any loss of cultural or social status. This produced theoretical and empirical analyses—which also appear in this book—indicating that the old differences between high and popular culture had been considerably reduced. Some even claimed—but no one in this book—that these differences had disappeared completely and that

America appeared to be developing a single, unbounded, although internally variegated culture that served both for diversion and for intellectual-aesthetic experience.

Some of the people making this argument were extrapolating from empirical findings about changes in cultural choices, which reflected changing tastes, alterations in the American class structure, and related revisions in the boundaries of popular and high culture. Other writers, notably conservatives, were, however, using what they viewed as the end of the popular culture–high culture distinction to claim that class and class differences were disappearing in America. Conservatives have always been very good at making empirical sounding ideological statements, but class differences remain in American culture, however *culture* is defined. Moreover, economic and political class differences became more pronounced again during the government-sponsored increases in income and wealth inequality of the 1980s and early 1990s, although the cultural consequences of the new rise in inequalities remain to be studied.

Some illustration of how changing tastes affect the conception of popular and high culture is provided by Peterson and Simkus, whose data on class and country music indicate that such music is no longer solely the preserve of rural and small-town low-income people. They also provide some suggestive evidence that, when class positions are assigned to taste levels, it is the class position of the audience, not the cultural qualities of the music, that determines the assignment—which says in yet another way that class shapes culture. To be sure, this is not quite the same for all culture, and it is probably less true of intellectual-aesthetic culture than it is of entertainment. For example, fiction is in some respects more diversified than country music, and the novels of Philip Roth are more complicated than those of popular writers like Sidney Sheldon.

By the criterion of complexity, Roth is "higher" than Sheldon, although the choice of the complexity criterion, generally offered by the supporters of high culture, is not coincidental. Ability to deal with literary complexity correlates with years of schooling and thus with class. However, class-correlated complexity levels are less relevant in determining who prefers what kinds of country music. (And what would sociologists say about taste and class in a society in which the educated strata choose Sheldon and country music while the uneducated prefer Roth and chamber music?)

While it is true that some old low-, middle-, and highbrow boundaries have fallen or been crossed, yet others remain, and will do so as long as there are differences of class, gender, race, and taste preferences that reflect them. For example, despite their frequent, albeit superficial efforts, art museums have not yet been able to attract lower-middle- and working-class audiences to come to see museum art.

III

I found this book particularly useful for thinking more about the differences between culture as entertainment and culture as intellectual-aesthetic experience. Although empirical social research has not often emphasized these differences, it is likely that some people's entertainment is others' intellectual-aesthetic experience, and vice versa. One problem has been a scholarly class bias, for scholars, especially in the humanities, have been writing about "our" intellectual-aesthetic culture and "their" entertainment. Sociologists have also been touched by this bias, and as a result they have not paid enough empirical attention to how highbrows entertain themselves or where lower-income groups get their intellectual-aesthetic culture. Nor have the similarities and differences between entertainment and intellectual-aesthetic experience, for all classes, been explored sufficiently.

The differences among these kinds of culture also complicate the general relation between culture and class, and this book provides considerable evidence that the relationship is hardly direct. The upper classes, whether defined by money or prestige, pay some of the bills for high culture (and use their class power to get governments to pay the rest), but they do not constitute a loyal audience for it. Their cultural preferences seem to be more for middlebrow cultures, whether for entertainment or intellectual-aesthetic experience. In a telling analysis, David Halle shows us that, although the working class tends to buy landscape paintings while the upper classes choose abstract art, the latter often see landscapes in the abstractions that they acquire. Thus, it appears that, literally or figuratively, just about everyone winds up with landscapes on their walls. Moreover, the upper classes seem to choose the same movies and television programs as other people for their electronic entertainment, although they may still do their boating on yachts while those of more moderate income opt for motorboats or go rowing.

In any case, high culture is the culture, not of the upper class, but of a professional stratum that earns its living by creating, distributing, analyzing, and criticizing the various works identified as high culture as well as of a small but loyal set of cultural amateurs, many of them in related professions, who add to the total high culture audience. Although they are amateurs, the latter view culture as if they were themselves professional cultural creators or critics, which may be why they are called *cultured* or *cultivated*. In this respect, they differ radically from other audiences of high culture—and of popular culture—who want to be treated and satisfied as audiences and do not care much about the intellectual-aesthetic questions with which creators grapple in their work. (I called the former *creator oriented* and the latter *audience oriented* in my *Popular Culture and High Culture*,[2] and I still think the distinction is useful.) The professional high culture audience is in some ways the successor of that group of people who, as Paul DiMaggio has reported,[3] were imported from Europe in the late nineteenth century by the Boston Brahmins to bring high culture to Boston and a new source of prestige to the Brahmins.

Although the study of high culture *institutions* is now getting under way in America, we still know very little about the *persons* who make these institutions function. We have not yet studied the social sources and inspirations of their intellectual-aesthetic directions or how and why they make the creative and other decisions they do. The news media cover only the fights they sometimes get into with boards of trustees, with the marketers who help concert halls and museums maximize audience size, and lately with the federal government. We also need to study the private cultural lives of this professional stratum. Presumably, they get their intellectual-aesthetic culture from their work, and perhaps their entertainment too, although, typically, we have not asked what they do for diversion—or even whether they practice what they preach about the virtues of high culture. (Similar questions could be asked about the professionals who create popular culture, in New York, Hollywood, and elsewhere, but that too will have to wait until sociologists of the professions develop a greater interest in the sociology of culture.)

Last, but perhaps not least, there is the relation between culture and prestige. Earlier in this century, the existence of people who chose their culture for reasons of prestige, that is, who went to the opera to be seen and went to sleep when the performance started, were a common subject of discussion and of criticism. This may have been an upper-class pattern only, or a highbrow stereotype of rich middlebrows, but while we know that the search and competition for prestige is not dead, we do not know much about how, where, and among whom it takes place today, in the lower as well as the higher classes.

Ordinary Americans consume more and more of their entertainment and intellectual-aesthetic culture inside the home, but presumably the furnishing of the house, the pictures on the walls, and, in the more educated classes, the books on the coffee table are still used to impress relatives, friends, neighbors, and other visitors. And we know even less about whether and how the poor, who do not have much money to spend on impressing anyone, use culture to obtain and compete for prestige. But then we remain ignorant about people's current prestige-seeking strategies in general. Furthermore, while we know that peer pressure, reference groups, and word of mouth still influence cultural choice, we do not know which peers, reference groups, and mouths are considered by different classes when choosing among the various kinds of culture.

The connections between culture and prestige are relevant, not only among consumers or audiences, but also among professionals, in part because there are taste-related status distinctions among kinds of cultural work. Creators of high culture still appear to have more status than those of popular culture, even though the latter are far more affluent. However, similar comparisons can be made in a variety of cultural fields. The equivalents of high culture and popular culture exist in architecture, in part because of its connection to art, but they can also be found in sociology.

Professional sociologists feel that they do better and more prestigious work than pop sociologists, and within professional sociology academics continue to look down their noses at market and applied researchers. Within the academy, the people who "do theory" are often accorded more prestige than those who carry out empirical studies and especially than those who write textbooks. To some extent the ranking is related to the perceived complexity of the cultural product, but it also has to do with the status of the final consumer. As in all professions, those who deal with higher-status clients outrank those who deal with lower-status ones—which is why writers of sociology textbooks for high school students rank low on the professional prestige scale.

IV

This book is also a work about boundaries, and I have already made passing references to cultural boundaries. Like other social arrangements, cultures have boundaries—and before the concept of boundaries became popular, sociologists talked about subcultures as a primitive way of dealing with such boundaries. Cultural *concepts* have boundaries too, or else they would melt into other concepts, and the occupational tool kits of sociologists of culture would be emptier than they are. Conceptual boundaries quickly become evident when sociologists and anthropologists discuss culture, but then social scientists protect their turfs as much as teenagers.

As a refugee from Nazi Germany who got out just in time, I have always had a healthy fear of boundaries. I am especially nervous at officially open borders that are guarded with guns, and I am not even calm at those that are guarded more peacefully. I bring up the distinction between guarded and open boundaries because it is also important for ethnographers, whose fieldwork begins with discovering whether the boundaries of the groups or institutions they want to study are guarded and from whom they must get permission to cross those boundaries. Much can be learned about groups and institutions by looking to see if their boundaries are completely open or guarded and, if the latter, how and why.

Many boundaries, especially guarded and closed ones, exist to protect inequalities and to make sure that the less than equal cannot enter or can do so only by paying proper deference. We still have to look at cultural boundaries to determine whether, when, and how their functions are connected to maintaining inequality.

Most of the cultural institutions discussed in this book are in one way or another commercial, which means that they are guarded mainly to collect monies and keep out people sufficiently unequal economically that they cannot pay the entrance fee. Still, as in many types of institutions, inequality is also measured by degree of purity and impurity. Governments are increasingly interested in promoting official culture, fiercely guarding kinds of moral purity that have influential political constituencies, while museums, which collect and show museum culture, take great pains to keep out what they consider to be impure, or nonmuseum, culture. The most open culture is probably folk culture and its latter-day versions, the noncommercial popular culture that people create—or adapt from commercial culture—for family and community ceremonies.

In its openness and absence of governmental or profit boundaries, folk or noncommercial popular culture is in some ways the cultural equivalent of civil society. Civil society is currently celebrated by social scientists, and rightly so, although some of the civil societies that emerged at the end of the 1980s in most Eastern European countries are at this writing turning into upper-middle-class political parties or cliques with too little interest in their economically less fortunate fellows.

xiv   Herbert J. Gans

Folk culture is also celebrated, especially when the folk have given it up and it is about to become museum culture, but noncommercial popular culture does not yet seem to have any intellectual celebrants.

One of the most significant distinctions among boundaries is between visible and invisible ones, for the latter are sometimes harder to cross than visible ones, as blacks trying to buy houses in the suburbs and scholars with working-class accents applying for faculty positions at "elite" universities know well. Prestigious organizations try especially to keep their boundaries invisible since it would be gauche if they were not. This is one reason why working-class visitors to museums are so often uncomfortable.

In an age of democracy and universalism, boundaries are made to be crossed, but as Alan Wolfe reminds us, there are socially useful groups that cannot survive without closed ones. Useful or not, we also seem to be stuck with in-groups and out-groups, but in a democracy what groups are entitled to closed or open boundaries needs continuous discussion. The current interest in boundaries may produce new insights and data for this discussion as well as for other social concerns.

However, we also need to remember that, in the end, boundaries are useful concepts mainly to the extent that they shed light on the groups and concepts that they bound. Otherwise, boundaries are universals, like time and space, and there are limits to what social researchers can say about them as universals. Moreover, even specific boundaries are finally of lesser importance, for groups and institutions—and the larger social structures—ultimately shape them, not the other way around. If we could do away with class and other kinds of inequalities, boundaries to enforce them might, dare I say it, wither away.

Notes

1. Given the wide variety of approaches to the issues engaged by the contributors to this book, I am representative of only some of the future readers, probably those of a more structural and empirical bent and on this side of the Atlantic Ocean. Conversely, the editors of the book cut a wider swath and in the beginning of their introduction to the volume also represent various symbolic and symbolic interactionist traditions, with special attention to those on the other side of the ocean. Although this division of labor is marvelously apt, it was completely unintended; I wrote my preface before I saw the first two sections of their introduction.

2. Herbert J. Gans, *Popular Culture and High Culture* (New York: Basic, 1974).

3. Paul DiMaggio, "Cultural Entrepreneurship in Nineteenth-Century Boston: The Creation of an Organizational Base for High Culture in America," in *Media, Culture and Society: A Critical Reader,* ed. Richard Collins, James Curran, Nicholas Garnham, Paddy Scannell, Philip Schlesinger, and Colin Sparks (Beverly Hills, Calif.: Sage, 1986).

ACKNOWLEDGMENTS

This volume reflects our recent theoretical wanderings, some of the felicitous affinities we have developed, and intellectual pleasures we have experienced, while working on our respective books *Money, Morals, and Manners* and *Marcel Mauss*. The volume also reveals emerging exchanges, spoken or veiled, between several of the sociologists involved in the project. These essays are offered with the hope of generating lively exchanges, innovative research, and common intellectual endeavors.

Six of the papers included here were written expressly for this volume. While the other papers were prepared for various audiences, they "naturally" complement the original six. One chapter was presented at the Mellon Colloquium Series on Cultural Diversity that was organized at Princeton University in 1990. Two were presented at a session on symbolic boundaries that was held at the International Sociological Association meetings in Madrid in 1990. Two were included in an issue of *Sociologie et Sociétés* that we guest edited in 1990. (One of these articles, that of Randall Collins, builds on a piece published in the *Journal of Family Issues* [vol. 9, 1988]. We thank Sage Publications for permission to reprint passages from this publication.) The remaining chapter has a story too complex to be told.

This project would not have been possible without the help of Doug Mitchell, Craig Gill, and Joseph H. Brown of the University of Chicago Press. Warm thanks go to all the contributors, who delivered their contributions in record time.

—Michèle Lamont and Marcel Fournier

ONE   Introduction

Michèle Lamont and
Marcel Fournier

If there is one fundamental proposition on which sociologists of culture agree, it is that, far from forming a unique society, humanity is made up of social groups that are differentiated by their practices, beliefs, and institutions. As Marcel Mauss wrote in his essay "On Civilization," "The domain of social life is essentially a domain of differences." Between groups and society, there always has been, and always will be, boundaries and differences. Examples are numerous: "Israel detests Moab, who cooks lamb in the milk of its mother, and it is why we still do not eat meat on Fridays. The Touareg feeds himself only from the milk of his she-camel and finds cow milk repulsive just as we find the milk of a mare repulsive. . . . I have not learned how to ski, while my young countrymen in the Vosges enjoy this activity." From this perspective, circumcision is nothing but a tattoo, a "tribal or even national symbol." Whether they create distinctions or interdictions, such symbols are expressions of a group's desire to "concentrate themselves, separate themselves from others."[1] Social scientists disagree on the importance of natural and symbolic factors in determining such boundaries, as illustrated recently by the debates surrounding issues such as sociobiology and essentialist feminist theories. However, one of the most important challenges that we face today is understanding how we create boundaries and what the social consequences of such actions are.

I

Three distinct approaches have been used by sociologists to conceptualize symbolic boundaries and their origins: while some locate them in people's heads or view them as the product of interactions between individuals, others argue that they are imposed by sociopolitical forces.

1

These approaches remind us of three major dimensions of cultural life, namely, the cognitive, communicative, and political dimensions. These three dimensions help us compare theories of symbolic boundaries while relating them to central sociological traditions.

The questions of inclusion and exclusion had such an importance for the École Sociologique Française that certain of its enemies referred to Durkheim and his collaborators as the "totem and taboo" clan. This group of intellectuals was primarily concerned with forms of human solidarity, and they shared a special interest for the study of morality. They have taught us that social groups survive through integration and normative action and that one of the principles of their unity is properly cultural or symbolic in nature. They have also taught us that all social groups delimit and structure their common social life. The best example of this is the distinction that is found in all religions between the sacred and the profane. Not only does this distinction create two spaces, two worlds, but it also imposes very elaborate rituals for the passage from one world to the next.[2]

In *Primitive Classification,* Durkheim and Mauss advanced a daring proposition suggesting a correspondence between classification and social organization: "It was because men were grouped, and thought of themselves in the form of groups, that in their ideas they grouped other things."[3] This proposition has been widely criticized, but the notion of classification has remained central to anthropologists and sociologists of culture and knowledge: human beings name and classify things and people. They create labels through contrast and inclusion.

The members of the École Sociologique Française had two objectives: to shed light on the relations of interdependence existing among various types of social facts and to demonstrate that one of the bases of social solidarity is "the agreement of spirits." Durkheim's last book, *The Elementary Forms of Religious Life* (1912), goes beyond the limits of the sociology of religion to address central issues in the sociology of knowledge. Its topic is collective representations—that is, the notions of time, space, numbers, causes, etc. that are "essential" and "remain at the foundation of the human intelligence."[4] In this book, Durkheim argues that culture is above all a way of knowing.

Whether structuralist or cognitive in orientation, the cultural anthropology of the past thirty years grows out of the tradition of the École Sociologique Française, renewing it methodologically while borrowing from linguistics and psychology. Even if Claude Lévi-Strauss rejected Durkheimian sociologism, he recognized his debt to Mauss, adopting the notion that studying a society essentially means shedding light on symbolic classifications, which are generally organized around binary oppositions.[5] Similarly, recent work in ethnoscience analyzes the organization of popular taxonomies in various domains (botanical, zoological, etc.).[6] Here again, the boundaries that separate groups are viewed as primarily symbolic or cognitive: they are divisions constituted by mental categories opposing various types of properties (high/low, male/female, nature/culture, right/left, and so forth). Finally, when Mary Douglas studies exclusion and pollution, she adopts the Durkheimian distinction of sacred and profane to apply it not just to religious life but to social life in general.[7] She argues that, while classifications play a growing role in the organization of social life, their production is increasingly the responsibility of specialists and professionals who define institutional criteria for labeling individuals as rational or criminal.[8]

The terms *label* and *labeling* immediately remind us of social psychology and, more specifically, of symbolic interactionism, which analyzes not the cognitive tools that people use to constitute for themselves a social identity but the social processes that lead to the constitution of identity. Facing us, we always find "the other" whose eyes and judgments we cannot escape. Particularly since the publication of Howard Becker's *Outsiders* in the early 1960s, we have realized that deviant acts lead to social exclusion only when these acts are socially defined as such.[9] Social life happens in the context of face-to-face interactions and of verbal and nonverbal communication. Erving Goffman has best shown that social life is a form of theatricalization with a front stage and a back stage, masks and makeup. His telling descriptions reveal that the distances or boundaries that separate individuals are never, even in total institutions, purely physical. They are symbolic representations that most often take the form of stigma.[10]

The processes of social integration and exclusion are rarely located exclusively at the level of interindividual exchanges. The macrosociological context, whether political or economic in nature, is also crucial: individuals are located within organizations and institutions, they belong to groups with interests, and they form political forces. Culture is not only a code or a mode of communication: it is also a form of domination, an ideology at the service of the dominant classes, as the Marxists used to say. The structural Marxism of Louis Althusser and Nicos Poutlantzas has qualified an approach that, when applied to culture, was far too simplistic: they stressed the autonomy of the political, ideological, and economic realms and shed light on the role of the ideological state apparatus while conceptualizing the boundaries that

divide individuals, groups, and collectivities as the product of domination and exploitation.[11]

The notion of domination is also central to the multidimensional
Weberian perspective; not only are there classes, but there are also
status groups that compete for the monopolization of resources and
political groups that mobilize themselves to promote the interests of
their members. Between these groups, there are boundaries that are
cultural or symbolic in nature.[12] On the other hand, domination and
authority are efficient only if they are legitimate. Violence is not only
physical. It is also symbolic, as Bourdieu later pointed out.[13]

II

As with all categorizations, the distinction between knowledge, communication, and domination is far too schematic: it distinguishes between approaches that are in reality quite fuzzy and often easily transgressed. We know only too well that, to use Marcel Mauss's words
again, "all oppositions between schools are futile games of the mind
or manifestations of an ongoing competition between professors, philosophies, or theologies. Truly great ethnologists have all been as eclectic in their choice of theoretical problems as they have been in their
choice of method, adapting the latter to the former."[14] Therefore,
boundaries in sociological theory are like boundaries in everyday life:
they are arbitrary even if we are reluctant to acknowledge them as such.
Once this is recognized, our challenge is to displace and transgress such
boundaries and develop a multidimensional conception of culture. As
Wittgenstein wrote, "In the domain of thought, certain important advances are comparable to the displacement of volumes from one book-
stack to the next: displacements are accomplished even if nothing
allows us to think that the new position will be the one that will
remain."[15] In the world of research, only a permanent questioning of
acquired positions can lead to genuine advances.

In the last twenty years, such corrective efforts were first defined in
opposition to an orthodox Marxism that many hoped to redirect or
transcend. For a large number of social scientists, the best way to
demonstrate that domination was not at the center of everything was
to analyze various types of resistance and various subcultures empirically.[16] The work of Jürgen Habermas in Germany, that of the Birmingham school sociologists in England, and the work of Michel Foucault and Pierre Bourdieu in France pushed sociology and anthropology
toward one another. These writings also indirectly brought into ques-

tion the traditional distinctions between macro- and micro-sociologies. Similarly, interpretative and hermeneutic approaches gained a greater following in our field.[17] In the sociology of science, the critique of positivism, on the one hand, and the influence of ethnomethodology, on the other, have brought the discipline toward an increasingly relativistic perspective, as illustrated by the work of Latour and Woolgar or Knorr-Cetina.[18] Instead of studying "social facts as social things," cultural sociologists became increasingly interested in describing various processes of social construction, focusing less on "why" and more on "how" things happen, thereby reviving both the symbolic interactionist tradition that had flourished in the Chicago school since the early part of the century and the influential phenomenological writings from the 1960s such as those of sociologists Peter Berger and Thomas Luckman.[19]

One of the most controversial and influential positions advanced today by sociologists is that of Pierre Bourdieu and his collaborators. Grouped in the Centre de Sociologie Européenne at the École des Hautes Études en Sciences Sociales (Paris), for the last thirty years this team of researchers has studied spheres of activity as different as literature, art, fashion, and sports in order to develop conceptual tools that would help us understand the nature of symbolic activity. They developed a theory of action (or of practice) that articulates with a theory of society (or of social classes). While opposing both objectivism and subjectivism, Bourdieu himself has borrowed the road of what he calls *structural constructivism* to propose a political economy of symbolic goods that takes into consideration the dynamic of social relations and that of various fields of activity.[20] According to Bourdieu, if there is a principle of organization to all forms of social life, it is the logic of distinction. In any differentiated society, individuals, groups, and social classes cannot escape this logic—which brings them together while separating them from one another. The boundaries that we create are symbolic, but they are also political as they "freeze a particular state of the social struggle, i.e. a given state of the distribution of advantages and obligations."[21] Cultural consumption plays a central role in this process. Therefore, analyzing the different relations that people have with cultural objects helps us understand domination better.

Bourdieu is only one of many social scientists who read power relations between groups through their relations with culture. For instance, again, British social historians and Birmingham school sociologists have considered how the working class defines its identity in opposition to those of other classes. Many American historians have followed this path in their study of popular culture, analyzing how historical forces construct race, class, and gender, thereby providing a more sophisticated understanding of hegemonic processes.[22] Similarly, under the influence of Derrida and Foucault, poststructuralists have highlighted how identity is defined relationally and how it is shaped by power relations among groups. Hence, they added a political edge to earlier semiotic writings that analyzed cultural codes and symbolic differences without reference to cultural politics. Likewise, post-Geertzian reflective anthropology and the new historicism in literary criticism read domination and hegemony out of ethnographic data or literary texts,[23] while students of postmodernism document the decline of cultural hierarchies and the collapse of universal symbolic boundaries.[24] Finally, in Afro-American studies and in women's studies, important debates opposing boundaries and nature, as well as constructivist and essentialist interpretations of ethnic and racial differences, are raging. All the *human sciences,* as Wilhelm Dilthey liked to call them, have been haunted by such concepts as identity, exclusion, and domination[25]—rarely in the past have so many social scientists and humanists been concerned with similar issues. The strong influence that the writings of Foucault, and more recently Bourdieu, have had on these disciplines has been sustained by the critical concerns that they share with Marxism in general and with the Birmingham school and German Critical Theory in particular.[26]

Scholars who have made the relation between culture and exclusion a central theme often unknowingly adopt either a Left-Weberian perspective that stresses the creation of status groups and the monopolization of resources or a Durkheimian perspective that centers on the exclusion generated by shared communal values. Unfortunately, they have too often ignored the connection between their newly discovered interests and the sociological tradition, stressing instead their affiliations with fashionable European theories that provide cachet to their own intellectual endeavors. We now need to overcome disciplinary, and particularly methodological, differences to take stock of our achievements and work toward systematically improving our understanding. We should also start drawing larger conclusions about processes of boundary formation that go beyond specific cases. It is with the goal of facilitating this enterprise that the original essays assembled here are offered.

At a time when the American upper middle class is increasingly isolated from other social classes,[27] when social inequality is growing rapidly,[28] when ethnicity and race are more and more at the center of social conflicts, and when the obstacles that women and minorities face in the workplace seem again to be increasing, understanding the nature and dynamics of symbolic boundaries is a particularly urgent task. One sociological contribution to this endeavor would be to provide some of the conceptual tools, such as the notion of symbolic boundaries, that can bring together strands of research that cut across literary criticism, history, anthropology, law, and political science as well as women's studies and Afro-American studies. In sociology proper, while a large number of constructivist studies and an even larger number of studies of inequality are available, rarely have American researchers brought these two research foci together in a systematic way.

III

Few of the essays assembled here deal with the role played by such institutions as the family, the military, or the school system in creating inequality. And few deal with the economic dimensions of inequality that were widely studied in the 1960s and 1970s by structuralists and Marxists alike. Instead, these studies focus on the properly cultural aspects of inequality that stratification specialists tend to neglect. They treat several of the dimensions along which distinctions are frequently made, whether they are types of activity (consumption of high culture, cuisine) or categories of persons (gender, ethnicity).[29]

These essays illustrate some of the main directions that cultural sociology has taken over the past decade. Over the years we have increasingly come to conceptualize culture as institutionalized repertoires that have as powerful an effect on the structuration of everyday life as do economic forces.[30] Accordingly, we have shown how the cultural is structural, conceptualizing culture as the structured categories by which we organize our actions.[31] We have also come to pay more and more attention to the effects of culture on the social positioning of individuals by analyzing how cultural signals are mobilized in exclusionary practices that result in the creation of status groups.[32] The process by which culture shapes groups has come under scrutiny in sociological studies of the roles played by symbolic boundaries in the definition of social identities. Other topics that have stimulated recent discussion include the process by which contradictory views of the sacred and the profane become institutionalized, how competing definitions of *legitimate culture* (cultural capital) are mobilized in group conflicts, and how various types of inequality are reproduced through boundary work.[33]

The organizing themes of the book cover many of these issues. The

first part is concerned with the institutionalization of cultural repertoires and the symbolic boundaries that define them. Focusing on the
institutionalization of artistic and moral categories, the papers in this
section analyze either the historical evolution of such categories or their
present conditions of development. The second part focuses on class
patterns of cultural consumption and indirectly on the specific ways in
which high and popular culture can be used in boundary work, that
is, in the creation of status groups. The third part is primarily concerned with how boundaries are built and used by groups whose identities are based on ascribed characteristics, namely, women and members
of ethnic minority groups. The final section discusses how phenomena
of exclusion manifest themselves in broader social systems and what
their political consequences are. Throughout the volume contributors
raise broad theoretical issues concerning the role played by culture in
the making of social inequality.

1. The Institutionalization of Cultural Categories

One of the most frequently studied oppositions characteristic of all
modern societies is that between "popular culture" and "elite" or "high
culture," which extends to the classification of artworks into "sacred"
and "profane" genres. In his early work, Paul DiMaggio showed that
such boundaries are the products of social history. More specifically,
he showed that, in the United States at the beginning of the twentieth
century, a "high culture model" was established in the visual arts (e.g.,
museums) and in music (e.g., symphony orchestras) by a distinct organizational system, the trustee-governed nonprofit enterprise.[34] Here,
DiMaggio analyzes differences in how this shift occurred in three other
domains: drama, opera, and dance. He shows that the very cultural
categories that are used by groups to "cultivate differences" themselves
become institutionalized over time.

Diana Crane addresses similar issues while redirecting the attention
to contemporary societies. She argues that, with the rehabilitation of
popular culture and the growing interpenetration of high culture and
popular culture, the arbitrariness of the high/low distinction is made
visible. Convinced that we have to define cultures in terms of the environments in which they are created, produced, and disseminated rather
than in terms of their content, Crane substitutes the distinction media
culture/urban culture for the classic distinction high culture/popular
culture. The dynamics of the cultural system are characterized by the
continuous tension between the domination of the core media cultures
and the proliferation of new cultural organizations in peripheral and

local cultures. Hence, Crane documents how institutional arrangements shape classification systems.

Joseph R. Gusfield traces the genealogy of some of our ideas about pollution and food by analyzing the moral crusade of the natural foods movement led by Sylvester Graham (of "Graham cracker" fame) in the 1830s, which developed a system of ideas associated with food avoidances and beliefs about the dangers to health from modern food technology. By comparing Graham's ideas with those found in the current "natural foods" movement in the United States, Gusfield provides a fascinating analysis of how the contrast between substantive and symbolic aspects of meaning are turned into statements about social boundaries between valued and disvalued behaviors and between healthful and diseased people. In the two cases that are considered here, the discourse on the body and food stresses the superiority of the natural over the artificial as well as the dangers present in commercial and rapidly changing societies where boundaries and social control are permanently challenged.

Nicola Beisel analyzes the institutionalization of cultural categories by discussing a different moral crusade, that of Anthony Comstock, who tried to redefine the boundary between obscenity and literature in the 1870s while leading a crusade against Walt Whitman and provoking the arrest of Alfred Knoedler, the owner of one of New York's leading art galleries. Simultaneously, Beisel examines the interesting theoretical issue of boundary formation. Following Stinchcombe, she suggests that people use existing ideologies to try to transform social structures and moral boundaries.[35] She shows that Comstock uses three sets of social categories to define polluting behaviors: youth, class, and ethnicity (or foreignness).

Each of these four pieces contributes in a different way to our understanding of the process of boundary formation. While DiMaggio and Crane focus on the institutional processes involved in the definition of boundaries, Gusfield and Beisel discuss how available cultural repertoires and contexts of interpretation are mobilized in boundary work. However, these contributions are concerned with only two of the various domains in which such boundary work occurs.

2. High Culture and Exclusion

Because the elite has privileged access to high culture, many of the available studies of boundary work have historically focused on how high culture is mobilized to evaluate or signal status or to create status groups and monopolize privileges: the work of Thorstein Veblen, W.

Lloyd Warner, and many others pointed us in this direction several decades ago.[36] Contemporary sociologists are now interested in developing a more fine-tuned understanding of these processes.

In his empirical study of four communities in the New York City region David Halle studies the experiential framework that people mobilize in their appreciation of abstract art. He finds that, if high culture penetrates only sections of the dominant class, it does not necessarily contribute to class reproduction: moving from one taste culture to another does not always require special knowledge that is unequally distributed across classes. Often it requires only a decision to favor one type of decoration over another. Consequently, art consumption does not necessarily generate social boundaries, as has been posited by cultural capital theory. Hence, Halle's findings shed doubt on approaches that suggest that culture is primarily a tool for domination and power or a basis for symbolic mastery.

In contrast to Halle, Richard A. Peterson and Albert Simkus argue that artistic taste continues to signify status. Using a refined classification of occupational status that takes into consideration the relative cultural capital of each occupation, they show that a hierarchy of cultural practices exists across classes in the United States, that is, that the higher-ranked occupational groups prefer classical music while the lower ones prefer country and western. However, musical tastes are not all clearly hierarchicalized as there is less and less consensus on the ranking as one moves down in the hierarchy of tastes, with an increasingly large number of alternative forms having more or less equal taste value. Therefore, the taste hierarchy is best represented not by a slim column of taste genres but as a pyramid with one elite taste at the top and ever more alternative forms as one moves down toward the base.

In contemporary societies, one could easily come to the conclusion that "democracy" in art is impossible. The fact that art museums continue to attract educated professionals, managers, and students tends to confirm this view. Vera Zolberg raises the question, Does this situation result from the nature of the collections or from the politics of art museums, which seek a high-status public? She argues that the recent proliferation of new art forms and styles has undermined the relation between artistic preferences and occupation or social status. Even though one of the goals of art museum administrations is democratization, this goal often remains unfulfilled as organizational cultures tend to devalue educative action. Zolberg explores the theoretical implications of her findings for the changing relation between cultural consumption and status boundaries.

3. *Gender and Ethnicity in Boundary Work*

If familiarity with high culture seems to be a basis for exclusion only in the higher social echelons, other status signals are used, although with unequal frequency, by members of all social classes. This is notably the case for gender and ethnicity.

Randall Collins contributes to our understanding of the production of symbolic boundaries in his examination of the sexual division of cultural labor. He argues that the production of cultural boundaries is a female specialty. For instance, the role of housewife is defined primarily in the realm of "status production" (cleanliness, presentation of food), while women most often find work in the culture-producing sector (as artists, writers, teachers, salespeople). As for the female white-collar working class, the role of cultural management includes a great deal of what Collins calls "Goffmanian labor": secretaries, salesclerks, and nurses are the first line of "organizational self-representation." Gender differences are associated not only with the opposition up/down but also with the opposition production/consumption and power/culture. However, far from living in a realm of illusion, women may well constitute the feature that keeps modern capitalism alive through their involvement in the production and consumption of status culture.

"Belief in difference invariably results in inequality," writes Cynthia Fuchs Epstein. Structural by definition, boundary distinctions are at first maintained by conceptual means: words and categories, such as male/female, white/black, are never innocent; rather, they convey often malleable connotations. They also prescribe attitudes and govern behaviors. Building on her influential argument against essentialism or cultural feminism, Epstein points out that dichotomous categories play an important part in the definition of women as "others" and that much is at stake in the labeling of behaviors and attitudes as feminine and masculine. On the other hand, the destruction of gender oppositions is always problematic because we all have a clear sense of cultural limits while the legitimate ways of transgressing these limits remain well codified and quite restricted. Those who violate gender boundaries in illegitimate ways often experience punishment in the workplace. This forces many women to reassure their male colleagues of their respect for traditional gender roles and of their commitment to family over work. Hence, Epstein opens the way for a more sophisticated analysis of the factors that prevent change in symbolic boundaries.

It is important not to treat particular symbolic boundaries, such as those based on gender or ethnicity, as discrete phenomena. John R. Hall raises the issue of commonalities between types of boundaries in his analysis of status situations. In the process of developing a provocative critique of Pierre Bourdieu's work, he concurs with Halle and others that culture is more fluid and complex than had been suggested by cultural capital theory and that we need to recognize the existence of heterogeneous markets and multiple kinds of cultural capital. Hall thus proposes a "cultural structuralism" that addresses the multiplicity of status situations. The question of ethnicity cannot be seen as secondary in the dynamics of distinction: "ethnic cultural capital" does not always reduce to class cultural capital. The same applies to the resources valued by status groups based on age, religion, community, or shared leisure time activity. Hall provides a critique of the notion of an overarching market of cultural capital that is particularly useful for understanding the interaction between what he calls *economic formations* and *cultural formations*.

4. Exclusion and the Polity

Despite the fact that differentiation is a crucial aspect of social life, individuals remain members of larger communities, that is, of societies or nations. The opposition between citizen/noncitizen is central: to be a member of a society or a nation is more than an attribute; it is a privilege and a responsibility. Societies establish their physical boundaries and give their members certain privileges or rights (suffrage, etc.). Jeffrey C. Alexander argues that we need to pay attention to the symbolic dimension of "civil society." He shows that "civil discourse" is binary and occurs at three levels (motives, relations, and institutions) to divide the world into "those who deserve inclusion" and "those who do not." Democracy goes hand in hand with rationality, openness, equality, and liberty: this is the "discourse of liberty" whose tenets are considered to be sacred. Every attack against any of these tenets raises repression and sometimes expulsion.

Alan Wolfe also argues that democracy is by definition inclusive or universalist: it is a way of taking in, rather than keeping out. On the other hand, sociology teaches us that such a view is idealistic: in fact, social life requires boundaries, membership rituals, privileged space, and other demarcations. For liberal sociologists, the question is then to establish how it is possible to share a democratic commitment to the universal rights of abstract agents given the limits to inclusion inherent in social life. Should the harm done by differences be tolerated for a richer world of meanings? What kinds of boundaries should be maintained, and which should we fight against? Contrary to poststructuralist theorists, Wolfe argues that boundaries are not always imposed by "the other" and that boundaries that are chosen by individuals should be respected. This should also apply to boundaries that are the product of a moral passage, that is, of an informed decision taken after considering options. It is precisely because boundaries are here to stay that we need to gain a more specific understanding of how and when they can be challenged.

IV

Together these essays enrich our understanding of the various facets of symbolic boundaries that shape the social fabric. In their own way, each contributor sheds light on the signals that are used to read status, on the mechanisms of cultural distinctions that operate in everyday life, and on the consequences of such processes for inequality. Several authors also build on or challenge influential theoretical contributions to cultural sociology. We hope that the empirical evidence they offer will generate fruitful discussions in sociological circles and elsewhere. More generally, we hope that this volume will initiate a dialogue on future research directions in the study of inequality, on the one hand, and culture and symbolic boundaries, on the other. Our goal here is not so much to provide a clear research agenda as to suggest ways of widening the discussion. Several lines of research appear to be particularly promising. For instance, it would be useful to ask more systematically, following Epstein and others, how and why different boundaries (e.g., gender, national, cultural, or racial boundaries) are equally important for different kinds of groups. Are there important differences in the boundaries that are drawn by groups whose identities are defined by shared achieved characteristics or, alternately, by shared ascribed characteristics? Are there variations in the boundary work produced by the members of different classes? Are there variations in the boundary work typical of old entrenched groups and that of newer groups, whether they be nations, voluntary associations, or professions? Answering these questions is essential to gaining a better understanding of the cultural dimension of the stratification system.[37]

Following Alan Wolfe, we should also raise questions pertaining to the fundamental nature of boundaries. What features make up the character of boundaries? Are rituals always essential to the creation of boundaries?[38] Are there differences in the types of transgressions or initiations that most often accompany particular types of boundaries?

Alternatively, which boundaries are temporary and which permanent? What causes certain boundaries to be stable and used at home and in the workplace—as described by Epstein in her chapter—while others are more influenced by contextual factors?[39] How do people move across interactions from one frame to another, for example, from drawing cultural boundaries to drawing gender or racial boundaries? To answer such questions a systematic comparison that could lead to a typology of boundaries might be useful. Such a typology could describe the similarities and differences between boundaries based on signals as varied as birthrights, credentials, citizenship, gender, and beauty and more generally on observable versus unobservable signals or on stable versus fluctuating character traits.

A third important set of issues pertains to historical changes in the importance of specific symbolic boundaries or to what Alexander calls the "construction, destruction, and deconstruction of civic solidarity." Epstein notes that gender boundaries become less important in periods of economic growth and when women are freed from strong community ties and are less integrated in family networks. What factors contribute to the deinstitutionalization of other types of boundaries? Are cultural differences losing importance in the multifaceted society in which we live? Is our cultural consensus weakening while contemporary American culture is becoming more loosely bounded? In the early 1970s, Herbert Gans analyzed how class distinctions are often mediated by other statuses (age, ethnicity, gender). Is this tendency becoming more prevalent? In other words, are boundaries based on moral, cultural, or socioeconomic status increasingly used to euphemistically draw gender, race, or ethnic boundaries at a time when norms against boundary work based on ascribed characteristics are gaining greater legitimacy? As much of the recent literature suggests, ascribed characteristics may truly be losing in importance.[40]

Even if groups and individuals create boundaries among themselves, the pressures of economic interests and the division of labor work to bring the walls down and to force us to live together. In this context, what are the factors that push us to segregate or integrate, to close boundaries or to view differences positively? Are all types of symbolic boundaries equally conducive to the creation of objective boundaries and discrimination? Are the different types of symbolic boundaries equally crossable, resisted, and open to conflict? To quote Hall, we need to develop a "comparative historical sociology of shifting, multiple configured status situations. . . . to better problematize the relation between reciprocity and hierarchy and to understand how individuals or groups can be in a situation of subordination while being linked by sets of duties and reciprocal obligations." In other words, we should return to the question that Claude Lévi-Strauss raises in the conclusion of his most recent book, *Histoire de lynx,* the question of the feasibility of producing alternative identities and differences from social communalities.[41] We hope that the essays offered here constitute a step toward the realization of this shared intellectual project.

Notes

1. Marcel Mauss, "La Civilisation: Eléments et formes," in *Oeuvres* (Paris: Minuit, 1969), 2:456–79, 471–72. Here and elsewhere, the English translation from the French edition is our own.

2. Emile Durkheim, *The Elementary Forms of Religious Life* (New York: Free Press, 1965), chaps. 6, 7.

3. Emile Durkheim and Marcel Mauss, *Primitive Classification* (Chicago: University of Chicago Press, 1963), 82.

4. Durkheim, *Elementary Forms of Religious Life,* 33.

5. Claude Lévi-Strauss, "Introduction à l'oeuvre de Marcel Mauss," in *Sociologie et anthropologie,* by Marcel Mauss (Paris: Presses Universitaires de France, 1950).

6. Stephen Tyler, *Cognitive Anthropology* (New York: Holt, Rinehart & Winston, 1969).

7. Mary Douglas, *Purity and Danger: An Analysis of Concepts of Pollution and Purity* (London: Routledge & Kegan Paul, 1966).

8. Mary Douglas, *How Institutions Think* (London: Routledge & Kegan Paul, 1986).

9. Howard Becker, *Outsiders: Studies in the Sociology of Deviance* (New York: Free Press, 1963).

10. Erving Goffman, *The Presentation of Self in Everyday Life* (Garden City, N.Y.: Doubleday, 1959) and *Stigma: Notes on the Management of Spoiled Identity* (Englewood Cliffs, N.J.: Prentice-Hall, 1963).

11. Louis Althusser, *Essays on Ideology* (London: Verso, 1984); Nicos Poulantzas, *Pouvoir politique et classes sociales* (Paris: Maspero, 1975).

12. Max Weber, *Economy and Society* (New York: Bedminster, 1968).

13. Pierre Bourdieu, *Outline of a Theory of Practice* (Cambridge: Cambridge University Press, 1977).

14. Mauss, "La Civilisation," 459.

15. Ludwig Wittgenstein, *Le Cahier bleu et le cahier brun* (Paris: Gallimard, 1965), 90 (our translation).

16. See, e.g., Paul Willis, *Learning to Labor: How Working Class Kids Get Working Class Jobs* (New York: Columbia University Press, 1981).

17. For an interdisciplinary perspective, see Paul Rabinow and William M. Sullivan, eds., *Interpretive Social Sciences* (Berkeley and Los Angeles: University of California Press, 1979).

18. Bruno Latour and Steven Woolgar, *Laboratory Life: The Social Construction of Scientific Facts* (Beverly Hills, Calif.: Sage, 1979); Karin D. Knorr-Cetina, *The Manufacture of Knowledge: An Essay in the Constructivist and Contextual Nature of Society* (Oxford: Pergamon, 1981).

19. Peter Berger and Thomas Luckman, *The Social Construction of Reality: A Treatise in the Sociology of Knowledge* (Garden City, N.Y.: Doubleday, 1966).

20. Pierre Bourdieu, "Social Space and Symbolic Power," *Sociological Theory* 7, no. 10 (1989): 14–25.

21. Pierre Bourdieu, *Distinction: A Social Critique of the Judgment of Taste* (Cambridge, Mass.: Harvard University Press, 1984), 477.

22. E. P. Thompson, *The Making of the English Working Class* (New York: Vintage, 1963). For a review, see Chandra Mukerji and Michael Schudson, eds., *Rethinking Popular Culture: Contemporary Perspectives in Cultural Studies* (Berkeley and Los Angeles: University of California Press, 1991). See also Lynn Hunt, ed., *The New Cultural History* (Berkeley and Los Angeles: University of California Press, 1989).

23. See, e.g., James Clifford and George E. Marcus, eds., *Writing Culture: The Poetics and Politics of Ethnography* (Berkeley and Los Angeles: University of California Press, 1986). For an analysis of these changes in anthropology, see Sherry Ortner, "Theory in Anthropology since the Sixties," *Comparative Studies in Society and History* 26, no. 10 (1984): 126–66. It would be as unfair to caricature contemporary American sociology as a narrowly positivistic discipline peopled by surveys and questionnaires as it would be to define contemporary cultural anthropology exclusively through the intellectual heritage of Evans-Pritchard.

24. David Harvey, *The Conditions of Postmodernity: An Inquiry into the Origins of Cultural Change* (Oxford: Blackwell, 1989).

25. Wilhelm Dilthey, "The Construction of the Historical World in the Human Studies," in *Selected Writings,* ed. H. P. Rickman (London: Cambridge University Press, 1976).

26. On the development of this interdisciplinary movement, see Michèle Lamont and Marsha Witten, "Surveying the Continental Drift: The Diffusion of French Social and Literary Theory in the United States," *French Politics and Society* 6 (1988): 17–23.

27. Robert Reich, "The Secession of the Successful," *New York Times Magazine,* 20 January 1991, 16–45.

28. Bennett Harrison and Barry Bluestone, *The Great U-Turn: Corporate Restructuring and the Polarizing of America* (New York: Basic, 1988).

29. Space limitations prevent us from examining the complex issues pertaining to racial boundaries.

30. Clifford Geertz, *The Interpretation of Culture* (New York: Basic, 1973); Ann Swidler, "Culture in Action: Symbols and Strategies," *American Sociologi-*

cal Review 51 (1986): 273–86; Robert Wuthnow, *Meaning and Moral Order: Explorations in Cultural Analysis* (Berkeley and Los Angeles: University of California Press, 1988); John R. Hall, *Gone from the Promised Land: Jonestown in American Cultural History* (New Brunswick, N.J.: Transaction, 1987).

31. Eviatar Zerubavel, *The Fine Line: Boundaries and Distinctions in Every-day Life* (New York: Free Press, 1991).

32. See, e.g., Jonathan Rieder, *Canarsie: The Jews and Italians of Brooklyn against Liberalism* (Cambridge, Mass.: Harvard University Press, 1985); Judith Gerson and Kathy Peiss, "Boundaries, Negotiations and Consciousness: Re-conceptualizing Gender Relations," *Social Problems* 32 (1985): 317–31.

33. See in particular Bourdieu's *Distinction*. For a discussion of this litera-ture, see Michèle Lamont and Robert Wuthnow, "Betwixt and Between: Re-cent Cultural Sociology in Europe and the United States," in *Frontiers of Social Theory: The New Synthesis,* ed. George Ritzer (New York: Columbia University Press, 1990). For a discussion of the various types of relations between power and culture, including symbolic boundaries, that are posited in this literature, see Michèle Lamont, "The Power/Culture Link in a Comparative Perspective," *Contemporary Social Research* 11 (1989): 131–50.

34. Paul DiMaggio, "Cultural Entrepreneurship in Nineteenth-Century Boston: The Creation of an Organizational Base for High Culture in America," in *Media, Culture and Society: A Critical Reader,* ed. Richard Collins, James Curran, Nicholas Garnham, Paddy Scannell, Philip Schlesinger, and Colin Sparks (Beverly Hills, Calif.: Sage, 1986).

35. Arthur Stinchcombe, "The Deep Structure of Moral Categories: Eigh-teenth Century French Stratification and the Revolution," in *Structural Sociol-ogy,* ed. Eno Rossi (New York: Columbia University Press, 1978).

36. Thorstein Veblen, *The Theory of the Leisure Class* (New York: B. W. Huelsh, 1912); W. Lloyd Warner and L. Hunt, *Social Life of a Community* (New Haven, Conn.: Yale University Press, 1941).

37. The following discussion builds in part on Marcel Fournier's ongoing study of Marcel Mauss's work and on Michèle Lamont's *Money, Morals, and Manners: The Culture of the French and the American Upper-Middle Class* (Chi-cago: University of Chicago Press, 1992).

38. In *La Noblesse d'état* (Paris: Minuit, 1989), Pierre Bourdieu shows the similarities between noble titles and academic titles.

39. Luc Boltanski and Laurent Thevenot (in *De la justification: Les Écono-mies de la grandeur* [Paris: Gallimard, 1991]) indirectly address the influence of situational factors on boundary work. They provide an analysis of conflicts and negotiation by looking at how individuals succeed in maintaining their status or honor when they are victims of injustice. They achieve this at the discursive level by drawing on various principles of justification to frame their own understanding of the situation against other understandings.

40. For example, Matthijs Kalmijn, "Status Homogamy in the United States," *American Journal of Sociology* 97, no. 2 (1991): 496–523.

41. Claude Lévi-Strauss, *Histoire de lynx* (Paris: Plon, 1991).

PART ONE   The Institutionalization
of Cultural Categories

TWO

Cultural Boundaries and
Structural Change: The
Extension of the High Culture
Model to Theater, Opera, and
the Dance, 1900–1940

Paul DiMaggio

Accounts of cultural boundaries in anthropology and sociology tend to portray them either as structurally rooted in differences among persons in caste, class, or race or, when such boundaries are based on differences in taste or aesthetic disposition, as emergent properties of interaction. Moreover, most work on cultural capital, which in modern societies is a key building material from which status hierarchies are fashioned, documents inequality in its possession across persons and groups or demonstrates its effects on various kinds of achievement and attainment, typically at the individual level.

Such work brackets the different, but equally important, topic, How is cultural capital valorized as prestigious? Why do some tastes and dispositions serve as bases of vertical distinction whereas others are dishonored or neutral with respect to status? This question drives us to examine institutional change. For the notion of cultural capital presupposes the existence of institutions with the power to establish authoritatively the value of different forms of culture: in effect, to create and to defend boundaries among varying kinds of aesthetic (or culinary or religious or habilimentary) products and practices. Although the transformation of such valuations into cultural boundaries among persons is an accomplishment of local interaction, the utility of such classifications is grounded in institutional systems that separate the products and practices to which they refer (DiMaggio 1991).

In other words, to be useful in creating boundaries among persons, distinctions of taste must be grounded in boundaries among forms of cultural practice. The effectiveness and robustness of such boundaries are themselves functions of the resources available to patrons and practitioners who wish to construct them. To illustrate this, let us consider the processes by which opera, the drama, and the dance were annexed to the high culture system in the United States.

Genre Distinctions as Organized Boundaries

The relation between art and society was transformed during the last half of the nineteenth century. Urban elites across the United States developed institutions that defined certain kinds of aesthetic culture as sacred, separated them from profane performance and exhibition, developed distinctive audiences and forms of organization, and articulated ideologies legitimating elite taste.[1]

To be sure, differences in taste had long been associated with social class in the United States. But they were of minor importance before the late nineteenth century. Without a distinct institutional system to define and reinforce boundaries between different forms of art, the classification of artworks into sacred and profane genres was constantly impeded by the eagerness of commercial entrepreneurs to attract the largest possible audiences. And as long as cultural boundaries were indistinct, "fashionable taste," far from embodying cultural authority, was suspect as snobbish, trivial, and undemocratic. Only when elite taste was harnessed to a clearly articulated ideology embodied in the exhibitions and performances of organizations that selected and presented art in a manner distinct from that of commercial entrepreneurs, that is, to what I call the *high culture model,* did an understanding of culture as hierarchical become both legitimate and widespread.

The instrument by which this was accomplished was the trustee-governed nonprofit enterprise. Under the guarantee system, which preceded it in music, patrons provided funds for series of concerts organized by musical entrepreneurs. They did not retain the power to hire and fire managers or performers, nor, in most cases, was their stake a long-term one. By contrast, trustees firmly commanded nonprofit institutions, charitable aims were embedded in their bylaws, and trusteeship collectively represented a permanent commitment. Given the time required to establish new etiquettes for behavior at exhibitions and performances, insulate high cultural from commercial performance and exhibition, define canons of art and music, and seal them off from both profane culture and the general public, the degree of control afforded by the nonprofit corporate form was essential. By 1900, nonprofit, trustee-governed art museums and symphony orchestras were well established in major urban centers; by 1930, they were common in cities across the United States.

This fundamental shift in the classification and organization of artistic production and distribution is acknowledged and understood (DiMaggio 1982; Levine 1988; Weber 1976; DeNora 1992). What is less well understood is how elite forms of organizing and understanding art were generalized from classical music and the visual arts to other forms. By 1940, the high culture model would extend beyond art and classical music to drama, opera, and the dance. However natural it appears to us today, its extension was neither automatic nor inevitable; it is a social change that requires explanation.

The Transformation of the American Stage

Of all the art forms to which the high culture model was extended, the stage was the most improbable: the most commercially successful; the one least in need, as it was organized during the nineteenth century, of elite patronage; and the one most attuned, by tradition and by its concrete and accessible character, to popular demand. Compared to music, drama's concrete thematic content, its reliance on the spoken word, is not easily etherialized; lacking the ambiguity of music or the visual image, theater did not lend itself to the transcendent, quasi-religious discourse employed to sacralize classical music or the visual arts.

To be sure, as Levine (1988) has demonstrated, the plays of Shakespeare, once performed throughout America to audiences of every social class, had been appropriated into elite culture by the end of the century, and the classical drama of Euripides was ensconced in the academy. But two or three exemplars do not an art form make: no large body of dramatic literature was readily available for sacralization. Moreover, the stage's association with artifice and inauthenticity, and the suspect reputation of actors as a class, militated against its emergence as a fine art. In 1900, few could foresee that in just thirty years critics and producers would be making fine distinctions on a broad scale between "mere entertainment" and the "art" or "intellectual" theater of "serious playwrights," many of them figures of the twentieth century.

The application of the high culture model to the stage can be seen as early as 1910, when the Drama Committee of Boston's Twentieth Century Club reported to the community on "the amusement situation" in that city. These civic reformers castigated the city's theater owners in terms reminiscent of earlier critics of commercial musical ensembles, but with an urgency informed by their conviction that the contemporary stage represented not just wasted opportunity but an active threat to public morals.

A chief sin of the theater owners was their failure to classify productions by quality and merit and thus to segregate the elevating from the less worthy. "It is notable," they complained, "that the different theatre managements, exclusive of those giving burlesque and vaudeville, make no attempt to establish a permanent clientele. . . . It is difficult, for instance, to understand what prompted the Shuberts, after opening their new theatre with two weeks of Shakespeare . . . , to put on for their second attraction as commonplace a musical comedy as 'The Midnight Sons.' " The managers were also faulted for violating the boundary between audience and stage. Efforts by guardians of public morality to ban "the first so-called 'barefoot dancers' " several years before were based not on a prudish fear of bare feet, they claimed, but on the recognition that "it was evidently the beginning of a further breaking down of those barriers that separate the audience from the performer upon the stage." Such theaters were guilty of "lowering public standards of morality and decreasing the average efficiency of the individual citizen." "A constant attendance upon such forms of entertainment—if long persisted in—cannot but make the spectator less able to enjoy genuine dramatic art." (Twentieth Century Club 1910, 3, 30–31, 8).

But what *was* "genuine dramatic art"? The American theater had been almost entirely commercial. Critical standards were weak, and a dramatic canon comparable to the standard repertoire of the symphony orchestras had not yet emerged. The absence of a well-defined legitimating aesthetic hindered efforts to "improve" the stage at least until the late 1920s (Twentieth Century Club, 14; Levine 1988).

The lack of ideological resources to define a canon is illustrated in the difficulties faced by the American Drama League, an organization devoted to the improvement of the stage, in choosing plays to sponsor in the 1910s. A sympathetic observer wrote, "By what tenets shall one decide what play to approve? By the tenets of things past? Then is experiment unduly handicapped. Or by the tenets of novelty? Then must all tradition and law be given up. . . . Some thought a play should be well-made; others that it should be uplifting in tendency. Some would bar too great frankness in the treatment of problems but would admit just enough frankness. . . . It is clear that there are no absolute tenets" (Dickinson 1917, 48–49). Discourse about theater in 1917, like discourse on art and music in 1850, depended on a moral frame of reference and was uncertain as to the aesthetic criteria to which the art should be subjected.

Between 1910 and 1940, efforts to create a noncommercial theater devoted to artistic principles advanced mightily. Such efforts took many forms. The earliest were local social dramatic clubs, analogous to the musical societies of the early nineteenth century, groups of wealthy men and women who put on elevated dramatic performances for their own and their friends' amusement.[2] These activities begot the "little theater movement," foreshadowed in short-lived efforts in New York and Boston in the 1890s, and beginning in earnest in Chicago in 1906 with Victor Mapes's "new theater" and Laura Dainty Pelham's ambitious restructuring of the Hull House Players in 1907. From there the movement spread to New York, Boston, and other American cities.[3]

At the peak of the little theater movement in 1929, there were over one thousand noncommercial stages throughout the United States. At their most ambitious, they produced "serious drama" for small audiences and helped define a dramatic canon that moved beyond Shakespeare and the classics to such modern playwrights as Shaw, Ibsen, Galsworthy, and, later, O'Neill and Odets. But for a handful of settlement-house, leftist, and rural theaters, the little stages never tried to serve any but a high-status public; except for the few that attracted substantial subsidies, their small houses did not permit them to charge admission prices that the working or lower middle classes could afford.

The little theater movement did not endure because it was trapped between the Scylla of commercialism and the Charybdis of dilettantism. Most drew exclusively on amateur acting talent, often hiring a paid director with professional experience. Few of the handful that paid performers offered a living wage.[4] After initial successes, some little theaters moved to larger houses, hoping to finance growth and professionalize with subscription revenues. Most perished in the attempt.

Many of the majority that remained amateur became exclusive social clubs.[5] Their repertoires devolved into what New York producer Norris Houghton, who reported to the Rockefeller Foundation on the regional stage in the late 1930s, described as "escapism . . . drama as entertainment. . . . There is nothing in the program of any of these community theatres to indicate whether it is living in South Carolina or Michigan, Arizona or Pennsylvania. . . . Their repertories are practically interchangeable. . . . As obsessed as Broadway's managers with 'what the public wants,' " the amateur theaters, by the entertainment standards of Broadway or the motion pictures, "do not give adequate return for one's money" (Houghton 1941, 131).

At first, rather than patronize theaters, many drama lovers organized audiences, establishing block buying or subscription schemes to guarantee profits to touring productions or independent producers. The Drama League of America, created in 1910, used a committee system to select productions for its members; eventually, it developed into a national service organization, sponsoring lectures, classes, and meetings and disseminating lists of recommended plays. The National Federation of Theatre Clubs also had brief success organizing a national audience for refined drama (Dickinson 1917, 55–56). The New York Theatre Guild, the most ambitious of these ventures, mounted its own productions and toured them to guilds it organized in six eastern and midwestern cities, the costs guaranteed by a twenty-five-thousand-member subscription audience.[6]

Such guarantee schemes failed to elevate the stage because they did not challenge its economic structure: although they sought higher-quality productions, they could not ensure that commercial producers would supply them (Dickinson 1917, 47). The Shubert Organization, miffed at the Theatre Guild's defection to their competitor Erlanger, created its own "high-class" subscription scheme, the Dramatic League, to compete with the guild (Poggi 1968, 133).

Some little theaters, however, established prototypes for organizing drama under the nonprofit form, and a few of them survived. Henry Jewett's Boston Repertory Company, established in 1916, was organized under a trust incorporated for "educational, literary and artistic purposes." Placing representatives of state and city education departments on its board to bolster its claims as an educational institution, the theater was exempted from local taxation and received considerable private subsidy from wealthy Bostonians (Duffus 1928, 300–302).

A few theaters prospered in the not-for-profit mold. The Cleveland Playhouse, established as an amateur group under professional direction in 1915, added paid actors in 1921 and by 1927 became fully professional, with its own theater and a budget of $100,000 (Mac-Gowan 1929, 18). Consciously modeled on the symphony orchestra, it was characterized by its director as "a resident producing theatre, professionally organized, and operated not for profit and trusteed by a representative group of people drawn from the cultural, social and business life of the city of Cleveland" (Houghton 1941, 68–73). Theaters in Detroit and Pasadena also successfully established themselves during this era as nonprofit organizations employing professional actors (MacGowan 1929, 77–78, 100). By 1929, the nonprofit organization was so firmly established in drama that Kenneth MacGowan, commissioned by the Carnegie Corporation to survey the field, could generalize that, "because [little theaters] are incorporated on a non-profit-making basis and devoted to an educational purpose, they have succeeded in escaping certain taxes, along with schools and art museums" (1929, 242).

Several little theaters affiliated directly with art museums. Patrons created the Goodman Theatre under the wing of the Chicago Art Institute, which provided a house. Little theaters were established by the Detroit Arts and Crafts Guild and the St. Louis Artists Guild, and the Little Theatre Society of Indiana was associated with the John Herron Art Institute (Dickinson 1917, 206–7; MacGowan 1929, 57). Because such sponsorship represented what one contemporary called "the association of drama, the poor drab of the arts, with her more pampered sisters," it was a matter of symbolic as well as financial importance (Dickinson 1917, 65). Thomas Wood Stevens, plucked from the Carnegie Institute Drama Department to run the Goodman in 1925, made the connection explicit: "The theatre has no special style or type of drama to promulgate, any more than the exhibition galleries of the Institute exist for any special group of artists. In each case the question is whether a particular old play is worth revival or a particular new play is suited to performance" (quoted in Duffus 1928, 289).[7]

The little stage had begun as an artists' theater staffed, ironically but out of economic necessity, by amateurs, grappling for a means of defining serious dramatic works and, among the more ambitious, trying to produce plays that could change the theater and, in some instances, the world. Between 1910 and 1940, the outlines of a dramatic canon had emerged more clearly; styles of elite patronage and governance had been pioneered and implemented effectively by a handful of successful institutions. If some little theater participants of the late 1930s were, as Houghton put it, "self-consciously striving for culture for the sake of appearances" (1941, 244), that in itself was evidence of the movement's success, for fifty years before the equation of theater with culture and its use as a source of distinction would have seemed very odd indeed.

Several factors explain the emergence of theaters devoted to art or (in the case of leftist, rural, and settlement-house theaters) social change rather than entertainment. As an object of patronage, theater was especially attractive to groups excluded from the governance of museums and orchestras: Jews and women were unusually prominent among the backers of early subsidized art theaters (although the former were excluded from the more social little theaters). A resurgence of interest in classical theater and the transformation of Shakespeare into a cult object helped define the contours of a dramatic canon.

The free theater movements in England, Ireland, Germany, and Rus-

sia touched the United States through the immigration of artists like
Max Reinhart and influential visits by the Irish Abbey Players and
especially, in the 1920s, Stanislavsky's Moscow Art Theatre. Many
actors found the European stages' artistic vision and method intrinsically appealing. Moreover, their aesthetic gravity and organizational
structure, in which directors and actors rather than managers played
the dominant role, were doubly attractive to actors who were attempting, with some success, to establish a claim to professional status
(McArthur 1984).

More crucial than these factors, however, was the evolving ecology
of public entertainment between 1880 and 1920, which opened niches
for noncommercial dramatic institutions that had previously been
closed. Of these changes, three were most important.

The first was the stratification of audiences and genres in the commercial stage. Whereas in 1850 theaters were differentiated less by
repertoire than by ambience and, to some extent, style of presentation,
by 1900 stages were increasingly segmented by class and rank. At the
bottom, burlesque appealed to audiences of working-class men and was
shunned by women and the well born. Variety entertainment, originally also a male preserve, was differentiated into vulgar and "progressive" vaudeville, as entrepreneurs like Tony Pastor and B. F. Keith
discovered that they could make more money by investing in fancy
houses, expunging "blue" humor from their shows, and hiring high-
priced and fashionable talent from the legitimate (i.e., dramatic) stage
(Gilbert 1940, 158).[8] As this occurred, dramatic presentations were
further differentiated as well. This stratification of commercial markets
accustomed the public to making qualitative distinctions among dramatic genres.[9]

Second, local control of the stage was sharply reduced during this
era. By 1896 the consolidation of "the Syndicate," a theater trust combining the interests of Marc Klew, Abraham Erlanger, Charles Frohman, and several other theater circuit managers, placed productions
under the control of a handful of New York–based entrepreneurs,
who bought up many local houses and controlled even more through
contracts. The Syndicate and its competitor, the Shubert organization,
drew more income from house management than from producing
plays. Rationalizing the market to optimize profit, they forced small
towns out of tour circuits, shrinking the supply of productions: the
number of legitimate theater houses fell from more than five thousand
in 1890 to about fifteen hundred twenty years later. The Syndicate
provided the towns it did serve with a standard and inferior product,

reducing the appeal of theater and, more important, making the commercial stage less accessible to and less readily accepted by many producers and directors, some of whom became active in the art theater movement for economic as well as artistic reasons.[10] For them, creating nonprofit theaters combined the pursuit of artistic goals with the struggle against a concrete and, to many, an odious foe.[11]

Finally, film administered the coup de grace to the theatrical road, creating a vast new public for dramatic entertainment and capturing much of the old one. Well before the advent of "talkies" in 1929, movies stole the working-class audience from the legitimate stage. As early as 1912, observers remarked that theater galleries, once swelling with the lower-income public, were empty; after 1920, theaters were built without galleries (Poggi 1968, 41). By the 1910s and 1920s, movies, offering entertainment for one-fifth the price of the legitimate stage, had captured the middle-income audience as well. In cities and small towns across the United States, new movie palaces were built, owners converted theaters to more profitable cinemas, and movie companies bought up other theaters and closed them down. Between 1910 and 1925, the number of legitimate theaters outside New York fell from 1,490 to 564 (MacGowan 1929, 71).[12] By 1940, only 148 legitimate theaters and only three professional stock companies were open outside New York; in most of the United States, live theater, if available at all, was restricted to sporadic tours and offerings of amateur and collegiate companies.[13]

To establish classical music as an insulated form of high culture, Henry Lee Higginson and his contemporaries had to alter the economics of production so that producing concerts was too costly to yield a profit. Only after the integration of production and presentation into a single organization, full-time employment of musicians, standards of musical craft that only a permanent orchestra could achieve, and relentlessly classical programs were established as norms did orchestras require subvention and endowment. The ideological work of T. S. Dwight and his colleagues and the increasing legitimacy of classical standards had prepared an elite concert public that made this transformation possible (DiMaggio 1982).

In the theater, industrial and technological change accomplished what cultural entrepreneurship had in music: with the exception of Broadway, commercial enterprise became a losing proposition. Without competition from commercial producers, those who would elevate theater to art inherited the stage by default. Lacking a powerful ideology and an established canon, however, they were unable to attract elite patronage to the same degree as museums or symphony orchestras. Relying on subscription and guarantee rather than endowment, most could neither employ professional actors on a full-time basis (and thus could not match the level of craft displayed in film) nor sustain their artistic aspirations with a consistently "highbrow" repertoire (the only alternative standard available to legitimate the noncommercial stage). Thus, the little theaters and the variations thereupon, with a few exceptions, failed to become permanent institutions.

If most little theaters failed as organizations, however, they effected change as a movement. The art theaters of New York, the amateur playhouses around the country, and their academic allies succeeded in developing a legitimating ideology and a canon and in convincing a substantial part of the elite public that the stage both required and deserved subsidy. Although the realization of their vision in a national system of nonprofit, trustee-governed theaters remained more than two decades away, a critical shift in the status of the stage had been achieved. By 1940, one could look toward the day, as Houghton did, when all America's great cities would be "ready to support a permanent professional theatre of the caliber of their permanent professional orchestras" (1941, 74).

The End of Commercial Opera

Whereas the elevation of theater to high art requires explanation, the most surprising thing about opera's adoption of the high culture model is how long it was delayed. Opera was a fashionable diversion of the wealthy from the 1820s, equipped with rudiments of an accepted canon and, after the rise of Wagner, a powerful legitimating ideology. As Lawrence Levine has demonstrated, during the late nineteenth century what was originally a widely available form of popular culture, performed by numerous touring companies in English and often in excerpt and parody, became a pastime of well-to-do urban audiences, presented in foreign tongues and subject to an elaborate aesthetic that devalued the forms and conventions that had made opera popular among Americans of all classes (Levine 1988, 85–104).[14]

Yet the organization of trustee-governed opera companies under the high culture model was not fully effected until the 1930s. Before that time, opera was usually supported through guarantee. Rather than integrate the functions of production and presentation within a single firm, as was the case with symphony orchestras, patrons controlled houses but contracted with commercial impresarios to hire talent and produce the shows. If theater tested the ability of the high culture model of organization to facilitate the segmentation and sacralization of even the most commercial and popular of art forms, opera tested the viability of commercial methods of organizing in the realm of acknowledged art.

Significant aesthetic issues were at stake. For one thing, so long as commercial entrepreneurs controlled the repertoire and made artistic decisions on commercial grounds, patronage of grand opera, if not the art form itself, remained suspect as a means of ostentatious display rather than a warrant of benevolence and aesthetic discrimination. If the patrons of the Metropolitan Opera were largely indifferent, as they were during the late nineteenth century, as to whether they supported Italian opera or German, and if they conversed incessantly at a volume that caused the single-ticket audience to rebel, could their aesthetic commitment be taken seriously?[15]

Second, so long as opera was produced by commercial entrepreneurs, the boundary between European-style "grand opera" and musical theater would remain indistinct. Many nineteenth-century Americans disapproved of opera presented in the original language, favoring English translation as more democratic and more congenial to authentic appreciation. Opera in English vied with opera in French, Italian, and German into the first decades of the twentieth century. And if opera in English was as good as opera in Italian or German, how did one distinguish between grand opera and opéra bouffe (which American companies often performed in the grand style), or between comic opera and the operettas of Gilbert and Sullivan, or between Gilbert and Sullivan and the productions of the American musical stage?

In other words, if opera was defined as "serious art," the *boundaries* of opera were open to contestation, and the movement of managers, designers, and even soloists back and forth between grand opera, light opera, musical comedy, and vaudeville did nothing to clarify them.[16] Only with the surrender of commercial entrepreneurs to the high culture model of integrated presentation and production under the authority of wealthy trustees was the continuum marked by grand opera and the popular musical stage sharply dichotomized and the aesthetic rectitude of opera's patrons broadly acknowledged.

The delay in opera's adoption of the nonprofit form was due largely to economic circumstance. Opera is the most expensive, and thus the riskiest, of art forms. The cost of hiring not just musicians, as the orchestras did, but also vocalists (including stars who earned $3,000 or more a week), dancers, a chorus, and set designers long precluded full-time employment of the sort that the orchestras pioneered. The risk of huge deficits made patrons unwilling to combine house owner-ship and opera production (lest a bad season jeopardize the hall itself) and, in many cases, unwilling to take financial responsibility for the productions, thus encouraging speculation that their interests were financial. Yet through the 1920s opportunities for profit created a core of commercial managers eager to take on the risk and chronically tempted to cut corners on sets and rehearsals.

So great was the sum of capital required just to guarantee a season of grand opera that patrons motivated by artistic principle were forced to turn to wealthy backers who required side payments in the form of prestigious boxes, reinforcing connotations of snobbery. And the cost of maintaining separate troupes for Italian, German, and French opera, combined with the public's desire for a balanced repertoire, led compa-nies to produce operas not only not in English translation but often not even in the language in which they were originally written; the spectacle of Wagner in Italian or Puccini in German simply stoked popular suspicion that only conspicuous display and a deficit of na-tional pride could account for recourse to the foreign tongue.

A case in point is the Boston Opera Company of department-store magnate Eban Jordan, Jr., son of the founder of the New England Conservatory. In keeping with Boston's tradition of cultural steward-ship, Jordan viewed the opera as similar in mission to the orchestra, professing a commitment to the art that appears to have been genuine. He vouched for the educational value of grand opera and, following the model of the Boston Symphony, banned encores and applause during the action on the stage. Yet, although Jordan built a hall at great expense, he never entirely divorced the project from commercial considerations. He anticipated that the hall, which he leased to the opera company, would yield a profit, and he organized the latter as a stock company (selling two thousand shares at $100 each) that would guarantee opera seasons rather than produce them itself (Eaton 1965, 10–12).

Despite the auspices under which it was founded (Jordan himself paid the deficits during the first several years), without a clear demarca-tion between philanthropy and commerce the Boston Opera main-tained a tenuous hold on both its good intentions and public loyalty. Jordan had aimed to avoid the star system and keep top ticket prices to $3.00, within the range of the middle class, but by the second season these goals had been abandoned (Eaton 1968, 79). Even the educational character of the enterprise met with skepticism: Mayor Fitzgerald supported tax exemption, but the state legislature denied it (Eaton 1965, 174). By 1914, the wealthy lost interest, and the middle class, to whom rising prices had made the opera less attractive, were no longer able to provide enough revenue to keep it open, even with annual subvention from Jordan and his allies. In 1915, an associate of Oscar Hammerstein tried, but failed, to mount a season. Four years later, Jordan sold the hall to the Shuberts.

Nothing better illustrates the evolution of opera organization than the history of the Metropolitan, the nation's oldest surviving opera institution. The Met was a product of social, rather than aesthetic or educational, ambition; its founders were men of new wealth who had been unable to obtain boxes at the old Academy Opera. The new house's boxes were many and opulent. As critic Henry Finck wrote in the *New York Evening Post*, "From an artistic and musical point of view, the large number of boxes . . . is a decided mistake. But as the house was avowedly built for social purposes rather than artistic, it is useless to complain about this" (Kolodin 1936, 11). Wealthy families obtained boxes by buying shares in the stock company that built and maintained the house; transfers of shares required ratification by the shareholders as a group.

The stock company provided a stage, a roof, and seats. Commercial entrepreneurs provided the operas. When profits failed to materialize, opera house backers were pressed to increase their guarantees; when profits were high, the impresarios paid the proprietors. The Metropolitan's shift from Italian to German opera in its second season was motivated by financial considerations: Henry Abbey, who had lost $500,000 during the first year, demanded a full guarantee for the second; by contrast, Leopold Damrosch offered Wagner on the cheap, economizing by using his own orchestra and less expensive German vocal talent (Kolodin 1936, 22–24).[17]

When fire destroyed much of the opera house, the corporation was reorganized and a new house opened in 1893. Italian and French opera dominated the schedule under Abbey and Maurice Grau, men experienced producing opéra bouffe and theater as well as touring virtuosos and grand opera (Grau 1909). Their aims were strictly commercial, and they were well rewarded. "Maurice never posed as a great musical thinker," his brother wrote. "He did not pretend to labor for art; he understood the public" (Grau 1909, 23; Kolodin 1936, 89). The patrons derived financial gain as well as prestige from their investment:

in 1903, a parterre box, purchased at $60,000 ten years earlier, had appreciated to $100,000 and could bring $12,000 a year on lease (Kolodin 1936, 87).

When Grau stepped down, investors, including three from the Metropolitan Opera and Real Estate Company board, formed a production company to back his successor, producer Heinrich Conried. The new company guaranteed the opera house owners $150,000 against losses (they in turn spent that much to improve the stage) and promised, as part of its lease, that no more than 40 percent of the productions would be Wagnerian. Conried's first season netted $60,000 in profit (Kolodin 1936, 91–99; Eaton 1968, 141–43).[18]

Opera production and the maintenance of an opera house were integrated under a commercial entrepreneur, not a nonprofit firm. In 1906, Oscar Hammerstein, who had made a fortune from cigar-manufacturing patents, real estate, and vaudeville, opened the Manhattan Opera House. With fewer, less visible boxes and better, cheaper seats for the middle class, Hammerstein's operation competed vigorously with the Metropolitan. Specializing in name stars and a French/Italian repertoire, Hammerstein had a profitable first season, to the disadvantage of Conried, who resigned a year later (Cone 1964, 164).

The Metropolitan responded by bringing production and presentation into closer alliance. William Vanderbilt, vice president of the Metropolitan Opera and Real Estate Company, bought out Conried's share in the production company, which was renamed the Metropolitan Opera Company and placed under the presidency of financier Otto Kahn. In 1908, the producing company's new leadership announced that the firm would no longer be conducted for profit: net revenues were to be dedicated to a pension fund for artists and "to other permanent uses for advancement of the Metropolitan Opera Company as an artistic institution." Kahn and Vanderbilt offered to purchase the stock of shareholders opposed to the change, and many withdrew. Two new directors from the Metropolitan Opera and Real Estate Company were named to the board, increasing the number of shared directors to four (Kolodin 1936, 131–33).

This arrangement might have placed opera patronage on the same disinterested plane as support for symphonic music, but Hammerstein's competition kept financial matters at the fore: during the 1909–10 season the Metropolitan Company lost nearly $300,000 while Hammerstein netted almost as much. Hammerstein's house and operas received praise, as well, from critics who did not perceive commercial enterprise as inimical to operatic art. (Indeed, when Hammerstein's company *did* become fashionable in its second season, the *Post* feared that the change "might tempt the manager from the path of artistic rectitude" [Cone 1964, 70–72, 123].)

Paradoxically, it was Hammerstein who echoed the arguments that American advocates of classical music and endowed orchestras had begun to employ during the 1860s and 1870s, telling the Philadelphia press that

grand opera is . . . the most elevating influence upon modern society, after religion. From the earliest days it has ever been the most elegant of all forms of entertainment . . . it employs and unifies all the arts. . . . I sincerely believe that nothing will make better citizenship than familiarity with grand opera. It lifts one so out of the sordid affairs of life and makes material things seem so petty, so inconsequential, that it places one for the time being, at least, in a higher and better world. . . . Grand opera . . . is the awakening of the soul to the sublime and the divine." (Cone 1964, 123)[19]

In contrast, the Metropolitan's Conried sounded like P. T. Barnum:

"[A manager] cannot force the public to like certain operas any more than you can force it to like certain dishes. Both are matters of taste. Knowing that the opera impresario has but to give the public what he thinks it will like, not what he thinks it ought to hear, I have tried to do the former." (Cone 1964, 138)

The Metropolitan's guarantors' response to Hammerstein was instinctive to businessmen of their day: they created a trust. Aping theater's Klew and Erlanger, they organized a chain of opera houses, united by board interlocks and partnerships between local and New York capital and extending from Philadelphia (where Hammerstein also maintained a house) to Chicago and Boston (where he threatened). Faced with such formidable competition for stars and performance rights, Hammerstein met his opponents at the bargaining table and came away $1.2 million richer. In return, he gave Metropolitan interests his physical properties, performance rights, contracts to many of his performers, the Philadelphia opera house, and a promise to refrain for ten years from producing opera in New York, Boston, Philadelphia, or Chicago (Kolodin 1936, 163–67; Cone 1964, 252–63, 274–79).

The stage was set, it seems, for a new way of organizing serious artistic work: nationally, along trust lines. Given opera's expense, the advantages of cost and risk pooling were clear, as Mrs. Jeannette Thurber, a Philadelphia patron, had recognized in her unsuccessful effort to create an American Opera Company under conductor Theodore

Thomas twenty-five years earlier. With the provocative Hammerstein gone from the scene, however, the combination did not long survive. Within a few years, business disagreements led to dissolution of the Metropolitan's relations with the Chicago and Philadelphia companies, and the Boston Opera shut its doors. The Metropolitan Opera Company engaged Arturo Toscanini as conductor and for twenty years operated at a profit.

Yet grand opera remained risky. To defray its expense, the Metropolitan required an audience of three thousand willing to pay for an orchestra seat three times the price of a theater ticket and twenty times the cost of admission to a motion picture. Without capacity audiences, opera is an economic house of cards, as the Metropolitan's backers discovered at the onset of the Great Depression.

Throughout the 1920s, the men who controlled the Metropolitan had resisted every effort exerted on behalf of either artistic reform or even modest overtures to the public. When long-time board member A. D. Juilliard died in 1919, he authorized the foundation he established to support the opera in any manner that did not result in private gain; but when the Juilliard Foundation attempted in 1924 to subsidize the opera company, with the hope of improving its repertoire and artistic standards, its directors turned them down lest the gift interfere with the company's autonomy (Kolodin 1936, 449–50). Several years later, when patron Otto Kahn tried to organize a campaign to build a new house more hospitable to artists and the general public, the Opera and Real Estate Company's directors, afraid that they might be forced to surrender their boxes, rebuffed him (Kolodin 1936, 362–72; Eaton 1968, 241–43).

Only when grand opera became a losing proposition did the Metropolitan adopt the form of the symphony orchestra. By 1931, the Metropolitan Opera Company had seen a $1.1 million cash reserve vanish in two years. Its future in jeopardy, it converted itself to a not-for-profit educational membership group, the Metropolitan Association. Prodded by the Juilliard Foundation, which subsidized its transformation in return for four seats on the Association board, the Metropolitan revamped its management, cut costs, and mounted a series of fundraising drives. Depicting itself as an institution in service to art, the community, and the nation, its backers employed such innovations as radio, a women's guild, and solicitations from the Broadway stage. (Irving Berlin, who had married the daughter of Metropolitan director Clarence MacKay, wrote a musical appeal into one of his Broadway revues [Kolodin 1936, 449–83].)[20] Under the goad of Juilliard's multi-stringed assistance and economic necessity, the Metropolitan lowered seat prices, used more American performers, and offered a supplementary season of English opera at popular prices (Eaton 1968, 250).

As the opera's social luster diminished, the Real Estate Corporation directors distanced themselves, treating their boxes as lucrative rental properties. In 1939, the Metropolitan Opera Association bought out the holdings of the Opera and Real Estate Corporation, enabling the latter to go out of business, uniting production and presentation under a single nonprofit entity, and eliminating ownership of boxes once and for all.[21]

Chicago's opera company, created during the war between the Metropolitan and Hammerstein, received lavish subsidies from that city's civic-minded business elite, adopted a distinctly nonprofit form by the mid-1920s, and hung on for another twenty years. San Francisco also maintained an active opera company during the 1920s, one organized as an association and supported by business leaders. But the Metropolitan loomed so large in American operatic life that its shift to the nonprofit educational form was decisive.

Once that occurred, opera's legitimacy rose markedly. As the head of classical repertoire for RCA Victor wrote in a 1936 promotional volume, "While in former years," opera "generally attracted large audiences primarily as a form of entertainment, today opera is commanding the attention of both layman and serious musician as an important and significant art form" (RCA Manufacturing Co. 1936). Opera also became incorporated into the national high culture system, taking its place next to the other high arts in university curricula, as a subject of study by middle-class amateurs, and, with the rise of foundation arts support, an object of organized as well as individual giving. Groups modeled on civic symphonies brought opera to such small cities as Flint, Michigan, where it was sponsored by the Community Chest, and Allentown, Pennsylvania. Most of these essentially amateur operations presented between one and three operas a year, usually in English. Some, like Allentown's, favored operettas or "the better" musical comedies over more demanding grand opera (Graf 1951, 152–61).

In the wake of the Hammerstein affair, an experienced observer prophesied that a "new Moses" would inaugurate a "musical renaissance" by creating a national circuit of interdependent stock houses to present "grand opera in English" throughout the United States (Grau 1910).[22] By the 1930s, no one believed that opera's salvation, much less its diffusion, lay in the hands of commercial enterprise. If America was to have opera, critics agreed, it would be organized in the same way as classical music and fine art.

Dance: From Ancillary to Art

If art theater faced the dilemma of indistinct boundaries and opera the problem of organizational form, the dance confronted both at once and, by World War II, had made only tentative steps toward their solution. At the turn of the century, dance could barely claim the mantle of art. Of what are today the two major forms of artistic dance, one, ballet, was merely "a shadow of grand opera," as Robert Edmond Jones put it (1930, 257). The other, aesthetic or "modern" dance, was inchoate, a hazy figure on the busy ground of the vaudeville stage. Practitioners of each were in moral and aesthetic disrepute.

Between 1900 and 1940, American artists in both ballet and the aesthetic dance would attempt to elevate their activities to the position of classical music and fine art—with much quarreling among themselves. Their strategies were markedly different. Aesthetic dance, which, starting from scratch, had much the harder time of it, sought ennoblement by association with the established arts, with modernism and physical culture, and with the wealthy. Ballet, by contrast, had to free itself from past associations and establish an identity distinct from its conventional role as an ancillary to opera.

Ballet had enjoyed a brief vogue around mid-century: Viennese ballerina Fanny Elssler's 1840s tour was a success unmatched until the arrival of Jenny Lind, and others followed in her wake.[23] But by the 1860s its popularity had subsided: the "unattractive and somewhat mature coterie of foreign choristers" who danced for grand opera companies were poorly trained, poorly rewarded, and of minor interest compared to orchestral and vocal elements.[24] Their lightly girded limbs called their virtue into question, especially with the incorporation of ballet in Broadway spectacle-extravaganza—lavishly produced fantasies in which mythic story lines knit together musical numbers and special effects—until "ballet was considered synonymous with the leg shows that also featured ranks of girls in tights" (Kendall 1979, 7; Freedly 1948, 65–79). (Indeed, the nineteenth-century public made few distinctions about the dance of any kind. In 1885, Allen Dodworth, New York's most prominent teacher of ballroom styles, bemoaned "a general failure to apprehend the difference between ballet and social dancing" [O'Neill 1948, 85].)

Not until the Metropolitan Opera and the New Theatre brought Anna Pavlova and Mikhail Mordkin to the latter's stage in 1910, and the attendant vogue, renewed by a Russian tour in 1911 and the arrival of Diaghilev himself with the Ballet Russe a few years later, would ballet approach the status it eventually gained.[25] But these events were one-shot commercial tours; they laid the groundwork for American ballet but did not establish it.[26] American dancers trained in ballet still had to make their careers in Europe or, like Joseph Smith, who danced at La Scala and introduced the "turkey trot" in the early 1900s, to ply a variety of genres (Moore 1948a, 187).

Meanwhile, a small circle of female vaudeville performers—Loie Fuller, Ruth St. Denis, Maud Allan, and a few others—were creating a new art form out of odds and ends of the commercial stage.[27] The coincidence of three developments made it possible for them to do so. First, the rapid expansion of commercial popular entertainments, from vaudeville to international expositions, had shaken traditions of stage dancing and provided a vast range of styles from which an innovator could choose, splicing together old-fashioned clog dances and cake-walks, social dance in many forms, Spanish styles, the exotic "Oriental dance" popularized by "Little Egypt" on the Chicago Midway in 1893, and the vaudeville "skirt dance."[28] Second, the craze for physical culture and "aesthetic gymnastics," associated with both eugenics and the feminist "free-dress" movement by American exponents of Delsarte's metaphysically elaborate system, provided a receptive elite (and largely female) public for forms of physical expression that were in many quarters still regarded as immoral.[29] Third, B. F. Keith's dedication of his Orpheum Circuit to "refined vaudeville" created a market for acts that, like the first interpretive dancers, could dance a calculatedly ambiguous line between the titillating and the aesthetic.[30]

The pioneers innovated on the New York vaudeville stage, then proceeded to Europe, where they won wide acclaim. After several years abroad, they took New York by storm. As their careers and styles matured, the hold of old-fashioned theater dance on their work weakened, and the influence of aesthetic gymnastics and Orientalism grew. Many of them left vaudeville (or tried to leave it) for the concert stage, presenting Sunday concerts and matinees to audiences of wealthy women or college students (Kendell 1979).

In their efforts to claim the prestige of art for an activity that contemporaries often had trouble distinguishing from "hootch dancing," aesthetic dancers sought to create a new vocabulary for understanding their work and to associate it by juxtaposition with what art museums

and orchestras had defined as the great traditions of Western civilization. They emphasized the physical and moral healthfulness of free and
unrestrained movement.[31] They emulated Grecian vases and mock-
classic painting in dress and gesture, claiming antique origins for their
new approach to dance. Some, like Isadora Duncan, who startled audiences by swaying to Chopin in 1900 and Beethoven's Seventh a few
years later, danced to the music of the greatest composers or depicted
stories drawn from the canvases of famous artists.[32] Their followers
succeeded in ensconcing dance, often in the form of "aesthetic gymnastics," in the curricula of the most prestigious women's colleges.[33] And
although many toured Keith's circuit, most tried to avoid vaudeville,
seeking livings in opera-house concert engagements, private soirees in
Newport or Manhattan, or even, like Duncan, performing with symphony orchestras. Few succeeded at this for very long: just three years
after Ruth St. Denis's national success with *Egypta* in 1911, she was
touring southeastern backwaters; for her, as for many others, teaching,
not concert life, was the alternative to vaudeville or musical revue
work.[34]

So new was aesthetic dance, and so rooted in the commercial stage,
that it seems not to have occurred to the innovators to follow the path
of orchestras and even theaters in seeking endowment and incorporation as trustee-governed nonprofit organizations. There were a few
patrons and guarantors, the ubiquitous Otto Kahn among them, and
many women of wealth who paid dancers to perform in their salons
or even pursued the "classical dance" themselves.[35] But in the 1920s—
when St. Denis's husband and partner, Ted Shawn, envisioned "American born and raised dancers, dancing to music by American composers,
with scenery and costumes designed by American artists, *and under the
direction and management of American business men*" (Chujoy 1953,
49; emphasis added)—dance was viewed as something less than an
incorporatable art. (Denishawn, as they called their school and company, solved its financial problems by serving as a tony ingenue hatch-
ery for D. W. Griffith and Cecil B. DeMille [Kendall 1979].)

Martha Graham, a Denishawn student, was one who hoped for an
alternative. After making her name in Shawn's *Xochitl*, a "Toltec" epic
in the tradition of the nineteenth-century spectacle-extravaganza, she
decried the absence of genuine American dance "as an art form." "Instead of an art which was the fruit of a people's soul," she complained,
"we had entertainment." Graham's solution was to eliminate the theatrical paraphernalia that had served her so well as *Xochitl* cycled through
the Pantages vaudeville circuit and to focus, instead, on "concert

dance"—"that performance where dance is the focal point" (Graham 1930, 250–51; see also Kendall 1979, 166–68). But Graham was unable at first to realize her vision. Not concerts but teaching berths at the Eastman School and a New York conservatory enabled her to leave the security of the Greenwich Village Follies and start her own company (Kendall 1979, 171–79).

Not until the creation of the American Ballet did the dance attain institutional proportions, and even Balanchine's company, despite the purity of its founders' motives, failed to emulate the high culture organizational model for many years (Chujoy 1953; Kirstein [1938] 1967). Balanchine, of course, specialized in ballet, not "modern dance," at a time when practitioners of the two approaches had little use for one another. But the difference was not as marked as it might seem: Balanchine was a choreographic innovator who drew on but was not fettered by the Russian balletic tradition; Lincoln Kirstein's Ballet Caravan, an offshoot of Balanchine's company, was even closer in spirit to the modernists. By the 1930s, the difference lay less in style per se than in pedagogy (Kirstein and Balanchine believed that classic training from earliest childhood was a prerequisite for any form of serious dance) and earnestness of purpose, criteria that made Martha Graham acceptable to Kirstein whereas most of her contemporaries were not. In turn, the ballet that Graham detested was not Balanchine's but the term *American ballet*, which "has been so exploited commercially, as to be useless and shabby at present—having no art value" (Graham 1930, 252).[36]

Why was Balanchine's company not organized as a nonprofit corporation? Kirstein and his partner, philanthropist Edward Warburg, both of whom were close to the Museum of Modern Art, knew all about trustee-governed organizations; until Balanchine rebelled, they had planned to incorporate their school and company under the sponsorship of a Hartford art museum, in part to keep it away from New York theatrical influence (Chujoy 1953, 25–29). They no doubt feared losing control of an organization with an innovative vision that few American patrons would understand, yet that is exactly what they lost during the American Ballet's unhappy tenure with the Metropolitan Opera in the late 1930s. Moreover, when they *did* relinquish control, Kirstein devoting himself to the school and the Ballet Caravan and Warburg resigning later to take responsibility for his late father's philanthropies, they gave the company to Balanchine himself, who was increasingly engrossed in Broadway and Hollywood projects, rather than to a nonprofit corporation (Chujoy 1953, 66). Kirstein claimed that patronage was a thing of the past, but he must have known better:

despite the depression's dampening effect, dozens of new art museums and orchestras sprang up during the 1930s, demonstrating that hard times had hardly eliminated cultural philanthropy. Rather, the answer must be that the dance, either interpretive or American ballet, was simply not sufficiently prestigious for endowment to be a viable strategy.

Kirstein called attention to the rise of the orchestra in just sixty years to a point at which America had "an endowed orchestral institution in almost every one of our fair-sized cities." "It is not too much to hope," he proclaimed, "that we may be able to have one day as many ballet organizations as there are orchestras." Oddly enough, however, he proposed that ballet emulate not the orchestras, with their trustees and endowments, but the organized audience schemes of the art theater, calling on American ballet companies to create "a strong combination with each other" to form a national booking office and "the creation of a definite provincial American *circuit* for dance-attractions as such" (Kirstein [1938] 1967, 47–48, 110–13).

Ballet was being taken more seriously as art by the 1930s, as the result of the Russian tours and the teachers they left behind, of Balanchine and Kirstein's efforts, and of the efforts of such other dancer-choreographers as Chicago's Ruth Page and Philadelphia's Ruth Littlefield. Proselytizers like Arnold L. Haskell, British publicist for the Ballet Russe de Monte Carlo, created the worshipful figure of the "balletomane," bringing to dance the intensity of quasi-religious devotion that nineteenth-century aesthetes had lavished on Beethoven (Haskell 1934).[37] In a sense, ballet was riding the coattails of opera, which, as we have seen, was becoming less commercial and ever more earnest. But the most successful ballets outside opera were still those that offered mixed programs to commercial crowds on tours backed by impresarios like Sol Hurok. Those unwilling or, because their style was academic or opaque, unable to take to the commercial circuit had but three options: teaching, opera, or, as the Ballet Caravan did, eking out an existence from subsidized tours of college campuses.[38]

However ambiguous their status, and however tentative, for different reasons, their claims to artistic prominence, ballet and aesthetic dance progressed during the 1920s and 1930s toward inclusion among the high arts. By 1938, Kirstein ([1938] 1967, 47) discerned "the first healthy signs of local American ballet companies" in a dozen American cities. According to a contemporary estimate, there were one thousand "professional creative dancers" at work in the United States and another three thousand students. Between 1926 and 1930 the number of dance concerts in New York and Chicago rose from thirty to more than one hundred. And between 1920 and 1930 the number of dance teachers and dance students (defined broadly, but excluding classes in ballroom dance) more than doubled, to 5,000 and 500,000, respectively (Keppel and Duffus 1933, 175–76).[39]

Yet if an increasing number of Americans could distinguish aesthetic dance and ballet from the dance of the Broadway revue and were willing to grant its artistic value and even to pay to see it, neither form would prosper so long as it depended on the commercial circuits. If a few of the dance students would seek to serve art, far more were "absorbed into the dance factories and films" or worked "as trick machines in Vaudeville," as Haskell (1934, 275) put it. Publicist and critic Oliver Sayler, bemoaning the condition of American dance in 1930, was nearly alone in calling for endowed dance institutions: "We must hunt a Maecenas," he wrote, but "we scan the environment without seeing a hint" of one (1930, 94). Practitioners of the dance would not wrest independence—from the entertainment industry and from the margins of opera—until, some forty years later, they learned how to employ the same organizational form by which the theaters established themselves as agents of art.

Conclusion

The processes by which high culture institutions expanded to encompass additional art forms are of interest because they demonstrate that the construction of the edifice of "high culture" and the constitution of certain artistic expressions as "cultural capital" took place not at once but rather over a period of many years. The stories of the progress of opera, theater, and the dance to "high cultural" status remind us that, even though systems of cultural classification present themselves as based on natural and enduring judgments of value, they are products of human action, continually subject to accretion and erosion, selection and change.

In each case, some combination of patrons and artists created boundaries that polarized what had been a continuum of aesthetic practice. The stories are similar in that, in order to bound themselves from related "popular" forms, opera, theater, and the dance all had to accomplish two things. The first was to free themselves from the grip of the marketplace (which ordinarily drives entrepreneurs to elide aesthetic distinctions in order to create larger audiences and discourages canon formation by providing incentives for presenters to differentiate their products). The role of the nonprofit organization was central to this process, for it provided sufficient autonomy from the market to make credible the professions of "disinterestedness" on which claims to high cultural status ride. Second, erecting boundaries required developing ties to the universities, which in the United States have been the dominant centers in which cultural authority has been institutionalized, as well as the organizations most responsible for engaging the interest of young people in elite culture.

Despite these commonalities, the particulars of the processes by which the content of drama, opera, and the dance became forms of cultural capital varied significantly. In theater, the popular end of the continuum was simply extinguished (or, more accurately, transformed into another genre, film) by technological change, leaving a vacuum. In opera, a profitable art became unprofitable in any form. In dance, the artists themselves were primarily responsible for creating innovations and ideologies that made a disreputable ancillary to other forms of performance a plausible contender in its own right. Even within the limited scope of aesthetics in the United States, no one set of generalizations characterizes the process of sacralization in all cases. Rather, every art form, from opera and the dance to film and rock and roll, has had practitioners, and often patrons, who have tried to elevate its prestige. Whether they have succeeded has depended on the shape of the opportunity space (the existence of competitors, commercial substitutes, or publics and patrons of new wealth) and the point in time at which such projects take shape, which determines the preexisting discursive and organizational resources available for imitation.

In effect, these observations treat artistic disciplines as independent units of analysis that can be subjected to systematic comparison. What is striking, however, in the stories I have told is the extent to which the institutions of cultural production constitute a field of interrelated parts. Theater, dance, and opera piggybacked, symbolically and organizationally, on the high culture forms that had been sacralized before them. Dance asserted its claims to art by conscious juxtaposition of novel movements to classical art and music; art theaters allied themselves with art museums; and when economic crisis struck, opera eventually turned to the orchestra for an organizational model. By 1910, the justifications developed by founders of the nation's first art museums and orchestras served as ready-made ideological resources that cultural entrepreneurs could employ across a range of other art forms. The organizational models they pioneered also served as resources for those who would clarify the boundaries of opera, theater, and the dance.

The art museums and orchestras retained a first-mover advantage that constrained the progress of other forms, however. For one thing, they commanded by far the largest share of donative resources throughout the period in question as well as the largest share of prestige, the coin with which the most generous potential donors could be recruited to boards of trustees. (Opera could rival them in a few cities, but not many.) Moreover, art and music, as first movers, participated centrally in the nationalization of high culture after World War I. They were the only arts disciplines that entered the humanistic (as opposed to professional) curriculum as core departments in most colleges and universities. They accounted for the vast majority of arts spending by philanthropic foundations between 1920 and 1940. Advocates of each mounted national appreciation campaigns, with clubwomen and public-school teachers as footsoldiers, that spread popular awareness of their canons (DiMaggio 1991).

By contrast, later movers were largely left out of these developments. Patronage for theater and the dance was hard to find and came largely from the new middle class and from those excluded from the governance of museums and orchestras. Opera was included in the curriculum under the aegis of classical music; dance was taught as part of physical education in women's colleges; drama remained largely a field of professional education.

Consequently, the late movers relied more on national institutions and initiative and less on locally influential people for their survival than did the museums and orchestras. The Metropolitan, which was for many years the only substantial and stable American opera company, developed the Opera Guild as a national support organization. Assistance for drama was organized in the 1930s by university-based professionals through the National Theatre Conference, with support from the Rockefeller Foundation. Concert dance relied on national tours of college campuses for many years. The rise of nonprofit, professional regional stages as fixtures of urban places was the result of a Ford Foundation project in the 1960s. The dance owed its expansion and institutionalization during the 1970s to the National Endowment for the Arts.

The greater openness of theater and the dance than of music and, until the rise of the postwar art market, of visual art to modernism was likewise a consequence of their late-mover status. (Opera was different because of its tradition of elite patronage and because it had established its canon years before.) Weaker ties to local elites who, in music and art, exerted a conservative influence on the museums' and orchestras' openness to innovation, the lack of partially autonomous academic disciplines with the cultural authority to define and sustain strongly bounded canons, and the fact that modernism was already on the horizon when art theater and the dance became institutionalized—all contributed to the weaker insulation of high cultural contents and their greater openness to change. Likewise, the absence of strong community-based nonprofit institutions ensured weaker boundaries between "serious" drama and dance and their commercial counterparts.

Indeed, the rise of art theater and the dance was shaped by the developing organization of commercial culture. As we have seen, the elevation of theater to an art form was due largely to the abdication of the stage by commercial interests after the rise of film. The emergence of aesthetic dance would have been impossible but for the development of "refined" vaudeville circuits in the century's first years. Even the status of opera as high culture, which might otherwise have been recognized only in the few cities that boasted active companies, was broadened by opera's adoption by commercial broadcasters and record companies (most of which included opera recordings on special classical "labels" like Victor's Red Seal).

One implication of this argument is that, as the scope of high culture broadened to additional forms of art, the distinction between sacred and profane culture became less dichotomous and more continuous. Although intellectuals wrote of the "seven arts" and "high culture," in fact, organizationally and ideologically, art, music, opera, drama, ballet, and the dance represented points on a spectrum, varying in prestige, institutional stability, and the degree to which each was insulated from commercial entertainments.

In the long run, these developments tended to erode the strong classification, "high" or sacred versus "vulgar," erected by the cultural entrepreneurs of the nineteenth century. By the 1920s, new aspirants to the title of *art*—not just theater and the dance but modern painting, photography, and film—had come to the fore. For the most part, their sponsors were in one way or another outsiders: Jewish Americans excluded from elite circles or women, often wealthy ones, rebelling against the stifling constraints of Victorianism. To the extent that they succeeded, they self-consciously moved outside the boundaries of urban upper-class status communities to create, or use, institutions that were national, rather than local, in scope: Kirstein's ballet and the Museum of Modern Art are examples of this. Although advocates of the new art forms and genres embraced a version of aestheticism similar to that of their predecessors and used the nonprofit form whenever they could afford to do so, they were more willing to apply the disinterested gaze of the connoisseur to modern and American aesthetic contents. Outsiders by gender, ethnicity, or simply personal idiosyncracy to the closed communities of post-Victorian wealth, these patrons, and the artists they supported, were more inclined than their predecessors to play with boundaries between art and market, between the culture of the elite and the entertainments of the street.

Notes

I gratefully acknowledge support for the research on which this paper is based from the Ford Foundation, the Rockefeller Foundation, and the John Simon Guggenheim Memorial Foundation. I am grateful to Brad Gray and Michèle Lamont for helpful comments on earlier drafts. Any errors of fact or interpretation are mine alone.

1. By *sacred* culture I mean not religious art and music but predominantly secular works (classical statuary, the symphonies of Beethoven) that cultural entrepreneurs began to talk and think about in new ways and to treat as if they embodied divine inspiration and as if the experience they provided their viewers or listeners was sharply disjoined from the mundane and interested world of everyday life. In other words, *sacredness* in this sense has less to do with the content of art than with the kinds of barriers—cognitive and organizational—that are built up around it.

2. These, in turn, came out of the wide vogue for parlor dramatics in the 1860s and 1870s, many of the forms of which (e.g., masques and tableaux) were prominent in the rural theater movement of the 1920s. For a probing discussion of American Victorian theatricality, see Halttunen (1982).

3. Of the numerous contemporary and subsequent accounts of the little theater, the most useful, on which this section principally draws, are Dickinson (1917), MacGowan (1929), Houghton (1941), and Poggi (1968).

4. Salaries at Maurice Browne's Chicago Little Theatre rose from $3.50 per week in the early years to $10.00–$16.00 later on; Jaspar Deeter gave actors at his Hedgerow Theatre in suburban Philadelphia room and board, expenses, and a share in net revenues, when there were any (MacGowan 1929, 96, 298).

5. Indeed, some of them started this way. Philadelphia's Plays and Players Club, which performed only for its distinctly blue-blooded membership, took as its goal "to associate the amateur histrionic talent and playwrights of the community for the advancement and production of amateur theatricals and for literacy and social intercourse" and to serve as "a promoting committee for

good drama" (Dickinson 1917, 73). According to MacGowan (1929, 85–86), the organization of little theaters as private clubs was particularly common in the Southeast.

6. The guild's activities contributed to the definition of a canonical set of "good" plays. Reporting on his fourteen-thousand-mile tour of American noncommercial stages, Kenneth MacGowan (1929, 73, 194) reported, "I found the Guild's repertory being repeated again and again all over the country."

7. Not surprisingly, the theaters that were organizationally closest to the high culture model were most similar to orchestras and art museums socially and aesthetically as well. The Goodman suffered mass resignations in the late 1920s because, in the words of one observer, "what 'the best people' think rather than what 'the people' feel is the standard of its activities; in other words, because its standards are parochial European, not autochthonous" (Browne 1930, 207).

8. The Keith-Albee-Orpheum vaudeville chain was known to entertainers as the "Sunday-school circuit." Not only did Keith, who began his vaudeville career in the late 1880s and whose devoutly Catholic wife participated in his business, ban off-color humor, but he forbid such audience practices as whistling, smoking, hollering, and spitting, conventional in working-class houses. By 1893, when Keith opened Boston's Colonial Theatre to vaudeville, even Chauncey Depew, gatekeeper of New York society, was induced to attend. By 1922, Keith's Cleveland Palace featured paintings by Corot and Bougereau in the lobby (Gilbert 1940, 204–9). If vaudeville theaters still rarely entertained the upper crust, they played to many women and children, and by 1910 several agents specialized in booking vaudeville acts into the private parlors of the wealthy (Grau 1910, 191).

9. On vaudeville, see Grau (1910), Gilbert (1940), and Toll (1976). On the stratification of commercial culture, see Kasson (1978), Rozenzweig (1983), Erenberg (1981), Peiss (1986), and Levine (1988).

10. A book on community drama notes that in "small communities . . . only through the medium of the motion-picture" are "occasional fleeting glimpses . . . caught of the plays which are thrilling large cities. . . . Towns far removed from dramatic centers are now realizing that if they are to have plays they must produce them" (Playground and Recreation Association of America 1926, 3).

11. The indispensable treatment of the Syndicate is Poggi's (1968) fine economic history of the American theater. Useful discussions appear in Grau (1910), MacGowan (1929), Toll (1976), and Lynes (1985). Thomas Dickinson, who authored the first survey of the little theater field in 1917, attributes "the first signs of insurgency in the theatre" to "those actors who felt the new business systems coming down around them and sought to escape their hampering control" (pp. 20–21).

12. I derive these figures by subtracting MacGowan's enumeration of New York City "first-class houses" from a count by *Billboard* of "legitimate theatres"

that MacGowan cites. Poggi (1968, 28) places the number of theaters outside metropolitan areas at 1,549 in 1910, 674 in 1925, and 400 in 1928.

13. For fine general discussions of the evolution of film and the impact of film on the stage, see Poggi (1968) and Sklar (1975). On the number of legitimate theaters and stock companies, see Houghton (1941, 14, 48). The number of stock companies does not include summer stock, which was only beginning to become popular in the late 1930s.

14. Levine (1988) brilliantly demonstrates the shift in opera's social constituency during the nineteenth century but overstates the degree to which issues of opera's definition, sponsorship, merit, and legitimacy were resolved by the turn of the century.

15. The Metropolitan, at the box level at least, had the character of an elite social club. The less desirable seats catered to the German opera audience, which protested the noisy carryings-on above them (Brenneise, n.d.). In fact, in 1893, the Metropolitan's owners *created* a private men's club, the Vaudeville Club, that satisfied their appetite for a form of entertainment that many of them undoubtedly savored more than opera—and, it was rumored, served as a means to sating even baser appetites at the expense of the women entertainers employed there (Shelton 1981, 25–26).

16. Although most leading opera artists were Europeans and had thus pursued purely operatic careers, their American counterparts often transgressed genre boundaries, as did some of the Europeans themselves. Thus, contralto Ernestine Schumann-Heink left the Met for musical comedy, and Rosa Ponselle reached that institution after a career in "minor-league vaudeville" (Eaton 1968, 141, 205). Joseph Urban, brought to America as set designer for the Boston Opera Co., joined Ziegfeld's Follies when the opera closed its doors (Cantor and Freedman 1934, 127–29). Earlier, singer Mary Lewis had moved from the Follies to the Metropolitan stage (Kolodin 1936, 334). When the Met canceled its production of *Salomé* in 1907, the prima ballerina, Bianca Froelich, simply took her dance to vaudeville. "Mlle. Dazié," a Cincinnati-born toe-dancer who made her mark on the popular stage as the mysterious "Domino Roue" (so named because, for a time, she wore a red mask at all public performances), worked for Ziegfeld and danced in the Hammerstein Opera's corps de ballet in the same year (Grau 1910, 251–52; Kendall 1979).

17. Kolodin says that Abbey lost $600,000, whereas Grau (1910, 22) puts the figure at $400,000, and Eaton (1968, 63) cites estimates of $500,000. Abbey's losses included those from touring as well as from the Metropolitan season, although the latter were predominant. On German opera, see also Damrosch (1926) and Eaton (1968, 69–70).

18. Opera's position amid the commercial and sacred polls of the entertainment field is illustrated by the fact that Grau's major competitors for the job included Charles Ellis, business manager of the Boston Symphony Orchestra, and the Frohman Brothers, Broadway producers and principals in the Theatre Trust.

19. Hammerstein's declaration cannot be dismissed as pure public relations,

for he did create an opera house more hospitable to a middle-class audience, introduced innovations in repertoire, and maintained high quality. The *Post*, e.g., wrote of Hammerstein in 1907, "So far he has worked for art, and for art alone, regardless of expense, and for this reason and because of his daring and pluck, he deserves complete success" (Cone 1964, 123).

20. Cornelius Vanderbilt IV mocked the campaign as "the brilliant idea of letting the masses finance entertainment for the upper classes" (Eaton 1968, 248).

21. According to Eaton (1968, 281–85), many of the original box holders never returned. The association needed the house to secure a real-estate tax exemption, which could not be granted to a private, for-profit corporation (the Metropolitan Real Estate Co.). Once they took over the house, New York mayor LaGuardia denied the exemption on the grounds that "an educational institution, to warrant exemption, must do things for the public, and that, the Met does not" (Sokol 1981, 31).

22. Grau's discussion of opera is notable for his apparent disregard of all the boundaries that would later become salient. Although he praises philanthropists, he makes no distinction between philanthropic and commercial ventures, nor does he distinguish clearly between opera in English and in the original language or between grand opera and light (using the former term to embrace the latter). His nominee as the "new Moses" is Milton Aborn, a former vaudeville comedian then managing a light opera company.

23. On the decline of interest in ballet in the 1860s, see Moore (1948a, 184–86). On Elssler, see Levine (1988, 108). In the fashion of her day, Elssler "combined classical ballet with English hornpipes and Spanish folk dances." Earlier ballet companies were even more eclectic: Alexander Placide and his wife, among the first ballet artists to perform in the United States, like many others mixed classic ballet, gymnastics, circus acrobatics, and pantomime in the 1790s (Moore 1948b, 34–36). As Levine (1988) notes, such eclecticism died out in music and art with the sacralization of classical music and classic visual art by the 1900s. But in ballet, where commercial impresarios held sway, it remained characteristic. During the 1910s and 1920s, stage revues frequently featured a ballet or "interpretive dance" number. And touring ballets ordinarily featured "American" dance numbers as well as classic ballet; in the 1930s, the Ballet Russe de Monte Carlo, under Sol Hurok's sponsorship, combined classic ballet and popular numbers into what one critic called an "artistic leg show" (Chujoy 1953, 36). Even Balanchine, in his first New York season, received the loudest cheers (from audiences, if not critics) for the single deviation from classic ballet, *Alma Mater*, which, the *New York Times* reported, "departs so slightly from the type of dancing that has been done for years in revue that it is of little consequence" (Chujoy 1953, 48). In other words, absent the high culture model of organization, neither the passage of time nor the evolution of aesthetic ideologies was sufficient to segregate popular and "high art" genres in practice.

24. This is Robert Grau's characterization of the Metropolitan Opera's

corps de ballet during the years that his brother Maurice managed the company (1910, 254).

25. The shift was initially subtle. Even in the 1910s, cosmopolitans like Agnes DeMille's playwright-director father, Cecil B. DeMille's brother and collaborator, "considered dancing at best exhibitionistic acrobatics, and certainly a field that offered neither intellectual nor spiritual challenge. . . . Worse, the woman dancer entered a field long and closely associated with prostitution" (DeMille 1952, 70–71).

26. Outside New York City, opera ballet remained associated with vice even after Pavlova. In 1910, an Indianapolis critic wrote of the touring Boston Opera Co.'s principal dancer, "One wonders what kind of a woman it is that will bare her body and exhibit it to public gaze. Art? One kind, perhaps, but there are some people brought up with ideas of modesty that will be willing to have this branch of their education underdeveloped" (Eaton 1965, 72).

27. The most important works on dance are Kendall (1979) and Ruyter (1979); see also Van Vechten ([1910] 1948) on Allan, Hastings (1948), Terry (1976), and Shelton (1981) on Denishawn, and Duncan ([1927] 1955).

28. The skirt dance was itself an eclectic innovation, influenced by blackface and, more important although less common, African-American minstrelsy (Winter 1948; Toll 1974). Its development was related to the shift in social dance from the collective forms of the early nineteenth century to "closed-couple dances," first the waltz and, by the 1890s, a freer assortment of two-steps and related dances (Erenberg 1981, 149–50).

29. François Delsarte was a French teacher of voice and pantomime who sought to develop a science of movement. His American followers, of whom Genevieve Stebbins was most notable, welded Delsartianism to the physical culture movement (Ruyter 1979; Sussman 1990, 15; Kendall 1979, 23–24). On the link to eugenics, see Kendall (1979, 107–11). On the origins of the free-dress movement, see Banner (1983, chap. 6).

30. This was especially true of dancers like Maud Allan and Ruth St. Denis, who combined aesthetic claims with refined commercial sensibilities. Allan, e.g., was noted for her performance of *Salomé*, based on the character of the opera by the same name. J. P. Morgan and confederates among the Metropolitan Opera House partners closed the Met's production of *Salomé* prematurely in 1907 because they regarded it as licentious, thus creating a small industry of imitators (including Hammerstein, who staged it the next season) eager to benefit from the character's simultaneous appeal to the artistic and the salacious. By 1908, the school of Mlle. Dazié (née Peterkin) turned out 150 *Salomés* monthly for vaudeville promoters (Kendall 1979, 74–75). Maud Allan rode *Salomé* to fame in Europe, but by the time she had returned to the United States, Carl Van Vechten reported that "New York has seen so many dances of this sort by now that there were no exclamations of shocked surprise, no one fainted, and, at the end there was no very definite applause" (Van Vechten [1910] 1948, 221–23).

31. Criticized in 1909 for appearing "without fleshing and in bare feet,"

Loie Fuller denounced the "hideous man-made lines of the corset" (DeMorinni 1948, 216). No one was better at appropriating the halo of high culture to dance than Isadora Duncan, whose own classical education and middle-class family background gave her an authority with which elite women could more easily identify. The first chapter of her autobiography is ample evidence of this. In a mere eight pages, she manages allusions to Rousseau, Dante, and Whitman as well as to her "Art" (the latter always capitalized). A few pages later she describes her "real education" as consisting of early exposure to Beethoven, Schumann, Schubert, Mozart, Chopin, Shakespeare, Shelley, Keats, and Burns, encompassing two separate canons within a single sentence. In 1930, after her death, Isadora's sister Elizabeth, her partner in dance education for many years, captured in a three-page essay all the essential elements of the dance ideology: aestheticism ("the universal connection of the dance with the other arts"); spiritualism (before Isadora "the religion of the human body had been forgotten"); physical culture and eugenics (dance education's "fundamental" aim is "to make a stronger and freer human race); and feminism ("Isadora brought a *new freedom* to the body and spirit") (pp. 245–47; emphasis added).

32. The problem, of course, was that, lacking unified elite sponsorship of the sort granted fine art and classical music, aesthetic dancers—who significantly made their greatest progress in New York, with its fragmented elite, and Los Angeles, which was too young to have an upper class, except for the movie magnates for whom dancers were a crucial industrial input—often found their claims derided. Robert Grau (1910) was typical when he wrote of the "present craze for dancing to the music of the great masters," "And yet, this latest craze does not seem to possess the elements of sustained interest desired by its exponents, nor can it be said that even the surroundings of a symphony orchestra and the selection of the scores of the world's greatest masters will overcome for any great length of time, the suggestive, if not questionable, type of costume—or shall I say the lack of such, which, after all, is the basic element by which these wholly unknown dancers had come to their fame" (p. 25). Grau noted that, when Maud Allan, famed for her bare-midriffed depiction of Salomé, appeared at Carnegie Hall, "a careful observer . . . would easily form the impression that sensationalism was the incentive for the management and the attraction as well from a box office point of view" (p. 251). Even Duncan's recreations of pictorial masterpieces could be misconstrued; for all the aesthetic gloss Isadora gave them, they were essentially more *vivants* resurrections of the *tableaux* popular among male patrons of 1880s dime museums and variety houses. Occasionally, such efforts met with resistance: when Ruth St. Denis first performed her *Radha* in Paris, the French Society of Authors and Composers prevented her from using Delibes's compositions, which had backed her in New York and London, because such "music was unsuitable for the decadent art of dancing" (Shelton 1981, 74).

33. Ruyter (1979) and Sussman (1990) describe the close links between the Delsartian movement, modern dance, and women's colleges, and Kendall

(1979) describes the profound influence of Delsartianism and the women's health movement on many of the leading female dancers of the first generation. Sussman points out that women's colleges initiated gymnastics curricula early, in defense against claims that higher education debilitated women, and became an important training ground for aesthetic dancers; as Kendall indicates, whereas the first generation (as usual excepting Duncan) came from poor families, by the 1910s art dancers were often wealthy women or their daughters. This change in the class origins of dancers, similar to the change in the backgrounds of actors during the same period (McArthur 1984), was a significant factor in gaining public acceptance of stage dance as an "acceptable" activity.

34. By 1935, in between performances at society salons and symphony orchestras, St. Denis was receiving New York City welfare checks to cover her rent; a teaching position at Adelphi College helped her regain financial stability (Shelton 1981, 100–103, 244, 250). When she was considering a concert career in the late 1920s, Agnes DeMille, who became a successful stage dancer and choreographer, was told by Sol Hurok that a debut concert series would cost her $3,000; she choreographed a revival of *The Black Crook,* the original spectacle-extravaganza of the 1870s, in Hoboken instead and worked in "third-rate moving-picture houses in Baltimore, Max Reinhardt's Chorus, a stock company . . . , a movie short, private parties, third-rate night clubs" (DeMille 1952, 131, 135–36).

35. The appeal of art dance, an ambiguously multivocal form, to wealthy women was essential to its survival. Ruth St. Denis's *Radha,* a kind of Oriental serpent dance, was originally rejected by vaudeville agents and managers, who regarded it as too close to vulgar "hootch and peep-show styles" for the increasingly respectable vaudeville stage. St. Denis was eventually given a slot at Proctor's between a prizefighter and some trained monkeys. Discovered by a wealthy woman spectator, she became popular among one set of New York socialites, who sponsored her in a series of private matinees, billed as a "Temple Dancer" and presented in rented theaters to the accompaniment of incense and genuine Hindus. Mrs. Fennelosa, the Salem-born daughter of the Museum of Fine Art's curator and Orientalist lecturer, attended the first performance, and, before long, St. Denis danced at Mrs. Gardner's Fenway Court (Shelton 1981, 58). Isadora Duncan, who had less patience with the commercial stage and none with variety, gravitated almost immediately toward Delsartean performances in private salons (Kendall 1979, 51–54, 63, 86–87).

36. As usual, more than aesthetics was at stake in the controversy between the interpretive or "modern" dancers, preponderantly women and staunchly feminist, and devotees of serious ballet. The latter's contention that disciplined dance training must start in childhood not only denigrated the skills of most of the former but, more profoundly, also implied that, having cast off their corsets, women must submit to a domination even more profound, entailing the shaping of their spirits as well as their bodies. Thus, Isadora Duncan wrote

of her only ballet lessons that, when her "famous ballet teacher . . . told me to stand on my toes, I asked him why, and when he replied 'Because it is beautiful,' I said that it was ugly and against nature and after the third lesson I left his class, never to return" (Duncan [1927] 1955, 21).

37. Although Balanchine and Duncan sniffed at Massine's ensemble, which catered to the catholic tastes of its audiences on the vaudeville circuit, Haskell depicted it as art personified. His *Balletomania* (1934) is a paean to ballet as an art form as well as to Massine himself; its theme is that "ballet is so much more than just a pleasant evening's entertainment; that like music or the drama it has endless varieties of shades and subtleties not as yet fully understood outside dancing circles" (p. xviii). Kirstein, too, applied the by-now classic language of aestheticism to ballet. Balanchine, he wrote, "in his serious work" (as distinguished from his Broadway projects) "has always avoided crass pageantry, showy stage pictures of living models, pictorial build-ups, and parades in which there is not *dancing* as such. . . . His movement is a continual homage to music. . . . Balanchine's greatest pleasure is derived from his collaborations with the scores of Gluck, Mozart, Chopin, Liszt, Tchaikovsky. . . . Balanchine has an inborn choreographic sense so acute as to amount almost to that of a painter's extra gift, giving him an eye so delicate that he can see color spectra past the range of his fellows . . . his choreography is not ever literally narrative; it seldom tells a consecutive story. . . . [his dances] have to be watched more closely than the ordinary corroborative mimicry which is easily familiar to superficial audiences. . . . Nor are his gestures 'symbolic'; they do not *symbolize* anything; they are in themselves deeply and completely lyrical" (Kirstein [1938] 1967, 22–23).

I quote at such length because Kirstein so well illustrates the established discursive resources that, by the 1920s, were available to sophisticated propagandists for aspiring art forms owing to the success of the classification projects of the late 1800s. Theme for theme, Kirstein recapitulates, with reference to dance, the arguments and valuative criteria used by T. S. Dwight and his contemporaries to elevate classical music: the distinction between serious and commercial endeavor; the identification of the latter with spectacle, a deformed and illegitimate kind of art; the identification of ballet with classical music by association (Balanchine as *collaborator* of Mozart and Liszt) and with the visual arts by a simile incorporating the Romantic ideology of genius (the "painter's extra gift . . . an eye so delicate that he can see color spectra" that we cannot); the devaluation of representation in favor of abstraction and "art as such"; the challenge to the reader to recognize Balanchine as better because he is more demanding, with the promise that readers may raise themselves above the mere "superficial audiences." Change a few words, and you can read Dwight on Beethoven, ca. 1865.

38. In their efforts to insulate the dance from the commercial theater world, both Graham and Kirstein avoided the established commercial booking agencies in favor of the Pond Lecture Bureau (Chujoy 1953, 78–79).

39. The growing legitimacy of dance is evident by comparison of Keppel and Duffus's *The Arts in American Life* (1933) to its predecessor, Duffus's *The American Renaissance* (1928), in which dance and ballet receive no mention.

References

Banner, Lois W. *American Beauty.* Chicago: University of Chicago Press, 1983.

Brenneise, Harvey. "Art of Entertainment? The Development of the Metropolitan Opera, 1883–1900." M.A. thesis, Andrews University, n.d.

Browne, Maurice. "Suggesting a Dramatic Declaration of Independence." In *Revolt in the Arts: A Survey of the Creation, Distribution and Appreciation of Art in America,* ed. Oliver M. Sayler. New York: Brentano's, 1930.

Cantor, Eddie, and David Freedman. *Ziegfeld: The Great Glorifier.* New York: Alfred H. King, 1934.

Chujoy, Anatole. *The New York City Ballet.* New York: Knopf, 1953.

Cone, John Frederick. *Oscar Hammerstein's Manhattan Opera Company.* Norman: University of Oklahoma Press, 1964.

Damrosch, Walter. *My Musical Life.* New York: Scribner's, 1926.

DeMille, Agnes. *Dance to the Piper.* Boston: Little, Brown, 1952.

DeMorinni, Clare. "Loie Fuller: The Fairy of Light." In *Chronicles of the American Dance,* ed. Paul Magriel. New York: Henry Holt, 1948.

De Nora, Tia. "Musical Patronage and Social Change at the Time of Beethoven's Arrival in Vienna." *American Journal of Sociology* 97 (1991).

Dickinson, Thomas H. *The Insurgent Theatre.* New York: B. W. Huebsch, 1917.

DiMaggio, Paul. "Cultural Entrepreneurship in Nineteenth-Century Boston." Parts 1, 2. *Media, Culture and Society* 4 (1982): 33–50, 303–22.

DiMaggio, Paul. "Constructing an Organizational Field as a Professional Project: U.S. Art Museums, 1920–1940." In *The New Institutionalism in Organizational Analysis,* ed. Walter Powell and Paul DiMaggio. Chicago: University of Chicago Press, 1991.

Duffus, R. L. *The American Renaissance.* New York: Knopf, 1928.

Duncan, Elizabeth. "Nature, Teacher of the Dance." In *Revolt in the Arts: A Survey of the Creation, Distribution and Appreciation of Art in America,* ed. Oliver M. Sayler. New York: Brentano's, 1930.

Duncan, Isadora. *My Life.* 1927. Reprint. New York: Liveright, 1955.

Eaton, Quaintance. *The Boston Opera Company: The Story of a Unique Musical Institution.* New York: Appleton-Century, 1965.

Eaton, Quaintance. *The Miracle of the Met: An Informal History of the Metropolitan Opera, 1883–1967.* New York: Meredith, 1968.

Erenberg, Lewis A. *Steppin' Out: New York Night Life and the Transformation of American Culture, 1890–1930.* Chicago: University of Chicago Press, 1981.

Freedly, George. "The Black Crook and the White Fawn." In *Chronicles of the American Dance*, ed. Paul Magriel. New York: Henry Holt, 1948.

Gilbert, Douglas. *American Vaudeville: Its Life and Times*. New York: Dover, 1940.

Graf, Herbert. *Opera for the People*. Minneapolis: University of Minnesota Press, 1951.

Graham, Martha. "Seeking an American Art of the Dance." In *Revolt in the Arts: A Survey of the Creation, Distribution and Appreciation of Art in America*, ed. Oliver M. Sayler. New York: Brentano's, 1930.

Grau, Robert. *Forty Years Observation of Music and the Drama*. New York: Broadway, 1909.

Grau, Robert. *The Man of Business in the Amusement World*. New York, 1910.

Halttunen, Karen. *Confidence Men and Painted Women: A Study of Middle-Class Culture in America, 1830–1870*. New Haven, Conn.: Yale University Press, 1982.

Haskell, Arnold L. *Balletomania: The Story of an Obsession*. New York: Simon & Schuster, 1934.

Hastings, Baird. "The Denishawn Era (1914–31)." In *Chronicles of the American Dance*, ed. Paul Magriel. New York: Henry Holt, 1948.

Houghton, Norris. *Advance from Broadway: 19,000 Miles of American Theatre*. New York: Harcourt, Brace, 1941.

Jones, Robert Edmond. "Toward an American Ballet." In *Revolt in the Arts: A Survey of the Creation, Distribution and Appreciation of Art in America*, ed. Oliver M. Sayler. New York: Brentano's, 1930.

Kasson, John F. *Amusing the Million: Coney Island at the Turn of the Century*. New York: Hill & Wang, 1978.

Kendall, Elizabeth. *Where She Danced*. New York: Knopf, 1979.

Keppel, Frederick P., and R. L. Duffus. *The Arts in American Life*. New York: McGraw-Hill, 1933.

Kirstein, Lincoln. *Blast at Ballet: A Corrective for the American Audience*. 1938. Reprinted in *Three Pamphlets Collected*. New York: Dance Horizons, 1967.

Kolodin, Irving. *The Metropolitan Opera: 1883–1935*. New York: Oxford University Press, 1936.

Levine, Lawrence W. *Highbrow/Lowbrow: The Emergence of Cultural Hierarchy in America*. Cambridge, Mass.: Harvard University Press, 1988.

Lynes, Russell. *The Lively Audience: A Social History of the Visual and Performing Arts in America, 1890–1950*. New York: Harper & Row, 1985.

McArthur, Benjamin. *Actors and American Culture, 1880–1920*. Philadelphia: Temple University Press, 1984.

MacGowan, Kenneth. *Footlights across America: Towards a National Theatre*. New York: Harcourt, Brace, 1929.

Moore, Lillian. "George Washington Smith." In *Chronicles of the American Dance*, ed. Paul Magriel. New York: Henry Holt, 1948a.

Moore, Lillian. "John Durang: The First American Dancer." In *Chronicles of the American Dance*, ed. Paul Magriel. New York: Henry Holt, 1948b.

O'Neill, Rosetta. "The Dodworth Family and Ballroom Dancing in New York." In *Chronicles of the American Dance,* ed. Paul Magriel. New York: Henry Holt, 1948.

Peiss, Kathy. *Cheap Amusements: Working Women and Leisure in Turn-of-the-Century New York.* Philadelphia: Temple University Press, 1986.

Playground and Recreation Association of America. *Community Drama: Suggestions for a Community-Wide Program of Dramatic Activities.* New York: Century, 1926.

Poggi, Jack. *Theater in America: The Impact of Economic Forces, 1860–1967.* Ithaca, N.Y.: Cornell University Press, 1968.

RCA Manufacturing Co. *The Victor Book of the Opera: Stories of the Operas with Illustrations and Descriptions of Victor Opera Records.* Camden, N.J.: 1936.

Rozenzweig, Roy. *Eight Hours for What We Will: Workers and Leisure in an Industrial City, 1870–1920.* New York: Cambridge University Press, 1983.

Ruyter, Nancy Lee Chalfa. *Reformers and Visionaries: The Americanization of the Art of Dance.* New York: Dance Horizons, 1979.

Sayler, Oliver M., ed. *Revolt in the Arts: A Survey of the Creation, Distribution and Appreciation of Art in America.* New York: Brentano's, 1930.

Shelton, Suzanne. *Divine Dancer: A Biography of Ruth St. Denis.* Garden City, N.Y.: Doubleday, 1981.

Sklar, Robert. *Movie-Made America.* New York: Random House, 1975.

Sokol, Martin L. *The New York City Opera: An American Adventure.* New York: Macmillan, 1981.

Sussman, Leila A. "American Women's Colleges and the Social Origins of Modern Dance." Tufts University, 1990. Typescript.

Terry, Walter. *Ted Shawn: Father of American Dance.* New York: Dial, 1976.

Toll, Robert. *Blacking Up: The Minstrel Show in Nineteenth-Century America.* New York: Oxford University Press, 1974.

Toll, Robert. *On with the Show: The First Century of Show Business in America.* New York: Oxford University Press, 1976.

Twentieth Century Club. Drama Committee. *The Amusement Situation in Boston.* Boston, 1910.

Van Vechten, Carl. "Maud Allan." 1910. Reprinted in *Chronicles of the American Dance,* ed. Paul Magriel. New York: Henry Holt, 1948.

Weber, William M. *Music and the Middle Class in Nineteenth-Century Europe.* New York: Holmes & Meier, 1976.

Winter, Marian Hannah. "Juba and American Minstrelsy." In *Chronicles of the American Dance,* ed. Paul Magriel. New York: Henry Holt, 1948.

THREE

High Culture versus Popular Culture Revisited: A Reconceptualization of Recorded Cultures

Diana Crane

The concepts of high culture and popular culture are ideal types that are generally used by sociologists to distinguish between different forms of recorded culture (Gans 1974). Unfortunately, this categorization, which is based on the content, style, and values expressed by these works, does not reflect the complexities of recorded cultures in contemporary societies. Generalizations about high culture and popular culture obscure rather than clarify the nature and effects of recorded culture because they rely on outmoded conceptualizations of both social structure and recorded cultures. Since high culture is considered to be superior to popular culture, appreciation of it has been used as a symbolic boundary to exclude those who prefer other forms of culture.

Differentiating between these two forms of culture in terms of content and style implies that cultural items can be categorized unambiguously in terms of one of these categories. A conception of recorded culture in which a single set of standards is used to differentiate between cultural objects is outmoded. At the present time, culture is pluralistic; many different aesthetic systems are operating in every cultural form. Consequently, the quality of a particular cultural object can be evaluated only within a particular aesthetic system; there are no universal standards of quality. In this situation, it is no longer appropriate to argue that the aesthetic systems used for certain forms of culture, such as the arts, are superior to those used for other forms of culture that are disseminated to larger and more heterogeneous audiences. Instead, as numerous studies in the sociology of culture have revealed, the boundaries between high culture and popular culture are fluid; the two forms of culture are socially constructed.

However, there is no generally accepted alternative system of classification between different forms of culture. From a sociological perspective, it is more meaningful to categorize recorded cultures in terms of the environments in which they are created, produced, and disseminated rather than in terms of assumptions concerning differences or the lack of differences in their style and content. I will argue that there are two principal types of recorded cultures, media culture and urban culture, that are embedded in the contexts in which they are created, produced, and disseminated.

These cultures are produced in two contexts: that of national culture industries and that of urban environments. The contents of each of these types of recorded cultures are equally diverse, but the contexts of production and dissemination are entirely different. Given the enormously superior resources of national culture industries as well as the transformation of the urban environments that formerly sustained urban cultures, the survival of urban cultures is seriously threatened.

Media Culture and Urban Culture

Media cultures are typically produced through arrangements between small and large firms and are distributed by large corporations that control markets of national and international audiences. "Core" media cultures, such as television, Hollywood film, and major newspapers and news magazines, are consumed by large and relatively undifferentiated audiences. "Peripheral" media cultures, such as book and magazine publishing, popular music, and radio, are consumed by large audiences in the aggregate that are highly differentiated in terms of specific tastes by life-style and subculture. In both cases, the characteristics of the content, the audiences, and even the effects on the audiences depend on corporate policies. These policies in turn depend on levels of profit and competition among these organizations at any particular time, which are constantly changing, as market conditions change.

In this century, the use of modern technologies to produce, record, or disseminate cultural objects has often been taken as an indication that such creators are producing popular rather than high culture.[1] This reflects the attitude expressed by members of the Frankfurt school that popular music is produced by means of technology in the same way that other products are produced by industrial technology. The use of technology is seen as implying standardized and interchangeable parts and the appearance of novelty through the alteration of superficial details. Gendron (1987) shows that members of the Frankfurt school erred. In fact, in music, technology has led to innovation, greatly expanding the possibilities for variation.

As Kealy (1982, 107) shows, the technology for recording popular music is extremely complex: dozens of microphones each with its own characteristic sound effects, a wide variety of electronic devices (such as amplifiers, dynamic range compressors and expanders, and frequency equalizers), and multitrack tape recorders that allow up to twenty-four channels of music to be recorded on one tape and that can record each musical instrument separately. Rock recordings consist of numerous layers of studio performances that are remixed and edited into a final version. These developments have greatly increased the musician's control over the final product. Some musicians view electronic studio equipment as a "musical instrument" in itself.

Because of the expense of using most technologies, access to them has often been controlled by organizations that have limited the autonomy of creators. The autonomous individual creator is a central feature of the ideology of high culture (Becker 1982; Zolberg 1990). Kealy argues that musicians record their work in three different types of situations, which vary in terms of level of autonomy. Big companies permit the least autonomy and small companies and independent producers the most.

By contrast, urban culture is produced and disseminated in urban settings for local audiences. Urban "culture worlds"[2] consist of the following: (1) culture creators and support personnel who assist them in various ways; (2) conventions or shared understandings about what cultural products should be like; (3) gatekeepers who evaluate cultural products; (4) organizations within or around which cultural activities take place, are displayed, or are produced; and (5) audiences whose characteristics can be a major factor in determining what types of cultural products can be displayed, performed, or sold in a particular environment.

Culture worlds differ in terms of whether they are dominated by networks of creators or by organizations, either profit-oriented small businesses or nonprofit organizations (Gilmore 1987). Each type of culture world also has different standards for evaluating cultural works. Further variations in standards occur as a result of social class differences. When the audiences for these forms of culture are drawn from the middle and upper class, the cultural products are usually defined as "high culture." Some of these cultural products are esoteric and aesthetically complex; others are not very different in terms of content from culture that is disseminated to national audiences by large corporations.

Through a process of cultural exclusion based on the use of high culture as a symbolic boundary, urban cultures that are aimed at local audiences drawn from lower-class or minority groups are typically not defined as high culture (e.g., black and Hispanic theater, graffiti, and mural painting in urban ghettos) and are generally ignored by critics and historians. These cultural products are sometimes as esoteric (e.g., jazz and hard rock) as avant-garde urban cultures disseminated to the upper and middle class. Alternatively, they may have political undertones (radical theater) or express ethnic chauvinism (street parades).

Culture worlds controlled by networks of creators are especially conducive to the production of cultural works that are either aesthetically original or ideologically provocative, or both. This is partly because the new networks that emerge along with new styles attract the young, who are likely to have fresh perspectives on culture, and partly because they provide continuous "feedback" among creators themselves and between creators and their audiences, which are likely to include creators of other types of culture as well as individuals who are familiar with conventions underlying such works (Crane 1987).

Culture worlds organized around small, profit-oriented businesses tend to encourage works that please rather than provoke or shock potential buyers. Some of these creators resemble the *artist-craftsman* in Becker's (1982) sense of the term; they prefer to produce works that are beautiful and harmonious rather than unique and provocative. Finally, culture worlds organized around nonprofit organizations are typically concerned with the preservation of existing artistic and ethnic traditions rather than the creation of new ones. The "creators" are often performers who reinterpret the works of creators who are generally dead.[3]

Within each culture world, cultural works are subjected to evaluation by gatekeepers. Mulkay and Chaplin (1982) discuss three models of how this process operates. If indeed high culture were intrinsically different from popular culture, then the model of aesthetic appraisal would apply to the gatekeeping process in culture worlds. According to this model, a cultural object is evaluated in terms of explicit aesthetic criteria and either succeeds or fails. This model implies the existence of universal standards of judgment that could be applied to all types of cultural products, at least within a particular cultural form, as well as consensus among gatekeepers about aesthetic criteria and about the evaluation of particular works. As Zolberg (1990) shows, this model also assumes that art objects are unique and are created by a single artist.

Sociologists have documented the wide range of factors that impinge on the interpretation of artistic works. The quality and meaning of a particular artwork may be assessed very differently from one historical period to another (Zolberg 1990). Even within the same period, evaluation and interpretation of the same work may vary greatly, depending on the aesthetic and social commitments of the observer (Crane 1987). Not only do perspectives differ widely within a particular art world, depending on stylistic preferences and commitments, but there are also many different art worlds, each with its own standards, its own gatekeepers, its own institutions, and its own public.[4] Consequently, the plausibility of the model of aesthetic appraisal is questionable, particularly in a period of cultural pluralism and incessant cultural change.

In fact, the gatekeeping process is especially problematic for network creators whose work is based on a new or revised definition of what constitutes a work of art. In order to succeed, members of a new network must obtain a nucleus of supporters or "a constituency" in the art world or on its periphery. In the art market, such constituencies are drawn from the following: (1) art galleries that display and sell artworks to private collectors; (2) art journals that provide forums for art critics; and (3) organizational patrons, including museums and corporations.

Given the implausibility of the first model (Mulkay and Chaplin 1982; Crane 1987), Mulkay and Chaplin propose two additional models. According to the model of cultural persuasion, each new group of culture creators develops new criteria for aesthetic judgment that are appropriate to their cultural products. If these new criteria are accepted by gatekeepers, the new group will be successful. In other words, culture creators have an effect on the gatekeeping system not as individuals but as members of groups that share criteria for creating and evaluating cultural products. The label *avant-garde* is attributed to a group of artists only under certain conditions. In order for members of a new art style to be defined as engaging in activities associated with an avant-garde, they must have some awareness of one another as a social group. The greater their self-awareness, the more likely their redefinitions of the various categories of artistic activity will be considered avant-garde by members of that culture world. In other words, the social context in which a new style appears is crucial for its perception as avant-garde.

Finally, according to the model of social influence, culture creators become successful because they are sponsored by influential gatekeepers. Success is engineered through a process of personal influence and the availability of material resources. The last two models are not mutually exclusive. The most successful artists generally acquire their reputations in the context of a new style. However, their prestige relative to other members of the style often reflects their success in obtaining powerful mentors such as critics, dealers, and curators. As the art world has increased in size, sponsorship by powerful galleries and collectors has become an increasingly important influence on acquisitions by museums (Crane 1987).

For most people, high culture is associated with cultural objects that received acclaim in the past, generally in previous centuries. As Halle's (1989) work shows, abstract art, which is the major form of avant-garde art in the twentieth century, evokes little interest among the public, even among the upper and upper middle classes. The public from all social classes prefers representational artworks that either were painted in previous centuries or, if painted in this century, imitate traditional styles of painting.

However, the inclusion of cultural objects in the canon of classic high culture was subject to the same kinds of selection processes that I have described for contemporary avant-garde culture. In some cases, classic high culture includes works that were part of popular culture in the period in which they were created. Literary works by Dickens and Balzac are examples that come to mind, as well as the majority of nineteenth-century operas.

Classic high culture remains popular despite the fact that it is often imbued with the ideological baggage of the period in which it was created. A well-known example is Mark Twain's racism. Nineteenth-century operas were recently described as validating "aesthetic, philosophic and political principles incompatible with our own, with views of society and behavior we itch to obliterate and dare not look in the eye for fear of what may be reflected there" (Osborne 1991).

At the turn of the century, the work of the French artist Marcel Duchamp was dedicated to demonstrating precisely the arbitrariness of our judgments of what constitutes art or high culture. By offering commonplace objects, such as urinals, as artworks, and by claiming to have created a new artwork by painting a mustache on a reproduction of the *Mona Lisa,* Duchamp attempted to undermine the concept of high culture by demonstrating that it was interchangeable with popular culture, thereby exposing it to ridicule.

His ideas have spawned a lively avant-garde tradition in the twentieth century in which an enormous range of objects from everyday life are "labeled" artworks by artists. Examples include paintings depicting Campbell's soup cans, comics, advertisements, bottles of excrement labeled *artist's shit,* a skinned rabbit, digging and filling a hole in a park, a painting of a blank wall, a tape recording of an artist's breathing, a printout from a computer programmed to count to infinity, and graffiti (Banfield 1984). The acrimonious controversy that grants to artists who work in this vein have aroused among legislators and the general public indicates how little consensus exists concerning the nature of contemporary high culture.

As we have seen, the wide range of styles that are identified with high culture today indicates that high culture cannot be identified in terms of its intrinsic content. Instead, high culture tends to be associated with specific social contexts, those that are relatively inaccessible to the average person, such as museums, art galleries, and symphony orchestras. As DiMaggio has shown, one of the strategies adopted by urban elites in the late nineteenth century was to make these types of organizations less accessible to the working class.

Presumably, if music videos, which have many of the characteristics of twentieth-century avant-garde art styles (Kaplan 1987), were shown only in art museums instead of on cable television, they would be defined as high culture rather than as popular culture. The reasons why Broadway theater is classified as high culture and television dramas as popular culture have more to do with differences in accessibility to the average person than with differences in content. According to H. Stith Bennett (1980, 3), "Popular things are widely distributed, things that anyone can come in contact with, things that are shared by entire communities."

The situation is even more ambiguous with respect to literature. While avant-garde art has its own specialized networks and organizations, fiction that is later defined as literature and as a classic is subjected to the same gatekeeping process as popular fiction. In fact, most future classics begin as bestsellers. Books that become bestsellers tend to be published by a few publishing houses that advertise frequently in the major popular literary review, the *New York Times Book Review* (Ohmann 1983).

Cultural producers whose resources are too limited to create and sustain culture worlds in which their work can be evaluated and disseminated to the public are unable to support claims that their cultural conventions produce works that deserve to be considered high culture. In the past, female creators and black creators have most frequently been unable to support such claims and have been relegated to the status of craftsperson, "folk" artist, or entertainer (another example of cultural exclusion using symbolic boundaries).

While middle-class male art communities are supported by an array of organizations such as art schools, journals, galleries, art centers, and museums, lower-class and minority art communities have few organizations devoted to their welfare and little access to middle-class organizations. These obstacles can be only partially surmounted, as indicated by Lachmann's (1988) study of the mural painting segment of graffiti painters in New York in the late 1970s.

These young black painters developed a system of apprenticeship where novices could learn the different techniques of painting murals on subway cars and a gatekeeping system in which peers evaluated one another's work at "writers' corners," located in nodal stations of the New York City subway system. These writers corners served to bring together muralists from different neighborhoods in a citywide community or network. In those settings, prestige and recognition were allocated. According to Lachmann (1988, 242),

Muralists' quantitative conception of style allowed them to develop a total art world, formulating aesthetic standards for evaluating one another's murals and determining which innovations of content and technique would be judged advanced in graffiti style. Comparisons of style were made possible by graffiti's mobility on subway cars. Writers' corners allowed muralists to associate with their peers, who constituted an audience with the experience and discrimination for bestowing fame for style.[5]

Needless to say, the "fame" of these muralists did not transcend the boundaries of their own community, which was eventually destroyed by the police. Black musicians have encountered similar problems. At the turn of the century, jazz originated as an isolated, lower-class culture world in which groups of musicians performed in clubs and black bars. In the 1940s and 1950s, middle-class black jazz musicians with formal musical training in conservatories created a succession of middle-class culture worlds in which they stressed technical mastery of instruments and self-conscious experimentation with musical conventions (Peterson 1972). Performances took place in the same locations as classical music: concert halls and academic workshops with audiences of middle-class whites. In spite of these developments, the debate over whether jazz is an art has never been resolved. Vuillamy (1977, 183) argues that the music establishment has failed to recognize all types of music that come from the African-American tradition. This tradition has produced a new musical language that is very different from the European musical tradition. Musical styles, such as jazz, rock, and soul, are dismissed because they do not conform to the criteria of the European tradition.

Vuillamy (1977) concludes that there are many different sets of aesthetic standards for creating what is loosely called "popular" music (see also Bennett 1980). As Vuillamy points out, this contradicts the widespread assumption that popular culture is a "homogenous category while high culture is subdivided into many different categories with strict boundaries" (1977, 182). The former is automatically assumed to be of inferior quality.

In both national and urban cultures, cultural producers are subjected to stringent gatekeeping systems, although the level of exclusion is considerably greater at the national than at the urban level. In the latter, there is more opportunity for the offbeat, eccentric, and esoteric to find a niche, but, on the other hand, the survival of urban cultures is always precarious, and the numbers of people who consume them regularly are much smaller.

The Interpenetration of High Culture and Popular Culture

There is continual tension between the tendency of the core media cultures to dominate the entire system, as organizations in this area merge to become increasingly gigantic conglomerates, and the continual proliferation of new cultural organizations in peripheral and local cultures. The extent to which cultural products or themes move from national cultures to urban cultures, or vice versa, is relatively undocumented. In the past two decades, avant-garde cultures in music and painting have frequently taken themes and images from national media cultures (Crane 1987). Popular music industries have found new musicians in urban working-class and minority rock music cultures.

While critics have tended to stress the effect of high culture on popular culture, the arbitrariness of these categories is indicated by the high frequency of collaboration, both past and present, across these so-called boundaries. Using examples from art movements in France at the turn of the century, Crow (1983) develops a complex argument that avant-garde artists in that period drew on ideas that marginal social groups had attached to popular culture artifacts. Reworking these ideas with their own aesthetic discoveries, they produced works that revitalized both avant-garde and popular cultures.

As the media and particularly television have assumed ever larger roles in our everyday existence, they have increasingly become the subject matter of artists who aspire to the avant-garde. Part of their motivation for using these themes is a strong desire to communicate with a larger audience than has in the past appreciated high culture. They choose to rework media images because they are familiar and therefore accessible to the general public (Rico 1990; Crane 1987).

Recently, these types of exchanges have been the subject of extensive museum exhibitions that have attempted to trace the interactions between painting and advertising, on the one hand, and painting and graffiti, comics, advertising, and caricature, on the other.[6] Again, the traffic is two-way, with painters adopting themes from popular culture and popular culture incorporating these themes as reworked by painters. Similar developments have been taking place in music, where young musicians repeatedly discovered that the musical vocabularies of hard rock and serial minimalism were not very different. According to Iain Chambers (1988, 610), "From the late 1960's onward, the music of Frank Zappa, of such German groups as Can, Amon Duul II, and Tangerine Dream, and in England, Henry Cow, Brian Eno, and even David Bowie, can be linked to the experiments in serial composition, repetition, and incidental 'noise' found in the work of Varese, Stockhausen, Cage, Riley, LaMonte Young, Glass and others."

A related development is that avant-garde artists are increasingly using the technologies that have been the basis for a great deal of popular culture. The cutting edge of the avant-garde is art that uses video, film, television, and photography. As these technologies become more accessible to those with limited means, the use of technology per se will cease to be the criterion for popular culture.

At the same time, the culture and behavior of the avant-garde are becoming increasingly frequent among creators who are identified with popular culture. Avant-garde strategies appeared in the behavior of the originators of punk music, such as deliberate attempts to provoke their audiences, intentional blurring of the boundaries between art and everyday life, and juxtapositions of disparate objects and behaviors (Henry 1984). As Kaplan (1987) has shown, some music videos create a kind of avant-gardist ambiguity and provocation, but often with glaring inconsistencies that undercut the effects. Finally, fashion designers have discovered that avant-gardist provocation is a means of attracting attention to their work (Crane 1988).

Media Culture, Urban Culture, and Cultural Exclusion

By grounding these different forms of culture in a particular environmental context, it is easier to identify their connections with elites and power structures and to avoid abstract generalizations about influence and impact. The elites that benefit from their control over these different types of culture are numerous and varied. There is a tendency in the literature to speak of a single elite or of *the* upper class or *the* upper middle class. In fact, all social classes today are internally fragmented into different life-styles or culture classes that at times intersect with different classes.[7]

Different elites control different forms of national culture. Faulkner (1983) has documented the existence of a Hollywood elite that controls national film culture. Other elites control publishing, television, and popular music (Coser et al. 1982; Gitlin 1983). The fact that all these elites can be categorized as upper middle class or upper class does not alter the fact that distinctive groups of people within these classes, with different kinds of ethnic, educational, and occupational experiences, control the production and dissemination of these cultures.

To what extent are these elites able to manipulate cultural messages, thereby excluding their audiences from access to certain kinds of information or worldviews? In general, national media cultures provide a means of defining reality for large segments of the population, although the extent to which this actually happens has been a subject of considerable controversy in the literature since this assumes a level of social integration that is not realistic. There is consensus in the literature that the content that enters core culture is characterized by a high degree of emphasis on certain themes, with certain topics receiving more attention than others. The larger the audience, the more stereotyped the material being communicated in order to facilitate comprehension by individuals from a wide range of backgrounds (Crane 1992).

However, reception theory has contributed a new understanding of the impact of popular culture, in which much more importance is assigned to the public. "Texts," either printed or visual, are considered to be "indeterminate," meaning that descriptions of people, places, and events are always incomplete. In order to make sense of the text, readers fill in the gaps, but because individuals differ in the ways in which they accomplish this task, a variety of interpretations emerges. Reception theory hypothesizes that readers belong to "interpretive communities," communities of readers who interpret the same text in similar ways because they share similar backgrounds and environments. For example, Radway's (1984) study of lower-middle-class women who were dedicated readers of romance novels also found that these women accepted some elements of these novels as "reality," as sources of information that could contribute to their knowledge of the world, and at the same time focused on certain aspects of the novels that contributed to their self-esteem as women and satisfied their personal needs for emotional "nurturance." Novels that did not fulfill these needs were considered "unsuccessful" by these readers. These women's interpretations of these novels were very different from the commonplace assumption that such novels are a form of "soft" pornography.

Fiske (1984) argues that texts become popular, not because they express a hegemonic worldview, but because they resonate with the public. Their messages fit with the ideas that people are using to interpret their social experiences at a particular time. The satisfaction of consuming popular culture is that of being reassured that one's interpretation of the world is congruent with that of others.

The fragmentation of peripheral national cultures means that content (e.g., popular music, magazines) is increasingly tailored to the interests and life-styles of narrowly defined demographic groups. The culture that these groups receive reflects their tastes, interests, and attitudes at a particular period in time. Consequently, it confirms rather than challenges their worldviews and self-images. Given the proliferation of life-styles and their links to residential communities that are extremely homogeneous in this respect (Weiss 1989), it seems likely that today life-styles, more than elite urban cultures, function as symbolic boundaries.

In urban cultures, one also finds different elites controlling different forms of culture (Gilmore 1987; Crane 1992). In some cities, members of upper classes, representing inherited wealth and social status, control boards of trustees of cultural organizations, such as museums, symphony orchestras, and opera houses, that preserve and disseminate classic forms of recorded culture (DiMaggio 1982). Groups that produce esoteric, avant-garde cultures tend to be controlled by academic and intellectual elites (Gans 1985). Lower-class and lower-middle-class urban cultures tend to be controlled by members of particular ethnic groups within those classes.

Since urban cultures are disseminated to class-based audiences, it is in this area that cultural exclusion has traditionally taken place. As DiMaggio (1982) has shown, the elite in nineteenth-century Boston constructed a high culture world consisting of organizations that they controlled and from which they excluded nonelites. Those who do not have access to certain forms of urban culture may be at a disadvantage in terms of upward mobility (Bourdieu 1984). However, at least in the United States, differences in life-style (home decoration, sports, etiquette, clothing, etc.) between social classes are probably more crucial for upward mobility than differences in the consumption of recorded culture.

A model of the organization of urban culture as controlled by elites applies best to older cities on the East Coast, but it is becoming increasingly inapplicable even there, and many midwestern and western cities never did exemplify it. In the past two decades, the influence of upper-class elites in eastern cities over organizations that preserve classic cultural traditions has declined, in part because of the increased geographic mobility of members of these elites, which produces declining commitment to particular cities, and in part because their financial resources are insufficient to support these organizations. As these organizations enlist other sources of support, new elites (corporate, political) are replacing previous ones. This means that new actors exercise control over the definition of recorded culture that is disseminated in these settings.

A recent exhibition at the Museum of Modern Art in New York ("Information Art: Diagramming Microchips," 6 September–30 October 1990) exemplifies this transformation. Supported by a corporation that manufactures microchips for computers, the exhibition was organized around the theme that microchips are works of art. Conflicts between "old" and "new" elites have begun to occur, as witnessed by the recent controversy over the exhibition of photographs by Robert Mapplethorpe. At the same time, cultural organizations are constrained to attract audiences that are larger and more representative of the population as a whole, which in turn affects their selection of cultural fare. At the other end of the social scale, as members of ethnic groups intermarry or move upward in society, their involvement with forms of ethnic urban culture declines.

In some cities, avant-garde and commercial cultures have been used as part of an "arts-based development strategy" in inner-city neighborhoods in order to expand urban economies by attracting corporate investment as well as tourists and suburban residents (Whitt and Share 1988). Analysis of these projects reveals that they are concentrated largely on the creation of nonprofit and profit-oriented organizations embedded in facilities for middle-class tourists and visitors. Most arts-oriented urban development projects neglect the urban cultures of the working class and tend to displace networks of avant-garde creators as a result of increases in property values.

There is also some indication that the nature of cities in general is changing in ways that are not favorable to the survival or growth of urban cultures. Given the high level of geographic mobility of the middle class, cities less and less represent communities of individuals linked to one another directly or indirectly by long-term social ties and committed to the survival of political and cultural institutions (Calhoun 1988). Newer cities consist of agglomerations of suburbs; there is no center in which cultural organizations could be clustered and no dominant elite with a strong commitment to the city to act as patrons. To the extent that urban subcultures are being replaced or displaced by suburban cultures built around shopping malls, there is less room for "alternative" cultures that appeal to small segments of the population.

Conclusion

To summarize, recorded cultures are more complex than the high culture/popular culture model suggests. I have argued that high culture is largely a phenomenon created and consumed in urban settings while popular culture is disseminated by national media industries. However, urban cultures include forms of culture created for the working class that do not fit the traditional definitions of high culture. In fact, the latter, as typically defined in the literature, corresponds most closely to classic culture transmitted by nonprofit organizations, but this represents only a small portion of the forms of culture created and disseminated in urban settings.

Popular culture disseminated to mass audiences no longer fits the stereotype of popular culture in the sociological literature. In fact, the types of culture disseminated by national media organizations both to mass audiences and to specialized audiences are becoming increasingly diverse. They also often resemble the products of urban cultures as avant-gardes assimilate both the technologies used to produce media culture and its images and themes while media innovators ransack the archives of all forms of culture in a desperate quest for unfamiliar images and themes.

While urban cultures remain most closely associated with social class, their usefulness for maintaining social boundaries between social classes is dwindling as urban social structures undergo drastic changes and control over urban cultural organizations, along with the power to define culture, shifts to corporate elites and government agencies. While media conglomerates are expanding to global dimensions, the social structures that supported urban cultures in the past are being transformed in ways that threaten their long-term survival.

Notes

1. In spite of the fact that they are able to work by themselves, photographers have encountered considerable resistance to their demands for serious consideration of their aesthetic achievements. At least part of this resistance stems from the fact that photography is made by machines (Christopherson 1974).

2. Becker (1982) uses the term *art world*. I prefer *culture world* as being more general and applying to a wider range of phenomena.

3. Profit-oriented organizations include Broadway theaters, the decorative arts (including fashion designers), craftspeople, and rock clubs. Nonprofit organizations include museums, opera, regional theater, symphony orchestras, gospel music choirs, and parades. These cultural activities are not necessarily the sole or even the primary purpose of the organization.

4. Examples of different types of art worlds include the New York avant-garde art world, cowboy art, which flourishes in the American Southwest, and various types of art worlds centered around collectibles (see, e.g., FitzGibbon 1987).

5. A few of these graffiti mural painters were given exhibitions in Manhattan galleries, largely because a group of white artists, the Neoexpressionists, were interested in exploring themes from popular culture in their work.

6. "Art and Advertising: 1890–1990," Georges Pompidou Center, Paris, 1 November 1990–25 February 1991; "High and Low: Modern Art and Popular Culture," Museum of Modern Art, New York, 1990.

7. A recent report documents the existence of forty distinct life-styles in the United States (Weiss 1989).

References

Banfield, E. C. *The Democratic Muse: Visual Arts and the Public Interest.* New York: Basic, 1984.

Becker, H. S. *Art Worlds.* Berkeley and Los Angeles: University of California Press, 1982.

Bennett, H. S. *On Becoming a Rock Musician.* Amherst: University of Massachusetts Press, 1980.

Bourdieu, P. *Distinction: A Social Critique of the Judgement of Taste.* Cambridge, Mass.: Harvard University Press, 1984.

Calhoun, C. "Populist Politics, Communications Media, and Large Scale Integration." *Sociological Theory* 6 (1988): 219–41.

Chambers, I. "Contamination, Coincidence, and Collusion: Pop Music, Urban Culture, and the Avant-Garde." In *Marxism and the Interpretation of Culture,* ed. C. Nelson and L. Grossberg. Urbana: University of Illinois Press, 1988.

Christopherson, R. W. "From Folk Art to Fine Art: A Transformation in the Meaning of Photographic Work." *Urban Life and Culture* 3 (1974): 123–57.

Coser, L., et al. *Books: The Culture of Publishing.* New York: Basic, 1982.

Crane, D. *The Transformation of the Avant-Garde.* Chicago: University of Chicago Press, 1987.

Crane, D. "Fashion Worlds: Anatomy of an Avant-Garde Fashion Tradition." Paper presented at the fourteenth annual Conference on Social Theory, Politics, and the Arts, American University, Washington, D.C., 28–30 October 1988.

Crane, D. *The Production of Culture: Media Industries and Urban Arts.* Newbury Park, Calif.: Sage, 1992.

Crow, T. "Modernism and Mass Culture in the Visual Arts." In *Modernism and Modernity,* ed. B. H. D. Buchloh et al. Halifax: The Press of the Nova Scotia College of Art and Design, 1983.

DiMaggio, P. "Cultural Entrepreneurship in Nineteenth Century Boston: The Creation of an Organizational Base for High Culture in America." *Media, Culture, and Society* 4 (1982): 33–50.

Faulkner, R. *Music on Demand.* New Brunswick, N.J.: Transaction, 1983.

Fiske, J. "Popularity and Ideology: A Structuralist Reading of Dr. Who." In *Interpreting Television: Current Research Perspectives,* ed. W. D. Rowlands and B. Watkins. Beverly Hills, Calif.: Sage, 1984.

FitzGibbon, H. "From Prints to Posters: The Production of Artistic Value in a Popular Art World." *Symbolic Interaction* 10 (1987): 111–28.

Gans, H. *Popular Culture and High Culture.* New York: Basic, 1974.

Gans, H. "American Popular Culture and High Culture in a Changing Class Structure." In *Art, Ideology, and Politics,* ed. J. Balfe and M. J. Wyszomirski. New York: Praeger, 1985.

Gendron, B. "Theodor Adorno Meets the Cadillacs." In *Studies in Entertainment,* ed. T. Modleski. Bloomington: University of Indiana Press, 1987.

Gilmore, S. "Coordination and Convention: The Organization of the Concert World." *Symbolic Interaction* 10 (1987): 209–27.

Gitlin, T. *Inside Prime Time.* New York: Pantheon, 1983.

Halle, D. "Class and Culture in Modern America: The Vision of the Landscape in the Residences of Contemporary Americans." *Prospects* 14 (1989): 373–406.

Henry, P. "Punk and Avant-Garde Art." *Journal of Popular Culture* 17 (1984): 30–36.

Kaplan, A. *Rocking around the Clock: Music Television, Postmodernism, and Consumer Culture.* New York: Methuen, 1987.

Kealy, E. "Conventions and the Production of the Popular Music Aesthetic." *Journal of Popular Culture* 16 (1982): 100–115.

Lachmann, R. "Graffiti as Career and Ideology." *American Journal of Sociology* 94 (1988): 229–50.

Mulkay, M., and E. Chaplin. "Aesthetics and the Artistic Career: A Study of Anomie in Fine-Art Painting." *Sociological Quarterly* 23 (1982): 117–38.

Ohmann, R. "The Shaping of a Canon: U.S. Fiction, 1960–1975." *Critical Inquiry* 10 (1983): 199–223.

Osborne, C. L. "Opera's Fabulous Vanishing Act." *New York Times,* 17 February 1991.

Peterson, R. "A Process Model of the Folk, Pop, and Fine Art Phases of Jazz." In *American Music: From Storyville to Woodstock,* ed. C. Nanry. New Brunswick, N.J.: Transaction, 1972.

Radway, J. *Reading the Romance: Women, Patriarchy, and Popular Culture.* Chapel Hill: University of North Carolina Press, 1984.

Rico, D. "For Los Angeles Artists, the Media Is the Subject." *International Herald Tribune,* 28–29 April 1990.

Vuillamy, G. "Music and the Mass Culture Debate." In *Whose Music? A Sociology of Musical Languages,* ed. J. Shepherd et al. London: Latimer, 1977.

Weiss, M. *The Clustering of America.* New York: Harper & Row, 1989.

Whitt, J. A., and A. J. Share. "The Performing Arts as an Urban Development Strategy: Transforming the Central City." *Research in Politics and Society* 3 (1988): 155–77.

Zolberg, V. *Constructing a Sociology of the Arts.* New York: Cambridge University Press, 1990.

FOUR

Nature's Body and the Metaphors of Food

Joseph R. Gusfield

"No diet comes without a larger social agenda."
Hillel Schwartz, *Never Satisfied*

"The doctrines which men ostensibly hold," wrote the British historian Leslie Stephen, "do not become operative upon their conduct until they have generated an imaginative symbolism" (Stephens 1927, 2:329; quoted in Schorer 1959, 25). "Imaginative symbolism" pervades the cultural frames by which human beings constitute their experience and provides the sense of order and understanding through which sense is made of events and objects. A study of symbols and their meanings is an essential part of sociological analysis and inherent in the study of cultures.

The human body is a perpetual source of meaning and an object of historical variation. It is an instrument of purpose and a goal of aesthetic perfection. It can be attractive or repulsive, glorified or transcended, covered with adornment or exposed and revealed. How the body is conceived and how human beings act toward it is as much a matter of culture and history as are the manners and morals of food habits and the canons of sexual behavior. The human body is at once both a physiological and anatomical entity and a cultural object.

An inquiry into the meaning of body is both a descriptive account of how men and women act toward their bodies and an analytic exploration of how such actions are linked to other aspects of life. "The body," wrote Jayme Sokolow, "symbolizes the struggle between order and disorder in all societies" (Sokolow 1983, 92). An analysis of the meanings of health and food is a search for such symbolisms and a hunt for possible social and political orders to which they might be related. This chapter is such a search, using the symbolism of nature and culture in a discourse on the natural foods movements of the nineteenth and twentieth centuries as a means for conducting that search.

Culture can be thought of as a set of possible meanings that can be drawn on to constitute experienced realities (Schutz 1967; Swidler 1986). There are many examples of how objects are differently constituted in differing historical contexts. How the object "child" is perceived has varied in Western history. At times children have been experienced as small adults and have had attributed to them the same motivations, understandings, and moral responsibilities as adults (Aries 1962). Another example of how culture constitutes the experience of objects and events is given in the very conception of art. To "see" artistic products as creative "for their own sake," as objects to be contemplated rather than as means serving some other end, whether religious, instructive, or decorative, is not inherent in the nature of artistic production. Such a notion did not emerge until the eighteenth century (Abrams 1985). Conversely, symbols and myths may appear as continuous archetypes, appearing again and again in history. Such is the "myth of the eternal return," of a golden age to which humans dream of returning (Eliade 1971; Frye 1957). Symbols such as nature or the primitive can occur frequently in history. They exist as part of the stock of symbols, ideas, myths, images, and legends available to be drawn on in any given period (Boas and Lovejoy 1935; White 1972; Stocking 1989).

The conception of culture as the a priori categories constituting the possibility of experience has presented a methodological problem for the sociological analysis of ideas. The key concepts of the sociologist have been, and I assert still are, those of social structure, hierarchy, and social group. The Marxist principle that existence determines consciousness has summed up a major part of the sociologist's weaponry. In the general intellectual movement of the social sciences in the past two decades that dogma has seemed less and less viable and its reverse increasingly relevant.

The relation between culture and social structure remains a major intellectual problem of sociological method. This chapter is one effort at reconciling concepts that are on the verge of divorce. In it I examine the concept of "nature" as it takes on divergent meanings in differing social contexts, with differing consequences and understandings in relation to the social structure and to the perception of the body. While "the body" is a common object, its symbolic properties, its meanings, may be distinctly different in different contexts.

The cultural symbols and meanings that order experience do not exist in a vacuum. They possess implications for living that operate for and against groups and institutions. In most societies such symbols and meanings are not shared by everyone. Concepts of health and of food, which will be analyzed here, are symbols of who and what we are and of who and what we are not. Such symbols take on meanings that, implicitly or explicitly, have a structural as well as a cultural meaning. Not only do they order experience, but they order it in distinction from other meanings and from others who manifest different meanings. In this paper, it is not only the meanings and symbols through which health and eating are espoused that is my theme. It is also the structural contexts that provide meanings that are more temporal and spatial than the cultural meanings and symbols. The contrasts between "folk medicine" and professional medicine and between natural foods and commercial foods provide different contexts of understanding. They create and maintain boundaries that define loyalties and provide distinctions that draw on and accentuate social conflicts and aspirations rooted in social structure. Eating is not only a physiological process. It is also a form of self-production through communication. We ingest symbolic forms.

Contrasts and conflicts between differing cultural and structural forms set the framework for this analysis of the natural foods movements of the nineteenth and twentieth centuries. A basic struggle between the hedonistic tenets of a market economy and the abstemiousness of philosophies and religions of self-control, between the needs for social order and the fears of social control, lies deep within American individualism. These form a context within which diet and health become differently interlocked in the movements of the 1830s and the 1950s.

The Counterculture of Popular Medicine

American movements to reform how we eat have always been set in the context of health. Historians and social critics interested in the forms of recreation, leisure, and play have discussed at length the similarities and differences in play within social structures. Varieties of entertainment, activities of play, and rules of morality between classes have been the focus of studies and critical essays (Burke 1970; Gans 1974; Thompson 1974). The customary terms used to describe such divisions have been those of a *popular* or *folk* culture and those of an *elite* or *high* culture. These contrasts have been drawn from a class or some other hierarchical order in which a more powerful group or institution, such as church officials or a social elite, attempt to control or change the behavior of those lower on the ladder of power and prestige (Rosenzweig 1983; Burke 1970).

The distinction is drawn in another fashion when scholars of medicine and health discuss the practice of medicine and the idea of health as it is pursued within and without the institutions of medical care embodied in doctors, nurses, clinics, hospitals, and patients. The distinctions are less those of class and more those of formal training and informal, untrained "folk belief." The terms become those of *professional* medicine and *folk* medicine. The latter is also discussed as *alternative* medicine and sometimes *quackery* (Starr 1982; Shryock 1931). I choose to retain the terms *elite* and *popular* in order to convey the more detached sense that these common terms, used in other arenas, help maintain.

The claim of science to have advanced human welfare through medical discovery is one of the most telling arguments for the idea of progress in the twentieth century. Civilization, through scientific research, has protected us against disease and deterioration and lengthened life while making it more comfortable. It is in the development of knowledge and technical equipment that health is improved and life extended. Contemporary institutional, professional medicine rests on the belief that there is a special body of knowledge and technical skill such that only those trained in it can help cure sickness and prevent illness. This is a definition of the medical institution. Specially accredited persons (doctors and nurses) and specially equipped arenas (clinics and hospitals) represent the institutionalized form of scientific medicine. It is by these persons and in these spaces that legitimate medicine should be practiced, and only in this way can health be achieved (Parsons 1951, chap. 10).

The triumphs of scientific research advanced and supported the claim of the professional to know more about and be more skilled at the prevention, diagnosis, and treatment of disease than the layperson, who lacked the training and the technology. Without the progress that science has made, the claims of a medical elite to legitimate authority would lack credibility and trust.

The medical institution and professional medicine emerge as attributes of culture, products of a historical development in which nature is overcome and improved on. Popular medicine claims to achieve health without doctors and medical institutions. (Risse et al. 1977). In this view health does not depend on scientific knowledge and a professional elite but is within the grasp of the ordinary person. It needs no special training or expensive equipment. The populace, the untrained, nonprofessionalized, are their own best physicians, their own best healers. The "natural man" is as much an authority in matters of health as is the Ph.D. and the M.D. If elite medicine is conceptualized as the legitimate institution, then popular medicine can be considered a countermedicine and part of a counterculture.

It is unwarranted to sum up all popular medicine in any single, easy description. That it is populist is inherent in the conception of it as nonprofessional. This and similar notions characterize many, although not all, of the dissenting medical reform movements of the nineteenth century and much of the alternative medicine of the twentieth. The situation today is not unlike that expressed by the sectarian leader of the botanic medicine of the early nineteenth century, Samuel Thomson. The study of medicine, Thomson wrote, is "no more necessary to mankind at large, to qualify them to administer relief from pain and sickness, than to a cook in preparing food to satisfy hunger" (quoted in Starr 1982, 52).

This distinction between popular and elite medicine marks a boundary essential to an understanding of natural foods movements. Such movements are part of popular medicine and need to be seen in contrast to practices and philosophies of medicine as it is conducted within elite institutions.

Food as Social Symbol and Metaphor

My use of culture and its embodiment in food is a perspective focused on the understanding of meanings. From this viewpoint, culture can be seen as symbol systems with which life is organized into a comprehensible set of actions and events. (Gusfield 1981). Clifford Geertz has stated this in an excellent fashion: "Both so-called cognitive and so-called expressive symbols or symbol-systems have, then, at least one thing in common: they are extrinsic sources of information in terms of which human life can be patterned—extrapersonal mechanisms for the perception, understanding, judgment and manipulation of the world. Culture patterns . . . are 'programs'; they provide a template or blueprint for the organization of social and psychological processes" (Geertz 1973, 216).

That food and drink are used as symbols of social position and status is an old theme in sociology. Thorstein Veblen's classic study of conspicuous consumption and status symbols created a mode of analysis that has been the staple of sociological studies of consumer behavior since its original publication in 1899 (Veblen 1934). More recently, the study of food and drink has been as attentive to the text (the content of consumption) as it has been to its context (the setting and the participants). Mary Douglas, probably the leading figure in this rebirth of interest in an anthropology of food, makes the distinction between food as material and food as symbol by referring to eating as a "field of action." "It is a medium in which other levels of categorization become manifest" (Douglas 1984, 30). In her own analyses of British meals and of the Judaic rules of *kashruth,* she has demonstrated how what is eaten and how it is eaten constitute a mode of communication and can be read as a cultural object, embodying the attributes of social organization or general culture (Douglas 1975).

Others have made use of somewhat similar orientations to the study of food. Sahlins's distinction between animals that are proper and improper to eat in Western societies laid emphasis on the "human-like" qualities attributed to "pets," such as dogs, horses, and cats, compared to animals perceived as less than human, such as pigs, sheep, and cattle (Sahlins 1976). Barthes's analysis of steak as a male food or sugar as symbolic of a "sweet time" again shows that food is a system of signs and symbols that can be read for their meaning—for what they denote as well as what they connote (Barthes 1973, 1979; see also Farb and Armelagos 1980, chap. 5). Lévi-Strauss's *The Raw and the Cooked* (1969) is, perhaps, the seminal work in this approach to the study of food as a symbol and as a medium of communication.

In his analysis of taste and social structure, Pierre Bourdieu presents both an empirical study of consumer habits and an interpretive theory that, applied to food and drink, sees in food or meals the communication and representation of more general orientations to life-styles. In his surveys of the French population, Bourdieu found sharp differences in both the foods eaten and the nature of meals among various classes and occupational groups. Among the working classes, the emphasis in eating is on the material and the familial. Guests not closely related to the household are seldom invited. The sequence of courses is unimportant. The changing of plates is minimal. The food itself is heavy and filling—a focus on plenty. There is a sharp division between male and female food and a lack of concern for food as creating health or beauty of body. Among the petite bourgeoisie and the bourgeoisie, the opposite is the case. The meal is an occasion for social interaction, it is regulated in manners and sequences and it is preoccupied with considerations of health and aesthetic consequences (Bourdieu 1984, 177–200).

Bourdieu reads these empirical differences as evincing the existence of distinctive class-based tastes, as parts of fundamental and deep-seated styles of life. In emphasizing the meal as an occasion for social relationships, the bourgeoisie deny the primary, material function of eating and maintain the integration of the family with the more disciplined areas of life. Order, restraint, and propriety may not be abandoned. In this they express an orientation to society as a matter of refinement and regulation, of a "stylization of life" that "tends to shift the emphasis from substance and function to form and manner, and so to deny the crudely material reality of eating and of the things consumed or . . . the basely material vulgarity of those who indulge in the immediate satisfactions of food and drink" (Bourdieu 1984, 196).

To describe a structural context is not to deduce the behavior from a social situation, as a direct response or solution to perceived social problems. Food and body can better be seen as possessing levels of meanings, as being polysemic (Turner 1967; Leach 1976; Gusfield and Michelowicz 1984). On one level, the relation between food and health can be read literally. At this level, the relation is physiological and does not reflect an attitude toward the social order. At other levels, however, it can be read metaphorically, as symbolizing the experience of the user, of the author, as symbolizing the other domains of understanding with which the literal is connected (Douglas 1975, 1984; Farb and Armelagos 1980). To see steak as a food symbolic of masculinity is to observe the symbolic properties with which it has become invested in some modern societies (Barthes 1973). The metaphoric attributes are connected by a common vision of the world, by a way of stylizing activity (Bourdieu 1984). It is these diverse yet connected levels and domains of meaning that constitute the object of my analysis of natural foods movements.

The Natural Foods Movement: Sylvester Graham and the 1830s

The American "natural foods" movement has its origins in the 1830s, a period of intense religious reawakening and deep concern over the immorality and crime associated with increasing urbanization (Nissenbaum 1980; Sokolow 1983; Schwartz 1986). These were also the years during which new public attitudes toward sexuality and alcohol were emerging and during which many were experiencing the transformation of American society from a traditional, hierarchical community to one of greater openness and individuality. The authority of past institutions, especially that of the family, was seen as declining, and generational conflict grew as family and apprenticeship played less and less of a role in determining career choice. It was especially the demise of familial and church authority that spelled danger and provoked fear in the minds of many, although it was also the source of satisfaction to others (Smith-Rosenberg 1978; Rothman 1971). It is against this background that the rise of the American natural foods movement in the 1830s can be understood.

Sylvester Graham is usually taken as the major figure in the development of the idea system associated with food avoidances and beliefs about the dangers to health from modern food technology. Graham, an ordained Presbyterian minister, was not a medical professional. He had, however, read and been influenced by two French physiologists, Bichat and Broussais, and by the American physician and health reformer Benjamin Rush. While serving as an organizer for the American Temperance Society, he came to prominence through his lectures on health in New York and Philadelphia during the cholera epidemic of 1832.

The physiological principles that Graham had received were coupled with an orientation toward modern life that emphasized the destructive effect of modern "refinements" on food, morality, and health. By the 1830s, Americans began to abandon self-sufficient farming, at least of their own food, relying instead on the increased commercialization of foodstuffs. Graham was particularly appalled at the production of bread outside the home. In order to appeal to consumers' palates, commercial bakeries used a refined flour to produce a bread that was whiter, less grainy, and less fibrous than the coarse, dark bread with which Americans were familiar. Graham was convinced that this loss of fiber was detrimental to health. In his lectures and writings he preached against the use of refined flour and against the consumption of white bread (Graham 1839). He developed a foodstuff called the "Graham cracker," still in use in American homes today, that retained the natural fibrous qualities of earlier breads.

Bread is, of course, a central part of the diet and, as a consequence, a frequent object of symbolization. The breaking of bread as a symbol of solidarity or the use of the wafer in the Eucharist are examples. In writing and speaking about the advantages of raw, unrefined flour, Graham waxed nostalgic over the associations of bread with home and hearth: "Who that can look back 30 or 40 years to those blessed days of New England's prosperity and happiness, when our good mothers used to make the family bread, but can well remember how long and how patiently those excellent matrons stood over their bread troughs, kneading and molding their dough? And who with such recollections cannot also well remember the delicious bread that those mothers used invariably to set before them? There was a natural sweetness and richness in it which made it always desirable" (Graham 1839, 2:448–49).

But Graham and the Grahamites went well beyond an attack on refined flour. Graham's scheme for the understanding of ill health was built on an assumed relation between excitation and debility (Nissenbaum 1980). The excitement that certain foods created was dangerous to the body. The refined flour produced in commercial agriculture deprived the body of needed coarse fiber. But it was not only the direct effects of diet on the body that alarmed Graham. It was also the effects of sexual desire and sexual intercourse on health. Limits to lust were essential to human health, as were limits to gluttony. Meat, spices, sugar, coffee, tea, and alcohol, like sex, were other forms of excitation that were also deleterious to the body. So too was the nervousness created by the pace of urban life. The resulting stimulation risked destroying a natural health that previous generations, and primitive peoples, instinctually knew and followed.

Graham's view of the debilitating consequences of "excessive" sexual stimulation and intercourse should be viewed against the growing Puritanism of American sexual norms. That Puritanism that Europeans frequently see as part of American culture did not emerge until the 1830s (Sokolow 1983; Smith-Rosenberg 1978). It is a product, in part, of the religious revivalism of the era but also a response to the immoralities perceived in the growing cities and among the increasingly diverse immigrant populations there. One study of Graham's influence and the rise of "Victorian" morality in America attributes both to an American response to modernization (Sokolow 1983).

Whatever the origins of Victorian morality, contemporary sexual morals were increasingly attacked. There was public admonition against masturbation and an expressed sense that sexual behavior and gluttony were out of control (Sokolow 1983, chap. 2; Schwartz 1986, chap. 2). Graham himself was one of the first public enunciators of the new sexual purity. His *Lectures to Young Men on Chastity* (Graham 1840) is among the early statements of the antimasturbation movement. That attitude toward masturbation and sex in general is significant for any consideration of the nineteenth-century purity campaigns. The connection between diet and sexuality is important to the symbolic character of the meanings implicit in each. Each involves a similar view of the body as a metaphor for social order and disorder in Graham's time. That connection is a central thread in my analysis.

Throughout his writing, and that of many of his followers, the contrast is drawn between a past of nature and a present of artificiality, of civilization. The processes by which food is grown, prepared, and processed for a commercial market of anonymous customers and the blandishments by which the consumer is induced into "luxury" are departures from a natural order of events. That natural order is healthier and safer than modern life, despite its technical innovations. Graham was opposed to the then-innovative use of manure as fertilizer. It was "unnatural." The process by which bread was baked from superfine flour "tortured it into an unnatural state" (Nissenbaum 1980, 7). The heightening of sexual appetites under modern conditions contrasted with a natural propensity for self-control.

Graham's use of *nature* was not simply an equation between the absence of the modern and his contemporary world. His is both an anthropological and a religious sense, although he was no primitivist[1] (Whorton 1982; Schwartz 1986). Nature is God's order, the laws of nature. That he finds them often followed where humans act instinctively, in primitive life or in the immediate past of rural farm life, does not mean that they may not also be disobeyed there as well. It is the disobeying of such laws of healthy living that constitutes the danger to health. Mankind, he wrote, is unwilling to affirm that in "the higher order of God's works . . . human life and health, and thought and feeling are governed by laws as precise and fixed and immutable as those that hold the planets in their orbits" (Graham 1839, 1:20).

In this fashion Graham was similar to many who thought about health in the nineteenth century. He equated the moral and the medical; good health and good character go together. By improving health you improved moral capacities; by improving moral character you improved health. The body was not a neutral physiological object but a field of moral contention. The self-discipline demanded by healthy diet was itself an act of moral virtue. It was a paradigm common in the nineteenth century (Schwartz 1986, chap. 2; Rosenberg 1962, chaps. 2, 7; Rosenberg and Smith-Rosenberg 1985; Pivar 1973, chap. 1). Graham expressed it this way: "While we continually violate the physiological laws of our nature, our systems will continue to be living volcanos of bad feelings and bad passions, which however correct our abstract principles of morality may be, will continually break out in immoral actions" (quoted in Pivar 1973, 38–39).

I dwell on Graham and his ideas far longer than seems warranted here. Two reasons prompt this attention. First, Sylvester Graham was among the leading medical reformers of his time. His ideas, and those of a number of other reformers and Grahamites, greatly influenced American conceptions of health and illness and of the uses of food. Not only did he spawn a number of journals, but his conceptions of how to avoid the risks of ill health were embodied in a number of Grahamite resort hotels. He had great influence on the American Seventh Day Adventists. One of these Grahamite followers was John Harvey Kellogg, whose invented food, corn flakes, was an endeavor to provide a vegetarian, fibrous, and safer food for the American breakfast (Carson 1957).

Second, and perhaps more important, Graham's ideas, both manifestly and in their latent meanings and symbolism, have much in common with the current natural foods movement in the United States. The way in which Graham perceived foods as sources of risk or safety and what he thought they symbolized about the consumer and about his or her society are remarkably similar to attitudes current in the natural foods movement today. For this reason it is useful to analyze Graham's thought more closely.

I find it helpful to conceive of Graham's ideas in the form of two sets of contrasts. The first (see table 1) is a contrast based on substances. The second (see table 2) is based on the added meanings Graham utilizes, the symbolic attributions of his thought. Here the distinctions reflect a view of the natural order as benign and conducive to health and of the social order (or disorder) as producing illness.

Table 1. Substantive Table of Healthy and Unhealthy

Healthy	Unhealthy
Unrefined	Refined
Coarse	Smooth
Pure	Additives
Raw	Cooked
Wheat bread	White bread
Organic	Fertilized
Water	Alcohol
Fruit juice	Tea, coffee
Chastity	Sexual intercourse
Natural	Artificial

Table 2. Symbolic Table of Healthy (Natural) and Unhealthy (Social) Orders

Natural Order	Social Order
Temperance	Indulgence
Serenity	Excitement
Natural desires	Induced desires
Sufficiency	Luxury
Self-control	External control
Home	Commerce
Moral economy	Market economy
Health	Disease
Nature	Civilization

Social Contexts and Structural Meanings

Tables 1 and 2 relate the various substantive matters, such as a prefer-ence for unrefined flour, to the personal and moral characteristics that are symbolized by the recommended eating styles, such as temperance. These meanings, however, also need to be seen in the light of what the contrasts imply for social structure. At another level of analysis, Graham and his followers are proferring advice that relates to the social order of their times. It is here that culture and social structure come together to form contextualized meanings. It is here that the contrasts between substantive and symbolic aspects of meaning are turned into statements about social boundaries between valued and disvalued be-haviors, between healthy and diseased people.

Graham has drawn us a picture of what it is that he finds objection-able and at the same time unhealthy in food and sex and in the social order emerging, in his view, in the America of the 1830s. With the market replacing the home as the source of production of food, the control of the individual and the family over their life stuff, their food, is passing into institutional hands—to commercial agriculture, to food technology, to impersonal, profit-oriented businesses. It is a market whose appeal to the consumer is that of taste and indulgence. With this transformation, a new kind of person is coming into existence— one who lacks the capacity for self-control. In the 1830s there was a growing abundance of food and at the same time a growing denuncia-tion of gluttony (Schwartz 1986). It is in this social order that Graham finds the sources of risk to health and to morality.

There is, however, a contrast to be protected and to which the new being—the consumer—can cling for safety. It is the natural order that men and women have known and that they are capable of following. It is not a Hobbesian but a Rousseauistic natural order. Human beings find no advantage in the growth of a larger, more technologically integrated social order and the material progress it brings. Health is an attribute of the past, of the unspoiled, unindulgent, and disciplined traditional American.

That this symbolism characterized more groups than the Grahamites was evident in the presidential election of 1840. Whig followers of William Henry Harrison used the distinction between the elite and the populace in drawing their candidate as a "log cabin" man, in contrast to the elite and polished Martin Van Buren. In the discourse of the campaign Van Buren's cuisine was contrasted to Harrison's plain and simple food, "chateau wine" to "log cabin cider": "The fable was the same. The simple, the home-grown, the coarse and blunt must triumph over the elegant, the manufactured, the refined and diplomatic" (Schwartz 1986, 36).

In his history of the Grahamite movement, Stephen Nissenbaum remarks on the irony that Graham's antipathy to the marketplace is coupled with a view of man as naturally capable of self-control. The latter tenet, he maintains, fits a "bourgeois philosophy" more consistent with the marketplace than a normal economy (Nissenbaum 1982).

I would agree with Nissenbaum that Graham's doctrines symbolize a view of the commercial institutions of his day as detrimental to human beings and of a natural order as superior and preferable to the social order. But the contradiction is as deeply rooted in conceptions of a consistent bourgeois philosophy as it is in Graham (Levine 1978). What my analysis of these ideas uncovers in the context of Graham's doctrine of health and risk is the individualism inherent in the glorification of natural man. As I will discuss below, Graham is critical of the weakened forms of social control and the consequent need for principles of self-discipline made necessary in the 1830s. What the developing commercialism and the weakened role of familial, communal, and religious authority led to was the release of appetite—of passion, feeling, and desire. Gluttony and lust were both the results and the sources of disease and illness.

Here Graham's enunciation of sexual purity is significant. It is by no means idiosyncratic to Graham. Others in the diet movement were similarly critical of American sexual practices and wrote various forms of advice to young men, including condemnations of masturbation and warnings about its ill and evil effects. (Smith-Rosenberg 1978).

Among these were William Alcott, Graham's leading "competitor" in the early 1830s, Russell Trall in 1856; James Jackson in 1862; and John Harvey Kellogg in 1888. Graham's published lectures on the subject were a way of fixing in print what he had been saying for two years in lectures to young men in colleges and in lyceums. He was addressing young men away from home and free to explore the new, uncontrolled areas of urban life.

It is this young man, unattached to institutions of family or church, unapprenticed to occupational supervision, to whom Graham and others directed their message of sexual purity. It was the young man, the unattached adolescent, who constituted the source of fear, a part of the "dangerous classes" who provided the disorders of urban crime and drunkenness. These young men were also the potential victims of the temptations to which urban, modern life exposed them (Boyer 1978; Schwartz 1986). They were the objects of the awakened and unchained desires that surrounded them in the urban environments.

The message of Graham and other sexual reformers was substantially the same. Control thyself. Sex is intended for reproduction, not for recreation. Indulgence, hedonism, and self-abuse contain the seeds of sickness—directly in poor health, even insanity, and indirectly in their effect on the future role of husband and father. Married couples, cautioned Graham, should limit intercourse to once a month. It is the stimulation and excitation that, within the scope of his physiological scheme, cause illness in the stomach and that diminish the individual's general vigor and fitness.

It is here, in the concept of excitation, that I find a linkage between Graham's temperance, sexual and diet theories, and exhortations. In all these, the temptations of indulgence and release surround the individual. The new foods, the sexual opportunities, the presence of alcohol, all damage the moral order of the community and the personal order of the individual. All the stimulation and arousal of desire have ill effects on health. The institutional controls of family, church, and work are declining.

The solution that Graham suggests is not a reformed institution but the emergence of heightened self-discipline and self-control. In the absence of authority, the social and moral order must depend on the internal mechanisms of discipline and order that the individual is capable of sustaining.

It is in this juncture of diverse programs at the nexus of self-control that I find the metaphoric, symbolic significance of natural foods in the nineteenth century. The linking concepts are "excitation" and "self-control." Excitation emanates from the outside, from the foods and markets and temptations available to the contemporary, urban population. In the inaugural issue of the *Graham Journal of Health and Longevity,* the editor writes, "The mental movement of the present is retrograde . . . the vehemence of passion is subduing the vigor of thought . . . Vehemence and impetuosity are, indeed, the characteristics of the age . . . continual and inordinate craving and eager grasping after every species of moral as well as physical stimuli . . . everything adopted to excite and dissipate" (29 March 1837, 1).

Such a description of contemporary society might have been written by Emile Durkheim as an example of anomie. It pictures a society in which communal, religious, and familial norms are either absent or unenforceable. In the consequent void anything is possible; everything is capable of realization. In such a society, the traditional institutional controls cannot be depended on to ensure righteous living. Discipline and control must depend on the self.

What is it that the body symbolizes as an object of health? Illness, like sexual immorality and intemperance, is both a sign and an effect of moral defection. It indicates the inability of the person to exercise resistance to physical desire and, at the same time, results in the debility and disease that constitute illness. Here is the theme of Christian perfectionism exemplified. Immorality is also unhealthy. Illness is failure to observe God's law and a sign of theological dereliction. As James Whorton points out, *stimulation* was a term in Graham's time used as much in a moral as in a physiological context: "The determination to promote godliness by suppressing animal appetites and passions, the Victorian antipleasure principle, was sufficiently far advanced as to have branded overstimulation, or nervous and mental excitation, as morally evil, the first step of gradual descent into drunkenness and debauchery" (Whorton 1982, 43).

The body is then an area of struggle between the tempting forces of market and city, which draw the person into immediate physical gratifications, and the laws of God and nature, from which the canons of good health and right living are derived. In a changed world of weakened tradition and institutional forces, it is to the self that one must look for sources of social and personal control.

This analysis of symbolic and metaphoric properties in the theory of health is not a form of reduction. I am not asserting that Graham and his disciples saw natural foods as a means to achieve sexual morality or a device for coping with urban crime and disorder. That is certainly not what the Grahamites assert. Rather, what I am claiming is that the theory of illness and health and the body as an object can be understood as "making sense" to the Grahamites and their audiences because those theories are embedded in a view of reality that fits their experience. Such "root hypotheses" or paradigms are seen in the lectures and books on sex and temperance and on physiology. In them the body is seen metaphorically. They are what Christians experiencing the decline in communal and family control could well have understood. It is here, in the view of the body as a manifestation of moral order and immoral disorder, that culture operates. It is in perceiving the situation of the times—in our case lessened authority and increased temptation—that social structure operates to give specific, situated meaning to cultural categories.

Implicated in that paradigm is a particular view of the place of the person in society. External social controls could not be depended on to produce people of moral rectitude because such controls were absent or unworkable. As Levine (1978), Rothman (1971), and others have pointed out, social rules in colonial America were enforced by in-stitutions, not persons. The nineteenth-century could not do so. One response might have been to attempt to rebuild or reinforce such in-stitutions. Rothman's analysis of mental asylums, poorhouses, peniten-tiaries, and hospitals describes just such attempts. But in the natural foods movements, and in health reform in general, there is no such attempt. It is to the individual, to the self, that Graham and his follow-ers looked.

The Natural Foods Movement: Popular Medicine and Counterculture, 1950–90

Interest in natural foods and nutritional health by no means disap-peared with the death of Graham, nor did health faddist sects. Graham influenced a number of disciples, and out of his ideas about grain cereals and the risks of meat eating emerged a modern commercial industry—that of breakfast cereals. John Harvey Kellogg and C. W. Post both were self-styled disciples of Graham's. Kellogg, a physician and Seventh-Day Adventist, became the director of a Grahamite sani-tarium, which he moved closer to conventional medical practice while still following Graham's principles of nutrition. He experimented with various grain products and, in 1900, invented the corn flake. Originat-ing in a perceived threat from the market, this product spawned a new industry. Kellogg was a most prolific writer during the almost fifty years in which he played a significant role on the American health scene. He wrote as well on matters of morals, continuing the sexual purity theme that the earlier natural foods advocates had also espoused (Carson 1957).[2]

Others continued to champion the cause of good nutrition as the avenue toward good health. Nevertheless, these efforts remain distinctly on the margins of medical institutions. Following the feats of bacteriological immunization and sanitation and the organization of medicine into a profession dominated by the paradigm of allopathy, the natural foods movement remained marginal to the central forms of food consumption in the United States (Gideon 1948, 200–207; Cummings 1940).

The Natural Foods Movement of the 1950s and After

Beginning sometime in the 1950s and continuing into the present, there has been a quickening of interest in nutrition as a means to achieve good health and prevent illness.[3] It is evident in the increased publication of books espousing the value of "natural foods" and criticizing current American eating habits. It is further evinced in the considerable increase in journals devoted to the topic and in the proliferation of a new enterprise, the "health food" or "natural food" industry. In 1990 there were 108 retail outlets listed in the San Diego County telephone directory under the rubric "Health and Diet Foods—Retail." This represents approximately one such outlet for every 23,148 people in the metropolitan area.

In referring to the movement, I recognize a wide range of organized and unorganized groups. These range from the strict vegetarian, who avoids sugar, refined flours, and all products grown with chemical fertilizers and containing additives and preservatives, who reads the books and journals advocating natural diets, and for whom diet is a central point in life (Kandel and Pelto 1980; New and Priest 1967), to the casual consumer who has adopted some aspects of the natural foods "program"—for example, using vitamins, purchasing only organic food products, or avoiding or limiting the intake of meat or sugar—without seeing himself or herself as belonging or subscribing to any movement.

The spread of a natural foods orientation in American society is also evinced in the adoption of certain foods into the world of commercial food distribution (Belasco 1989). For a long time, granola could be obtained only in shops specializing in health or natural foods. Sometime in the 1970s, American supermarkets began to stock the granola produced by the small companies servicing the natural foods stores. By the late 1970s, even the biggest companies were producing and marketing granola. And, in the last few years, there has been some trend toward stocking cereals and other commodities in an unpackaged, bulk form, long a characteristic of the natural foods store as well as of urban groceries before World War II.

The differences between the two forms of retail establishment is, perhaps, one clue to the symbolism of the current natural foods movement and, at the same time, evidence of the similarities to its nineteenth-century analogues. The movement of the 1830s is similar in many ways to that of the 1950s. Each finds risks and safeties in the same places and from highly similar vantage points. Each symbolizes safe and dangerous foods in the same framework or paradigm. While the differences between the two forms of distributing food have been somewhat attenuated, they still persist. You and I know very well what to expect from a store that specializes in "natural foods."

One of the most striking aspects of the contemporary American health food or natural food store is the large number of products closer to the point of primary production—products in a raw, natural, and unprocessed state. Spices, cereals, and dried fruits are more likely to be found in bulk in a natural foods store than in a supermarket. The absence of complex packaging in a natural foods store is clear. The customer is closer in time to the natural state of the products. The variety of such products is also much greater—not just several brands of tea or honey but forty or fifty. The varieties within standard categories are in turn large and varied. Nationally known brands do not dominate the shelves. The number of different spices is far greater than those found in conventional groceries. The contrast between localized, specific distribution and the mass production of the supermarket is evident.

Two products, or forms of product, are conspicuous by their absence or limited presence. One is animal products—meats, poultry, and fish, but especially red meat. The other is canned goods. Both would have been symbols of progress in an earlier period. Animal products represented progress because they are part of the diet of affluent populations—expensive to produce and transport, especially meat. Canned goods represent the triumph of preservative technology over nature and the natural process of decay. It is almost superfluous to point out the absence of frozen foods for immediate consumption and, especially, of processed white bread, the great "bête blanc" of natural foods enthusiasts and the symbol, in its "sweet smoothness," of commercialized food industries and of modern civilization (Gideon 1948, 200–207).

To a certain extent, to walk into a natural foods store is to walk back into an earlier American form of merchandising, one that gives the consumer a sense of greater closeness to, and control over, the product. Yet such merchandising demeans the very qualities of safe packaging, diminished fear of adulteration, high animal content, and long shelf life that had been heralded as the signs of a progressive food technology. These qualities, as well as those of a progressive agriculture using chemical fertilizers and effective pesticides, become qualities of risk that in other circumstances are signs of safety and well-being. The availability and approval of nonpasteurized milk is again a symbol of the superiority of the natural over the artificial and processed.

In another way the natural foods store and its merchandising practices hearken back to an earlier era of a small-scale economy. Until recently, when major American food industries began to adopt natural foods and the country began to be health and food conscious, the necessary agricultural and merchandising groups had represented a wide variety of small producers who had either produced for a small and local market or occupied a very marginal place in the national distribution network. It is quite true that the spread of the consumer movement to natural foods depended on the preexistence and generation of the natural foods industry (Miller 1990). However, to some extent, these had been in existence before the 1950s.

The similarities between Sylvester Graham's nostalgic sense of a traditional America and that of the contemporary health foods movement are evident when the writings of leading Grahamite gurus are compared with such journals as *Vegetarian Times, Holistic Health, Whole Earth News, New Age, East/West,* and *Prevention.* One of the most popular and widely read of contemporary gurus has been Adelle Davis, whose book *Let's Eat Right and Keep Fit* was first published in 1954, was reissued in a revised edition in 1970, and is still in print and on sale at bookstores today (see Davis 1970). Although there are differences in what foods are included and stressed in a diet, and although there are differences in how authors apportion blame, Davis's book is surprisingly akin in its basic outlines to much of the natural foods movement's general program and philosophy and to Graham's pronouncements in the 1830s. However, while this is true at one level of meaning, it is not so at other levels of meaning and symbolism.

For both Graham and Davis, the appearance of a technology of refining, packaging, and preserving food has increased the risk of illness and disease. In the procedures of processing, of increasing agricultural yield, and of preserving food beyond short periods, and in the service of commercial gain, the natural qualities of food have been allowed to disappear. The fibers, vitamins, and minerals essential to physical and mental health are removed from our diet. It is up to the consumer to find ways, through improved diet, to restore them. All her flour, Davis writes, is stone ground, whole wheat, organically grown. She bakes her own bread from flour purchased at a local health foods store. She believes that the refining machinery creates such friction that the flour is precooked (Davis 1970, 101).

The distinction between the safeties of the past and the risks produced by the present commercial and technological society are referred to at many points by Davis. The raising of hens in shaded cages blocks the healthful properties of sunlight. So too frequent bathing robs the skin of oils that enable sunlight to work its healthful properties: "Sunshine would be an excellent source of [vitamin D] if it were not for the fact that people are surrounded by smog, wear clothes, live in houses and have bathtubs and hot-water heaters" (1970, 139). Davis does think that, despite the better health of primitives, Indians, and earlier American families, being bath-happy and soap-happy is progress. Yet her description casts much doubt.

This broad distinction between the modern world of civilized, cultured, refined man and an earlier world of primitive, rural, rawer people is implicit and often explicit in Davis's work, as it was in Graham's. The processes of working on the raw food in its original state—of adding modern technology and convenience to nature—accentuate the risk of illness. Whatever transforms food from its "natural" state is harmful (Belasco 1989). "By wholesomeness I mean the kind of food our grandparents and all our ancestors before them ate at every meal. *Just plain food*" (Davis 1970, 228; emphasis added).

Davis uses research studies conducted by nutritionists, but she is also often skeptical of academics and medical personnel, seeing in the former people whose research is supported by the food industry and in the latter people who ignore nutrition. The focus of medicine is disease, not health, she writes. "The purpose of medicine is to help the sick person get well. . . . The purpose of nutrition is to maintain health and to prevent illness" (1970, 18). Like other writers in this movement, she presents instances in which the "common man" knows better and is proved better than the wise doctors and professors. Such an approach is paradoxical since she was herself a trained chemist and dietician.[4]

An ad in the *Vegetarian Times* presents the same message of the virtue of the primitive and natural as superior to the civilized and scientific. It describes Lavilin as "free of aluminums and other harsh chemicals," yet effective, and as having been developed by scientists who were alarmed by the wide use of aluminum in deodorants and who "re-discovered the herbal flowers Arnica and Calendula, known for centuries to be soothing and anti-bacterial" (May 1986). These "natural extracts" decrease the bacteria that create odors.

At this level of specific advice on what to eat and what to avoid, the current health foods movement is of a piece with its earlier manifestations. It gives advice to individuals on how to help themselves. Graham lived in an America just beginning to recognize national and regional organization, in a society where medicine was just beginning to assume licensure. Food production was just beginning to pass from the domain of the self-sufficient family to become the commercial and technological concern of the marketplace. Those processes have become full-grown in our time, yet the basic advice remains the same. In one sense the glorification of natural foods is symbolic of efforts to control the forces of destruction, to find safety through our own means and not through dependence on the established order of social institutions. In its apolitical course, the current movement differs considerably from the counterculture movements of the 1960s—at least in the uses it makes of natural foods. Yet in its challenge to professional medicine and to the large and highly capital intensive food industries, it projects an image of both a counterculture and a consumer revolt. To borrow a term used by Warren Belasco to describe the movements of the 1960s, the natural foods movement is one phase in the counterculture process of creating and espousing a *countercuisine* (Belasco 1989).

The countercultural and counterstructural elements in the health and natural foods movements of the 1950s are even more prominent in the ideological symbolism of food in the counterculture of the 1960s. During the 1960s, many elements of the natural foods syndrome were taken over by the cultural side of the counterculture movements. Two differences mark this phase of the health foods movement. First, it was no longer primarily a health movement. Advice about what to eat and what to avoid were set within the general ecological movement rather than appearing within the paradigm of maintaining health and curing illness. Second, advice concerning health often carried ideological overtones, expressing opposition to many aspects of American political and cultural life (Belasco 1989). For example, the antipathy to white bread, a staple of both nineteenth- and twentieth-century natural foods movements, became explicit opposition to white supremacy in particular and political or cultural hegemony in general.

Politically, however, the 1960s health foods movement displayed its strongest affinity with the movement for ecological reform. Frances Lappe's *Diet for a Small Planet* was widely read during the late 1960s and sounded a theme common to many popular journals, such as the *Whole Earth Catalog*. What was implicit in the 1950s became an explicitly programmatic message of opposition to the food industries and to business interests, which are seen as responsible for the destruction of the ecological balance of the earth. Thus Lappe remembered, "Previously when I went to a supermarket, I felt at the mercy of our advertising culture. My tastes were manipulated. And food, instead of being my most direct link with the nurturing earth, had become mere merchandise by which I fulfilled my role as a 'good' consumer" (p. 8).

Yet forms of the 1950s movement persisted and can be found today both within the medical establishment itself and within the new age and other such movements. The health consciousness of the 1980s shows a similar concern with nutrition, this time supported by medical research on the effects of cholesterol, fiber, red meat, and overweight on health. Here too, as in holistic medicine, the movement is toward finding sources of illness in defective life-styles and forms of eating (Lowenberg 1989; Zola 1978; Carlson 1975).

Contexts of Meaning: The 1830s and the 1950s

There are two highly significant ways in which the current movement beginning in the 1950s differs, at least manifestly, from its nineteenth-century precursor. One is what I call its more evident populism. By this I mean the rejection and condemnation of professional institutions to which Americans conventionally look for advice on health. The philosophy of self-help is accompanied by a rejection of medicine and often of academic and scientific writings. In its explicit antipathy to institutionalized medicine and science, the movement of the 1950s manifests its countercultural character as an alternative medicine.

The antipathy to organized, professional medicine was less strident in Graham, although medicine was only just beginning to become an organized profession. Graham was one among a number of medical sectarians and reformers of his age. Part of their appeal can be attributed to the harsh treatment and poor rates of success of professional medicine. As practiced in the mid-nineteenth century, professional medicine often involved "heroic" therapy—drugs that produced excessive discomfort and heavy amounts of bleeding (Starr 1982, 94–102; Shryock 1931, 178–79).

A second difference between the current movement and that of the nineteenth century is the area of sexual behavior. Sex (at least safe sex) is no longer a source of danger or sexual desire an avenue to disease. And some writers—for example, Davis—hint at a positive relation between good eating habits and sexual fulfillment. But sex per se is not a theme in the present movement. But at another level the current movement is similar in demanding a rejection of indulgence. As lust is to sex, so gluttony is to hunger. The food industries promote the hedonistic use of food with no regard for health. Sugar then is the enemy, even in its unrefined, raw form. Sweets are anathema, the source of illness and bad teeth (Garten 1978). Among the terms in use in American life for pleasurable indulgence are symbols of sugar: "a sweet time." In his paper on food as symbol, Roland Barthes (1979) recalls the American popular song "Sugar Time" as the expression of joy and pleasure.

To live well and be fit, the natural food advocates are saying, requires, at symbolic levels, a self-oriented person, one unswayed by the institutional order and deaf to its lures. It requires self-control. A more extreme advocate, writing in the holistic medicine journal the *Well-Being Newsletter*, states this clearly, discussing the general rule that one should eat only those foods close to their natural state: "Is the Hygienic diet for you? Only you can answer this. It demands discipline and self-control, but it offers vigorous health and vitality" (Forrest 1985).

The continuity between the nineteenth- and the twentieth-century movements appears to me to reflect an individualism that may be unique to the American cultural scene (Lukes 1973). The imagined idyllic state of nature implies and leads to a rejection of social controls and social institutions. In this structure of thought, human beings are considered able to and are exhorted to depend on their own knowledge and abilities to achieve self-control. They are warned to eschew the advice of professionals and the supposed values of technological progress. Now, however, the behavior that the movement calls forth is not political but market oriented. In the terms of Hirschman's (1970) description of consumers in a free market, such behavior is neither protest nor loyalty. It is exit.

The ideal of character is the independent consumer, uncontrolled by either the commercial market or the trained professional. The values and the knowledge of scientific professionals, of government, of food technology, are not trusted. They are seen as increasing risks to health. The industrial world and agricultural technology preach a gospel of indulgence and luxury. That way lies danger. Health and safety depend on the individual's capacity for self-control. Civilization produces risk; nature is the source of health.

It would be an error to see this philosophy as a form of amoral anarchism. While it emerges from a context of opposition to institutional structure, it also commands a code of moral discipline that is viewed as sterner and tighter than the hedonistic ideal that the market enjoins. To follow the diet of the natural foods movement is to engage in an exercise, a ritual, in a display to self and others of that moral character. Health is the reward. In this respect the movement recalls the past and a "hard primitivism" of moral and physical steadfastness. The social order produces illness; the natural order creates health. Health is a product of "right living" and illness a sign of immorality, of a deficient life-style.

Where the two movements, that of the 1830s and that of the present, part ways is the way in which each views the institutional structure of society. For the movements of the nineteenth century, excessive eating and drinking and the diminished restraints on sexual practice symbolize a social life in which the moral order has lost the authority to enforce what nature, in God's law, demands. Illness is the outcome of the loosened social structure. The appeal to self-control is made within the context of what is perceived to be a weakened and delegitimized set of social rules. The body physical, as well as the body social and the body politic, is out of control, and only the will of the individual can regain control.

In the contemporary movement, the substantive message is remarkably similar, but the context, and thus the meaning, is very different. It is the institutions themselves and their power that is to be avoided. Medicine, science, and the marketplace of food industries are too commanding, too powerful, and too much the source of conventional wisdom. They are distrusted and delegitimated in the movement's insistence on naturalness. What is signified and symbolized in the contemporary health movement is a return to control over one's body. What is signified and symbolized in the Grahamite movement is the attempt to restore moral authority.

This alienation of natural foods users from the conventional and the dominant in eating is analogous to other related movements. Examining a variety of magazines with health foods concerns is to enter a world of holistic medicine, of the healing powers of quartz crystals, of yogic and tantric rites, of forms of nonprofessionalized psychotherapeutic self-transformation that are today grouped under the rubric *new age*. Both movements seek a return to a past, but the pasts they seek differ. For Graham and his followers, the past was a traditional structure of well-observed and understood laws and the power vested in traditional authority. That past could not be fully recovered because the institutions of authority could not be revived. But the laws those institutions enforced still applied, and a Christian perfectionism was possible, if not through institutions, then through socializing the individual. A healthy mind meant a healthy body and a moral character.

For the contemporary movement, the past is more directly hallowed. What is envisioned is a world of individuals who carve out for themselves areas of detachment from the strong and overpowering institutions that surround them. Only in themselves and in their control over their lives and their intake can they find the health and the political morality with which to prevent disease and illness. What the Grahamites sought, the contemporary movement sees as having been found and now lost.

But the nineteenth century was open to a view of nature as an ordered system for which religion provided both an understanding and a source of effective rules. Moral purity and physical purity were synonymous, and the body was the expression and symbol of the individual's fealty to both. In a world where few institutions embodied that ideal, the burden of health is thrown on the individual, as is the burden of social behavior.

The contemporary movement is more secularized, less sacral in tone and content. We are faced with a world that both restrains and permits, that stimulates the appetites and provides the professional elites to treat the effects of appetite. Nature becomes the symbol of opposition. It describes a morality and a source of knowledge that stems from an instinctual and unsocialized self that civilization, in its appeals and hierarchies, seems to have lost. Modern life is thus to blame for so much of the evil surrounding us.

The movements of the nineteenth and twentieth centuries are alike in some other respects. Most important, both substitute a planned, ordered system of eating for one that is haphazard and spontaneous. Meals cannot be unplanned periods of simple gratification. The questions of what to eat, when to eat, and how to eat must all be thought through and deliberately answered. The body, like the office, the factory, the home, is brought under the control of the rationalized soul, the central symbol of modern life and the modern social system. Here is the paradox of the antimodernism of the health foods movement. Its counterculture is committed to the dominant value of the modernist project.

For both movements, the organic, raw, grainy world of the un-cooked, the unprocessed, the virginal and untouched, has a hallowed aura. *Civilization* is a word that spells danger, disenchantment, and distrust. John Harvey Kellogg used the word to describe the origins of much that he thought ails us. In a phrase that all natural foods enthusiasts would have relished, he referred to certain illnesses as products of the "civilized colon" (Whorton 1982, 221).

Notes

This chapter is part of a chapter on health movements, which in turn is part of a book in progress, tentatively titled *The Idea of Regress: Studies in the Antimodern Temper*.

1. "Graham was too little the Leatherstocking and too much the Presbyte-rian to embrace the primeval. He proposed rather a civilized rejection of civili-zation, a return not to the tribal primitive but to primitive Christianity" (Schwartz 1986, 32).

2. John Harvey Kellogg and his brother William developed the cereal busi-ness bearing their family name but eventually quarreled over the character of the product. William wanted to improve the taste of the cereals and market them without reference to their healthful propensities. John remained commit-ted to the idea of natural foods as health foods. William was able, however, to gain legal control of the business and moved the enterprise away from its Grahamite origins (Carson 1957).

3. After the 1950s, the movement develops a number of derivative branches and additions. While the central advice, even when supported by medical re-search, remains relatively unchanged, its symbolic meanings shift in accordance with the large movements with which the movement becomes associated. These are discussed below.

4. The natural foods movements of the 1950s and the 1960s were de-nounced by many medical authorities and nutritionists as frauds or as just plain wrong. For examples, including bibliographies, see Whalen and Stare (1975) and Herbert and Barrett (1982).

References

Abrams, M. H. "Art-as-Such: The Sociology of Modern Aesthetics." *Bulletin of the American Academy of Arts and Sciences* 38 (1985): 8–33.

Aries, Phillipe. *Centuries of Childhood: A Social History of Family Life*. New York: Vintage, 1962.

Barthes, Roland. *Mythologies*. St. Albans: Paladin, 1973.

Barthes, Roland. "Toward a Psychosociology of Contemporary Food Consumption." In *Food and Drink in History,* ed. R. Forster and O. Ranum. Baltimore: Johns Hopkins University Press, 1979.

Belasco, Warren. *Appetite for Change: How the Counterculture Took on the Food Industry, 1966–1988*. New York: Pantheon, 1989.

Boas, George, and A. O. Lovejoy. *Primitivism and Related Ideas in Antiquity*. Baltimore: Johns Hopkins University Press, 1935.

Bourdieu, Pierre. *Distinction: A Social Critique of the Judgment of Taste*. Cambridge, Mass.: Harvard University Press, 1984.

Boyer, Paul. *Urban Masses and the Moral Order in America, 1820–1920*. Cambridge, Mass.: Harvard University Press, 1978.

Burke, Peter. *Popular Culture in Early Modern Europe*. London: Temple Church, 1970.

Carlson, Rick. 1975. *The End of Medicine*. New York: Wiley, 1975.

Carson, Gerald. *Cornflake Crusade*. New York: Rinehart, 1957.

Cummings, Richard O. *The American and His Food: A History of Food Habits in the United States*. Chicago: University of Chicago Press, 1940.

Davis, Adelle. *Let's Eat Right to Keep Fit*. New York: Harcourt, Brace, Jovanovich, 1970.

Douglas, Mary. "Deciphering a Meal." In *Implicit Meanings,* ed. Mary Douglas. London: Routledge & Kegan Paul, 1975.

Douglas, Mary. "Standard Social Uses of Food: Introduction." In *Food and the Social Order: Studies in Three American Communities,* ed. Mary Douglas. New York: Russell Sage, 1984.

Eliade, Mircea. *The Myth of the Eternal Return*. Princeton, N.J.: Princeton University Press, 1971.

Farb, Peter, and George Armelagos. *Consuming Passions: The Anthropology of Eating*. New York: Pocket, 1980.

Forrest, Stephen. "Principles of Practical Nutrition." *Well-Being Newsletter* 2 (November–December 1985): 5.

Frye, Northrop. *Anatomy of Criticism*. Princeton, N.J.: Princeton University Press, 1957.

Gans, Herbert. *Popular Culture and High Culture*. New York: Basic, 1974.

Garten, Max. *"Civilized" Diseases and Their Circumvention*. San Jose, Calif.: MaxMillio, 1978.

Geertz, Clifford. "Ideology as a Cultural System." In *The Interpretation of Cultures,* ed. Clifford Geertz. New York: Basic, 1973.

Gideon, Siegfried. *Mechanization Takes Command*. New York: Oxford University Press, 1948.

Graham, Sylvester. *Lectures on the Science of Human Life*. 2 vols. Boston: Marsh, Capen, Lyon & Webb, 1839.

Graham, Sylvester. *Lectures to Young Men on Chastity*. Boston: George W. Light, 1840.

Gusfield, Joseph. *The Culture of Public Problems: Drinking, Driving, and the Symbolic Order*. Chicago: University of Chicago Press, 1981.

Gusfield, Joseph, and Jerzy Michelowicz. "Secular Symbolism: Studies of Ritual, Ceremony and the Symbolic Order in Modern Life." In *Annual Review of Sociology*, vol. 10, ed. Ralph Turner and James Short. Palo Alto, Calif.: Annual Reviews, 1984.

Herbert, Victor, and Stephen Barrett. *Vitamins and "Health Foods": The Great American Hustle*. Philadelphia: George F. Stickley, 1982.

Hirschman, Albert. *Exit, Voice and Loyalty*. Cambridge, Mass.: Harvard University Press, 1970.

Kandel, Randy, and Gretel Pelto. "The Health Food Movement." In *Nutritional Anthropology*, ed. N. Jerome, R. Kandel and G. Pelto. Pleasantville, N.Y.: Redgrave, 1980.

Lappe, Frances M. *Diet for a Small Planet*. New York: Ballantine, 1971.

Leach, Edmund. *Culture and Communication*. Cambridge: Cambridge University Press, 1976.

Levine, Harry Gene. "Demon of the Middle Class: Liquor, Self-Control and Temperance Ideology in 19th.-Century America." Ph.D. diss., Department of Sociology, University of California, Berkeley, 1978.

Lévi-Strauss, Claude. *The Raw and the Cooked*. New York: Harper & Row; Vintage, 1969.

Lowenberg, June. *Caring and Responsibility: The Crossroads between Holistic Practice and Traditional Medicine*. Philadelphia: University of Pennsylvania Press, 1989.

Lukes, Steven. *Individualism*. Oxford: Basil Blackwell, 1973.

Miller, Laura. "The Commercialization of a Social Movement: The Natural Foods Movement as Lifestyle and Politics." Paper prepared for the Seminar in Social Movements, Department of Sociology, University of California, San Diego, 1990.

New, Peter, and Rhea Priest. 1967. "Food and Thought: A Sociological Study of Food Cultists." *Journal of the American Dietetic Association* 51 (1967): 13–18.

Nissenbaum, Stephen. *Sex, Diet and Debility in Jacksonian America: Sylvester Graham and Health Reform*. Westport, Conn.: Greenwood, 1980.

Parsons, Talcott. *The Social System*. Glencoe, Ill.: Free Press, 1951.

Pivar, David. *Purity Crusade: Sexual Morality and Social Control, 1868–1890*. Westport, Conn.: Greenwood, 1973.

Risse, Guenter, Ronald Number, and Judith Leavitt, eds. *Medicine without Doctors*. New York: Science History Publications/USA, 1977.

Rosenberg, Charles. *The Cholera Years: The United States in 1832, 1849 and 1866*. Chicago: University of Chicago Press, 1962.

Rosenberg, Charles, and Carroll Smith-Rosenberg. "Pietism and the Origins of the American Public Health Movement." In *Sickness and Health in America*, ed. Judith Leavitt and Ronald Numbers. Madison: University of Wisconsin Press, 1985.

Rosenzweig, Roy. *Eight Hours for What We Will.* Cambridge: Cambridge University Press, 1983.

Rothman, David. *The Discovery of the Asylum: Social Order and Disorder in the New Republic.* Boston: Little, Brown, 1971.

Sahlins, Marshall. *Culture and Pratical Reason.* Chicago: University of Chicago Press, 1976.

Schorer, Mark. *William Blake: The Politics of Vision.* New York: Vintage, 1959.

Schutz, Alfred. *The Phenomenology of the Social World.* Evanston, Ill.: Northwestern University Press, 1967.

Schwartz, Hillel. *Never Satisfied: A Cultural History of Diets, Fantasies and Fat.* New York: Anchor, 1986.

Shryock, Richard. "Sylvester Graham and the Health Movement." *Mississippi Valley Historical Review* 18 (1931): 172–83.

Smith-Rosenberg, Carroll. "Sex as Symbol in Victorian Piety." In *Turning Points: Historical and Sociological Essays on the Family,* ed. John Demos and Sarane Boocock. Chicago: University of Chicago Press, 1978.

Sokolow, Jayme. *Eros and Modernization.* London and Toronto: Associated Universities Press, 1983.

Starr, Paul. *The Social Transformation of American Medicine.* New York: Basic, 1982.

Stephens, Leslie. *History of English Thought in the Eighteenth Century,* vol. 2. London: Putnam, 1927.

Stocking, George, Jr. "The Ethnographic Sensibility of the 1920s and the Dualism of the Anthropological Tradition." In *Romantic Motives: Essays on Anthropological Sensibility,* ed. George Stocking, Jr. Madison: University of Wisconsin Press, 1989.

Swidler, Anne. "Culture in Action: Symbols and Strategies." *American Sociological Review* 51 (1986): 273–86.

Thompson, E. P. "Patrician Society, Plebeian Culture." *Journal of Social History* 7 (1974): 382–405.

Turner, Victor. *The Forest of Symbols: Aspects of Noembu Ritual.* Ithaca, N.Y.: Cornell University Press, 1967.

Veblen, Thorstein. 1934 [1898]. *The Theory of the Leisure Class.* New York: Modern Library.

Whalen, Elizabeth, and Frederick Stare. *Panic in the Pantry.* New York: Atheneum, 1975.

White, Hayden, "The Forms of Wildness: Archeology of an Idea." In *The Wild Man: An Image in Western Thought from the Renaissance to Romanticism,* ed. Edward Dudley and Maximillian Novak. Pittsburgh: University of Pittsburgh Press, 1972.

Whorton, James. *Crusaders for Fitness: The History of American Health Reformers.* Princeton, N.J.: Princeton University Press, 1982.

Zola, Irving. "Medicine as an Institution of Social Control." In *The Cultural Crisis of Modern Medicine,* ed. J. Ehrenreich. New York: Monthly Review Press, 1978.

FIVE

Constructing a Shifting
Moral Boundary: Literature
and Obscenity in Nineteenth-
Century America

Nicola Beisel

In 1872 Anthony Comstock approached the leaders of New York
City's Young Men's Christian Association to ask their support for a
campaign to rid New York's streets of obscene literature. Robert Mc-
Burney and Morris Jesup, both influential and wealthy businessmen,
responded, helping Comstock found the New York Society for the
Suppression of Vice (NYSSV). The NYSSV was remarkable for the
wealth and prestige of its supporters, over 80 percent of whom were
either upper or upper middle class. In its first twenty years, 16 percent
of New York City's millionaires who were also in the Social Register,
citizens who possessed both vast wealth and the highest social prestige,
gave money to Comstock's campaign (Beisel 1990a; Boyer 1968; Johnson 1973). Leaders of the NYSSV included Samuel Colgate, William
Dodge, Kilian Van Rensselaer, and David Dows. The support of these
wealthy and influential citizens enabled Comstock to lobby successfully
for federal and state laws against obscenity. The federal Comstock
Laws, passed in 1873, made it illegal to transport obscene materials
through the mail and made Comstock a special agent of the Postal
Service. Comstock used this office, and that of secretary of the NYSSV,
to secure evidence against, obtain warrants against, and prosecute those
who violated the obscenity laws.

But the laws did not clearly specify what materials were subject to
prosecution. The Comstock Laws forbade the mailing of devices that
caused, or information about, contraception or abortion, but regarding
"obscene" material the law forbade the distribution of any "obscene,
lewd, or lascivious book, pamphlet, picture, paper, writing, print, or
other publication of an indecent character" (Comstock [1883] 1967,
209).[1] Given virtually unlimited license to define obscenity as he
wished, and often supported by the courts, which upheld his judgment

in over half his arrests, Comstock was constrained largely by what he could convince his supporters to accept as legitimate targets of an antiobscenity organization (Johnson 1973, 195).

Obscenity proved to be a moving target. Comstock began his campaign by arresting the purveyors of what he called "libidinous" pictures and writings, materials for which nobody proffered the defense that works with literary or artistic merit were being censored. However, in 1879 Comstock discovered obscenity in "the classics," largely by encountering translated editions of Ovid and Boccaccio that were being produced to replace the more common obscenity that had been suppressed. The number of vendors of salacious classics that were arrested is not known, although in 1881 Comstock did report the arrest of two New Jersey book merchants who sold an English edition of an "Italian book," illustrated with "lewd pictures," one of whom promoted his wares by telling young men, "You must not leave this on the parlor table, nor let ladies see it" (NYSSV 1883, 8). Comstock claimed that a "purely technical" point allowed these merchants to escape conviction but asserted that the trial had "a salutary effect upon those inclined to parade this filthy matter as a specialty" (NYSSV 1883, 8). That "respectable" booksellers might forgo selling potentially illegal wares because they feared arrest, and the reputation of being an obscenity vendor, is a plausible claim.

Comstock's diatribes against classic literature are important for what they portended. Comstock turned his eye to high culture and in 1883 started Boston's New England Society for the Suppression of Vice (NESSV, later renamed the Watch and Ward Society) on their career of book censorship by urging them to suppress a new and unabridged edition of Walt Whitman's *Leaves of Grass*. The NESSV stopped the publication (in Boston) of Whitman's book and suppressed (although it did not entirely halt) its circulation; ultimately, their stranglehold on the sale of books in Boston earned that city a reputation as the book-banning capital of the country.

This chapter will analyze the formation and movement of the boundary between literature and obscenity in the late nineteenth century. I will argue that the moral boundary between obscenity and literature was constructed from ideologies about other social categories, namely, those of youth, class, and ethnicity, and that the boundary around obscenity moved steadily into the realm of literature as Comstock subtracted the categories of ethnicity, class, and youth from his original definition of what constituted obscenity.

The Moving Boundary as a Theoretical Issue

Understanding the shifting boundary drawn between literature and obscenity by Comstock and his supporters requires that we consider the nature of boundaries and how the construction of moral boundaries might allow for their movement. One approach to understanding moral boundaries has been to consider them as part of the symbolic order of society. Mary Douglas argues that pollution taboos manifest the general social order and that "polluting" matter is matter out of its proper place. Concern about the pollution of the physical bodies of individuals, Douglas argues, reflects a larger concern about the integrity of the "body politic" ([1966] 1984, 124). This approach to boundaries implies that boundary formation is the response of an entire society and that the boundary itself represents consensus about the limits of socially acceptable actions.

Douglas also discusses boundary formation as a process reflecting divisions within society, not just the boundary around it. Ideologies about polluting sexual behavior reflect beliefs about the nature of social order or about relations between parts of society ([1966] 1984, 4). Carroll Smith-Rosenberg (1978) uses Douglas's perspective on pollution to examine Victorian sexual beliefs, in particular, the hysteria about adolescent male masturbation spread by male moral reformers in the mid-nineteenth-century United States. She argues that the body is a metaphor for society and that attempts to control bodily functions and desires indicate an attempt to control or protect social groups or institutions. Sexual reform is a consequence of the transition to an industrial society, which created anxiety about social disorder; at the same time, the gradual decay of the apprenticeship system generated particular anxiety about adolescent males. Fears of adolescent male sexuality, and advice to parents on its control, make sense given the urbanization of American society and the fears about the social order that this engendered.

The theory that concern about bodily pollution indicates concern about social order clarifies Comstock's rhetoric about obscenity. Comstock called the literature of which he disapproved "carrion" or "filthy matter" that would "poison and corrupt the streams of life" (Comstock [1883] 1967, 26, 141; NYSSV 1878, 11). He likened a child to a glass of distilled water and equated evil reading with dropping ink in the glass (Comstock [1883] 1967, 240). Comstock used metaphors of disease, describing the lust induced by reading obscenity as a cancer that struck at society (Comstock [1883] 1967, 132). If concern about pollution reflects concern about social order, as Douglas and Smith-Rosenberg assert, then understanding Comstock's censorship requires a search for allusions to underlying social concerns in his rhetoric.

However, recognizing that pollution rhetoric points to social concerns, or even to attempts to control potentially dangerous social groups, does not help us understand how the boundary around obscenity crept steadily into the realm of literature in the late nineteenth century. While pollution rhetoric may reflect social cleavages, this perspective does not explain how the rhetoric itself is constructed or, more important, how rhetoric is used so that its intended audience understands what social conflicts are at issue and how they should react to them. In the writings of Douglas and Smith-Rosenberg, the process of constructing and using metaphors seems somewhat magical; bodily metaphors reflect widely shared concerns about structural instabilities in society. What is magical about the process is the absence of human actors using existing ideologies, or constructing new ideologies, to explain social conflict. The moving social boundary between obscenity and literature suggests that boundaries are actively constructed and reconstructed in the face of both changing social conditions and shifting public receptiveness to censorship rhetoric. To understand the boundary between literature and obscenity we must think of it as something actively constructed by people and not as a passive reflection of underlying social structures or tensions.

From what are moral boundaries constructed? In his discussion of the changes in moral categories occasioned by the French Revolution, Stinchcombe argues that analysis of a moral order should proceed by examining the "basic or pervasive categories of the normative system." The social categories (and moral obligations) of wife and child, for example, are understood by examining the roles of these family members in religion, property, and politics. Thus, Stinchcombe argues that one should analyze social and moral categories as combinations of other categories (which he calls "deep structures"). By combining deeper social categories, which Stinchcombe calls "ideological raw materials," people make sense of (and rules for) different social situations (1982, 68).

Stinchcombe's work implies that social categories, such as class and family, exist as structures in part because of the moral and cultural meanings attached to the categories. Sewell (in press) refines this point in his discussion and critique of Giddens's (1984) work on structuration. Sewell argues that social structures have a dual nature—that they consist simultaneously of resources and rules. Resources, such as factories in capitalist society or Hudson Bay blankets in a Kwakiutl potlatch, are resources because of the cultural meanings attached to them and the rules about their use. Structural change is possible, Sewell argues, both because the reproduction of resources is never certain (e.g., a field planted one year may fail the next) and because human agency makes cultural rules transposable—a rule about one situation may be applied to another. Because social categories are constructed both from moral obligations and from the mobilization of resources, they are simultaneously cultural/symbolic and material. The work of both Sewell and Stinchcombe implies that a moral boundary, such as the boundary around obscenity, can be analyzed by examining the social categories, and ideologies about those categories, that were invoked by its construction. The movement of the boundary between obscenity and literature suggests that the social categories used to construct the boundary between obscene and acceptable material changed.

Comstock's crusade against obscene literature, and his gradual redefinition of his target, allows us to examine the mobilization of cultural rules about social categories in the process of boundary formation. While the formation and movement of moral boundaries has been (and is) the object of a number of political movements, Comstock is significant both for the scope and the endurance of his crusade. In the course of his forty-year career he arrested over thirty-six hundred people for various crimes against public morality. His cases set legal precedents in censorship law; the Comstock Laws are best known as the device that was used to restrict the circulation of contraceptive information and contraceptives until the 1920s (Reed [1978] 1983; Blatt 1989).[2]

In the analysis that follows I will argue that Comstock originally constructed the moral boundary between obscenity and literature by using three sets of social categories: youth (and beliefs about the effects of sexuality on children and the family); class, used to argue that the upper class was being polluted by lower-class sexuality and culture as well as in assertions that sexually titillating material threatened the social position of upper-class youths; and ethnicity, which Comstock invoked to argue that foreign influences were responsible for the pollution of American culture. Comstock attempted to move the boundary between obscenity and literature by subtracting one or more of the categories of class, foreignness, and youth from the definition of obscenity. Comstock originally defined *obscenity* as the indecent products of lower-class culture sold by foreigners to upper-class youths. In seeking to suppress "the classics," he argued that the literature was prurient and aimed at a youthful audience, but since such literature was part of upper-class culture, he could argue only that it was written by foreigners and reflected the depraved nature of their societies. Suppressing Whitman involved another subtraction: Whitman was an American writing for an elite audience, which left Comstock with the sole argument that *Leaves of Grass* appealed to and spawned sexual corruption.

Categories for Constituting Obscenity
Youth and Sexual Vulnerability

Censorship could be justified, and funds to pursue offenders generated, only if the sources, targets, and effects of obscene reading could be explained to potential supporters and defenders. Comstock's primary justification for his early censorship activities was that obscene materials corrupted children. Furthermore, vendors of obscenity sought and exploited the curiosity of youths to market their wares. The materials had devastating effects on their young audience; children, Comstock asserted, were "ruined" by exposure to obscenity. Ruin was occasioned by sexual arousal and partly resulted from the social consequences of illicit sexual behavior. But obscenity was also damaging because it besmirched the innate innocence of children: "No language can describe the utter disgust and loathing with which pure minds must regard the traffic, and yet so shrewd and wily are the dealers, so hidden their mode of advertising their wares . . . that in hundreds of our schools, seminaries, and colleges, yes, in thousands of the most refined and Christian homes of our land they have succeeded in injecting a virus more destructive to the innocency and purity of youth, if not counteracted, than can be the most deadly disease to the body" (NYSSV 1875, 10–11).

Obscenity was dangerous not only because dealers targeted children but also because children's innate innocence did not protect them from corruption. Instead, innocence made children especially vulnerable. Comstock took pains to argue that even seemingly pure children, whose parents had attempted to impart moral virtue, were vulnerable to the temptations of obscenity:

That children may be so instructed as to the danger, so strengthened in principle by right teaching, and so ennobled by pure surroundings, as to cast from them the temptation and scorn the wretch who would stealthily lead them to vice, we have no doubt; but . . . how many are utterly corrupted in imagination, with vilest images—before confiding parents have dreamed of the danger! And this is the most disastrous element of the evil—it attacks specially and fatally the youth. . . . Mature years are comparatively safe from this contamination; youth is imperilled by its faintest breathing, and what shall be the society of twenty years hence if the boys and girls of today are smitten with this leprosy? (NYSSV 1877, 7–8)

Comstock appealed for support by playing on parents' anxieties about their offspring's future. Furthermore, parents could be blind to children's indiscretions. For example, Comstock argued, "No boy is safe. How do you know that [your son's] last pocket-money did not go out in answer to just such a bait as this?" (NYSSV 1876, 11).

Obscenity threatened children because of sexuality, specifically, because obscene materials would arouse sexual feelings and behaviors that endangered children's physical and mental health. While the theme of protecting children dominated Comstock's writings, "youth" can be understood as a component in creating the boundary between obscenity and literature only in the light of nineteenth-century sexual ideologies.

Comstock frequently alluded to "the secret vice," a referent to beliefs, shared by physicians and laypersons, that frequent sexual activity, especially masturbation, had severe (possibly fatal) health effects (Haller and Haller 1974; Hare 1962; MacDonald 1967; Neuman 1975). Obscene materials induced masturbation, which led to a greater thirst for obscenity, a cycle of addiction that, Comstock argued, devastated boys:

The boy's mind becomes a sink of corruption and he is a loathing unto himself. In his better moments he wrestles and cries out against this foe, but all in vain; he dare not speak out to his most intimate friend for shame: he dare not go to parent—he almost fears to call upon God. Despair takes possession of his soul as he finds himself losing strength of will—becoming nervous and infirm; he suffers unutterable agony during the hours of the night, and awakes only to carry a burdened heart through all the day. (NYSSV 1877, 9)

Comstock frequently asserted that obscenity was a "death trap" for youths (Comstock [1883] 1967, 131). It was a commonplace in late nineteenth-century discussions of prostitution that suicide was the inevitable fate of fallen women. Comstock borrowed from ideologies about prostitution to argue that suicide was the only escape from the life of "disgusting scenes before the mind" and "disease, wounds, and putrefying sores" that befell a male "victim of lust" (Comstock [1883] 1967, 132–33; Hobson 1987; Walkowitz 1980).

Sexuality, Comstock argued, also led to murder. Three boys in a neighboring city who had raped and murdered a "young and beautiful maiden" were evidence of the effects of unbridled lust (Comstock [1883] 1967, 133). Individuals were harmed when lust disgraced families and caused disease in children, but Comstock also claimed that lust could destroy society: "I repeat, lust is the boon companion of all other crimes. There is no evil so extensive, none doing more to destroy the institutions of free America. It sets aside the laws of God and morality; marriage bonds are broken, state laws ignored, and dens of infamy plant themselves in almost every community, and then reaching out like immense cuttlefish, draw in, from all sides, our youth to destruction" (Comstock [1883] 1967, 132–33).

The sexual corruption of youths had two consequences. A beloved child might become a failure and a family disgrace. The society as a whole, Comstock argued, faced the loss of the entire next generation if obscenity and lust spread unchecked. In constructing the boundary between obscenity and literature, Comstock relied on ideologies about the effects of sexuality on youths and on appeals for the preservation of an essential social group, the children.

Policing Class Boundaries

Comstock also justified censorship by appealing to parental concerns about their children's class position. The argument that obscenity led to unbridled sexuality, which caused severe health effects, was rendered somewhat unbelievable by Comstock's accompanying assertion that 75 percent or more of boys in schools were afflicted by the secret vice (NYSSV 1880, 10–11). Appeals to the consequences of sexual debauchery on children's social positions were more credible. Comstock insinuated that children could fail to assume the social class of their parents because of the "moral assassination and spiritual death" that resulted from improper reading and asserted that obscene literature would lead to associations with "low companions."[3] Lust led children, both male and female, to the brothel (NYSSV 1878, 11). Bad books encouraged youthful rebellion, including inappropriate marriages. *Traps for the Young* tells the story of two boys, sons of "respectable" families, who, as the result of reading obscene literature, came to shameful ends—one married a servant girl, and the other escaped the restraints of home by running away to New York City (Comstock [1883] 1967, 139). While all children could be victimized by improper reading, Comstock emphasized that rich children were not immune: "Where does this evil exist? Where are these traps set? I reply, everywhere. Children of all grades in society, institutions of learning in all sections of the land, and the most select homes, are invaded by the evil of licentious literature" (Comstock [1883] 1967, 136). In these arguments Comstock played on upper-class anxieties about the stability of their class position. High social position did not make elite children immune from the approaches of, or exploitation by, depraved people:

A beautiful little girl, not quite 14 years of age, was returning from one of the select schools up-town to her home. While waiting for a car a miscreant approached her and handed her a paper parcel, telling her to take it home and look at it alone by herself. This sweet, confiding child took the parcel home to her mother first. The mother opened it and was shocked beyond expression to find that several pages of the most abominable matter had thus been placed in the hands of her beloved child. (NYSSV 1884, 7–8)

In such passages Comstock implies that pornographers were motivated, in part, by the satisfaction of corrupting wealthy children. High social position thus made rich children more, rather than less, vulnerable to obscenity and lust.

Comstock raised anxieties about class position when he argued that wealth did not negate children's innate sexual urges, which, if not controlled, could render any child a victim of lust. Inner weakness, particularly sexual weakness, could lead to youthful depravity and loss of social position. In a story about the corrupting effects of obscene literature, Comstock tells of a boy sent to boarding school who receives an advertisement for obscenity and, out of curiosity, sends away for it. While the boy is ashamed of the package that arrives in the mail and considers discarding it, the devil urges him to open it:

So urged, the boy breaks the seal and lets the monster loose. The hideous appearance at first shocks the pure mind, and the poor victim would fain put it out of existence. But the tempter says, "it can't hurt you; you are strong. Look it over and see what it is. Don't be afraid." Thus beguiled a second look, and then a mighty force from within is let loose. Passions that had slumbered or lain dormant are awakened, and the boy is forced over a precipice, and death and destruction are sure, except the grace of God saves him. (Comstock [1883] 1967, 135–36)

In such stories Comstock hints that class distinctions are surface distinctions only and provide little protection against universal human weakness. Thus, Comstock's rhetoric about obscenity invokes class in two ways. Class as a social structure is employed as a boundary that must be maintained between elite children and those "miscreants" seeking to corrupt them.[4] But at the same time Comstock plays on the permeability of this boundary. The social distance between classes is not so great that "pure" children are inaccessible to pornographers, but, more important, in at least one sense elite children are not so different from the miscreants. Obscenity dealers would have little effect on children in the absence of innate sexual desires that, if unleashed, could lead any child to a life of lust and dissipation.

Aliens, Foreigners, and the Sources of Obscenity

While Comstock's discussions of youth and class attempted to create anxiety about the intended audience for obscene publications, discussions of foreigners attempted to locate their source. In much the same way that Comstock blamed the spread of lust on the permeable boundary between elite children and their social inferiors, he justified censorship by playing on fears of foreigners and aliens. In the first public report issued by the NYSSV, Comstock noted, "Of the entire number of persons arrested, 46 were Irish, 34 Americans, 24 English, 13 Canadian, 3 French, 1 Spaniard, 1 Italian, 1 Negro, and 1 Polish Jew, showing that a large proportion of those engaged in the nefarious traffic are not native American citizens" (NYSSV 1875, 6). The following year Comstock cited similar statistics, commenting, "It will be seen at a glance that we owe much of this demoralization to the importation of criminals from other lands" (NYSSV 1876, 11). In the crusade against pornography, Comstock argued that obscenity was spread by foreigners, implying that it was foreign to American culture.

Comstock played on the permeability of social boundaries between immigrants and the native elite. The search for potentially dangerous foreign influences on elite children did not have to extend far beyond the home, where an increasingly immigrant servant class served the families of the wealthy (Solomon 1956). The literature on masturbation often blamed the vice on the influence of servants (Neuman 1975). Comstock played freely on anxieties about the help, arguing, for example, that elite mothers should devote less time to social activities and more to their children because "this gift from heaven is not a small thing, to be intrusted to some ignorant and often vicious servant girl" (Comstock [1883] 1967, 245).

When Comstock appealed to anxieties about immigrants, he referred to a bigger problem than immoral servants. The upper class of New

York felt besieged by immigrants, and with good cause. By 1890, 80.5 percent of New York City's white population were either immigrants or immigrants' children (U.S. Department of the Interior 1895, clxii). The voting power of immigrants eroded the political power of the upper classes, who reacted with charges that immigrant political hacks were robbing the city treasury and ruining the city's credit (Blodgett 1984; Higham [1955] 1988; Jaher 1982; Teaford 1984). By blaming the spread of obscenity on a growing immigrant working class, Comstock appealed to widespread fears that the political and social power and influence of the native elite was being eclipsed.

In the years after the Civil War, racism directed against African-Americans, especially the belief that blacks possessed an almost animalistic sexuality, was rampant (Hall 1983). Comstock played on immigrants as a more immediate threat, but his most extraordinary story about corrupt and corrupting servants involved a black man:

A Professor in charge of a leading high school told, in one of our meetings in the West, of an incident occurring in his own school, where a colored man in livery was driven in an elegant carriage to the door of his school, who alighted and entered bearing a tray with some 15 or 20 handsomely addressed envelopes, purporting to be wedding cards, and for the same number of the young ladies, daughters of some of the first families in that city. After the man had gone, he opened one of these envelopes and found most obscene and seductive matter, to poison their minds and ruin them body and soul. (NYSSV 1880, 9)

The significance of this story is in its statement about the fragility of the boundary between social classes. Comstock is asserting, not only that servants could corrupt elite children, but also that servants could consciously use the trappings of their position to corrupt girls. Instead of invoking deference and respect, symbols of class status could facilitate sexual corruption. Worse, they could become a vehicle of pollution in the hands of one presumably trusted by an elite family—in this case either the servant or the driver, or both.

But another argument about institutions and the pollution of youths is being made in this example. The servant has besmirched two institutions intended to protect morality and social purity. Marriage, which Comstock regarded as fundamental to social order, became a vehicle for sexual perversion through the device of using wedding invitations to spread obscenity. Boarding schools, institutions intended to protect children from the moral dangers of the city, became a means to their destruction. In addition to playing on the social categories of youth, class, and ethnicity, Comstock argued that the rupture of social boundaries caused the pollution of institutions.

Breached Boundaries: The Pollution of Institutions

Comstock frequently argued that whole institutions were threatened by vice. His discussions of gambling-crazed clerks, imposters who aped the manners of the wealthy, and obsessively masturbating boys implied that people's appearances might be deceptive (Comstock [1883] 1967, 57–64). But Comstock also discussed how institutions might not be what they appeared, in particular, how institutions might not offer the protection that people sought in them. Obscene literature was spread through many conduits, but Comstock asserted that it was distributed primarily through the market pornographers found in schools (NYSSV 1878, 6). Obscenity dealers operated by buying the names of children residing in exclusive boarding schools from postmasters (Comstock [1883] 1967, 134). School catalogs, which listed students' names and addresses, were a second source of names. These lists were used to send advertisements for obscene literature to schoolchildren (NYSSV 1875, 11). Almost all elite schools, Comstock asserted, were afflicted: "There is scarcely a prominent school or seminary for either sex in our land in which there could not be found if an exhaustive search were made, more or less of this literature familiarity with which enfeebles the mind, destroys the body, and ruins the souls of its victims" (NYSSV 1876, 15).

Schools posed several dangers. First, the sheer concentration of children created a market for obscene literature utilized by pornographers. Second, good children were exposed to bad ones at school. Comstock often wrote of tracing bad books to one or two troublemakers (Comstock [1883] 1967, 139). Sexually corrupt (and corrupting) teachers were a third problem. One particularly interesting case was that of Professor G. H. Gautier, a professor of French in "several of the leading institutions of learning," who imported "the vilest books, pictures, and articles ever made" and showed them to his pupils (NYSSV 1877, 8).[5]

But the gravest danger in boarding schools was lack of parental supervision of children's activities. Nineteenth-century literature on masturbation frequently alluded to this danger, founded on the belief that only ceaseless parental vigilance protected children from vice (Neuman 1975, 4). Comstock's stories of youths being "ruined" in boarding

schools played on these fears, as well as on fears that the schools,
founded as a means to ensure upward mobility, would be responsible
for morally (and, consequently, economically) wrecking children:

What is more beautiful in all the world than the youth of manly form, elastic
in physical exuberance, his face radiant with the bloom of a pure blood, a
countenance bespeaking a conscious rectitude and an unyielding integrity.
How many such youths can be found in the various households of the land!
How proudly the father of such a boy places him in some select institution of
learning, where he can be qualified for future positions of trust and honor! He
cheerfully makes every needful sacrifice. How the mother's heart beats with
suppressed emotion as he leaves for the first time the parental roof! After he
is gone, how the fond parents console each other in the assurance that all is
well; there need be no fears for him; character is too well established. . . . Wait
a little. The boy's name comes to the knowledge of such miscreants as we
arrest. What then? . . . the susceptible mind of the boy receives impressions
that set on fire his whole nature. His imagination is perverted. A black stain is
fixed indelibly upon it, and conscience, once a faithful monitor, is now seared
and silenced. The will, which once raised a strong barrier against solicitations
to evil, no longer asserts itself, and our bright, noble boy too often becomes
but a wreck of his former self. (NYSSV 1878, 11)

The threat of obscenity spreading in boarding schools hit at a particularly vulnerable spot in the psyche of upper-class parents, for the
boarding schools were founded, in part, to shield children from the
vices of cities with rapidly growing populations. The sheer size of
the cities and the growth of slums made parents ever more concerned
about influences on their children; thus, boarding schools in little country towns were attractive because of their isolation from the city (Levine 1980; McLachlan 1970). Not only were the schools intended to
be a haven from immorality, but they served as well to impart culture
and refinement to children of the newly wealthy (Baltzell [1958] 1979;
Roy 1984, 1989). Comstock's mention of the father making sacrifices
to send his son to school implies that the schools were thought of as
a means of upward mobility. That children could be corrupted in these
schools was probably Comstock's most potent threat.

While schools were the most fertile ground for spreading vice, it
spread as well in other institutions, including churches and respectable
businesses:

A sexton of a church manufactures his licentious photographs in a room separated from the parish school only by folding doors, employs men or boys to
sell them on the street as they walk about in the crowded thoroughfares. A

dealer in jewelry passing among the trade supplies the young men with libidinous microscopic charms. Still others, frequenting the steps of banking houses in Wall and Broad Streets, furnish the sons of the wealthy classes with expensive specimens of the highest licentious art. . . . Newsboys on railroads, porters in steamboats and hotels, boys and young men in schools and colleges all spread the contagion, and in such stealthy form as oftentimes to escape detection. (NYSSV 1876, 8)

In constructing the boundary between obscenity and literature, Comstock thus mobilized the social categories of youth, class, and ethnicity to justify censorship. Obscenity was a threat primarily to elite youths that ordinarily came from the lower classes and from foreigners. Comstock attempted to make his argument more believable, and the threat of obscenity more compelling, by arguing that social institutions intended to guard both morality and children were being perverted by obscenity and lust.

The Pollution of Literature: Literature as Pollution

In 1879 Comstock discovered a new problem. While the assault on obscenity had so far been waged as a war against corrupting influences seeping from the lower classes and polluting the children of the elite, he was now faced with the problem of pollution emanating from within upper-class culture itself. The new problem was "the classics." Comstock claimed that obscenity dealers, fearing arrest for circulating older forms of obscenity, were issuing translated, abridged, and illustrated editions of "classic" literature, in particular, works by Ovid and Boccaccio. His attempts to justify the suppression of these salacious editions evolved into a campaign against the writings of living (but unnamed) French novelists and, ultimately, a temporarily successful campaign against Walt Whitman's poetry.

Comstock recognized that the authority he gleaned by virtue of his experience suppressing common obscenity did not translate into a jurisdiction over books that were considered great literature. On encountering translated, abridged, and illustrated classics, he consulted publishers and book dealers "of high standing." These presumably more knowledgeable men responded to the sullied classics by telling Comstock, "Any man that does that ought to be prosecuted" (NYSSV 1879, 16). Comstock also sought justification for his actions in the law, which, he asserted, allowed the censorship of materials that "corrupt the minds of the youth and awaken lewd and libidinous thoughts, if sold so as to be liable to fall into their hands" (NYSSV 1879, 16).

Still, Comstock seemed to realize that prudence (and the social class of his supporters) dictated that he could not argue that the classics were inherently polluting and should thus be suppressed. Opting for confinement rather than eradication, Comstock made the argument that the classics were acceptable if they were kept from circulating among the general public: "This society has never interfered with any work of art, classic, or medical work, except to maintain and keep them in their own special sphere. We do not feel that it is interfering with a classic, when we punish a man in the courts for prostituting said book, and making an obscene article of it to serve his own base purposes" (NYSSV 1879, 17).

In constructing the boundary around the "special sphere" of the classics, which delimited obscene and acceptable uses of such works, Comstock again invoked the vulnerability of youths and the threat of foreign influences. But the process of moving the boundary between obscenity and literature so that translated classics would be counted as morally unacceptable forced Comstock to change his arguments about social class and the effects of literature. In censoring common obscenity, Comstock argued that he was erecting a barrier between polluting materials and the pure children of the elite. Classic literature, however, was a symbol of sophistication. As part of the cultural capital of the upper class, the classics were not mere status symbols. They were part of "high" culture, a sphere endowed with the power to elevate and purify those who consumed it (Levine 1988). Thus, in making arguments that the abridged and translated classics were obscene and should be suppressed, Comstock was forced to concede that the classics were not inherently bad. However, when used in certain ways by certain audiences, they were both polluting and polluted.

Just as he had argued that common obscenity was most dangerous to children, Comstock attempted to restrict the circulation of the classics by making arguments about the effect of such literature on youths. While consumption of the classics may have been suitable for elite adults, Comstock argued that children were imperiled by salacious classics in much the same way that they were by common pornography. This "literary poison" that was being "cast into the fountains of social life" was making youths "weak-minded, vapid, sentimental, lustful, [and] criminal" (NYSSV 1880, 11). Furthermore, Comstock argued, so-called classics were being marketed in the same way that other obscene material had been, namely, by sending advertisements to children in schools. The marketing of these abridged and translated works to youths was one of Comstock's chief justifications for their suppression (NYSSV 1879, 16).

Comstock's discussions of the effects of classics on children were fraught with contradictions. While Comstock clearly wanted to acknowledge the aura that surrounded such literature and probably feared that censoring classics would offend his supporters and undermine his work, his arguments revealed considerable hostility toward the literature. Yet he seemingly could not decide whether the classics were inherently polluting or whether only translated classics caused moral decay. Sometimes he argued the former. After comparing classic literature to strychnine made palatable by a candy coating, he concludes, "This cursed literature corrupts the thoughts, perverts the imagination, destroys the will power, renders impure the life, defiles the body, hardens the heart and damns the soul. . . . The practice of spreading impure literature among the young is fast sinking them to the level of ancient heathendom" (NYSSV 1883, 8).

But Comstock's diatribes against the classics were tempered by the acknowledgment that such literature might have legitimate uses. This concession largely had to do with the social class of people who consumed classic literature. *Class* meant different things in discussions of the classic literature and common obscenity. Street pornography, peddled by lower-class miscreants, threatened elite youths with moral ruin that would result in their falling from the top of the class hierarchy to the bottom. The classics, when misused, threatened the same result. Comstock conceded that classics could be tolerated as long as they were used to satisfy the legitimate demands of elite audiences, but problems arose when corrupted classics fed illegitimate desires: "These works, heretofore carefully concealed from public view, and kept by booksellers only to meet what some consider the legitimate demand of the student, or gentlemen's library, are now advertised and sold by certain parties as 'rich, rare and racy' books, 'amorous adventures,' 'spicy descriptions,' 'love intrigues on the sly,' etc." (NYSSV 1879, 16).

What was the proper place of the classics? Comstock attempted to resolve this question by arguing that such works should be confined to the "literary world," implying that only people who could read the classics in their original language should be permitted to. Thus, the classics should be the sole property of the educated. Comstock made this argument most explicitly in *Traps for the Young*, in which he quoted a letter from a professor of English literature who wrote to Comstock about the claim that translations of classic works, in this case by Boccaccio, should be confined to the literary world:

You concede too much. The book you are really writing about is an English book, having no "use in the literary world," for you are writing about a translation. You seem to me to admit that an English version of Boccaccio has the rights of a classic. That is not true. The plea for freedom in the circulation of classics is good only for Boccaccio in the Italian original. The translation is an English book, which no scholar wants, which nobody wants, for a literary or educational purpose. If there are scholars who want to know the beautiful Italian of Boccaccio, they must, of course, learn to read Italian. (Comstock 1883, 174)

While common obscenity was inherently bad and Comstock sought to eradicate it altogether, the classics were polluting when they left the libraries of educated gentlemen. Furthermore, the classics were polluted by those who attempted to popularize them by issuing translations that could be read by all classes. While cultivated people might have a legitimate use for the classics, "they are clearly illegal when so prostituted from what has heretofore been thought their proper and legitimate place" (NYSSV 1879, 16).

While those who could speak foreign languages might be allowed to read classic literature, Comstock played on fears of foreigners and foreign culture to justify his attacks on both literature and street pornography. While Comstock had argued that foreigners were more likely to be the criminals that attempted to sell common obscenity to pure, elite, native-born children, in discussions of the classics Comstock argued that foreign culture could be inherently polluting. Comstock argued that Italian classics were "celebrated the world over for their indecencies" and implied that such works had caused and would cause the collapse of nations (NYSSV 1883, 7): "In recognizing the claims of art and the classics, we do not recognize the right of any man to explore the records of corruption of past ages, and then serve up that which has helped destroy the nations of old, as a sweet morsel for the youth of our land" (NYSSV 1883, 8). Comstock's campaign against foreign authors was not confined to ancient civilizations. He argued that modern French and Italian novels translated into "popular and cheap forms" were also evil, for "many of these stories are little better than histories of brothels and prostitutes, in these lust-cursed nations" (Comstock [1883] 1967, 179). While Comstock condemned foreign novels, it is not clear that he did much about them, although he did encourage supporters in other cities to peruse the shelves of their public libraries and agitate for the removal of offensive literature (NYSSV

1886, 12). Moving from dead authors to living ones allowed Comstock to look for modern literature (unprotected by the aura of "the classics") that might be encompassed in definitions of the obscene. In 1882 Comstock's quest to protect youths from sexuality in print or pictures brought him to the books of one of America's greatest poets—Walt Whitman.

Leaves of Grass and Fig Leaves

Comstock's attack on Whitman represented a final shift in the boundary between obscenity and literature. While obscenity had first been defined as something emanating from foreigners and lower-class people that would pollute respectable children by arousing forbidden sexual desires, Whitman was the quintessential (although controversial) American poet, whose work had many upper-class admirers. Furthermore, while Comstock justified much of his forty-year career in the antivice movement on the grounds that he was protecting children, he never claimed that Whitman's poetry was sold to youths. What was left to Comstock was solely the claim that sexuality in high culture was demoralizing. Under the heading of "Semi-Classic," Comstock noted, "Another 'classic' for which exemption is named, is an attempt by an author of our own time to clothe the most sensual thoughts, with the flowers and fancies of poetry, making the lascivious conception only the more insidious and demoralizing" (NYSSV 1882, 6).

Comstock clearly wanted to suppress Whitman's poetry, but he recognized that this was a difficult case to make to his supporters. While Comstock later risked a public battle over whether photographic reproductions of French Salon nudes were obscene (Comstock 1887; Beisel 1990b), he did not attempt to censor Whitman publicly. Instead, he turned to allies in Boston and tried to prevent the publication of Whitman's work.

Comstock's allies were to be found in the New England Society for the Suppression of Vice (NESSV). Antivice work in Boston began in 1875 when Comstock visited the Monday Morning Minister's Meeting, a group that funded Comstock's trips to Boston to arrest obscenity dealers. The NESSV was officially incorporated in 1878. Like the New York antivice society, the Boston organization was led by a number of prominent businessmen, and by the end of the 1880s it was supported by a substantial proportion of Boston's upper class (Beisel 1990a). But in the beginning it was a faltering organization. Until January 1882 the leaders of the NESSV employed Comstock as their agent, so much of what was accomplished in the way of suppressing obscenity in Boston happened at the hands of Comstock.

In 1882 the leaders of the NESSV employed Henry Chase as their new agent and shortly thereafter voted that Chase should consult with the assistant state attorney, Mr. Barrows, regarding the prosecution of persons who sold "one or more of several books." The books at issue included Balzac's *Droll Stories*, Whitman's *Leaves of Grass*, and Boccaccio's *Decameron* (*Minutes* of the NESSV [hereafter *Minutes*] 6 February 1882). At the next month's meeting, the Committee read a letter from Comstock, apparently regarding Whitman's poetry, and unanimously voted that "'Leaves of Grass,' the volume of Walt Whitman's poems, is a work tending to corrupt the morals of the young. They therefore make their appeal to the publishers, James Osgood & Co., to withdraw said work from circulation or to expurgate from it all obscene and immoral matter" (*Minutes*, 6 March 1882). The NESSV found a willing ally in the district attorney's office. On 1 March 1882, the district attorney, Oliver Stevens, contacted the publishing firm of James R. Osgood and Company, which was producing a new edition of *Leaves of Grass*. Osgood was a well-known firm, and it reacted with alarm on being informed by the district attorney that "we are of the opinion that this book is such a book as brings it within the provisions of the Public Statutes respecting obscene literature, and suggest the propriety of withdrawing the same from circulation and suppressing the editions thereof" (Harned 1896, 163). Osgood immediately contacted Whitman, telling him that they did not yet know what portions of the book were objected to by the district attorney but that they "are, however, naturally reluctant to be identified with any legal proceedings in a matter of this nature" (Harned 1896, 163). Before agreeing to publish with Osgood, Whitman had informed the firm that his "sexuality odes" might be controversial, and the terms of his publication agreement included the understanding that these poems would be published in their entirety (Harned 1895). But on being threatened with prosecution Osgood began negotiating with Whitman about altering his poems. Whitman expressed willingness to delete some passages, until he was told that two entire poems, "A Woman Waits for Me" and "Ode to a Common Prostitute," would have to be removed. When Whitman refused to delete these poems, Osgood refused to print his book. Whitman took his book to Philadelphia, where the furor aroused by its suppression in Boston made it an enormous financial success (McCoy 1956).

Shortly thereafter, the NESSV issued their *Annual Report* for

1881–82, in which they stated, "The District Attorney has at our instance notified a number of booksellers that a certain immoral book, which had hitherto been freely exposed for sale, comes within prohibition of the law, and that any further sale will render the dealer liable to prosecution. A prominent publishing firm has, in consequence of a similar official notification, agreed to expurgate one of its books containing much indecent matter" (NESSV 1881–82, 4).

Forcing Osgood to halt the publication of *Leaves of Grass* was a triumph for the NESSV, but not one publicly acknowledged. While the *Annual Report* of the NESSV hinted at their role in suppressing Whitman, the society did not admit that it had been the force behind the censorship of Whitman until 1895 (McCoy 1956, 95). This may have been the result of unfavorable public opinion about the arrest (Blatt 1989).[6] However, the president of the NESSV, Homer Sprague, did not shy from expressing his opinion of *Leaves of Grass*. In September 1882 Sprague published an article in *Education* magazine. In it he constructed the problem of obscenity in the same terms used by Comstock, arguing that obscenity was a "malignant" and "hydra-headed" evil fed by the "strongest appetites and passions." Like Comstock, Sprague used "classic" literature to make the rhetorical bridge between "debasing pictures" and "filthy songs" and Whitman's poems. Although the NESSV had chosen to persecute Whitman rather than the dealers of translated classics, Sprague argued that translated classics, in which was stored "the vilest . . . Greek, Italian, or French obscenity," threatened to ruin the "afterages" (Sprague 1882, 72–73). Finally, like Comstock, Sprague's only charge against Whitman was that sexuality rendered his work indecent—although it was neither explicitly marketed to youths nor the product of foreign culture or a foreigner. Without mentioning Whitman by name, Sprague commented on the poet by saying, "Next come the dirt-eaters, each rolling before him his darling morsel of literary filth; disgusted with artificialities and linen decencies, and finding nutriment in *Leaves of Grass,* but not in fig-leaves; so much in love with Nature that, like the poor human earth-worms in Xenophon, they wish to do in public what others do in private, [and] abolish all laws against indecent exposure" (Sprague 1882, 74).

While the leaders of the antivice movement attempted to shift the boundary between obscenity and literature far enough to include Walt Whitman and were indeed able to use their power and influence to suppress the poet in Boston, they were not very successful in their attempt to use obscenity laws to purify high culture. In the 1880s neither the NYSSV nor the NESSV was able to generate much support for the contention that sexuality in high culture justified its suppression. The NESSV was a struggling organization both before and after the censorship of Whitman. While a cooperative district attorney helped the leaders of the NESSV suppress Whitman, it was not until 1883, when the organization began to campaign against gambling and corruption in city government, that it found a cause that united Boston's upper class behind them. In 1890 the NESSV again pursued the issue of obscenity in culture, attacking obscenity on the stage—in theaters frequented by the working classes. From the late 1890s until the 1920s the NESSV censored with impunity, but they were not able to do this until they had developed a strong base of support within Boston's upper class (Boyer 1963).

Conclusion

I have argued that the moral boundary between literature and obscenity was constructed in the late nineteenth century from the raw materials of already existing social structures and the ideologies that supported them. Comstock began his campaign against obscenity by defining forbidden works as those that could corrupt youths because of their sexual content, arguing that the reproduction of the elite was threatened because moral depravity occasioned by obscene reading could cause children of the upper class to fail to assume the class position of their parents. The boundary between literature and obscenity was also justified on the basis of ethnic divisions in nineteenth-century American society: Comstock argued that much obscene literature was spread by foreigners and was the product of foreign culture. The movement of the boundary between literature and obscenity resulted from omitting the claim that foreigners were the source of, and youths the audience for, pornography. The crusade against Whitman rested solely on the charge that his work contained and spawned sexual depravity.

The efforts made by Comstock and his allies in Boston to shift the boundary between obscenity and literature lead to some insights about the formation and maintenance of moral boundaries. Mary Douglas's theory that pollution rhetoric manifests existing social cleavages is indeed useful for understanding Comstock's crusade against obscenity. But this approach fails to help us understand the movement of the boundary between obscenity and literature precisely because it fails to acknowledge the role of active, thinking (and, in this case, mobilizing) human beings whose actions maintain and transform social boundaries (Giddens 1984; Sewell, in press). While Douglas asserts that a society's symbolic order reflects its social order, this approach to understanding moral boundaries grants cultural categories too little autonomy from social structures. The assertion that a society's symbolic order (represented by moral rhetoric) reflects its social cleavages means that cultural change can occur only in reaction to structural change. This becomes particularly problematic when we realize, as we must when examining the career of moral crusaders such as Anthony Comstock, that people use existing ideologies to try to transform social structures and moral boundaries.

In another sense, however, Douglas's work on pollution grants the symbolic order too much autonomy from social structures. Comstock's rhetoric about obscenity supports Stinchcombe's (1982) assertion that moral categories are constructed from other social categories. The ideologies that support and maintain social categories and social cleavages are the materials that thinking human beings use to make sense of and change their world. The symbolic order is not wholly autonomous from the social structure, for the same human agents who use ideological structures to make sense of the world also use their experiences in the world to challenge (and transform) ideological structures.

Notes

1. This quotation is from the law as amended by Congress in 1876. The original Comstock law, passed in 1873, did not explicitly list "writing" as a thing that could be suppressed.

2. The most important legal precedent for censorship resulting from Comstock's activities was the decision handed down by Judge Blatchford against D. M. Bennett, which formed the basis of obscenity law in the United States for more than fifty years (Blatt 1989, 119). I discuss the restriction of contraception and abortion in Beisel (1990b).

3. In *Traps for the Young*, Comstock tells the story of a judge's son who runs away from home in pursuit of the exciting life he read about in adventure stories. The boy was fatally beaten in a drunken brawl in a saloon, but before he dies tells the good woman who nurses him about how his reading had led to relationships with low associates (Comstock [1883] 1967, 30–32).

4. The language used by the leaders of the NYSSV implies that those who sought to corrupt respectable children were lower class. For example, the Reverend T. B. McCleod spoke in support of the actions of NYSSV in 1881 by saying, "Our country is increasing most rapidly in population, and with the increase there is a corresponding increase in crime. While many earnest and upright men are up among the rigging endeavoring to keep our ship afloat and in the right course, there are others below seeking to scuttle the vessel"

(NYSSV 1881, 22). This passage contains an implicit reference to immigrants, who were swelling the country's population and were concentrated in the working classes. The reference to those "below" who endangered the ship probably refers to those at the bottom of the class structure.

5. Comstock did not reveal that Gautier was convicted of sodomy as well as of dealing in obscenity or that the NYSSV had appealed to Governor Alonzo Cornell to keep him imprisoned: "He was at time of arrest and had been for years prior thereto a Professor of French and Languages in several of our best Institutions of Learning in New York and Brooklyn. While so engaged and enjoying the confidence of our best families he was in the habit of showing most obscene and filthy books, pictures, etc., to the boys to excite them, and then he practiced the Italian vice on them." (This quotation is taken from Sotheby's sale catalog, 29 October 1986. Item 27 was this letter from Comstock to Alonzo Cornell regarding an inmate whose friends were expected to appeal for his pardon.)

6. The extent of opposition to the suppression of Whitman's poems is disputed in the historical literature. Blatt asserts that Benjamin Tucker challenged the censorship of Whitman by obtaining several copies of *Leaves of Grass* and selling them openly, but another source claims that the threat of prosecution made Boston book dealers circulate the book as secretly as possible (see Blatt 1989, 142; and Kennedy 1895).

References

Baltzell, E. Digby. *Philadelphia Gentlemen: The Making of a National Upper Class.* 1958. Reprint. Philadelphia: University of Pennsylvania Press, 1979.

Beisel, Nicola. "Class, Culture, and Campaigns against Vice in Three American Cities, 1872–1892." *American Sociological Review* 55 (1990a): 44–62.

Beisel, Nicola. "Upper Class Formation and the Politics of Censorship in Boston, New York, and Philadelphia, 1872–1892." Ph.D. diss., University of Michigan, 1990b.

Blatt, Martin Henry. *Free Love and Anarchism.* Urbana: University of Illinois Press, 1989.

Blodgett, Geoffrey. "Yankee Leadership in a Divided City: Boston, 1860–1910." In *Boston, 1700–1980: The Evolution of Urban Politics,* ed. Ronald P. Formisano and Constance K. Burns. Westport, Conn.: Greenwood, 1984.

Boyer, Paul S. "Boston Book Censorship in the Twenties." *American Quarterly* 15 (1963): 3–24.

Boyer, Paul S. *Purity in Print: The Vice Society Movement and Book Censorship in America.* New York: Scribner's, 1968.

Comstock, Anthony. *Traps for the Young.* 1883. Reprint. Cambridge, Mass.: Belknap, 1967.

Comstock, Anthony. *Morals versus Art.* New York: J. S. Ogilvie, 1887.

Douglas, Mary. *Purity and Danger*. 1966. Reprint. New York: Routledge & Kegan Paul, 1966.

Giddens, Anthony. *The Constitution of Society*. Berkeley and Los Angeles: University of California Press, 1984.

Hall, Jacqueline Dowd. "The Mind That Burns in Each Body: Women, Rape, and Racial Violence." In *Powers of Desire: The Politics of Sexuality,* ed. Ann Snitow, Christine Stansell, and Sharon Thompson. New York: Monthly Review Press, 1983.

Haller, John S., and Robin M. Haller. *The Physician and Sexuality in Victorian America*. Urbana: University of Illinois Press, 1974.

Hare, E. H. "Masturbatory Insanity: The History of an Idea." *Journal of Mental Science* 108 (1962): 1–2.

Harned, Thomas B. "Whitman and His Boston Publishers." *Conservator* (December 1895), 150–53; (January 1896), 163–66.

Higham, John. *Strangers in the Land*. 1955. Reprint. New Brunswick, N.J.: Rutgers University Press, 1988.

Hobson, Barbara Meil. *Uneasy Virtue: The Politics of Prostitution and the American Reform Tradition*. New York: Basic, 1987.

Jaher, Frederic C. *The Urban Establishment*. Urbana: University of Illinois Press, 1982.

Johnson, Richard C. "Anthony Comstock: Reform, Vice, and the American Way." Ph.D. diss., University of Wisconsin, 1973.

Kennedy, William S. "Suppressing a Poet." *Conservator* (January 1895), 169–71.

Levine, Lawrence W. *Highbrow/Lowbrow: The Emergence of Cultural Hierarchy in America*. Cambridge, Mass.: Harvard University Press, 1988.

Levine, Steven B. "The Rise of American Boarding Schools and the Development of a National Upper Class." *Social Problems* 28 (1980): 63–94.

McCoy, Ralph E. "Banned in Boston: The Development of Literary Censorship in Massachusetts." Ph.D. diss., University of Illinois, 1956.

MacDonald, Robert H. "The Frightful Consequences of Onanism: Notes on the History of a Delusion." *Journal of the History of Ideas* 28 (July–September 1967): 423–31.

McLachlan, James. *American Boarding Schools: A Historical Study*. New York: Scribner's, 1970.

Neuman, R. P. "Masturbation, Madness, and the Modern Concepts of Childhood and Adolescence." *Journal of Social History* 8 (1975): 1–27.

New England Society for the Suppression of Vice. *Annual Reports*. Boston, various years. (The NESSV became the Watch and Ward Society in 1890.)

New England Society for the Suppression of Vice. *Minutes of Executive Committee Meetings*. 1878–88. Private Collection.

New York Society for the Suppression of Vice. *Annual Reports*. New York, 1874–92.

Reed, James W. *The Birth Control Movement and American Society: From Private Vice to Public Virtue*. 1978. Reprint. Princeton, N.J.: Princeton University Press, 1983.

Roy, William G. "Institutional Governance and Social Cohesion: The Internal Organization of the American Capitalist Class, 1886–1905." *Research in Social Stratification and Mobility* 3 (1984): 147–171.

Roy, William G. "The Social Organization of the Corporate Class Segment of the American Capitalist Class at the Turn of This Century." Paper presented at the conference "Bringing Class Back In," University of Kansas, April 1989.

Sewell, William H., Jr. "Towards a Theory of Structure: Duality, Agency, and Transformation." *American Journal of Sociology* (in press).

Smith-Rosenberg, Carroll. "Sex as a Symbol in Victorian Purity: An Ethnohistorical Analysis of Jacksonian America." *American Journal of Sociology* 84 (1978): S212–S248.

Solomon, Barbara M. *Ancestors and Immigrants*. Cambridge, Mass.: Harvard University Press, 1956.

Sprague, Homer B. "Societies for the Suppression of Vice." *Education* (September 1882), 70–81.

Stinchcombe, Arthur L. "The Deep Structure of Moral Categories: Eighteenth-Century French Stratification, and the Revolution." In *Structural Sociology,* ed. Eno Rossi. New York: Columbia University Press, 1982.

Teaford, Jon C. *The Unheralded Triumph*. Baltimore: Johns Hopkins University Press, 1984.

U.S. Department of the Interior. Census Office. *Report on the Population of the United States at the Eleventh Census: 1890,* pt. 1. Washington, D.C.: U.S. Government Printing Office, 1895.

Walkowitz, Judith. *Prostitution and Victorian Society*. New York: Cambridge University Press, 1980.

PART TWO High Culture
and Exclusion

SIX

The Audience for Abstract Art: Class, Culture, and Power

David Halle

The audience for abstract art has been idealized in much twentieth-century theory. Unexamined notions of the superior capacities—intelligence, aesthetic sensibilities, and so on—of those who admire abstract art, as compared with those who do not, abound. For example, Le Corbusier ([1921] 1986, 102) wrote that "the art of our period [above all cubism] is performing its proper functions when it addresses itself to the chosen few. Art is not a popular thing, still less an expensive toy for rich people . . . but is in its essence arrogant." Ortega y Gasset ([1925] 1972, 69) commented that, because abstract art had eliminated the "human element" that attracted the masses, it could be appreciated only by a minority who possessed "special gifts of artistic sensibility." Ingarden ([1928] 1986) argued that, the more abstract the work of art, the greater the intellectual effort required by the audience. Benjamin ([1936] 1969, 234, 239) explained the broad unpopularity of Picasso's work as a result of the fact that "the masses seek distraction" whereas art "demands concentration from the spectator." Clement Greenberg ([1939] 1961, 14–15) maintained that abstract art appealed only to the most "cultivated" segment of society—"the avant-garde"—who engaged in the process of "reflection" necessary to appreciate abstract art; by contrast the "masses," as well as most of the rich and the middle class, had been seduced by "kitsch," which "predigests art for the spectator and spares him effort." And Bourdieu (1984, 4) wrote that the working class requires art to be practical, an attitude incompatible with the "detachment and disinterestedness" needed to relate to abstract art.

Given these shared assumptions about the audience for abstract art, it is surprising to discover that in fact we know very little about what happens when people look at abstract art. No one has ever asked, in a systematic way, what people who like abstract art see in it, what goes on in their minds when they view it. Sociological surveys have done little more than document that some people like abstract art and others do not. Bourdieu, for example, asked respondents to name their favorite painter from a list that included Leonardo da Vinci, Renoir, Kandinsky, and Picasso.[1] Sociologists have scarcely asked why people like (or dislike) abstract art, let alone investigated the experiential process involved. Thus, the view that admiring abstract art involves some kind of superior experiential act rests on flimsy ground.

Understanding what occurs when people look at abstract art is not just a matter of filling a gap in our knowledge. Abstract art is unarguably the central component of twentieth-century art and a central component of twentieth-century culture in general. As a result it has stimulated some of the most influential theorizing about modern culture. Indeed, few important theories of modern culture do not also imply a view of the audience for abstract art. Likewise, a theory of modern culture that does not fit the case of the audience for abstract art would probably be in serious trouble. Thus, analysis of the audience for abstract art constitutes a critical case study for debates about modern culture.

In what follows I will first point out how a particular image of the way that the audience for abstract art relates to the works is entailed by the theory of cultural capital. I will then present data that cast doubt on the validity of this image. Finally, I will suggest that we should reconsider theories, of which the theory of cultural capital is just one (important) example, that see art and culture as basically about power and domination.

The Theory of Cultural Capital and the Audience for Abstract Art

Consider how a particular image of the audience for abstract art—in fact the idealized image of the superior capacities of those who like abstract art—is embedded in the theory of cultural capital. To make this clear I will briefly summarize the theory of cultural capital, as put forward by two of the most interesting sociologists of culture, Pierre Bourdieu in France and Paul DiMaggio in the United States. (Their versions are similar but not identical; see Bourdieu 1968, 1984; DiMaggio 1987; and DiMaggio and Useem 1978, 1981.)[2]

First, it is argued that appreciation of, and familiarity with, the high arts is a trained capacity. In Bourdieu's words (1984, 2), "A work of art has meaning and interest only for someone who possesses the cultural competence, i.e. the code, into which it is encoded . . . a beholder who lacks the specific code feels lost in a chaos of sounds and rhythms, colours and lines." Those who acquire this capacity acquire what is called "legitimate taste" or a taste for high culture.

Second, it is argued that the taste for high culture, the capacity to understand or decode high art, is unequally distributed among social classes, for this capacity (which constitutes "cultural capital") is taught above all in the educational system, especially at the higher levels. It is also taught in the modern family, but primarily in the families of the upper middle and upper classes. Thus, the working class and the poor, who typically come from families of modest social origins and are less likely to receive higher education, have little chance of acquiring the capacity to appreciate the high arts. Here we have the origin of the two fundamental tastes in modern society—the taste for high culture, which is associated with the dominant classes, and the taste for popular culture, which is associated with the dominated classes. (In this argument, *dominant class* or *upper and upper middle classes* tend to refer to capitalists, managers, and professionals; *dominated class* or *working class* or *popular classes* tend to refer to blue-collar workers and lower-white-collar workers, the latter composed mainly of clerical, secretarial, and retail sales employees.)

Finally, it is argued, competence in the high arts operates to preserve and reproduce the class structure in two main ways. First, familiarity with high culture is used as a criterion for access to the dominant class. Thus, those wishing to enter the dominant classes are well advised to acquire, especially through higher education, competence in the high arts, for this is the cultural capital that will be so crucial for their mobility. Second, familiarity with and participation in high culture builds solidarity among the dominant classes. For example, attendance at common cultural events and discussion of common cultural phenomena creates class solidarity.

It is apparent how a particular, and idealized, image of the audience for abstract art is embedded in this theory. Those who like abstract art do so because of their "cultural capital"—the extensive intellectual and experiential training that they bring to bear on the works. In turn, viewing and liking abstract art (as a component of high culture) is used by the dominant class as a criterion for access to, and strengthening solidarity within, its own ranks.

The cultural capital argument is problematic in at least two major ways. First, "high culture" (including the taste for abstract art) is not as widespread among the dominant classes (in the United States or in

France) as the theory implies, as I have argued elsewhere (Halle 1989; see also Peterson and Simkus, this volume). While it is true that the survey data we have show that the dominant classes are more likely than the subordinate classes to participate in high culture, items of high culture do not in fact appear to be of great interest to most of the dominant classes. On the contrary, high culture seems to appeal only to a minority. For example, a survey (Ford Foundation 1974) conducted in the early 1970s of exposure to the arts in twelve major U.S. cities showed little interest among blue-collar workers in high culture. Only 4 percent had been to a symphony concert in the past year, only 2 percent had been to the ballet, and only 1 percent to the opera. Yet the managers and professionals surveyed were only somewhat more interested in high culture. Among managers only 14 percent had been to a symphony concert in the past year, 4 percent to the ballet, and 6 percent to the opera. Among professionals only 18 percent had been to a symphony concert, 9 percent to the ballet, and 5 percent to the opera. These figures scarcely suggest that managers and professionals as a group are avid consumers of high culture.[3] This raises serious doubts about the importance of high culture as a criterion for entry into, and continued membership in, the dominant classes.[4]

The same picture of the limited penetration of high culture among even the dominant classes emerges from a reexamination of Bourdieu's data in France. For example, to probe his hypothesized difference between the taste of the dominant classes and the "popular aesthetic" of the dominated classes, Bourdieu asked members of each group whether they thought a "beautiful" photograph could be made from an object that was socially designated as meaningless (such as a cabbage), or repulsive (such as a snake), or misshapen (such as a pregnant woman). The idea was to probe the ("legitimate") taste of the dominant classes, which, Bourdieu argues, stresses "formal" qualities of objects and so is more likely to hold that any object can in principle be "formally" presented as beautiful. (The taste of the "popular" or "dominated classes," by contrast, Bourdieu argues, stresses "function" over "form.") Bourdieu (1984, 37–38) did find that only about 5 percent of the least-educated section of the working class thought that a cabbage would make a beautiful picture and only 8 percent thought that a pregnant woman would. But the dominant classes were scarcely, as a group, convinced of the aesthetic potential of these objects. Only 27 percent of the most highly educated section of the dominant classes thought that a cabbage would make a beautiful picture, and only 29.5 percent thought that a pregnant woman would. This implies a picture of the high arts as being a minority taste even among the dominant classes.

Thus, if high culture in the United States and France has penetrated only sections of the dominant classes, it is less clear to what extent it functions to reinforce the existing class structure.[5]

In this chapter I want to focus on a second problematic component of the theory of cultural capital—the nature of the experiential relation between audience and cultural work. In the case of abstract art this involves the as yet undemonstrated idea that viewers who like abstract art bring to bear on the works lengthy intellectual training received in the family or in the educational system (or in both), which they use to "decode" the works. At issue is the nature of the experiential act undertaken by the viewer of abstract art. At stake are three questions. Does a liking for abstract art involve specialized knowledge that is difficult to acquire and that can therefore serve to limit access to the social circles of the dominant class? Do these viewers merit the special status assigned them in so much twentieth-century cultural theory? More broadly, is culture fundamentally about power and domination, as the theory of cultural capital suggests?

The Research

The data that I will consider are based on interviews about abstract art with residents of a sample of houses drawn from four areas in the New York City region. Two of these areas are middle or upper middle class (one in the city, one in the suburbs); two are working and lower middle class (again, one in the city and one in the suburbs).

I chose a random sample of houses from each area and then interviewed residents in their homes. The analysis here is based on research in 160 residences, forty from each area. The interviews focused on the heads of the households. Spouses living together—the vast majority (86 percent) of the cases in the sample—were jointly defined as heads of household; where possible, I interviewed both spouses. The response rate (defined as the percentage of interviews obtained with at least one head of household in each residence sampled) was 62 percent.[6] In the bulk (90 percent) of the cases the heads of households interviewed owned their residence.

The upper-middle-class urban neighborhood contains the expensive townhouses of Manhattan's Upper East Side, from Sixtieth to Eighty-sixth streets and between Second and Park avenues. The upper-middle-class suburban area includes Manhasset, Flower Hill, and Plandome—three adjoining affluent suburbs on Long Island's North Shore, whose residents often commute to jobs in Manhattan. (For convenience I will refer to these three suburbs as Manhasset.) In the urban Manhattan and suburban Manhasset sample, the largest number of the heads of households who are in the labor force have managerial or professional occupations or own (small or large) businesses.[7] These occupations (capitalists, owners of small businesses, and managers or professionals) fall squarely within the domain of what Bourdieu refers to variously as the "dominant classes," the "upper tier" of the class structure, or the "upper and upper middle classes."

The urban working- and lower-middle-class neighborhood is Greenpoint, Brooklyn. The residences there are modest—row houses or small, free-standing homes. The sample was drawn from two adjacent sections, one mostly Polish, the other mostly Italian. The suburban working- and lower-middle-class neighborhood is Medford, on Long Island, just off the expressway and some sixty miles east of Manhattan. Medford was built by developers in the late 1950s and the 1960s and was intended to be inexpensive. The houses here are modest—most are simple ranches. In both the Greenpoint and the Medford samples, most of the heads of household (male and female) who are in the labor force have blue-collar or lower-white-collar (clerical and secretarial) jobs. These occupations fall squarely within the "dominated classes," "working class," or "popular classes" as defined by Bourdieu. For convenience I will refer to Greenpoint and Medford residents and their homes as "working class."[8]

The interviews were based on a schedule composed of both open- and close-ended questions. I also took a full set of photographs of the interior of each dwelling.[9]

Definition of Abstract Art

First, the definition of abstract art. This is a topic of some debate in twentieth-century art (although probably not as much as it should have been). For example, although some artists, such as Kandinsky ([1912] 1947) and Mondrian ([1937] 1945), were willing to refer to their works as *abstract*, other artists, such as Naum Gabo (1956), were not.[10]

Still, a particular definition of abstract art is accepted (implicitly or explicitly) by most twentieth-century writers as well as by those interviewed in this study. Thus, few respondents interviewed—either working or middle class—had difficulty, when asked, in deciding what was abstract art (or *modern art,* which they often used as a synonym—see the note to table 1 below). Abstract art, for most of them, had two features. First, it eschews easily recognizable images of the external world—it is "nonrepresentational." Second, it is presented as "art"; for example, if it is a picture, it is usually framed, hung on a wall, and considered of aesthetic value. This definition, broadly accepted elsewhere, will serve here.

Who Has Abstract Art?

Abstract art is, indeed, an elite taste. It is almost absent (in original or reproduction) from the working-class households I interviewed (see table 1). Only two households in suburban Medford and none in Greenpoint had art they identified as abstract, and the degree of abstraction was moderate. For example, a Medford woman displayed a framed poster, acquired from the liquor store where she works, advertising Paul Masson wines. The poster was, in the owner's words, "abstract but not heavy-duty abstract." It depicts a recognizable, although distorted, wine glass whose contents have the unlikely colors of orange and blue. Even among the upper middle class in Manhasset, only one-third of the households displayed any abstract art. And not one house-

Table 1. Whether Abstract Art Is Present in the House, by Type of Neighborhood in Which the House Is Located*

	Neighborhood			
Presence of Abstract Art	Upper-Class Urban (Manhattan)	Upper-Middle-Class Suburban (Manhasset)	Working-Class Urban (Greenpoint)	Working-Class Suburban (Medford)
Homes with any abstract art (%)	60	33	0	5
Homes without abstract art (%)	40	67	100	95
Total (%)	100	100	100	100
	(N = 40)	(N = 40)	(N = 40)	(N = 40)

Note: Respondents were asked if they had any "abstract art." Some respondents, especially among the working and lower middle class, were unsure about the term *abstract art;* in that case, the question was reworded with *modern art* substituted for *abstract art.* This almost always clarified the question to respondents, whose answers then made it clear that they understood *modern art* as a synonym for *abstract art.*

*$p < .001$ (chi-square test).

Table 2. Attitude of Residents toward Abstract Art, by Type of Neighborhood in Which the House Is Located*

Attitude to Abstract Art	Neighborhood			
	Upper-Class Urban (Manhattan)	Upper-Middle-Class Suburban (Manhasset)	Working-Class Urban (Greenpoint)	Working-Class Suburban (Medford)
Like abstract art (%)	84	40	25	33
Dislike abstract art (%)	16	55	41	40
No opinion (%)	0	5	34	26
Total (%)	100	100	100	99
	($N=62$)	($N=51$)	($N=55$)	($N=57$)

Note: Respondents who said they liked some, most, or all abstract art were classified as liking abstract art. Respondents who said they disliked all or almost all abstract art were classified as disliking abstract art.

*$p < .001$ (chi-square test).

hold there featured abstract art in the sense of making it the dominant motif in a room (rather than being the motif of one or two items displayed in a room with other, representational pictures). By contrast, 60 percent of the Manhattan households displayed abstract art. And twelve (30 percent) featured abstract art in at least one room, in the sense just defined.

The comments of residents, when asked whether they liked or disliked abstract art, followed a similar pattern (see table 2). Abstract art is not particularly liked among the working-class or the upper-middle-class suburban residents. It was liked by only 25 percent of the residents in Greenpoint, 33 percent of those in Medford, and 40 percent of those in Manhasset. Again, Manhattan residents are different. A large majority, 84 percent, said they liked abstract art, while only 16 percent disliked it.

Why People Dislike Abstract Art

What do people have against abstract art? A common objection is that the artists are charlatans who cannot draw and cannot paint. Abstract art, in short, is a fraud. This is one of the two main criticisms made by working-class people. It is also common among suburban residents of Manhasset (it is the third most common objection there, but in frequency not far behind the two most common objections) and is found too among the minority of Manhattan residents who are critical of abstract art (see table 3). The view is typically expressed with vehemence. Here are some examples. A female Greenpoint resident in her mid-twenties: "It [abstract art] looks like someone stepped on it." A Medford carpenter who sees abstract art when he renovates the vacation homes of wealthy people in the Hamptons on Long Island: "The paint fell off the truck and they cut the asphalt off and hung it on the wall. That's abstract art to me. I just see confusion."[11] A Manhattan architect: "Abstract art? It's a zero! It's something foisted on us by charlatans and sold by charlatans. At least Picasso and Klee had it in them to do something else. When they painted their own children, they didn't give them three heads. Gottlieb, Motherwell, they're frauds. Jackson Pollock is the worst. Abstract art became a highly intellectual thing. But art has to have an immediate feeling. If I see a Rembrandt,

Table 3. Main Reasons for Disliking Abstract Art, by Type of Neighborhood in Which House Is Located

Main Reasons for Disliking Abstract Art[a]	Neighborhood			
	Upper-Class Urban (Manhattan)	Upper-Middle-Class Suburban (Manhasset)	Working-Class Urban (Greenpoint)	Working-Class Suburban (Medford)
The artists are charlatans, frauds (%)	20	21	30	36
Has no meaning (%)	40	28	13	14
Ugly (%)	30	4	9	0
Harsh, cold, unemotional (%)	0	25	0	0
Too complex to understand/ ultramodern (%)	0	0	48	50
Other (%)	10	22	0	0
Total (%)	100	100	100	100
	(N = 10)	(N = 28)	(N = 23)	(N = 23)

[a]These are the reasons given by respondents who were classified in table 2 as disliking abstract art. Some respondents gave more than one reason, in which case their top two reasons for disliking abstract art were included here.

it has an immediacy. You don't have to have someone writing a book about it."

Another complaint is that abstract art has no meaning. This is one of the two main objections among upper-middle-class residents of Manhasset. A Manhasset man in his fifties: "It doesn't have any message for me." A Manhattan woman in her forties: "They [abstract paintings] don't mean anything. Take the German expressionists. I'm not German, and to look at it it's ugly. It doesn't say anything to me." A Manhasset woman in her sixties: "I stand looking at two blobs, trying to find a meaning in it. The meaning is that they can get fantastic sums of money for the works!"

The other common criticism among upper-middle-class Manhasset residents is that abstract art is "cold," "harsh," and "unemotional." A Manhasset man who deals in Japanese art: "Abstract art doesn't affect me visually and it doesn't affect me emotionally. It leaves me cold." A Manhasset woman: "I don't really like it [modern art]. It's too harsh, it's not soft. It doesn't reflect nature. I like things to be warm and comfortable."

Finally, there is a pair of objections found among the working class that imply that abstract art is an item of high culture that is beyond their understanding and part of an alien cultural world. Thus, some of these residents object either that abstract art is too complex to understand or that it is too modern, "ultramodern." These working-class people do not care for abstract art but believe that this is because they are not equipped to understand it and do not move in cultural circles that might. Such respondents are similar in outlook to the significant group of working-class respondents (34 percent in Greenpoint, 26 percent in Medford—see table 2) who say that they have no opinion on abstract art (again, mostly because they feel that they do not know much about it).

These findings will not surprise those who believe that abstract art is the domain of an intellectual and cultural elite who alone are capable of appreciating it. Indeed, it will confirm their view. Why should working-class residents or even most upper-middle-class suburbanites possess the skills to appreciate abstract art?

It is residents of Manhattan's East Side who offer an almost perfect group for examining the widely posited model of the audience for abstract art—an audience with superior capacities who engage in some kind of special (and superior) and experiential act when they view the works. They live close to four of the most important art museums in the world: three specialize in Modern Art (the Museum of Modern Art, the Guggenheim, and the Whitney), and the fourth (the Metropolitan) recently opened a major modern art wing. Their occupations are a mix of two main types—either the upper echelons of business, which offers the economic means to purchase art, or the creative arts themselves. Examples of respondents in the creative arts include an Oscar-winning filmmaker, a well-known photographer, the director of an advertising agency, an architect, and a dealer in "primitive art." Several of the respondents in business are also intimately involved with art. For example, a company director's first wife knew many of the major figures on the French art scene—Braque painted a wedding portrait for them, her grandmother had been Raoul Dufy's mistress—and he himself had bought the works of early pop artists such as Warhol and Lichtenstein before they became famous; a lawyer is on her firm's art committee, which purchases work for the offices. Indeed, almost all these residents are interested in art and attend galleries and museums at least from time to time. Thus, given New York's dominance of the modern art scene since World War II, this audience is as likely as any residential group in the United States (with the possible exception of neighborhoods composed mainly of artists) to fit the model.

Why People Like Abstract Art

Abstract Art as Decoration

Theorists of abstract art have offered a number of opinions as to what it is to appreciate abstract art. Some say that it is to comprehend the artist's intentions, others that it is to receive pleasure from the art, others that it is to relate in an imaginative manner to the works. Yet these writers were agreed, as was the modernist movement in general, on what would *not* count as appreciating abstract art. They were united in opposition to art that was "decorative." For example, Kandinsky ([1912] 1947, 68) warned against producing "works which are mere geometric decoration, resembling something like a necktie or a carpet." Mondrian ([1937] 1945, 14) cautioned that "all art becomes 'decoration' when depth of expression is lacking." Indeed, the critique of merely decorative art was one of the cornerstones of modernism. The Austrian architect Adolf Loos ([1908] 1966, 226–27), in a famous pronouncement, declared that "cultural evolution is equivalent to the removal of ornament from articles in daily use." And Frank Lloyd Wright (1931, 78) said, "Any house decoration, as such, is an architectural makeshift, however well it may be done."[12]

It is, then, salutary to discover that, of the East Side residents who

Table 4. Main Reasons for Liking Abstract Art, by Type of Neighborhood in Which House is Located

Main Reasons for Liking Abstract Art[a]	Neighborhood			
	Upper-Class Urban (Manhattan)	Upper-Middle-Class Suburban (Manhasset)	Working-Class Urban (Greenpoint)	Working-Class Suburban (Medford)
Decorative/design:				
Pure decorative/ design (%)	37	35	57	68
Decor (how the arts fits with the room) (%)	15	15	7	0
Permits imagination to wander (%)	33	25	14	21
Other (%)	15	25	21	11
Total (%)	100	100	99	100
	(N = 52)	(N = 20)	(N = 14)	(N = 19)

[a]These are the reasons given by respondents who were classified in table 2 as liking abstract art. Some respondents gave more than one reason, in which case the top two reasons given for liking abstract art were included here.

like abstract art, the largest number (52 percent) say that it is the design or decorative qualities in the works that attract them (see table 4). They like the colors, lines, shapes, or overall effect. (This is also the main reason why residents of Manhasset like abstract art.)

Of those who talk in this way, about one-third focus explicitly on what can be called *decor*—on how the art fits with, or improves the look of, the room. For example, a woman discussed a large (six- by four-foot) painting that dominates her living room: "That's a painting we love. We have a sedate room, and that painting explodes. It gives the room light." (Interviewer: "What does it mean to you?") "It doesn't really mean anything. The artist usually says, 'It isn't supposed to have meaning.' I've learned not to ask artists about meaning." A man in his early fifties discussed the various abstract paintings that hang in his bedroom: "I like them because they are colorful. They brighten up the wall [sections of which are painted grey, with a central section painted salmon]. I aimed for colorful art because of the greyness of the wall and the greyish carpet." The home of the lawyer who is on the art committee that chooses the paintings for her law firm is dominated by abstract and primitive art. She likes abstract art because "I like the colors. I think of art in semidecorative terms. I think of how it will blend into the room. To me lines and colors are important in themselves. For instance [discussing a large, bright tapestry by Sonia Delaunay] I like the vibrant colors—the dark sinks and recedes. And we wanted a tapestry to absorb sound since we had taken up the carpets."

In themselves, these comments about decor hardly demonstrate that abstract art has meaning only for someone who has a lengthy cultural training. Nor do they support the notion of a clear class difference underlying the experiential act of liking abstract art, especially since there is a conventional view that associates the working class with choosing "art" specifically in order to fit with the room furnishings (*sofa art,* as it is sometimes dismissively called).

However, residents for whom abstract art is decorative more commonly focus on the design qualities of the art without, as in the cases just cited, explicitly linking these to the room where the art is displayed. The dealer in primitive art: "To me [abstract art is] basically design— pure design and decorative design. My favorite is Klee—it's the design that I like." A Manhattan woman, a photographer, in her early sixties: "Being a mathematician, I love Mondrian. I see balance and color in the paintings. I feel comfortable with them." A Manhattan man who heads an advertising agency, describing an abstract painting hanging in the formal living room: "I like the effect it creates—its iridescence, luminosity. It's very attractive. And I like the color." A Manhattan woman who is a professional sculptor: "I love it [abstract art]. It's so clear, everything else seems so fuzzy. It seems to come down to the central forms and shapes. I think it's very beautiful." The Manhattan venture capitalist for whom Braque painted a wedding portrait, discussing a Stella hanging in his living room: "Why do I like it? It's one of the best colored Stellas of its period. I like this sort of abstract art. I like the colors and the way it looks."

These comments, all of which fall within the domain of the decorative, raise difficult problems for evaluating the quality of the experience undergone in viewing abstract art. Abstract art may, for these viewers, be decorative, but surely, it will be said, it is not, for all of them, merely decorative. Does not the notion of *decorative* dissolve into various categories (in addition to the distinction made already between *decor* and *purely decorative*)? Is there not a difference—among those who see abstract art as decorative, between viewers with an "artistic" and viewers with a "nonartistic" eye? In liking the decorative qualities of abstract art are not some of these residents training on the works a set of mental faculties (aesthetic and otherwise) that are qualitatively superior to those that the working class and the less talented or educated sections of the upper middle class bring to bear when they regard decorative items?

These are not questions that can be delved into further here. What can be said is that few of those who argue that the experiential act of looking at abstract art is superior to that of looking at representative art have delved into them at all, and those who have did not resolve the problem. Among the latter, Clement Greenberg is an interesting example. He recognized that, even for the artists, modern art was closely associated with the decorative. Indeed, he argued (1957, 40–45) that modern painting was almost inevitably "decorative": "Decoration is the specter that haunts modernist painting." For Greenberg, then, the task of the modern artist was somehow to infuse decoration with art. But how did one know if an artist had successfully infused the decorative with art? Here Greenberg lapses into subjectivism, veiled in obscurantist language, often suffused with an evaluative language drawn from cuisine. For example, discussing artists who in his opinion have failed to infuse the decorative with art, Greenberg complains that one artist's oils have a "saccharine color and gelatinous symbolism"; another artists's colors resemble "stale Florentine sugar." As Donald Kuspit (1979, 180) has written, "Greenberg's use of the qualitative terms of cuisine is itself inherently emotional; they are not unequivocally descriptive terms. It is impossible to say they are accurate, only that they are evocative. . . . Of course, one can argue that the rhetoric of cuisine is a kind of perceptual shorthand, but it is hard to say what intuitions it abbreviates."

Thus, there may be, among the audience for abstract art, an avant-garde or "artistic" attitude toward decoration, on the one hand, and an unsophisticated or mass attitude toward decoration, on the other. However, until some clear criteria are offered that would enable an observer to distinguish those comments or actions of respondents that indicate "avant-garde" or "artistic" attitudes toward decoration from those that indicate unsophisticated or mass attitudes, the argument is not convincing.

(Note that my argument in this chapter is about the audience for abstract art, not the artists. I do not want to suggest that, for the artists who produced abstract art, the art was primarily decorative, although some writers—e.g., Gombrich (1979, vii)—have flirted with this more radical idea.)[13]

The Creative Response?

The second most common reason that East Side residents give for liking abstract art does seem to support the stereotype of the audience for abstract art. Abstract art, they say, permits the imagination to wander. It allows a creative response to the work. Far less than representative art does it guide, determine, and fix the viewer's response. (This is also the second most common reason given by Manhasset residents who like abstract art.) Thirty-three percent of Manhattan respondents who liked abstract art gave this as the main reason, as did 25 percent of respondents in suburban Manhasset.

Consider some examples of East Side respondents who expressed this view, about abstract art in general or about particular works. A woman in her early forties: "I like abstract art. It gives you a lot to think about. I like to have on my walls things that make you dream a bit, that are not realistic." A man in his mid-forties: "I like abstract art because it doesn't pin you down. I can look at the lines and colors and see all kinds of things. Chagall is my favorite artist: I like the imagination in his work." A man in his mid-fifties, discussing an abstract painting: "There are two ways of looking at this. That's what intrigues me about it."

The idea that "great art" is distinguished by its ability to unleash the creative imagination of the audience is widespread (see, e.g., Willett 1971). Thus, this kind of relation between the spectator and the art looks more promising for the argument that enthusiasts of abstract art engage in some kind of superior experiential act (as compared with those who dislike abstract art or prefer representative art).

It would, however, be a mistake to stop here. The question arises as to what images respondents create when they view their abstract art. On what objects does their imagination settle when it is turned loose by abstract art? Respondents who said they liked abstract art because they could look at it creatively were asked what images came to mind as they looked creatively at their works. Their answers were striking. Over half saw landscapes, in one form or another. As they gazed at the works they seemed to see the ocean, waves, the beach, clouds, the sun, mountains, meadows, and so on. For example, a Manhattan man said: "I see clouds floating." A Manhattan woman (talking about a whitish painting): "I look at this and I imagine it's the snow of the Russian steppes." A Manhasset woman on an abstract painting by a Mexican artist: "It reminds me of the Yucatan. If you look at it, it's almost like the excavations of an old city." A man who liked the ambiguity in his abstract paintings: "I look at this and I wonder, 'Is this in the midst of a haze, or is it a spot on Jupiter with the clouds around it?' Or take this picture. Am I at the top of the Grand Canyon looking down at the Colorado River, or am I down by the river looking up, with the sun coming over the top?"

The problem with accepting these comments as evidence that these respondents relate in a distinctly creative way to their abstract paintings is that landscapes are by far the most popular topic of the paintings displayed in all four of the neighborhoods studied. They constitute 35 percent of all the paintings displayed in Manhattan houses, 32 percent of those in Manhasset, and 32 percent of those in Greenpoint and Medford. The landscape motif is pervasive among the working class and the upper middle class. Elsewhere, I have analyzed the content and meaning of these landscapes (Halle 1989). Here I want to make the point that the minority who allow their imaginations to wander over abstract paintings appear to come to rest at the same point as almost everyone else—the landscape. This scarcely counts as creativity, unless one wants to maintain that the landscapes discerned by these residents are more creative than others. This is an argument that would have to be substantiated.

Conclusion

The findings presented here, at least for the critical case of abstract art, cast doubt on the claim of cultural capital theorists that it is lengthy training acquired in one's family of origin or in the educational system that produces the tastes, knowledge, and capacities that underpin an interest in high culture. If abstract art is, for most of its audience, about decoration, then the apparent gap between those who like abstract art and those who do not looks less like a chasm than a crack. Everyone (the working class, the middle class, and the upper middle class) displays purely decorative motifs—lines, colors, and so on—in their homes. Wallpaper, drapes, and china in the homes of the working as well as the middle and upper middle classes frequently present these motifs. Thus, moving from one taste culture to another may not require elaborate cultural training; rather, it may be a simple step, involving little more than the decision to use abstract art in decoration.

The question remains as to why such decisions have been taken primarily by members of the middle and upper middle classes. It may be a result of elaborate prior training, as the theory of cultural capital insists. But it may also be a consequence of other factors that do not require elaborate prior experience—for example, a passing acquaintance, gained from the popular press (recall the famous symposium in *Life* magazine [11 October 1948] that presented the case for and against abstract art) or from viewing the homes of friends and acquaintances. Indeed, it is just as likely to be acquired after entry into the middle and upper middle class as it is to be a condition of gaining entry into those classes. The discovery that most of those who like abstract art do so because of its decorative qualities leaves room for all these possibilities, while the theory of cultural capital suggests only the first.

If acquiring a taste for abstract art is difficult, then the taste for high culture might serve as a barrier to class mobility. On the other hand, if deciding to display abstract art does not require any more cultural knowledge than the decision, made by someone of modest social origins who becomes a wealthy corporate lawyer, to put on a three-piece suit, then abstract art seems a less likely cultural barrier.

Culture, then, may be more fluid and complex than implied by theories that see it as being primarily about domination and power. Indeed, attempts to assimilate cultural power to the model of economic and political power may be a mistake. In his now classic essay "The Power of the Powerless," Havel (1985) has pointed out that, even when East European societies were dominated by the Soviet Union and by local Communist parties, the way in which the populace related to the power structure was too complex to fit a model of a dictatorial elite imposing its attitudes on the rest. My study suggests that the model of one group exercising cultural power over another is not the only model for understanding modern Western culture either.

Notes

1. Bourdieu asked respondents three questions about abstract art. In addition to the question cited in the text, he asked respondents whether abstract art "interested them" as much as "the classical schools." And he asked what people thought of the view, "Modern painting is just slapped on anyhow; a child could do it." The last question does begin to get at some of the experiential issues.

It is true of many other areas of modern culture that sociological surveys have often done little more than establish who does and who does not engage in the particular behavior or attitude in question. As Herbert Gans (1986, 33) has written, "The fact is that we still know virtually nothing about people and tastes. . . . Surveys can usually afford only to ask people about their most frequent activities and their general likes and dislikes, therefore producing find-ings about general tendencies. . . . The ethnographic and life-history data that can identify fundamental patterns of cultural choice and that are needed prerequisites to surveys have not yet been produced." Marxists too have said little about abstract art, as Zolberg (1990, 56) has pointed out.

2. Perhaps the main difference between Bourdieu and DiMaggio is that Bourdieu holds that separate tastes are associated with each social class. DiMaggio, at least in his recent work (1987), holds that the taste for popular culture is common among all social classes but that only members of the higher social classes also have a taste for high culture.

3. The same pattern emerges from other surveys of involvement in culture and high culture in the United States. Involvement with high culture does vary with socioeconomic level, above all with level of education. Those with college degrees are more likely than those without to have *some* interest in high culture. Yet only a minority of even the college-educated population spend much leisure time in these ways. For example, a study (Wilensky 1964) of men in a variety of occupations in Detroit found that, although only 1 percent of blue-collar workers read a "quality" newspaper every day, only 11 percent of engineers did so either. Even among professors and lawyers, a highly educated group, only a minority read a "quality" newspaper (42 percent of all professors and 36 percent of all lawyers). See also Robinson (1977).

4. These doubts are strengthened by case studies of the still heavily male-dominated upper echelons of the corporate structure. For instance, in the United States, knowledge of sports (which is hardly difficult to acquire or unevenly distributed in the class structure) seems at least as important as knowl-edge of the high arts for individual success in the corporate hierarchy (see Kanter 1979).

5. For an interesting discussion of the uneasy relation between Bourdieu's data and his theory, see Gartman (1991). For the argument that, in addition to familiarity with high culture, other cultural traits—especially moral traits (such as honesty and respect for others) and social traits (such as power and membership in certain social clubs)—are important for gaining access to domi-nant class circles, and for a very interesting attempt to specify which such traits are most valued in the United States and France, see Lamont (1992). See also Lamont and Lareau (1988).

6. The response rates for each area are as follows: Medford, 68 percent; Manhasset, 67 percent; Greenpoint, 60 percent; Manhattan, 53 percent. In Greenpoint, the response in the predominantly Polish section was 74 percent, while that in the predominantly Italian section was 39 percent.

7. Thus, among males heads of household in the Manhattan sample who were in the labor force, 47 percent had upper-white-collar occupations, 18 percent were capitalists (defined as owners of a business that employs at least five people), and 35 percent were owners of small businesses (employing less than five people). Among female heads of household in Manhattan, 36 percent had upper-white-collar occupations, 14 percent owned small businesses, 14

percent had lower-white-collar jobs, and 29 percent were housewives (home-makers) (another 7 percent engaged in unpaid volunteer/charity work). Among male heads of household in the Manhasset sample who were in the labor force, 46 percent had upper-white-collar occupations, 43 percent owned their own businesses, and 11 percent were blue-collar workers. Among female heads of household in Manhasset, 37 percent were homemakers, 32 percent had upper-white-collar occupations, and 32 percent had lower-white-collar occupations. Note that the data are for current paid occupation or (if the person has retired) for last paid occupation.

8. Among employed male heads of household in the Greenpoint sample, 60 percent had blue-collar occupations (*blue collar* here includes doormen and first-line supervisors), 10 percent had lower-white-collar occupations (*lower white collar* is defined as clerical, secretarial, or retail sales jobs), 10 percent had upper-white-collar occupations (*upper white collar* is defined as managerial or professional occupations), and 20 percent owned small businesses (defined as employing five persons or less). Among female heads of household (here a female spouse, like her husband, is considered a head of household), 45 percent had lower-white-collar occupations, 9 percent had blue-collar occupations, 12 percent had upper-white-collar occupations, 3 percent owned their own businesses, and 30 percent were homemakers. Among employed male heads of household in the Medford sample, 47 percent had blue-collar occupations, 25 percent had lower-white-collar occupations, 12 percent had upper-white-collar occupations, and 16 percent owned small businesses. Among female heads of household, 55 percent had lower-white-collar occupations, 9 percent had blue-collar occupations, 18 percent had upper-white-collar occupations, and 18 percent were homemakers. As with Manhattan and Manhasset, the data refer to current paid occupations, except for retired persons, who are classified by their last paid occupation before retiring.

9. In the overall project, I analyze the full range of art and cultural items in the houses studied. (Thus, I analyze portrait art and family pictures, primi-tive art, abstract art, religious art and iconography, and landscape art.) Here I will focus on abstract art.

10. Thus, Gabo, the Russian Constructivist, opposed the use of the word *abstraction* in art, considering it a "false terminology."

11. It might be argued that these critical working-class comments can be seen in terms of notions of cultural resistance (Willis 1990; Scott 1990). At any rate, these comments certainly do not support a "Frankfurt sociology" notion of the working class as dominated and passive.

12. The full Wright quotation is, "Any house decoration, as such, is an architectural makeshift, however well it may be done, unless the decoration, so called, is part of the architect's design in both concept and execution." See also Le Corbusier ([1921] 1986).

13. Thus, Gombrich (1979, vii) wrote, "Only the 20th. century has wit-nessed the final elevation of pattern-making into the autonomous activity of 'abstract art.' "

150   David Halle

References

Benjamin, Walter. "The Work of Art in the Age of Mechanical Reproduction." 1936. In *Illuminations,* trans. Harry Zohn. New York: Schocken, 1969.

Bourdieu, Pierre. "Outline of a Sociological Theory of Art Perception." *International Social Science Journal* 20 (1968): 4.

Bourdieu, Pierre. *Distinction: A Social Critique of the Judgement of Taste.* Cambridge, Mass.: Harvard University Press, 1984.

DiMaggio, Paul. "Classification in Art." *American Sociological Review* 52 (1987): 440–55.

DiMaggio, Paul, and Michael Useem. "Social Class and Arts Consumption: The Origins and Consequences of Class Differences in Exposure to the Arts in America." *Theory and Society* 5, no. 2 (1978): 141–61.

DiMaggio, Paul, and Michael Useem. "The Arts in Class Reproduction." In *Cultural and Economic Reproduction in Education,* ed. Michael Apple. Boston: Routledge & Kegan Paul, 1981.

Ford Foundation. *The Finances of the Performing Arts: A Survey of the Characteristics and Attitudes of Audiences for Theater, Opera, Symphony, and Ballet in 12 U.S. Cities.* 2 vols. New York, 1974.

Gabo, Naum. "Russia and Constructivism." 1956. Reprinted in *Gabo: Constructions, Sculpture, Paintings, Drawings, Engravings.* London: Lund Humphries, 1957.

Gans, Herbert. "American Popular Culture and High Culture in a Changing Class Structure." *Prospects* 10 (1986): 17–38.

Gartman, David. "Bourdieu's *Distinction.*" *American Journal of Sociology* 97 (1991): 421–47.

Gombrich, Ernest. *The Sense of Order.* Oxford: Phaidon, 1979.

Greenberg, Clement. "Avant-Garde and Kitsch." 1939. Reprinted in *Art and Culture.* Boston: Beacon, 1961.

Greenberg, Clement. "The Crisis of the Easel Picture." 1948. Reprinted in *Clement Greenberg: The Collected Essays and Criticism,* vol. 2, *1945–1949.* Chicago: University of Chicago Press, 1986.

Greenberg, Clement. "Milton Avery." *Arts* (December 1957): 40–45.

Halle, David. "Class and Culture in Modern America: The Vision of the Landscape in the Residences of Contemporary Americans." *Prospects* 13 (1989): 373–406.

Havel, Václav. "The Power of the Powerless." In *The Power of the Powerless,* ed. John Keane. London: Hutchinson, 1985.

Ingarden, Roman. *The Ontology of the Work of Art.* 1928. Reprint. Columbus: Ohio State University Press, 1986.

Kandinsky, Wassily. *Concerning the Spiritual in Art.* 1912. Reprint. New York: Wittenborn, 1947.

Kanter, Rosabeth Moss. *Men and Women of the Corporation.* New York: Basic, 1979.

Lamont, Michèle. *Money, Morals, and Manners: The Culture of the French and the American Upper-Middle Class*. Chicago: University of Chicago Press, 1992.

Lamont, Michèle, and Annette Lareau. "Cultural Capital: Allusions, Gaps and Glissandos in Recent Theoretical Developments." *Sociological Theory* 6 (1988): 153–68.

Le Corbusier. *Towards a New Architecture*. 1921. Translated by Frederick Etchells. New York: Dover, 1986.

Loos, Adolf. "Ornament and Crime." 1908. Reprinted in *Adolf Loos*, ed. Ludwig Münz and Gustav Künstler. New York: Praeger, 1966.

Mondrian, Piet. "Towards the True Vision of Reality." 1937. Reprinted in *Plastic Art and Pure Plastic Art*. New York: Wittenborn, 1945.

Ortega y Gasset, José. "The Dehumanization of Art." 1925. In *Velasquez, Goya and the Dehumanization of Art*, trans. Alexis Brown. New York: Norton, 1972.

Robinson, John. *How Americans Use Time*. New York: Praeger, 1977.

Scott, James. *Domination and the Arts of Resistance*. New Haven, Conn.: Yale University Press, 1990.

Wilensky, Harold. "Mass Society and Mass Culture." *American Sociological Review* 29 (1964): 173–97.

Willett, Frank. *African Art*. New York: Praeger, 1971.

Willis, Paul. *Common Culture*. Boulder, Colo.: Westview, 1990.

Wright, Frank Lloyd. "The Cardboard House." In *Modern Architecture: The Kahn Lectures for 1930*. Princeton, N.J.: Princeton University Press, 1931.

Zolberg, Vera. *Constructing a Sociology of the Arts*. Cambridge: Cambridge University Press, 1990.

SEVEN

How Musical Tastes Mark Occupational Status Groups

**Richard A. Peterson
and Albert Simkus**

The arts have been used to mark social class distinctions in capitalist societies, as has been noted by scholars ranging from Max Weber, Emile Durkheim, and Thorstein Veblen to David Riesman, Irving Goffman, Herbert Gans, Pierre Bourdieu, and Mary Douglas. And a number of recent studies have shown in detail how the idea of fine art *as high culture* was propagated by nineteenth-century moral entrepreneurs to serve as a basis for marking social class position.[1]

While the evidence of the first half of this century suggests strong links between social status and cultural taste, there is growing evidence that there is no longer a one-to-one correspondence between taste and status group membership in advanced postindustrial societies like the United States. Evidence on this point comes from a number of sources. Persons who attend elite arts events are most likely to come from the higher-status ranks of society,[2] yet, even among the highest-status groups, only a minority participate in the elite arts.[3] In her comparative study of upper-middle-class persons in four cities in France and the United States, Michèle Lamont shows that, while there are clear markers of status distinctions, a taste for the fine arts does not work as a universally recognized marker of status distinction.[4] Further, David Halle suggests that, even though taste in visual arts varies by social class, most of those who choose works of elite art do so for prosaic reasons of fashion and not because they consciously hold elite aesthetic standards.[5]

Are we to conclude that the arts no longer signify status? We think not, and to suggest the continuing use of the arts in signaling status distinctions we will, for the sake of brevity, consider just one important kind of status, *occupational status*, and one aspect of taste, *musical taste*. We will employ a sophisticated methodological technique so that the rankings of occupations and of types of music depend not on the conventional judgments of critics but on the evaluations of a representative sample of the U.S. population.

Occupation as a Measure of Status

Researchers hold widely divergent views of the contribution of occupation to the formation of values and tastes. For example, Bensman and Lilienfeld argue that the work that adults do for half their waking hours fundamentally structures all aspects of their lives.[6] Similarly, Collins writes, "Occupations are the major basis of class cultures; these cultures, in turn, along with material resources for intercommunication, are the mechanisms that organize classes as communities, i.e., as status groups."[7] Yet Davis asserts that "occupational stratum simply does not have the diffuse and strong effects on our nonvocational attitudes and opinions that sociologists have generally assumed."[8] Numerous other studies, while not as extreme, generally support each of these disparate contentions.[9]

The 1982 national Survey of Public Participation in the Arts (SPPA), which was collected for the National Endowment for the Arts by the U.S. Census Bureau, is uniquely appropriate for addressing this debate.[10] Before turning to find out whether occupations have distinctive musical tastes, we need first to define our measure of occupational groups and our categorization of musical tastes carefully. We also need to introduce our statistical means of delineating the relation between occupational status groups and musical tastes.

Music as a Measure of Taste

Attendance at classical music and opera performances is generally considered a good indicator of high culture musical taste,[11] and occupational groups have been shown to have quite different rates of classical music and opera attendance, as indexed both by surveys of the general population and by analyses of attenders of arts events.[12] Yet arts activity depends on the availability of the arts, which varies widely by the size of city and the region of the country. What is more, it varies by the life stage of persons. Urban college students, for example, have much higher participation rates than do urban professionals (who are married and have children) who are just five years older and presumably share much the same tastes.[13]

To avoid the problems associated with participation, our measure of musical taste is based on the respondents' stated aesthetic preferences. In the SPPA survey all respondents were asked which of thirteen types of music they enjoyed. Thus, there is a measure for every respondent. In bypassing the problem of the variation in the availability of activities, this alternative makes the choice very easy, for respondents could (and most did) choose more than one category of music. The follow-up question, however, is ideal for our use. It asked respondents to say which kind of music they liked the best; thus, there is a single measure for each respondent.[14]

Taking a strict cultural capital definition of taste,[15] we might have assigned a 1 to all persons choosing either "classical music" or "opera" and a 0 to persons choosing all other forms. This technique, however, would allow no way of clearly differentiating among the occupational groups that do not often choose classical music or opera.

Alternatively, we might rank all music choices in terms of presumed aesthetic merit. Although Shils, Gans, and others have distinguished among highbrow, middlebrow, and lowbrow musical tastes, neither the relative rankings of the types of music nor the relative distances between ranks are self-evident.[16] While "classical" music, for example, is widely known to rank higher than "country and western" music[17] and both the blues and country music are often nurtured in opposition to "bourgeois aesthetic,"[18] there is no a priori basis for ranking those musical tastes that would be expected to rank somewhere in the middle, such as "folk," "big band," "rock," and "mood/middle-of-the-road" music. Also, if "classical" music ranks above "musicals," exactly how much higher in its aesthetic appeal is it? To solve these problems, we made use of a statistical technique—discussed below—from which we may derive a set of scale values for both musical tastes and occupational status groups that best predict the pattern of association between the two variables.

This study focuses on the boundary-marking function of musical taste. While useful in showing the process of boundary marking, the present data set was not designed to get at the dynamics of the process. Do persons in the higher occupational status groups attend classical music concerts, one might ask, because they have learned to enjoy the music and in the process affirm their high status, or are they indifferent to the music and attend primarily to affirm their high status? While not created for this purpose, the study does provide two ways of beginning to frame an answer to this very important question. These are pursued in Appendix A.

Defining Occupational Status Groups

American survey researchers conventionally categorize the thousands of job titles into occupational categories using the scheme developed for the Bureau of the Census in the 1930s.[19] In this scheme physicians and economists as well as social workers and exotic dancers are grouped together as *professionals,* and professionals, thus defined, are ranked above the category called *managers,* which includes not only the directors of multinational corporations but also supervisors of fast-food outlets. In his study cited earlier, Davis aggregated even these broad groups together.[20] It is little wonder that occupational groups thus defined are not found to have distinctive patterns of cultural choice.

In defining occupational status groups we have grouped together occupations that involve the same job conditions and the same level of requirements for social and cultural skills. The groupings have been made after taking a fresh look at the classification of occupations in the light of the wide range of research and writing on occupation and social class that suggest the ways that boundaries between occupational groups are being redefined in practice.[21]

On this basis we define nineteen occupational status groups that, between them, include the total documented employed civilian labor force.[22] Representative job titles for each of the occupational status groups are given in table 1. The order of the groups in table 1 is simply a matter of convenience because the method of analysis we employ does not attach a priori importance to the logical links among occupational groups or even the rank ordering of occupational categories. For a more detailed discussion of the criteria used in placing specific job titles in each of the occupational status groups, see Appendix A. Before engaging in the empirical analysis, we made predictions about the relative status levels of each of the occupational groups. The interested reader can find these summarized in Appendix B below.

A Method for Simultaneously Ranking Occupations and Tastes

In order to scale statistically music genres into a taste hierarchy and scale the occupational status groups, we use log-multiplicative models developed by Leo Goodman.[23] This model takes the music genre choices of the nineteen occupational status groups and progressively reorders the occupations and the taste choices so that occupational status groups with the most similar patterns of music choices are adjacent and the music genres chosen by the most similar patterns of occu-

Table 1. Representative Occupations in Each of the Occupational Status Groups

---

Higher Cultural. Architects, lawyers, clergymen, librarians, academics.

Lower Cultural. Social workers, teachers below college, religious workers, public relations.

Artists. Actors, authors, dancers, editors, musicians, painters.

Higher Technical. Chemical engineers, actuaries, chemists, geologists, physicians, dentists.

Lower Technical. Accountants, computer programmers, chiropractors, pharmacists, registered nurses, health technicians, dietitions.

Higher Managerial. Owners, managers, administrators, officials, superintendents, with incomes greater than $30,000 in 1981.

Lower Managerial. Owners, managers, administrators, officials, superintendents, with incomes less than $30,000 in 1981.

Higher Sales. Insurance agents, real estate agents, manufacturing sales, stockbrokers.

Lower Sales. Newsboys, retail salesclerks, hucksters, peddlers.

Clerical. Bank tellers, file clerks, mail carriers, typists, office machine operators, ticket agents, receptionists, meter readers.

Skilled Manual. Bakers, brickmasons, bulldozer operators, carpenters, machinists, mechanics, printers, painters, plumbers, phone installers.

Semiskilled, Transport. Truck, taxi drivers, deliverymen, forklift operators, railroad switchmen.

Semiskilled Manual. Factory operatives, gas station attendants, laundry workers, weavers.

Laborers. Craft helpers, warehousemen, fishermen, construction laborers, garbage collectors.

Skilled Service. Dental assistants, nursing aides, practical nurses, barbers, cosmetologists, airline hostesses.

Protective Service. Policemen, sheriffs, firemen, watchmen, marshals, bridge tenders.

Unskilled Service. Janitors, maids, waiters, orderlies, porters, cooks.

Farmers. Farm owners and family, farm managers.

Farm Laborers. Farm workers, farm foremen, farm service laborers.

---

pational status groups are adjacent. Thus, the technique simultaneously ranks each of the variables in terms of the other.

In addition to reordering occupations and tastes to form the most parsimonious empirical ranking, the method provides a measure of the relative distance of each of the musical genres from each other. Thus, for example, three music genres may be ranked in order, but two may be quite alike while the third stands out as having a quite distinctive scale value. Turning to table 2 below, we see such a case. Folk music and musicals turn out to be high ranking in taste, but classical music is distinctively higher in the hierarchy than this pair. Finally, the method provides a measure that indicates how distinct are the choices of each occupational status group. The better the ranking of occupational status groups and musical tastes, the higher the score; the more nearly random the rankings, the lower the score.

Results

The Taste Order of Musical Styles

The first question to consider in looking at the results is whether a meaningful preference order of musical styles emerges from the process of log-multiplicative modeling, and the answer is clearly in the affirmative. It is possible to predict with reasonable accuracy the pattern of musical tastes for each of the occupations.[24]

Moving to specifics, table 2 shows the order of musical styles inherent in the data and revealed by the model. The left-hand column shows the relative position of the ten musical forms for the total sample. Classical music is clearly at one extreme of the taste ranking.[25] Country and western music is clearly at the other end. Its distance from the next lowest form is roughly the same as the distance between classical music and folk music at the other end of the taste hierarchy. Table 3 shows the cognate ordering of the nineteen occupational status groups. The three columns of data on the right-hand side of table 3 show that, indeed, the log-multiplicative model has roughly ordered the occupational groups on the classical music measures and ordered the country and western music measure in the opposite direction.[26]

There is nothing inherent in the statistical manipulations that identify one end as "higher" and the other end as "lower" taste. Classical music, however, has for a century been ascribed high aesthetic value

Table 2. Log-Multiplicative Scale Scores for the Ten Types of Music Liked Best

	Total Population		
	Two Dimensional		Whites:
Musical Taste	Scale 1	Scale 2	Scale 1
Classical	.51	.31	.50
Folk	.37	.04	.35
Musicals	.31	.14	.26
Jazz	.14	.16	.27
Mood/MOR	.07	−.61	.03
Big band	−.05	−.07	−.03
Rock	−.26	.11	−.29
Hymns/gospel	−.31	.03	−.36
Soul/blues/R&B	−.35	.53	−.28
Country music	−.44	−.63	−.44

Note: MOR = middle-of-the-road. R&B = rhythm and blues.

Table 3. Occupation by Music Taste Scale Scores and Select Music Choices

| Occupational Group | Music Taste Scores Total Sample | | | Classical (%) | | Country Best (%) | Not One Best (%) |
	Scale 1	Scale 2	Whites Alone	Best	Attend		
Higher Cultural	.39	.50	.43	28.9	39.4	8.9	13.3
Lower Cultural	.31	.29	.35	18.9	38.1	7.1	7.8
Higher Technical	.27	-.24	.23	18.0	26.6	13.5	10.1
Artists	.26	.99	.30	24.5	34.6	12.2	14.6
Higher Managerial	.22	-.78	.16	9.8	22.9	19.5	7.5
Higher Sales	.15	-.51	.12	11.0	20.7	20.5	11.9
Lower Technical	.13	-.35	.11	8.3	23.4	23.4	7.7
Skilled Service	.04	.47	.02	8.9	17.6	17.9	8.8
Lower Sales	.02	-.26	.00	4.3	14.7	19.3	4.3
Clerical	.01	-.12	-.00	6.3	15.2	20.8	7.3
Lower Managerial	-.00	-.32	-.00	3.6	13.1	21.5	8.9
Protective Service	-.03	-.17	-.01	9.2	9.9	26.2	7.7
Farmers	-.12	-.22	-.14	3.0	8.6	30.3	4.9
Unskilled Service	-.14	.38	-.09	4.2	9.8	20.2	2.3
Skilled Manual	-.22	-.33	-.23	3.4	6.3	36.4	6.4
Semiskilled Manual	-.26	.14	-.25	2.5	4.6	30.4	6.0
Semiskilled Transportation	-.26	-.16	-.31	2.6	4.3	32.5	4.1
Laborers	-.30	.43	-.28	.0	4.8	20.7	2.4
Farm Laborers	-.47	.27	-.42	.0	6.3	42.6	2.1
Average	.00	.00	.00	6.6	14.0	23.1	7.1

and country music low.[27] The left-hand columns of tables 2 and 3 provide further support for the assertion that classical music and country music define the taste hierarchy from high to low. The professional and managerial occupation scores have the same sign as classical music, while the lower manual occupations have the same sign as country and western music, indicating the direction of the affinity between the hierarchy of occupational status groups and the taste hierarchy of music genres.

Focusing again on the left-hand column of table 2, folk music ranks a strong second to classical music. Although the term *folk* was not defined for respondents, from an examination of the pattern of answers we infer that, when respondents answered that they liked "folk music" best, most had in mind a taste for the wide range of traditional ethnic, national, and regional musics of peoples around the world or the acoustical music roughly based on such music.[28] Musicals and jazz come next, followed by a large gap between these and the taste score of mood/middle-of-the-road music and big band dance music, which together are near the midpoint in the ranking. Again there is a large distance between these two and the next three types of music, rock, hymns/gospel, and soul/blues. It is interesting that, while these three forms are seen by their adherents as clearly distinct, they share musical affinities[29] and, from the evidence of this analysis, are most often chosen by persons of comparable occupational rank.

DiMaggio and Ostrower have noted that blacks and whites of comparable status levels often choose different forms of music.[30] Using the same data set as the present study, they made a detailed analysis of music choices and participation in arts activities and suggested that blacks of all levels choose jazz and soul/blues more often than whites in order to show their identification with black heritage and culture. At the same time, some high-status whites choose jazz and, to a lesser degree, soul/blues, while virtually all lower-status whites shun these musics. Peterson suggests that high-status whites choose jazz as a form of art music.[31] If this is true, a log-multiplicative model based on the white respondents should show the prestige score of both jazz and soul/blues to be substantially higher.[32] The right-hand column of table 2 shows the results for sample whites alone. The overall distribution of song genres is the same except that, as predicted, jazz has moved up and is here slightly above musicals and soul/blues has moved up to be above both rock and hymns/gospel.[33] This finding, that the ranking of musical tastes by occupational status groups varies somewhat by race, is in line with prior research, but it does put in question the assertion that the obtained ranking for the entire sample is universally agreed on in the U.S. population—a point to which we will return below.

The Order among Occupational Status Groups

The scores for occupational status groups are shown in table 3. The rank ordering of occupational groups in the first dimension of the two-dimensional model for the entire sample (the left-hand column of figures) is virtually the same as for the one-dimensional model for white respondents (the third column from the left).[34] Thus, the two can be considered at the same time.

The scores in table 3 show that the taste ranks of occupational status groups cluster in three distinct ranges. The top seven groups have clearly positive taste scores, the bottom seven groups have clearly negative taste scores, and the five occupational taste groups in the middle have taste scores near zero. For the convenience of comparing this table with the next two, which show the arts participation and the demographic characteristics of the occupational status groups, the occupational status groups are listed in the same order as in table 3, and lines have been drawn separating the three clusters of occupations just identified.

The first substantive observation is that the order of occupations indicated by these scores is quite consistent with the ranking we had expected, including the deviations we predicted from the conventional ordering. See Appendix B for details of our predictions.

The top cluster of occupational status groups includes all five of the professional occupations plus Higher Managers and Higher Sales, corresponding roughly to what Bourdieu calls the dominant class.[35] Our division of the professions into five groups has also proved fruitful. While all five kinds of professionals fit into the upper cluster of occupations, they range widely and in the order we predicted, with the Higher Cultural Professionals at the top and the Lower Technical Professionals at the bottom.

The middle cluster of occupational groups, those with taste scores near zero, are all white-, pink-, or blue-collar functionaries, namely, Clerical workers, Lower Sales, Lower Managerial, Higher Service workers, and Protective Service workers. The taste rank of the two groups of service workers is dramatically at variance with conventional expectations, which place service workers at, or near, the bottom of all manual workers. Yet, as we have predicted, Higher Service workers score at the top of the middle cluster of occupational groups, and Protective Service workers are in the middle cluster as well.[36]

The lower cluster of occupational status groups consists of the four categories of manual workers, Lower Service workers, and the two rural-based groups, Farmers and Farm Laborers. The order within the cluster is not in accord with the standard ranking but fits our predictions better. Lower Service workers rank above all four groups of manual workers. That this higher rank is not an artifact of the particular measure of taste is suggested by the fact, shown in table 5 below, that Lower Service Workers' incidence of activity in all art forms is equal to or higher than that of all other lower-cluster occupational groups. At the same time, their relatively high rank cannot be attributed to their education or income because, as can be seen in table 5, their education and income are quite low even when compared to others in the lower cluster of occupational groups. Farmers show tastes closer to those of their rural work associates than to their urban managerial counterparts. Finally, Skilled Manual workers who are conventionally seen to occupy a status well above other manual workers[37] have taste scores that are only just slightly above those of less skilled manual workers.

In each case, the divisions that we have made between higher and lower within the various conventional occupational categories have created dramatic differences in taste rank among managers, sales persons, and technical professionals. Only the split between Higher and Lower Cultural Professionals has made for differences that leave the two in adjacent taste ranks, and their difference in scores of .08 is not inconsiderable.[38]

The Arts Activities of Occupational Status Groups

It is useful to check the validity of our chosen measure of taste, preferred music genre. It is, of course, an expression of opinion and may not reflect behavior. Moreover, musical taste may not reflect taste in the arts generally. Accordingly, to see how generalizable the ordering of occupations by musical taste is, participation data for all the art forms available in the data set were examined. These data are displayed in table 4.

As shown in table 4, the level of participation in arts activities is closely associated with the taste rank of occupational groups. The seven occupational groups in the top cluster rank in the top seven on all the seven public arts participation measures from attending classical music

Table 4. Occupation by Arts Activities

	Classical	Opera	Show	Jazz	Play	Dance	Art Museum	Novel, Poetry
Higher Cultural	39.4	12.0	45.0	17.9	37.8	10.8	59.4	84.3
Lower Cultural	38.1	8.3	42.5	20.2	32.3	13.7	48.3	89.5
Higher Technical	26.6	8.7	36.5	15.1	26.3	7.4	45.0	75.7
Artists	34.6	14.0	36.8	25.0	28.4	12.5	57.4	82.5
Higher Managerial	22.9	5.4	38.1	14.0	22.9	7.5	39.3	73.7
Higher Sales	20.7	6.4	37.0	16.0	24.5	7.7	41.2	67.1
Lower Technical	23.4	5.0	31.8	15.0	22.0	9.5	37.3	74.2
Skilled Service	17.6	4.9	26.9	8.3	10.4	5.5	23.6	60.8
Lower Sales	14.7	5.4	18.7	11.5	12.7	5.9	25.6	67.1
Clerical	15.2	2.6	23.9	11.0	14.1	5.7	25.0	68.7
Lower Managerial	13.1	3.9	22.5	11.3	14.5	5.4	29.4	58.5
Protective Service	9.9	.5	12.4	8.9	7.9	2.5	20.3	61.8
Farmers	8.6	.5	9.6	1.6	4.3	1.6	13.9	44.9
Unskilled Service	9.8	2.9	13.1	11.1	8.6	3.5	16.8	53.4
Skilled Manual	6.3	1.2	10.9	8.0	5.9	1.7	14.4	41.5
Semiskilled Manual	4.6	.9	7.5	5.8	3.9	1.3	9.6	39.9
Semiskilled Transportation	4.3	1.0	6.2	6.7	5.0	1.0	9.8	33.2
Laborers	4.8	1.0	6.7	11.1	5.8	1.4	14.7	42.8
Farm Laborers	6.3	.0	4.7	6.3	7.0	.0	14.8	38.3
Average	14.0	3.3	20.3	11.0	13.1	4.8	24.3	60.4

performances to attending art museums, and the same is true, with one reversal, for the lone private arts activity, reading novels or poetry. The exception is that slightly more Clerical workers report reading novels or poetry than do Higher Sales workers. This reversal is probably due to the gender composition of the two occupational groups. Women generally read more than men do, and 29 percent of the Higher Sales workers are women, while 83 percent of clerical workers are women. Focusing on the top group of occupations, the Higher Cultural professionals rank one, two, or three on all the arts activities, while Lower Cultural Professionals and Arts Professionals rank nearly as high across all art forms.

The five occupational status groups in the middle cluster show average rates of arts participation, except for Protective Service workers, whose rates are considerably below the mean for the sample as a whole, even though, as table 5 below shows, their average educational attainment and income is above that of all other groups in the middle cluster of occupations. Since the job of these service workers is to protect lives, property, and the public order, and since they may interact in an authoritative capacity with higher-status persons, we predicted that they would cultivate higher tastes and have higher rates of arts participation, rates comparable to the skilled service workers. It may be that, in those situations where protective service workers interact with high-status persons, they do so in highly structured situations in which their successful performance depends mostly on following an explicit set of rules and not much on their sociocultural skills. Thus, unlike other service workers, they do not need to cultivate higher-status tastes.[39] Focusing on police and guards, who with firemen make up the large proportion of Protective Service workers, Mary Karpos suggests an alternative explanation for the low rates of arts participation among these Protective Service Workers. She finds evidence from several sources that they are loathe to interact freely in public, where they may be confronted by those whom they have previously had to arrest or reprimand.[40] This explanation draws further support from the fact that Protective Service Workers' private arts consumption (via reading, television, radio, and records) is much higher than their public arts consumption and is more nearly commensurate with their education and income.

The seven occupational groups in the lowest cluster tend to have the lowest rates of participation in arts activities. The rates of participation for Farmers is generally lower than would be expected by their taste rank, which reflects the lesser availability of arts activities in rural and small town areas. But relative isolation may not be the whole answer, for Farmers also show low rates of participation in individual, rural, and sedentary leisure activities.[41] Long work hours and advanced age are likely contributors to their pattern of low participation.

Are These Markers of Occupational Status Groups?

If, as we have seen, musical taste is a marker of occupational status, it is probably also to some degree a marker of other statuses such as gender, race, age, income, education, and region. Indeed, the data show clearly that country music is most preferred by those with a little education, blacks are more likely than whites to choose jazz, young people are more likely than older people to like rock music, etc. Are the differences between occupation groups just a reflection of the differential representation of these other status groups in the occupational status groups? The relevant variables for which we have data—age, gender, race, income, and education—are shown in table 5.[42]

Age. The mean ages of the nineteen occupational status groups cluster near the total sample average age of 38.6 years. No group averages more than five years above or below the grand mean except Farm Owners-Managers, whose mean age is ten years older than the average. Clearly, the taste rank of occupational status groups is not consistently affected by age. This holds true even though the different age groups have quite distinctive patterns of musical taste. Classical music, big band music, and hymns/gospel are chosen more often by those who are older, rock is chosen almost exclusively by the younger age groups, and both country and mood/middle-of-the-road music are chosen by those who are neither very young nor very old.[43]

Gender. Women and men make somewhat different choices of music[44] and are differently distributed in the various occupational status groups. Thus, gender may influence the ranking of musical tastes. As can be seen from table 5, they are under- and overrepresented in occupational status groups in our high-, middle-, and lower-status cluster of groups. Of the three, however, they are most conspicuously underrepresented in the lower cluster of occupational status groups and are found most frequently in three of the occupational groups in the middle cluster of occupations.

Log-multiplicative modeling performed separately for each gender revealed that, while men and women tend to make somewhat different aesthetic choices and tend to be found in different occupational status groups, women and men in the same occupational group make the

Table 5. Occupation by Demographic Variables

Occupation	Education	Income ($)	Age	Female (%)	Black (%)	Cases (N)
Higher Cultural	18.1	33,194	41.8	32.7	4.8	251
Lower Cultural	16.9	33,393	38.2	74.0	7.7	520
Higher Technical	16.9	39,005	38.2	9.6	2.9	312
Artists	14.7	29,545	38.2	40.4	2.9	136
Higher Managerial	14.9	45,540	43.1	27.4	3.4	704
Higher Sales	14.5	36,448	41.4	29.5	4.0	376
Lower Technical	14.9	32,629	38.6	55.0	7.0	889
Skilled Service	12.5	25,651	38.5	86.3	8.2	182
Lower Sales	12.7	26,707	38.0	66.4	3.4	443
Clerical	12.8	27,920	37.2	83.4	8.8	2,494
Lower Managerial	13.0	20,833	41.1	37.4	6.5	596
Protective Service	13.1	28,640	40.6	13.9	11.4	202
Farmers	11.8	26,540	48.7	20.7	.5	188
Unskilled Service	11.5	21,390	36.6	69.5	19.8	1,562
Skilled Manual	11.8	26,738	39.9	8.4	6.6	1,613
Semiskilled Manual	10.9	23,498	38.1	48.1	13.5	1,529
Semiskilled Transportation	11.2	24,417	39.9	11.7	12.9	420
laborers	11.2	23,234	34.3	14.4	15.8	584
Farm Laborers	10.1	20,157	35.1	24.2	12.5	128
Total sample	12.8	27,846	38.6	47.9	9.6	13,129

same patterns of music choices; thus, the skewed gender distribution across occupational groups has not affected the rankings of occupation and musical taste.

Race. African-Americans represent 9.6 percent of the total sample. They are underrepresented in all the occupational groups in the higher cluster of occupations. They are both over- and underrepresented in the middle cluster, and they are overrepresented in all the occupations in the lower cluster except for Farmers and Skilled Manual Workers.

African-Americans in lower-status occupations are much more likely to choose jazz and blues than are their white occupational peers, as noted above. Thus, as DiMaggio and Ostrower have noted[45] and our findings corroborate, the historically African-American musical genres operate quite differently in marking social status for African-Americans and for whites. In one way or another, thus, future studies using music tastes as a status marker will need to take these racially specific patterns into account.

Income. Average annual income varies from $20,157 for Farm Laborers to $45,540 for Higher Managers. While six of the seven top-ranked occupational groups are the only ones to average over $30,000 and the lowest-ranking occupational group also has the lowest income, there are many groups whose income is out of line with their taste rank, and the correlation between the first-dimension scale scores and income is .75. Within the three broad groupings of occupations, however, there is very little association between aesthetic rank and income, and the disjunction between taste rank and income is roughly in line with predictions deriving from Bourdieu and Passeron's formulation of the inverse distribution of economic and cultural capital.[46]

Education. Average years of schooling varies from tenth grade for Farm Laborers to two years of graduate school for Higher Cultural Professionals. The three highest taste-ranking groups are the only ones having average educational levels beyond four years of college. At the other extreme, Farm Laborers average just two years of high school, and all the seven bottom-ranked occupational groups average less than a high school education. As expected from all prior research, years of schooling is closely associated with the taste rank of the occupational group. The correlation between the scores for the first dimension of the two-dimensional-scales scores for the entire population and the average educational level of the occupational groups is .91. Managers, Lower Technical Professionals, and Protective Service workers all have lower taste scores than would be predicted from their level of education.

The high correlation of education and income with occupational status group—.91 and .75, respectively, in this study—has led a number of researchers to conclude that occupation is not very important in marking status.[47] This is true only in the special sense that, controlling for the effects of education and income simultaneously, occupation has little independent effect on status.[48] It may be convenient to use years of schooling as a proxy for other more complex conceptions of status, but this does not mean that occupation is unimportant in determining status. It is, after all, largely through occupational attainment that the fruits of education are actualized. There are, for example, no physicists with a grade school education or well-educated Laborers with incomes comparable to those of comparably educated Higher Managers. The education needed to perform occupational functions and the level of remuneration received are inexorably tied to the nature of the occupation, and, thus, it is artificial and misleading to consider only the *net* effects of occupation, after controlling for these other two variables intrinsic to its meaning. For this reason, the conventionally used statistical procedures that partial the variance in a dependent variable among independent variables are not in accord with the view of occupational groups developed here.

The Second Dimension of Taste and Occupational Groups— Race and Gender

To this point we have focused on the results for the first dimension of the log-multiplicative model. Before discussing the implications of our findings for better understanding the use of music tastes in marking status-group boundaries, it will prove fruitful to consider the second dimension. For the second dimension, the log-multiplicative model considers the relations among the occupations and musical genres with all the relations accounted for in the first dimension removed. In effect, it asks, the first dimension aside, Is there any statistically significant relation between occupational status groups and music taste genres? The music taste scores on the second dimension are displayed in table 2, and those for occupations are displayed in table 3. In examining these tables together, recall that occupational groups and music genres of like sign are associated with each other.

The ordering among occupations is dramatically different from that in the first dimension, and five of the six lowest-ranked musical forms on the first dimension are at the extremes of the second dimension, but with different signs. Big band, mood/easy listening, and country and western, together with Higher Managers and Higher Sales, all are high and positive; hymns/gospel, soul/blues, and classical music, together with Artists, Higher Cultural, Skilled Service, Unskilled Service, and Laborers, all are high and negative.

We believe that there are two related ways of understanding the pairings in the second dimension. Both have to do with the racially distinct patterns of choosing the African-American-based music genres noted above. First, a number of Artists, together with the more venturesome High Cultural Professionals, seek out and cultivate what they consider déclassé urban musical forms—soul/blues and hymns/gospel—while many among the Higher Managers and their work associates, the Higher Sales workers, choose the aesthetically least challenging of musical forms—big band, mood/middle-of-the-road, and country music.[49] Second, African-Americans are most overrepresented in two of the groups lowest on the second dimension—Unskilled Service Workers and Laborers. As noted above, the music taste choices of blacks differ significantly from those of whites in the same occupation, and these race-specific patterns may account for the characteristics of the second dimension.

Discussion

Clearly, the reformulation of occupational status groups has worked well. The various groupings of occupations, as predicted, have distinctive patterns of aesthetic preferences and rates of arts participation. Just as important, musical taste does act as a status marker helping establish and maintain status boundaries. These findings should be taken into account in future research on the cultivation of differences.

Beyond these clear, if conventional, results, there are two unexpected findings that suggest the need for theoretical reformulation of the received idea of status hierarchy. The first has to do with the shape of the status hierarchy. The second draws attention to the distinctive and undertheorized characteristics of groups at different levels of the hierarchy.

Hierarchy as Pyramid Rather Than as Column

In effect, the taste scale developed here has discriminated better at the upper end of the occupational prestige hierarchy than further down. In each of the subsamples tested, classical music emerged as clearly the most prestigious, while the ranking further down the line varied greatly from one gender-, race-, and age-specific subsample to another.[50] This may be because of the nature of the survey instrument,[51] but it may also reflect the realities of the use of music to mark boundaries in the United States today.

Our results suggest that there is general agreement among Americans that classical music anchors the upper end of the taste hierarchy and thus constitutes cultural capital. At the same time the data suggest that there is less and less consensus on the ranking as one moves down the hierarchy of taste. Instead, there may be an increasingly large number of alternative forms having more or less equal taste value. As indicated by the results of this analysis, below classical music we find folk, then jazz, followed by middle-of-the-road and big band music near the middle, with rock, religious music, soul, and country music all near the bottom.

Insofar as this is a fair description of the underlying structure of tastes, the taste hierarchy represents not so much a slim column of taste genres one on top of the other as a pyramid with one elite taste at the top and more and more alternative forms at about the same level as one moves down the pyramid toward its base. In addition, as one approaches the bottom, musical taste serves to mark not only status levels but also the status boundaries between groups defined by age, gender, race, region, religion, life-style, etc. at roughly the same stratum level.[52]

The Omnivore-Univore Hypothesis

While the image of a pyramid helps conceptualize the unranked taste distinctions that are found among the nonelite tastes, there is still some difficulty in identifying the highest-ranking occupational status groups with elite taste. Even among the occupational status group with the highest taste rank, Higher Cultural Professionals, only 28.9 percent say that they like classical music best (see table 3), and more say that they like country and western music best than say that they like opera best! What is more, 13.3 percent of the Higher Cultural Professionals could not choose one kind of music that they like the best. Does this mean that taste in music is losing its efficacy as a status marker for the elite? Perhaps, but we think not. It may just mean that the image of the taste-exclusive highbrow, along with the ranking from "snob" to "slob," is obsolete.

There is mounting evidence that high-status groups not only participate more than do others in high-status activities but also tend to participate more often in most kinds of leisure activities.[53] In effect, elite taste is no longer defined as an expressed appreciation of the high art forms (and a moral disdain or bemused tolerance for all other aesthetic expressions). Now it is being redefined as an appreciation of the aesthetics of every distinctive form along with an appreciation of the high arts.[54] Because status is gained by knowing about and participating in (that is to say, by consuming) all forms, the term *omnivore* seems appropriate.[55]

One indicator of the profound change in the formulation of taste that is taking place, and bringing the omnivore to the fore, is a comparison of the coverage of country music in elite literary magazines. In the 1920s, elite magazine authors were shocked to find country music still flourishing in the hills and in the economically backward sections of the country. By the 1930s, it was romanticized as a fast-disappearing relic of a simpler purer past. In the 1970s, authors mocked the clothes, the accent, and the retrogressive unliberated lyrics. But, by the 1980s, elite magazine authors seriously instructed their readers in the music's aesthetic and introduced the music's most creative exponents in words touching on genius.[56]

If the omnivore is at the top of the taste pyramid, how should we characterize those at its base? It is clear from table 4 that occupational status groups near the base tend to have a lower incidence of all activities. This suggests the term *inactive*, but this is unfair because the SPPA survey asked few questions about nonelite leisure pursuits. Looking again at the far-right-hand column of table 3, it is clear that the lower-status occupational groups much more often are able to choose one genre of music that they like the best. Tentatively, the best appellation would seem to be *univore*, suggesting that those near the base of the pyramid tend to be actively involved in one, or at best just a few, alternative aesthetic traditions.

Putting together the ideas of omnivore-univore and pyramid in place of columnar hierarchy, there seems to be a contradiction. The apex of the pyramid is singular and its base variegated, yet high-status omni-vores choose many genres, while univores at the bottom tend to choose just one. But these two ideas can be fit together. The omnivore, we suggest, commands status by displaying any of a range of tastes as the situation may require, while the univore uses a particular taste to assert differences from others at approximately the same level holding a differ-ent group affiliation. Thus, the elaborated musical taste code of the omnivore member of the elite can acclaim classical music and yet, in the proper context, show passing knowledge of a wide range of musical forms. At the same time persons near the bottom of the pyramid are more likely to stoutly defend their restricted taste preference, be it religious music, country music, the blues, rap, or some other vernacular music, against persons espousing another of the lower-status musical forms.[57]

Appendix A
Taste as Status Marker or as Arts Appreciation

It is possible to use the available data to begin to address the question of arts participation as status marker versus arts participation as arts appreciation in three distinct ways. The first is to compare the proportion of each occupational group who say they like classical music best (table 3) with the proportion who have attended a classical music concert in the past year (table 4). Looking at the occupations with at least 10 percent attenders—all of the top eleven groups—the proportion of attenders is always higher than the proportion of those who like the music best. Since some in each group said they liked opera best and even more said that they liked no one form the best, the higher rate of attendance cannot simply be taken as an index of attendance strictly for status-affirming reasons.

The results are at least suggestive because the difference between liking best and concert attendance varies widely between the occupational groups. For three groups—Higher Managers, Lower Managers, and Lower Sales—attendance is more than three times greater than the measure of liking. The elevated incidence of concert attendance of these three groups cannot be explained by their unusually high choice for opera or for "no one form best." Their elevated incidence of attendance over professed liking, thus, may well represent a higher rate of attendance for purely status-affirming reasons. These three groups are cognate to French occupational groups that Bourdieu identifies as having lower cultural capital relative to other high-status occupational groups.[58]

Second, it is possible to compare the proportion in each occupational status group who attend public arts events with the proportion who consume the same art form in private via recordings and television.[59] It is assumed that public attendance may be for both status enhancement and for appreciation while private consumption is more likely engaged in for reasons of arts appreciation. This assumption is an oversimplification for numerous reasons. For example, public attendance depends on the arts activity being available, and home consumption may be engaged in to impress guests or to build familiarity with the arts that can be presented as taste for status enhancement. Data on classical music, opera, ballet, and nonmusical plays were examined. The relative incidence of public attendance versus private consumption (via records or television) varies widely from one occupational status group to another and from one art form to another, with no clear picture emerging.

Third, in an exploratory study, Ganzeboom contrasts what he calls the "information-processing" and "status-seeking" theories of differential high cultural activity.[60] The data available to him allowed for only equivocal conclusions. The SPPA, with its much larger sample and richer set of questions, made it possible to pursue the question further. Hayes, using the SPPA data set and our nineteen-fold classification of occupational status groups, made parallel path analysis of private and of public arts consumption. Income was found to have no direct effect on either public or private arts participation, while education was found to have the same moderate positive effect on both public and private consumption. In line with the hypothesis that public arts participation is engaged in for reasons of status as well as for appreciation, early arts socialization had a greater effect on private than on public arts consumption, and occupational prestige had more of an effect on public than on private arts consumption.[61]

Clearly, the dynamics of public versus private arts consumption is poorly understood and deserves further study as one means of getting at the dynamics of arts participation for status seeking and status marking versus participation for reasons of appreciation.

Appendix B
Criteria Used in Creating Occupational Status Groups

This appendix provides a more detailed discussion of the criteria used in placing specific job titles in each of the occupational status groups. The nineteen occupational status groups, together with representative job titles, are given in table 1.

Professionals

Jobs generally classed as professions are divided into five categories. *Cultural Professionals* are those whose job is to create, evaluate, interpret, teach, disseminate, and preserve ideas having to do with the nature of human existence and the relationships between people. All have the right to do this by reason of their formal training, certification, and evaluation by their peers. In many situations, their standing is signaled by the display of cultural capital. *Higher Cultural Professionals* such as clergymen and academic scholars have the authority to create and evaluate such ideas, while *Lower Cultural Professionals*, including social workers and schoolteachers, primarily apply and teach ideas according to the standards created and supervised in a bureaucratic fashion. For this reason, the period of training (ideally a doctoral degree) is generally much longer and the standards of certification higher for higher cultural workers than for Lower Cultural Professionals.

While increasing the number of categories means that unlike occupations can be separated, it creates another problem because persons who perform quite different kinds of work are still included together in some job categories. Lawyers provide a case in point. Because they shape and interpret the symbolic order that comprises the laws of social interaction, and because in the course of their work they must display cultural capital, they are classed as higher cultural professionals. Yet many lawyers simply apply the law and thus should be classed as lower cultural professionals, while other lawyers who deal with property law act more like technicians than cultural professionals. This data set, like most others, does not allow a more fine-grained partitioning of lawyers. They are all classed as higher cultural professionals on the grounds that their professional training is lengthy and their occupational ideology leads them to act like other culture makers. In this way, their professional socialization differs from that of lower cultural professionals such as social workers.

Technical Professionals are those who manipulate the physical world or who, like physicians, think of and manipulate the human body as a physical object. All have the right to do this based on their formal training, certification, and evaluation by their peers. *Higher Technical Professionals* such as engineers, geologists, and dentists require advanced graduate training and are given broad latitude in the scope of their work. *Lower Technical Professionals* such as registered nurses and accountants require technical education beyond high school and may be licensed by the state but generally work under the supervision of higher technicians or managers in a highly bureaucratic setting.

Artists create and recreate expressive symbols such as paintings, novels, and symphonic performances. Many artists, including painters and writers, compete for work in an open and rapidly changing market of aesthetic goods and services; those in the performing arts—dancers, actors, musicians—see their job opportunities wane as their bodies atrophy. While many have extensive years of schooling beyond high school, there is in the United States today no academy that authoritatively marks professional status or limits the number of job candidates for the performing arts. For this reason it is impossible to distinguish higher and lower artists on the grounds used for cultural and technical professionals.

Managers

Managers wield power by their control over other workers and their ability to allocate resources. While the distinction is conventionally made between the ownership and the control of the means of production, many employee-managers have far greater power than do most owner-managers, so we do not make this distinction here. It would be best to distinguish higher from lower managers by the span of control, by the value of resources commanded, or by the level of risk taken in wielding power. Unfortunately, no such measures are available in many data sets, including ours. For managers, however, income may be used as a proxy for the amount of power wielded on the job because, for managers, remuneration is closely associated with authority level and enterprise size. For this reason we have divided *Lower* and *Higher Managers* on the basis of their family income for the year preceding the survey.[62]

Salespersons

The task of salespersons is to convince others to purchase particular goods or services. To a greater or lesser extent, Salespersons must use not only a knowledge of the product but also a wide range of interpersonal skills to persuade their prospective customers to buy. For this reason salespersons are often compensated according to the monetary value of sales they make. Salespersons vary from street vendors to stockbrokers. *Higher Salespersons* are those like stockbrokers, manufacturers' representatives, and real estate agents who require a relatively high level of technical knowledge, trust, and expertise, who sell expensive goods and services, or who sell at wholesale to higher-status individuals. *Lower Salespersons* are those who—like retail salesclerks and peddlers—sell to the general public.

Clerical Workers

Clerical Workers process information and aid its transmission. Examples include bank tellers, meter readers, and office machine operators. In societies where few are able to read, some clerks are able to gain great power by controlling the flow of vital information; in advanced industrial societies with high rates of literacy and a battery of increasingly sophisticated clerical machines, the work of clerical information workers is increasingly like that of many persons in "manual" occupations.[63] At the same time, it is difficult to categorize persons into distinct clerical strata realistically. In market economies with high levels of average education, the variation in the skills and responsibilities among clerical occupations varies greatly across workplaces.[64] There is no clear basis, therefore, on which to distinguish higher and lower levels of clerical workers if only the information provided by detailed census categories for occupations is available.

Production/Construction Workers

Production workers are conventionally subdivided into three groups related to the amount of skill required on the job. We retain these distinctions, subdividing one to take into account the nature of the social interactions required on the job. *Skilled Manual Workers* include all the traditional craft occupations such as carpenters and machinists, whose work has not been substantially deskilled by the introduction of machinery. It also includes those high-skill manual jobs that have emerged in the twentieth century, including telephone installers and crane operators.

Because, as drivers, their work generally involves greater contact with the public and less close supervision or control by the pace of machines, *Transportation Workers* are separated from *Semiskilled Operatives*—those who typically work at machines or on assembly lines in a factory or shop context.

Unskilled workers—here called *Laborers*—are involved in heavy physical labor in construction or dirty work like garbage collection requiring no great training or skill. Laborers work under the close direct supervision of foremen or craftspersons.

Service Workers

Traditionally, service workers were attached to households and performed routine manual tasks that otherwise would have been done by family members. Such jobs included maid, cook, butler, and night watchman. Service workers are conventionally ranked below other nonfarm manual workers or below all but laborers.[65] While household size has grown ever smaller throughout the twentieth century, the service sector of the economy has grown rapidly as the kinds of jobs that were done by servants are now performed by an ever proliferating number of independent occupations. Some of these new job categories are unskilled, while others require technical education and involve direct social contact with high-status individuals or involve the tasks of keeping law and order. We distinguish three kinds of service workers.

Protective Service Workers may be licensed to shoot weapons, direct the flow of traffic, detain persons, and enter the property of others in order to safeguard persons and property. Their warrant to intervene and control the actions of others in the name of the general good is usually signaled by the wearing of distinctive uniforms and special badges. Examples of Protective Service Workers include police officers, firemen, and guards.

The nonuniformed service workers can be divided into two sections on the basis of the importance attached to the skills they perform or the intimate nature of their service. *Skilled Service Workers* have undergone special training, and many are formally certified to perform the service. Examples include barbers, dental assistants, and cosmetologists. *Unskilled Service Workers* are generally expected to be inconspicuous in the performance of their service and require little education or training. Examples include maids, orderlies, and waiters.

Farm Workers
Farm workers are kept separate from nonfarm occupations because they live in relative isolation from other people, they work outdoors under conditions largely structured by the exigencies of the weather, and they tend to consider farming more a way of life than a job. For farm owner/managers—here called *Farmers*—the job is often romanticized as the "family farm/ranch, which is the backbone of the American way of life." Both farmers and farm laborers are largely isolated from others in the performance of their work, but farm management requires more education and involves interacting with a range of persons in managerial and sales positions. For *Farm Laborers* the way of life is more often enforced by the exigencies of poor education and poverty, compounded in many cases by exploitation based on ethnic or racial discrimination.

Appendix C
Expected Musical Tastes of the Nineteen Occupational Status Groups

We suggest here the expected musical taste level of each of the nineteen occupational status groups based on the findings in two bodies of literature. The first is the research on cultural capital inspired by the work of Pierre Bourdieu and his colleagues.[66] The second is the wide range of studies inspired by the seminal works of C. Wright Mills and Everett Hughes that detail job characteristics and social relations on the job.[67]

Professionals generally depend on cultural capital in marking status boundaries and thus should rank higher in musical taste than managers, who depend more on economic capital and organization resources; these two elements of what Bourdieu calls the dominating class should rank above all the dominated classes in musical taste.[68] On the basis of previous evidence and theorizing, it is possible to rank some occupational groups relative to others, but not completely to order all nineteen groups relative to each other. The rationale for our expected ordering of occupational groups follows.

Higher Cultural Professionals should rank the highest of all occupational groups because they are the arbiters of cultural capital. By showing taste, they are able to consolidate their claim to elite social status. *Lower Cultural Professionals* should rank next because their jobs involve maintaining the moral order and their occupational status depends on maintaining the aesthetic status quo. *Artists* produce the expressive symbols some of which eventually become the mark of the highest taste. Yet they are often rewarded for deviating somewhat from the conventional standard of taste.[69] Such "bohemianism" is predicted to lead artists to select as their favorite from a wide range of musical genres, and thus their average taste level will not be as high as the more conventional cultural professionals.[70]

Higher Technical Professionals depend for their livelihood on the ability to make crucial decisions about physical objects or people treated as objects; thus, cultural capital is not important on the job, but it is still important in their claim to elite status. *Lower Technical Professionals* are classed as professionals by convention, but their work involves the manipulation of objects or persons as objects under the supervision of others; also, their focused technical education does not inculcate elite tastes. Lower technical professionals may thus rank well down the line of all occupational groups.

Higher Managers present something of a problem because they include both high-income owners and managers. Possessing economic capital, owners should not need as much cultural capital as professionals. Managers, however, require cultural capital to show their readiness for advancement to positions of greater authority, where they mingle with high-status professionals. Because of this need to show conventional high taste, higher managers may well rank as high as higher technical professionals. *Lower Managers* are less financially successful. These are not the captains of industry and organization but the supervisors of clerical or manual workers. Cultural capital may be of some benefit in relating to their superiors but is of little use in relating to their subordinates.

Since the jobs held by salespersons require continual impression management, it behooves them to have tastes roughly comparable with those of their clients. This means that the rank of the two types of sales workers should be very different. *Higher Salespersons* continually interact on a familiar basis as quasi equals with professionals and higher managers; therefore, their rank should be roughly comparable with the average of the groups discussed above. Since *Lower Salespersons* deal with the general public, they should have tastes comparable to the average of the entire sample. Clerical workers, as noted above, now perform tasks little different from those of many factory operatives, but they work in offices rather than factories. They are expected to dress and act "presentably" to the general public. They should rank in the middle with lower sales workers.

Production and construction workers have manual jobs out of the view of high-status people and the public at large. The work of some requires great skill, but their jobs do not require them to interact with high-status persons; thus, they have no reason to develop high-status tastes. Since they know that their work is held in low esteem and they interact primarily with persons of their own occupational group, they may nurture tastes based in their ethnic or class origins that are contrary to elite tastes.[71] Accordingly, the four kinds of production and construction workers should be near the bottom of the taste hierarchy.

Skilled Manual Workers—craftsmen—have been called "blue-collar aristocrats."[72] Although given specific tasks to accomplish, they have great discretion in how to do the work. Their skill is often certified by craft, government, or organizational tests. Their income is high and their jobs more secure than those of other manual workers. Musical taste and the other elements of cultural capital should be unimportant to skilled workers except insofar as their relatively affluent middle-class life-styles bring them into contact with higher-status persons.[73] Their musical taste, therefore, should rank quite low, but still somewhat higher than those of other manual workers. *Semiskilled Manual Workers*—operatives—typically work at machines under close supervision in shops or factories. Their job security is low, and while they may belong to labor unions, their identification at work is likely to be with their gender and ethnic peers. Their tastes should be at the average of manual workers. *Transport Workers* are conventionally classed with semiskilled operatives. This is appropriate to their skill level, but their jobs as drivers mean that they have greater discretion in performing their tasks and often require them to interact with lower managers and members of the general public. Their taste level should therefore be above that of operatives and almost as high as that of craftsmen. *Laborers* perform unskilled heavy or dirty manual work, often under the supervision of skilled manual workers. They have no social contact with the public at large, and their taste preferences should rank lowest of any urban workers.

Service workers are conventionally ranked below other nonfarm manual workers or below all but laborers.[74] On the basis of the status of those they serve, however, we expect wide differences among the three sorts of service workers that we have identified. *Skilled Service* workers interact with the general public, but the performance of their job depends on projecting something of the higher status of the technical persons whom they represent in delivering their services. Their rank, thus, should be higher than all "manual" workers. *Unskilled Service* workers perform routine tasks and are expected to be inconspicuous. Their rank should thus be lower than any group mentioned above but higher than that of factory workers. *Protective Service* workers are paid to protect life and property and represent law and order in their official actions. On this basis, their taste level should be somewhat above the average of all occupational groups because it is the lives and property of the well to do and of corporations that most protective workers are paid to safeguard.

By reason of their rural residence, farmers have historically had the least contact with cosmopolitan tastes. *Farm Laborers* are, thus, both isolated and unskilled. They are most likely of all groups to nurture tastes of ethnic, religious, or racial origin and should occupy the bottom rung on the taste hierarchy. By reason of their managerial functions, *Farmers*—farm owners and managers—should rank with other managers. Yet because of their isolation and contact primarily with farm laborers, they should rank just above farm laborers. Farm owner-managers historically have developed distinctly different cultural tastes from those of the farm laborers with whom they associate. The nineteenth-century landed aristocracy of Europe and plantation owners of the

American South provide vivid cases in point, but cognate patterns of isolation probably operate in the United States today, albeit to a lesser degree, where American farmers employ a number of nonfamily members.

Notes

We gratefully acknowledge the useful comments on earlier drafts made by Karen Campbell, Daniel Cornfield, Paul DiMaggio, Terrill Hayes, Jennifer Jasper, Sue Hinze Jones, Mary Karpos, Michèle Lamont, Oscar Miller, John Mohr, Claire Peterson, and Karl Erik Rosengren. Thanks also to Miller and Dee Warmath for facilitating the data analysis. The data for the study were made available through the generosity of Thomas Bradshaw, research director of the National Endowment for the Arts. His predecessor, Harold Horowitz, is gratefully acknowledged for his support Richard Peterson at the National Endowment for the Arts, Washington, D.C., while he began development of what became the Survey of Public Participation in the Arts.

1. See, in particular, John Berger, *Ways of Seeing* (New York: Penguin, 1972); Paul DiMaggio, "Cultural Entrepreneurship in Nineteenth-Century Boston," pts. 1, 2, *Media, Culture and Society* 4 (1982): 33–50, 303–22, and "Cultural Boundaries and Structural Change" (this volume); Lawrence W. Levine, *Highbrow/Lowbrow: The Emergence of Cultural Hierarchy in America* (Cambridge, Mass.: Harvard University Press, 1988); and Tia DeNora, "Musical Patronage and Social Change in Beethoven's Vienna," *American Journal of Sociology* 97 (September 1991): 310.

2. Paul DiMaggio and Michael Useem, "Cultural Democracy in a Period of Cultural Expansion: The Social Composition of Arts Audiences in the United States," *Social Problems* 26 (1979): 180–197, and "Social Class and Arts Consumption: The Origins and Consequences of Class Differences in Exposure to the Arts in America," *Theory and Society* 5 (1978): 132–49.

3. On this point, see Richard Peterson, *Arts Audience Statistics and Culture Indicators: A Review of Contemporary Approaches* (Washington, D.C.: National Endowment for the Arts, 1980). In addition, Michèle Lamont and Annette Lareau ("Cultural Capital: Allusions, Gaps and Glissandos in Recent Theoretical Developments," *Sociological Theory* 6 [1988]: 153–68) cite a number of researchers who find no clear link between status and taste.

4. Michèle Lamont, *Money, Morals, and Manners: The Culture of the French and the American Upper-Middle Class* (Chicago: University of Chicago Press, 1992).

5. David Halle, "The Audience for Abstract Art" (this volume).

6. Joseph Bensman and Robert Lilienfeld, *Craft and Consciousness: Occupational Technique and the Development of World Images* (New York: Aldine de Gruyter, 1991).

7. Randall Collins, *Conflict Sociology: Toward an Explanatory Science* (New York: Academic, 1975).

8. James A. Davis, "Achievement Variables and Class Cultures: Family, Schooling, Job, and Forty-nine Dependent Variables in the Cumulative GSS," *American Sociological Review* 47 (1982): 569–86.

9. The evidence is not, however, as ambiguous as it first appears; the works showing the importance of occupation, on the one hand, tend to be ethnographic case studies of selected occupational specialties (e.g., Bensman and Lilienfeld, *Craft and Consciousness*) or essays about the grounds for distinctions among social classes and "taste cultures" (e.g., Herbert Gans, *Popular Culture and High Culture* [New York: Basic, 1974]; and Collins, *Conflict Sociology*, 61–75). The studies showing occupation having little or no effect on patterns of cultural choice, on the other hand, tend to be statistical analyses of survey data that look for the effects of occupation net of the effect of other social class–related variables, most notably, income and education (see, e.g., Norval D. Glenn, *Social Stratification* [New York: Wiley, 1969]; and Davis, "Achievement Variables"). Surveys that do not partial the effects of education and income from occupation tend to show a close association between occupation and taste (see, e.g., William H. Form and Gregory P. Stone, "Urbanism, Anonymity, and Status Symbolism," *American Journal of Sociology* 62 [1957]: 504–14; and Pierre Bourdieu, *Distinction: A Social Critique of the Judgement of Taste* [Cambridge, Mass.: Harvard University Press, 1984]).

10. The survey was administered to samples monthly throughout 1982, but only during the two months of November and December 1982 were respondents asked all the musical choice and arts-related questions. Thus, only the data from these two months could be used for this study. Full details of the SPPA are provided in John P. Robinson, Carol A. Keegan, Terry Hanford, and Timothy A. Triplett, *Public Participation in the Arts: Final Report on the 1982 Survey* (College Park: University of Maryland, 1985). Paul DiMaggio and Francie Ostrower ("Participation in the Arts by Black and White Americans," *Social Forces* 63 [1990]: 753–78) provide an excellent illustration of how the data can be used to answer sophisticated research questions.

11. Bourdieu, *Distinction;* DiMaggio, "Cultural Entrepreneurship," and "Cultural Boundaries."

12. On surveys of the general population, see DiMaggio and Useem, "Cultural Democracy"; on analyses of attenders of arts events, see DiMaggio and Useem, "Social Class and Arts Consumption."

13. Michael Hughes and Richard A. Peterson, "Isolating Cultural Choice Patterns in the U.S. Population," *American Behavioral Scientist* 26 (1983): 459–78.

14. A very small number of persons chose "none" or "other" or, refusing the request to choose, said "all equally." Because too few persons chose "opera," "bluegrass," and "barbershop" as their favorite musical form, anyone choosing these categories was eliminated from the analysis.

15. John Mohr and Paul DiMaggio, "Patterns of Occupational Inheritance of Cultural Capital" (paper delivered at the eighty-fifth annual meeting of the American Sociological Association, Washington, D.C., 1990).

16. Edward Shils, "The Mass Society and Its Culture," in *Culture for the Millions,* ed. Norman Jacobs (Princeton, N.J.: Van Nostrand, 1961), 1–27. Gans, *Popular Culture and High Culture.*

17. Richard A. Peterson and Paul DiMaggio, "From Region to Class, the Changing Locus of Country Music: A Test of the Massification Hypothesis," *Social Forces* 53 (1975): 497–506; John S. Reed and Philip Marsden, *Leisure Time Use in the South: A Secondary Analysis* (Washington, D.C.: National Endowment for the Arts, 1980), 2–10.

18. Charles Keil, *Urban Blues* (Chicago: University of Chicago Press, 1966); Richard Peterson, "Between Art and Pop: What Has Sustained Country Music?" (paper delivered at the eighty-fifth annual meeting of the American Sociological Association, Washington, D.C., 1990).

19. Alba Edwards, *A Social-Economic Grouping of the Gainful Workers of the United States* (Washington, D.C.: U.S. Census Bureau, 1938).

20. Davis, "Achievement Variables and Class Cultures."

21. In forming the occupational groups we have taken into account five lines of theorizing and research. These include (1) the issue of power and knowledge in the control of the means of production raised by the debate over the rise of a "new class" of experts and bureaucratic functionaries (see Ivan Szelenyi and Bill Martin, "The Three Waves of New Class Theories," *Theory and Society* 17 [1988]: 645–67; Charles Derber, William Schwartz, and Yale Magrass, *Power in the Highest Degree: Professionals and the Rise of the New Mandarin Order* [New York: Oxford University Press, 1990]); (2) the growing importance of licensing and certification in some occupational spheres (see Randall Collins, *The Credential Society* [New York: Academic, 1979]; Eliot Freidson, *Professional Powers: A Study of the Institutionalization of Formal Knowledge* [Chicago: University of Chicago Press, 1986]); (3) the split in the upper classes between those occupations controlling primarily economic capital and those relying more on cultural capital (see Bourdieu, *Distinction;* Pierre Bourdieu and L. Boltanski, "Changes in Social Structure and Changes in the Demand for Education," in *Contemporary Europe: Social Structure and Cultural Patterns,* ed. S. Giner and M. Scotford Archer [London: Routledge & Kegan Paul, 1977], 197–227); (4) the growing importance of the control over the dissemination of information (James R. Beniger, *The Control Revolution* [Cambridge, Mass.: Harvard University Press, 1986]); and, finally, (5) the social ecology of the workplace—whether occupational incumbents deal primarily with technical questions, with people of their own occupation, with the general public, or with persons with greater power, economic capital, or cultural capital (Bensman and Lilienfeld, *Craft and Consciousness;* David Halle, *America's Working Man* [Chicago: University of Chicago Press, 1984]; Rick Fantasia, *Cultures of Solidarity* [Berkeley and Los Angeles: University of California Press, 1988]).

22. In saying "documented," we recognizing that our classification misses those many thousands of workers in the United States who are employed in illicit and illegal activities in criminal occupations.

23. We have cross-tabulated the data for the SPPA respondents on the basis of our nineteen occupational groups by the ten categories of musical preference. The frequencies in this table were then fit by a multidimensional form of the log-multiplicative model II developed by Leo Goodman and explained in his "The Analysis of Cross-classified Data Having Ordered and/or Unordered Categories: Association Models, Correlation Models, and Asymmetry Models for Contingency Tables with or without Missing Entries," *Annals of Statistics* 13 (1985): 10–69.

This model has a great advantage over other models in that it requires no a priori assumptions about scale values or even the ordering of the categories of occupation and musical preference. Estimated parameters for this model provide scores for those categories that provide the best fit for the observed pattern of row-by-column association. These scores are normalized to have a mean of zero, and the sum of squared differences from the mean are constrained to equal one. The information provided by these scores involves the relative differences among category scores, not the absolute value of these scores. The version of the model employed here permits the estimation of more than one dimension of row and column scores, allowing us to estimate scores for several underlying bases of the observed table of associations (Goodman, "Analysis of Cross-classified Data"; Mark Becker and Clifford C. Clogg, "Analysis of Sets of Two-Way Contingency Tables Using Association Models," *Journal of the American Statistical Association* 84 [1989]: 142–51).

Thus, the logic of our analysis involves a conformity inductive method since our statistical procedure inductively discovers the optimal scale values for occupational status groups and music genres, and we observe the degree to which the resulting scales conform to our theoretical expectations.

24. The "deviance" (deviance is the likelihood-ratio chi square and can be partitioned and interpreted in a manner analogous to explained variance in a regression model) of the first scale under this model is 57 percent of that under the baseline model of independence between occupation and music preference. (The deviance under this model is 302.0 with 136 degrees of freedom, while that under the baseline model is 703.4 with 162 degrees of freedom.) Thus, the major portion, but not nearly all, of the relation between occupational group and music preference can be predicted on the basis of unidimensional scales of occupation and music taste.

The addition of a second dimension of row-column scores to the original one-dimensional model reduces the deviance by an additional 18 percent of that under the baseline model. The deviance for this two-dimensional log-multiplicative model is 179.1 with 112 degrees of freedom, so that only 25 percent of the baseline deviance remains unaccounted for.

25. As noted earlier, too few people chose opera as their favorite type of music for it to be included in the statistical modeling. Opera may rank as high as or higher than classical music.

26. Since the method seeks out the ordering of occupations that best fits

the pattern of choices on all ten types of music simultaneously, it is not surprising that the ordering of any given music genre is not perfect. In addition, special factors may be at work in some cases. For example, few blacks chose country and western music as their favorite, and, at the same time, blacks are overrepresented in several occupations, including lower service workers and laborers. This has had the effect of depressing the proportion of these two occupational groups reporting country and western music as their favorite music genre in table 3.

27. On classical music, see DiMaggio, "Cultural Entrepreneurship"; Levine, *Highbrow/Lowbrow*, 32. On country music, see Peterson and DiMaggio, "From Region to Class"; Reed and Marsden, *Leisure Time Use*, secs. 2.4–2.11.

28. Respondents might infer the term *folk music* to refer to the secular music of their own ethnic, national, or religious background. Since foreign-born persons who are most likely to make such a choice cluster in the lower-ranked occupations, their choice of "folk" would have given it a rank near the bottom among music genres. Thus, we infer that such people did not choose this genre. It is more likely that those persons who do like the music that represents their particular heritage tend to refer to it by that name and not by the generic term *folk*. The small number of responses (less than 1 percent of the sample) of this kind, including "Hungarian," "Yiddish," and "Irish music," were coded "other."

29. Bill C. Malone, *Southern Music/American Music* (Lexington: University of Kentucky Press, 1979).

30. DiMaggio and Ostrower, "Participation in the Arts," 35.

31. Richard Peterson, "A Process Model of the Folk, Pop, and Fine Art Phases of Jazz," in *American Music: From Storyville to Woodstock,* ed. Charles Nanry (New Brunswick, N.J.: Trans-Action Books; New York: Dutton, 1972), 135–51.

32. The one-dimensional model for whites accounts for 60 percent of the deviance under the baseline model for whites, only 3 percent above the explained deviance for the test modeling the entire sample. This lends modest support to the idea that the differing choice patterns of whites and blacks systematically reduced the explained variance in the initial total-sample modeling.

33. The number of blacks in the sample was too small to allow for a comparable race-specific ranking using black respondents.

34. Three pairs of adjacent occupations switch their order. These include higher technical and artists; farmers and unskilled service; and semiskilled transport and laborers. In no case is the numerical distance of the shift as large as those for the music genres discussed above.

35. Bourdieu, *Distinction*, 23–24.

36. M. Therese Stafford ("Occupational Sex Segregation and Inequality in the United States" [University of Texas at Austin, 1990, typescript]) provides evidence that supports our finding that some service workers have high prestige

and also that there is a wider range between upper and lower service workers than for any other occupational group. Dividing each of the eight conventional nonfarm categories of occupations into three levels based on their SES scores, she shows that the difference between upper and lower service workers is almost twice as great as that for any other occupational category.

37. Lemasters, E. E. *Blue-Collar Aristocrat* (Madison: University of Wisconsin Press, 1975), 28; Bensman and Lilienfeld, *Craft and Consciousness,* 7–8.

38. The program for the log-multiplicative modeling is new, and, as of this writing, we know of no computer program that can estimate the threshold of statistically significant differences between scale scores.

39. It is hard to get a picture of the leisure pursuits of protective service workers—and the other non-high-status occupations as well—because this survey, which focused primarily on the arts, did not ask questions about such activities as gun collecting, CB radio, sports participation, home brewing, hunting, fishing, and volunteer work. In addition, the survey lumped together activities of quite different sorts. For example, does "exercise" refer to aerobics or muscle building, and does "attend sports" refer to the likes of polo or professional wrestling? In addition, the survey grouped quite different activities. For example, "home and auto repair" and "hiking, camping, and boating."

40. Maryaltani Karpos, "Leisure Lifestyles of the Armed and Dangerous" (Vanderbilt University, 1991, typescript).

41. In an analysis of the leisure activities of the occupational status groups not discussed here, farmers rank lowest or very near the lowest on television viewing, exercising, hiking, camping and boating, and game playing.

42. As Judith Blau (*The Shape of Culture* [Cambridge: Cambridge University Press, 1989]) and Michèle Lamont ("The Refined") clearly show, the different regions of the country have quite distinct tastes, and a thorough analysis will need to take region into account.

43. Edward L. Fink, John P. Robinson, and Sue Dowden, "The Structure of Music Preference and Attendance," *Communication Research* 12 (1985): 301–18.

44. Marshall Greenberg and Ronald E. Frank, "Isolating Cultural Choice Patterns in the U.S. Population," *American Behavioral Scientist* 26 (1983): 439–58; Fink, Robinson, and Dowden, "Structure of Music Preference," 310.

45. DiMaggio and Ostrower, "Participation in the Arts," 760–62.

46. Pierre Bourdieu and J.-C. Passeron, *Reproduction in Education Society, and Culture* (Beverly Hills, Calif.: Sage, 1977), 74–76.

47. Glenn, *Social Stratification,* 28–32; Davis, "Achievement Variables and Class Cultures," 580.

48. Occupation, as conventionally measured, may be a less powerful predictor simply because education is better measured as "years of schooling" and income is better measured as "dollars earned" than occupation is measured by the conventional groupings of occupations. Thus, a more sensitive construction of occupational categories along the lines developed in this research may show

occupational group to be a more powerful predictor in a wide range of research arenas.

49. Country music is not conventionally considered bland in the sense that middle-of-the-road music is (Malone, *Southern Music/American Music*), but the style had attracted many new fans when the survey was made in 1980 and was chosen by more persons than any other form. Many of these new fans were the followers of the likes of Kenny Rogers, Crystal Gayle, and Lee Greenwood. Peterson ("Between Art and Pop") has called these "soft-shell" fans, in contrast with the followers of George Jones, George Straight, and Loretta Lynn, whom he terms "hard-core" fans. Some of the latter, in fact, would have chosen bluegrass rather than country and western as their favorite, thus further increasing the soft-shell representation among those who choose country and western music.

50. This finding is reflected not only in the analysis reported here but also in analyses not reported.

51. The SPPA survey used in this study was created to understand the dynamics of participation in the fine arts better and may not, therefore, have adequately canvassed the range of popular and quasi-folk music choices available as alternatives to art music.

52. This substantive conjecture is in line with the research findings of Judith Blau, "High Culture as Mass Culture," *Society* 23 (1986): 65–69, and "The Elite Arts, More or Less de Rigueur: A Comparative Analysis of Metropolitan Culture," *Social Forces* 64 (1986): 875–905; DiMaggio, "Cultural Entrepreneurship," and "Cultural Boundaries"; DiMaggio and Ostrower, "Participation in the Arts"; and Peterson, "Process Model."

53. DiMaggio and Useem, "Social Class and Arts Consumption"; Richard A. Peterson and Michael J. Hughes, "Social Correlates of Five Patterns of Arts Participation," in *Contributions to the Sociology of the Arts,* ed. Elit Nikolov (Sofia: Bulgarian Research Institute for Culture, 1984), 128–36; Robinson et al., *Public Participation in the Arts;* Paul DiMaggio, "Classification in the Arts," *American Sociological Review* 52 (1987): 440–55.

54. Richard A. Peterson, "Audience and Industry Origins of the Crisis in Classical Music Programming: Toward World Music," in *The Future of the Arts: Public Policy and Arts Research,* ed. David B. Pankratz and Valerie B. Morris (New York: Praeger, 1990), 207–27.

55. The word *dilettante* has been suggested, but this connotes a person who dabbles in a number of aesthetic forms and performs for a more or less disinterested elite audience. The omnivore has more in common with the "other-directed" character type described by David Riesman in his *The Lonely Crowd* (New Haven, Conn.: Yale University Press, 1950). What the two have in common is that they change to fit the circumstances of their immediate surroundings. The two are different in that Riesman's character characteristically found safety in adapting the blandest of tastes and values while the omnivore may display a range of quite different tastes as the circumstances demand.

56. This brief review is based on an informal reading of dozens of "outsider" articles written about country music over the past eighty years. A detailed analysis of this special genre could reveal a great deal about the construction of taste and about the changing images of country vs. city and North vs. South.

57. Musical tastes may well operate in a way roughly parallel to Bernstein's findings for linguistic codes (see Basil Bernstein, *Class, Codes and Control* [London: Routledge & Kegan Paul, 1977], vol. 3). Bernstein distinguishes between the elaborated linguistic code of the well-educated English elite and the restricted linguistic code of the poorly educated working class.

58. Bourdieu, *Distinction*.

59. Terrell H. Hayes, "Public and Private Arts Consumption: Thoughts on a Single Conception Model" (Vanderbilt University, 1991, typescript).

60. Harry B. G. Ganzeboom, "Explaining Differential Participation in High-cultural Activities: A Confrontation of Information-processing and Status-seeking Theories," in *Theoretical Models and Empirical Analyses: Contributions to the Explanations of Individual Actions and Collective Phenomena*, ed. Werner Raub (Utrecht: E. S. Publications, 1982).

61. Hayes, "Public and Private Arts Consumption."

62. While it is expedient to use income in differentiating higher and lower managers, this means that for these two manager job categories income is confounded with occupation at the level of the individual.

63. Beniger, *Control Revolution*; Robert T. Michael, Heidi I. Hartmann, and Brigid O'Farrell, eds., *Pay Equity: Empirical Inquiries* (Washington, D.C.: National Academy Press, 1989).

64. Toby L. Parcel, "Comparable Worth, Occupational Labor Markets, and Occupational Earnings: Results from the 1980 Census," in *Pay Equity: Empirical Inquiries*, ed. Robert T. Michael, Heidi I. Hartmann, and Brigid O'Farrell, 134–52.

65. Davis, "Achievement Variables and Class Cultures"; Glenn, *Social Stratification*.

66. See esp. Bourdieu, *Distinction*; Pierre Bourdieu, "The Social Space and the Genesis of Groups," *Theory and Society* 14 (1985): 723–44; Pierre Bourdieu and Jean-Claude Passeron, [1970] *Reproduction in Education, Society and Culture* (Beverly Hills, Calif.: Sage, 1977 [1970]); Bourdieu and Boltanski, "Changes in Social Structure," 209.

67. C. Wright Mills, *White Collar* (New York: Oxford University Press, 1953); Everett C. Hughes, *Men and Their Work* (Glencoe, Ill.: Free Press, 1958).

68. Bourdieu, *Distinction*, 116.

69. Charles R. Simpson, *SoHo: The Artist in the City* (Chicago: University of Chicago Press, 1981); Howard S. Becker, *Art Worlds* (Berkeley: University of California Press, 1982); Bensman and Lilienfeld, *Craft and Consciousness*, 32.

70. Sample artists do prove to have much more wide-ranging tastes than any other group, and the exclusion of this occupational status group from the

study would have markedly increased the predictive power of the statistical model we have employed.

71. Halle, *America's Working Man;* Fantasia, *Cultures of Solidarity;* Paul Willis, *Common Culture* (Boulder, Colo.: Westview, 1990).

72. Edgar E. LeMasters, *Blue-Collar Aristocrats* (Madison: University of Wisconsin Press, 1975).

73. Halle, *America's Working Man,* 220–28.

74. Davis, "Achievement Variables and Class Cultures," 81; Glenn, *Social Stratification,* 28–32.

EIGHT

Barrier or Leveler? The Case of the Art Museum

Vera L. Zolberg

"The role of the museum is to expand the elite."
Director of an American art museum

". . . provide an elite experience for everyone."
Joshua Taylor

"Culture is what remains when all else has been forgotten."
Edouard Herriot

For those who believe that culture is the preserve of the "happy few," that sensitive minority of whom Stendhal considered himself the spokesman, no one else—neither the unschooled worker and peasant nor the insensitive, newly wealthy philistine—is capable of appreciating the arts. Unlike the majority who reduce the arts to monetary value, the happy few value the arts in the disinterested manner appropriate to an aristocracy. In these terms, the idea that the arts could ever reach a broader public is utopian.

The world has changed since the first part of the nineteenth century, when Stendhal was active: despite inadequacies, in industrialized countries workers no longer constitute an uneducated mass; businessmen and bankers are well schooled; elite patronage or market value alone does not determine the success or failure of artworks. Modern countries, whether liberal democracies or authoritarian states, are committed to making previously elite-based art forms available to all who wish access to them. Indeed, these publics should be educated to *want* such access. From being a private good or a matter of personal taste, cultural capacity has come to be considered a right of citizenship that redounds to a nation's standing in the world.

If this characterization is correct, then how can it be that studies of cultural institutions, such as art museums, show that, despite their commitment to democratization, they seem not to reach out beyond the highly educated? For, despite the impression of crowding, it appears that the public for serious music, theater, and art museums continues to be drawn disproportionately from those who have had at least some university education. Their relative failure forces us to ask whether the democratization of art is really a high priority. In this essay, I look at how two countries, France and the United States, make the arts available to or keep them away from their citizens. Both nations share a democratic tradition, but they emphasize different rationales for their cultural policies. In the United States, bringing art to a large public has tended to be justified on the grounds that it has moral or civic value; in France, cultural policy, democratizing or not, has been directed toward the symbolic task of glorifying the nation (Mesnard 1974).

It may seem inappropriate to focus on art as a way of understanding social structure and mobility. After all, is it not the educational institution that is directly related to social status? I argue that the art museum provides an appropriate object for study because, beyond the function manifestly assigned them, of preserving aesthetic values, art museums are said to create and reinforce inequalities in society (Bourdieu and Darbel [1969] 1990). For the United States, Paul DiMaggio has demonstrated that the boundaries between high art and popular art were created in the nineteenth century through policies of newly founded institutions of high culture, art museums and symphony orchestras (DiMaggio 1982). In France, Pierre Bourdieu has argued that artistic taste is more than an idiosyncratic pleasure; it is a cultural weapon in the battle around the persistence of structures of social reproduction (Bourdieu [1979] 1984).

As convincing as Bourdieu's arguments may be, others insist that emphasizing the exclusionary nature of cultural capital neglects the fact that individuals emerging from dominated groups have, nevertheless, succeeded in acquiring scarce capital and using it effectively. Some have questioned his interpretations because he omits certain types of data (Robinson and Garnier 1985), pays insufficient attention to mediating processes (Swartz 1981; DiMaggio and Mohr 1985), exaggerates the status-related bases of taste (Halle 1987, and this volume), and neglects cross-national differences (Lamont 1989).

It is not my intention to resolve all aspects of the ongoing debate among these scholars, but their discussions inform my analysis of art museums in France and the United States. I begin by presenting aspects of these museums in turn, from the perspective of the relations between social inequality and the mission assigned to art museums vis à vis their publics, the art museums' treatment of their visitors, and the perceptions of different sectors of the public of these institutions. Beyond statements of intention, I take the standing of and structures of education in the art museums as indicators of the institutions' commitment to democratization. I then consider how a narrow interpretation of the role of public education may enhance the structures of inequality in both France and the United States. Finally, I suggest research strategies appropriate to filling persistent gaps in knowledge and to understanding the relation between the arts and social status.

The American Art Museum: A Tradition of Welcome to the Public?

American art museums are extremely heterogeneous: they range from huge "public" institutions with encyclopedic collections to small galleries; they may encompass a variety of works or be specialized to the point of displaying the oeuvre of a single artist; some have no permanent collection at all. Considered as educational institutions, some American art museums merely provide walls, lighting, and labels for pictures, and others have institutionalized elaborate programs of organized docent-led visits, didactic displays, video presentations, and lecture series. In spite of their diversity, however, they have some things in common.

Founded and governed by men of wealth as personal possessions, art museums came to be staffed by individuals who sought to transform them into professionally run organizations with high-quality art collections that are relatively autonomous of trustee control. At the same time, in return for public aid, direct and indirect, they became committed to providing service to a broad public. These two goals have been reiterated by reformers who call for both democratization and professionalization. In times of scarcity, when hard choices have to be made, budget cutting has almost always been made first in the public mission, whereas collecting is preserved.

Beset by these conflicting claims, American art museums seem to achieve one goal only at the expense of another. Nevertheless, large public art museums, most of them supported by a combination of private and local governmental funds, have a considerable track record in education and, like other bureaucratic organizations, have for a long time evaluated their performance by counting how many visitors and members they attract.

The simple fact that museums draw large numbers of visitors, especially since the Second World War, should not be taken uncritically as an indicator of substantial democratization. In reanalyzing over three hundred audience studies from a variety of cultural institutions, government agencies, and performing arts groups, DiMaggio, Useem, and Brown (1978) found that, on the whole, although museums in general attract a more representative portion of the American public than do live arts performances, which draw a more affluent and well-educated audience,[1] art museums were not bringing in a public representative of lower-status groups. Those who frequent art museums tend to be better educated, better off, and older and are more likely to be professionals than those who visit history, science, or other museums.[2] Recent surveys by the U.S. Census Bureau generally confirm the finding that art museums continue to attract professionals, managerial employees, and students but repel operatives, laborers, and service workers (Robinson 1985).

These findings raise the question as to whether this is simply because of the nature of their collections or because they deliberately seek a high-status public. Although it is impossible to answer directly, in the United States museum people themselves cast doubt on their openness to individuals lacking facility in dealing with what Pierre Bourdieu has termed the *cultural capital* of legitimate art (Bourdieu [1979] 1984). In order to gain greater perspective on the achievements or failings of art museums in America, it is helpful to look at art museums abroad.

Barriers in French Art Museums

Until recently, reaching out to welcome visitors was an activity in which most European art museums lagged behind many museums in the United States. Especially since World War II, however, France, among other nations, has tried to expand the art museum public and enlarge the pool of art lovers more generally. It was in part to this end that Pierre Bourdieu and his associates were asked to conduct a major study of art museums in France and several other European countries (Bourdieu and Darbel [1969] 1990). They asked whether the postwar influx of large numbers of visitors indicated that valued cultural capital is more sought after, better understood, and more available to deprived strata than in the past. Their incisive response was that this is not the case. On the one hand, in art museums in France, Greece, Poland, Spain, and the Netherlands, Bourdieu and his associates consistently found that, despite the wide range of political orientations, the governments of all these countries favored as an ideal the opening of access to high culture for all. On the other, however, none really succeeded in this mission. Since the research of Bourdieu and his associates set the agenda for further study and debate, it is worthwhile to reexamine their findings and see if they still hold.

It is important to bear in mind that museum attendance is almost always a voluntary activity involving visitors who are already aware of the institution's existence and accessibility. Yet even among the already self-selected visitors, rather than a unique experience whereby each individual "receives" artworks in an idiosyncratic manner, the visitors interviewed were found to have experienced art according to the social attributes they shared with others: among the most salient of those were family background, educational attainment, occupational status, and small-town or big-city dwelling.

Overrepresented were highly educated individuals, who came to museums well informed about what works were in the collection. They were likely to have preplanned their visit so as to focus on specific works and were more familiar with the names of more artists, schools of art, and styles than any of the other groups. Their museum experience was a comfortable one: they felt at ease, remained longer than other visitors, preferred being far from crowds, and came either alone or with an equally competent friend. On the whole, they avoided tour guides or docents and museum publications such as guidebooks, relying on their own prior reading or on more scholarly reference works.

Visitors of middle-class occupational status made up the next largest category. They acted eager to grasp what they could, even if they were not as sophisticated as better-educated visitors; they read guidebooks, pursued docents, and absorbed information. In contrast to the ease of the aristocratic dilettante, the middle-class visitor acts like a pedant, the sure sign of a parvenu (Bourdieu [1979] 1984). By wearing their aspiration to cultural knowledge on their sleeves, they reveal that they accept the legitimacy of their "betters" and their own denigration, hence becoming accomplices in their subordination.

The effects of deprivation are even more noticeable among lower-class visitors, for whom the museum experience was most unsettling. In their eyes, the art museum had the solemn qualities of a cathedral, not the inviting cathedral of Abbot Suger, who intentionally designed the Basilica of Saint-Denis to be as attractive as possible to the many, filling it with extravagant sights and sounds—a Disneyland, but with real gold and precious stones. Rather, it was like the austere Cistercian abbey from whose sanctuary Saint Bernard had vituperated against gold objects as distractions from devotion and excluded frivolous communicants. Whatever the art museums' intentions, the poorly educated felt ill at ease in sacral-appearing halls, their walls hung with darkened oil paintings. Blue-collar workers on rural dwellers were unprepared for the esoteric qualities of the works and unable to understand poorly marked directions, inadequate labels, and seemingly hostile guards. If anything, the least educated were more comfortable when surrounded by family members or friends. They preferred to visit folklore museums whose handicrafts encompassed the type of skill and refinement they could admire and understand. Not daring to ask questions of tour guides for fear of exposing their ignorance, they failed to use the few services museums offered in those times.

The research of Bourdieu and others, commissioned or supported by the cultural services of the countries studied, has led to efforts to overcome some of the museums' features and open them to more visitors. Although not necessarily as a result of his findings and recommendations, public galleries are now more likely to combine the paintings of "high art" with homelier objects such as furniture and ceramics, thereby contextualizing rather than fetishizing the works. In recent years, partly as a result of the increasing leisure time of a more educated public with freedom to travel, combined with the eagerness of localities to attract them, museums are now advertised on television, special exhibits even featured on news broadcasts and other media. These are practices that have become common in the United States as well.[3] It would be incorrect, therefore, to assume that the conditions that Bourdieu found many years ago hold for all time, in all places, under different institutional and political conditions. It is necessary to go beyond his findings and probe into whether and how art museums today differ.

It may be a sign of the art museums' success in attracting large numbers of visitors that some observers in recent years have begun to criticize them for turning fine art into mass entertainment. This accusation has been leveled in particular at the Centre Pompidou in Paris. By comparison with the usual French art museums, the Centre Pompidou was unique in its commitment to attracting a large public by providing the freedom of a supermarket or cafeteria of events and exhibitions in a relaxed setting. It shows unusual art forms as elements used by fine artists in their works (newspaper cuttings or cigarette wrappers in collages), new styles (pop art), new art forms (photography or video art), and marginalized art (of ethnic, gender, or racial minorities that do not conform to the aestheticizing discourse and representations of modern art). The Centre also presents movies and houses the leading center for experimental music, a major public library and reading room, an interactive children's museum, restaurants, and gift shops.

These strategies, intended to attract and please new publics, especially unschooled museum goers, might be expected to overcome the elitism of ordinary museums and bring in a more popular audience. The site of some of the most detailed research on French art museum publics, the Centre enables us to evaluate this situation. But the results are disappointing. As Claude Pecquet and Emmanuel Saulnier put it, the Centre Beaubourg has little in common with the project of bringing the masses to school, as had been the late nineteenth-century aim of French political reformers such as Jules Ferry. The reason, they say, is that "Beaubourg is not national but Parisian in its orientation . . . , because the Centre has absolutely no popular ambition . . . but is exclusively oriented in an elitist direction, and, finally, because Beaubourg has no pedagogic vocation but is dedicated to what is immediately playful, aestheticizing, and consumerist" (Pecquet and Saulnier 1979, 172; my translation).[4]

Congruent with this observation, a study of the Centre Pompidou's visitors found that, despite their large numbers, the museum still did not provide visitors with the hoped for democratizing experience. Instead, visitors tended to carve out a minimuseum for themselves corresponding to the cultural baggage that they had brought with them. Nathalie Heinich notes that "the specific audiences for the principal activities have approximately the same characteristics as the audiences for these activities elsewhere: the art gallery audience is similar to art gallery audiences everywhere and the library users are like other library users" (Heinich 1988, 210).

Heinich's findings agree with other more general studies of French cultural practices: "Cultural activities (music, theater, museums, etc.) separate the most educated from the less educated French people" (Mermet 1985, 350). This pattern is confirmed in relation to occupations, in that 60 percent of museum goers are executives or professionals and 49 percent are middle management. The proportions drop dramatically for lower-level salaried employes, skilled workers, and unskilled and farm-related workers.

Faced with new, unfamiliar art forms, those of modest social origin are obliged to acquire expertise in interpreting them. They might learn the appropriate discourses for understanding fine art and acquire familiarity with high culture through formal schooling, but coverage of the arts is poor in public schools, either in France or in America, a subject to which I return below. But without formal education, cultural "catch-up" seems doomed in advance. It is at this point that museum education should come into action.

Museum Education Compared: A Devalued Profession

The museum educator is supposed to be the advocate of the viewer, whereas the curator is the advocate of the artwork. It does not bode well for its educational mission to know that, in the hierarchy of status internal to the art museum, educators are outclassed by curators (Eisner and Dobbs 1984, 7). For whereas professionalization has almost always meant increasing curatorial competence (as indicated by the fact, e.g., that curators are increasingly expected to hold the Ph.D. in art history), democratization (the public education function) has until recently remained largely a volunteer activity, under the administrative oversight largely of women with master's degrees (Zolberg 1986). Educators deal with schoolteachers and school bureaucracies, not with major donors and museum trustees or administrators, only a few of whom are committed to the public service project.

Attractive surroundings, labels, gallery lectures, video presentations, and pamphlets may be the stock in trade of most large art museums, but the question both in Europe and in the United States remains as to whether art museums are reaching the least reachable or whether they should even try to do this. Whether in the highly centralized, government-funded French museums or in the decentralized American museums, which depend on a mixture of public and private funding sources, art museum people seem to share similar views of their public. A French museum man has written, "If works of art are allowed to express their natural eloquence, the majority of people will understand them; this will be far more effective than any guidebook, lecture or talk" (cited in Bourdieu and Darbel 1990, 1).

The attitude does not seem very different in the United States. An American museum educator critical of his museum said, "Not for nothing is the 20th century art museum likened to the Cathedral and Temple of ages past. It is in the priests' interest to keep the meaning of art a mystery." The director of a major art museum in a large American city stated, "I honestly don't know what museum education departments are supposed to do." Some museum people believe that education is something that "you have got . . . or you ain't got . . . and you are not going to train it into a person" (Eisner and Dobbs 1984, 6, 7, 44).[5] The director of a university art museum admitted in a public forum, "I find it difficult to be a populist. . . . I slightly freeze up. The real crises of what face us are not museums at all, but education. More and more are being worse and worse educated. . . . Processes of education shouldn't go on in the museum; in fact, the entry of people could be done best after written or oral general examination" (Zolberg 1986b, 194). Each time a "blockbuster" event for art museums takes place, drawing in crowds of new visitors, complaints about the public's lack of preparation are renewed.

As the statements cited above indicate, in the view of museum professionals the public must be highly motivated, well educated, and presentable, or the museum owes them little, if anything. The recurrent theme is the (near) inherency of artistic judgment. This belief undergirds the maintenance of unclear definitions or specifications of how to understand and evaluate art, with the result that its ineffable quality makes it an appurtenance of a quasi aristocracy. Art is supposed to be grasped by some innate quality of the human spirit, through something akin to grace. Therefore, museums have only to make art available to the public since those with this special gift need no more, whereas those lacking it cannot be reached in any case. They conform to Bourdieu's observation that, "of all the objects offered for consumers' choice, there are none more classifying than legitimate works of art, which, while distinctive in general, enable the production of distinctions ad infinitum by playing on divisions and sub-divisions into genres, periods, styles, authors etc." (Bourdieu [1979] 1984, 16).[6]

Museum people sometimes assert that there is no need for specialists in education since everyone in an art museum, by the very nature of the institution, is an educator. Why try to develop the profession of museum educator and follow the path of colleges and schools of education, clogged with empty requirements that succeed only in limiting their students' access to the liberal arts? As in the field of education more generally, where teaching a subject is held in higher regard than teaching a pupil, many art museum people assume that, if students are not prepared to learn, there is little point in wasting scarce resources on them. Related to this outlook is that educating the pupil requires a grasp of teaching techniques, but at the cost of having little substance or content to convey (Bloom 1987; Hirsch 1987). Since in America the art museum educator is viewed as a technician at best and in any case is subordinate to the real purpose of the museum as directors and trustees tend to see it, which is to acquire and care for artworks, then democratization has a long way to go.

Observing that there was little sign of innovativeness in educational programs in the art museums they surveyed, Eisner and Dobbs (1984) suggest that this is due to a dearth of career opportunities for museum educators. It produces low morale and withdrawal of the most ambitious from the field. An American museum director notes, "There is no system of accrediting museum educators. There is no system of establishing a measurement of an achievement in the field. There is no career track in most education departments and we find, and it is a source of a lot of talk and discussion, educators wanting to move out of education as quickly as possible because of a certain sense of unworthiness or dead endedness. There is this mood in the field that has been there for the last several years" (Eisner and Dobbs 1984, 13).

In France, the profession of museum educator is even less developed than in the United States. Art museum staff members receive training in art and administrative regulations but hardly any at all in museum education. In a 1979 publication by the Direction of French Museums, unlike the space and detail devoted to curators, restorers, and guards, less than a page was devoted to the museum educator (or *animateur*) as an autonomous professional. This does not mean that "animation" (including exhibits that appeal to a broad public) is considered unimportant. The author, Freches, refuses to take a stand favoring either a relatively closed institution or a totally open one. As he put it, "Animating a museum should not end up by threatening the very raison d'être of the institution, founded to preserve and present a patrimony. But this should under no conditions justify excluding the public or reducing it only to elites" (Freches 1979, 165; my translation). By 1986 the situation of the *animateur* had not greatly improved. A Ministry of Culture publication laying out a development program for museums reminds curators that they are obligated to educate the public in an active manner, reaching out, especially to young people. They are urged to do this both on the museum's premises and through itinerant programs (museo-buses). But there is little guidance on how actually to carry out this task. Only the relatively new occupation of *animateur* comes close to providing information to museum staff about how to educate the public. *Animateurs* are expected to hold a diploma in that field or obtain training while studying art or general education (Ministry of Culture 1986, 51–60).[7]

The fact is that, with few exceptions, both in France and in the United States, the adult groups that art museums serve are rarely sought out by the museum; rather, they select themselves. When it comes to schoolchildren, American art museums rarely reach out beyond certain schools, public or private, the bulk of which are located in relatively prosperous neighborhoods or suburbs. The biggest losers are the students who are least prepared for the fine arts, as they are for education more generally, having "inherited" little cultural capital in the form of esteemed artistic knowledge and taste (Bourdieu [1979] 1984, 81). But is this really as important as proponents of democratization make it out to be? I consider next the relation of artistic taste to social status and mobility.

The Arts and Social Status: A Continuing Debate

The relation between social status and taste is acknowledged by nearly all scholars, but there is considerable disagreement as to exactly how they are related and with what consequences for the individual and society more generally. The questions these scholars raise aim to help specify the conditions under which different forms of taste are likely to be salient and to fill the "gaps and glissandos" that plague attempts at understanding the links between culture and society (Lamont and Lareau 1988).

Among the most prominent analysts, Herbert J. Gans treats cultural behavior as depending on opportunities limited by class and educational background. In an updated reanalysis of his now classic *Popular Culture and High Culture* (1974), Gans notes that, in spite of changes, "the majority of class differences in the use of culture remain strong" (1985, 32). Richard A. Peterson has read similar data differently, arguing that taste does not correspond precisely enough to such social structural elements as class, occupation, education, region, or ethnicity for them to account for the patterns of cultural choice that he and others have discerned (Peterson 1983). Although both Gans and Peterson conceive of culture as values that may take the form of consumable goods and serve as social indicators, for Peterson cultural choice seems to be more open ended and related to a quest for individualistic life enhancement; for Gans aesthetic preferences are a human right to potentially uplifting pleasure. Neither considers its possible feedback effects on the individual's social standing, a formulation that is a central component of Bourdieu's analysis of taste ([1979] 1984).

Bourdieu is not alone in suggesting that social mobility depends on the acquisition of certain trappings: wealth, insignias, educational certificates (Marshall [1950] 1965; Goblot 1967; Jencks 1972; Hirsch 1987). Despite convergences in their ideas, they and their followers engage in an ongoing debate concerning the relations between taste and social power. This debate is oriented by divergent assumptions concerning the nature of the individual in society, the interactions of culture and power, and the degree of rigidity of social reproduction.

Some assume that achieving higher status is adequately explained by the individual's rational choice—in James S. Coleman's (1988) terms, by voluntarist action. Although Bourdieu does not exclude rationality and strategic behavior from his analysis, his conception of the individual is quite different. Because, as he sees it, cultural capital is not only "out there" but becomes part of the individual, he regards the materials and symbols of status not simply as objects to be acquired but, as did Durkheim to some extent, as integrated into the individual's being. Because in his terms the individual is the outcome of the interplay of native propensities and social forces, Bourdieu rejects purely individualistic or psychological models of the causes of social behavior (Lukes 1985, 286). The integrating focus of the micro-environment of interaction with the macro-structure of society is situated in his concept of *habitus*.

Crucial in enabling individuals to manipulate cultural capital convincingly, habitus connotes one's total social baggage. Its character varies among social fractions; it is socially valued or devalued by comparison with the habitus of others. Whereas cultural capital encompasses a broad range of symbols, information, and meanings representing education, language, and mathematical forms, it is through their habitus that individuals expend or manipulate the capital that comes their way or are hampered from doing this effectively. Its components are multiple and intertwined in their social origin: body size and shape, education, and demeanor, as played out in a particular arena of opportunity combining macro-social and -political trends on the one hand, and intellectual traditions on the other.[8] One of the important implications of his formulation is that knowledge of the content of culture is only the beginning of understanding: more critical is the manner in which individuals behave in relation to culture and how their deportment is perceived by others.[9]

More recently, Peterson and Simkus (this volume) find that the relation of musical tastes to the occupations they analyzed converges with Bourdieu's predictions, especially with respect to the social categories that Bourdieu treats as the "dominant class." But Bourdieu's formulation has not gone unchallenged. Two sets of doubts that are pertinent to this essay have been leveled. First, he seems to imply that social reproduction is so inheritable and unchangeable that reform to diminish its impact is illusory. Although inequality in most modern countries is no longer tied to official policies of genetic or racial criteria, according to Bourdieu it may be maintained by familial socialization, serving as a proxy for race and other biological definitions. Passage through other institutions, especially schools, supports this initial status.

A second criticism is implied by those who, observing that traditional elite culture has been challenged by an explosion of cultural styles, believe that hierarchically ordered symbols of culture have lost their monopoly over what constitutes high culture. So many new art forms and styles have appeared on the scene that art that was once clearly appropriate to a museum (oils on canvas, marble or bronze statuary) no longer monopolizes the domain of high culture. It has been joined by works that would not have been considered art in the past: soft sculpture, tattered remnants of straw and other detritus, replicas of soup cans, or piles of bricks (Zolberg 1990). These works continue the tradition of the avant-garde movements that overthrow successive art and taste establishments.

One implication of this phenomenon, suggested by David Halle's ethnographic studies of Americans who own artworks, is that taste is not as closely tied to status as Bourdieu suggests. Halle found that a liking for the landscape genre cuts across all status groups, while a preference for abstract art is rare even among the most dominant groups. Moreover, the ability even of collectors of abstract art to express any understanding of it is extremely limited. This leads Halle to question the validity of claims by Bourdieu that assimilate cultural capital to economic and political power.

Bourdieu's formulation does not, however, require that members of dominant social categories actually understand difficult art in any depth; indeed, they are expected to distance themselves from giving the impression of knowing too much. They are amateurs, not specialists. In habitus, it is manner that counts, not pedantry. Indeed, they may reject some modern art out of hand without threatening their position; in fact, they may use their rejection as a means of enhancing their position. More important, if Bourdieu and his associates are correct, it is precisely the dominant who are in a position to help set the rules of legitimacy for art forms and styles. But this includes not only the content but also the manner of presenting that expertise. People of high social origin are expected to have an easy familiarity with fine art, but they are not expected to verbalize this knowledge as if they were experts. Since they already have these qualities, it is in their interest to promote the myth of "natural" ability.

In these terms, subordinate classes are in a no-win situation. If they accept the claim to legitimacy of dominant groups and their culture, then their ability to rise depends on acquiring expertise in that culture to gain social recognition. But if they learn it too well, they run the risk of being denigrated as overly eager—"greasy grinds" (Bourdieu [1979] 1984).

While Halle's (this volume) argument on behalf of a more dynamic interpretation of concepts such as habitus and cultural capital that take into account the fluid character of artistic taste is convincing, it does not follow that, because art museums try to provide something for everyone, their exclusivity has been undermined. If that were the case, then the failure of the Centre Beaubourg and many American museums to provide "an elite experience for everyone" (see the epigraphs to this chapter) would be unimportant. Such a conclusion, as I show next, is premature.

Art Museums, Education, and Social Mobility

Ostensibly educational institutions serve as mediators for socializing children and youths to fill production and citizenship roles. This is a relatively narrow set of functions. Sociologists of education have come to believe that education should be understood more broadly as involving not only schooling in a narrow sense but also acculturation, or integration, into a common culture of society (Jencks 1972; Karabel and Halsey 1977; Bernstein 1971; Bourdieu and Passeron [1964] 1979). Educational certificates help people advance into valued careers that play a part in determining social status. In France, the most important of these certificates is the *baccalauréat*, which marks graduation from secondary school and, until recently, served as a virtual passport into elite higher education. Without it, there was no opportunity to attain entry into high-level professions.

The indispensability of the *baccalauréat* was recognized in an influential work written in 1912 by Edmond Goblot (although not published until 1928) that has become a minor classic in the French literature on social stratification (see Goblot 1967). Goblot presented the Janus-headed nature of this linchpin of French education. Conceiving of the *baccalauréat* as the major barrier that separated the bourgeoisie from the people, he argued that, once it was obtained, it served to incorporate the talented of whatever background into the elite, thus leveling preexisting social inequalities.

By taking greater account of less clear-cut barriers, studies by Bourdieu and others raise questions about the adequacy of this conceptualization. Goblot had given little or no consideration to the fact that, although the *baccalauréat* was based on seemingly concrete essay questions, written and oral, what counted as acceptable responses were not only "correct" information but also manner: rhetorical skill, a sense of measure, a certain conception of human psychology and consciousness of self. These criteria encompass *general* culture, that which enables one to convey culture in the sense of "what remains when all else has been forgotten," as Edouard Herriot remarked (cited in Prost 1968, 249). But these are qualities that come from socialization in a series of institutions and experiences, of which the school is only one. In this broader sense, a passing grade depends on the kind of family-based cultural capital that Bourdieu later analyzed.

From a different standpoint, after the Second World War the influential English theorist T. H. Marshall argued in favor of social inclusion for all as the basis for the existence of a democratic state. To this end he advocated the evolutionary growth of three sets of rights by which individual opportunities were to be enlarged: legal, political, and economic. By having access to education, individuals would be prepared for active participation in productive employment and for exercising their roles as citizens.

Well meaning as it is, Marshall's analysis is no less faulty than Goblot's in that he did not recognize that merely making opportunities *theoretically* available is insufficient to achieve democratization, because the capacity for "reception" of school culture by members of social categories is already biased by the effects of their social origins. Materially, this means that the poor are likely to suffer from inadequacies of their educational institutions. Furthermore, Marshall did not foresee changes in modern economies that quickly render obsolete specialized vocational education rather than more general preparation for new forms of work as well as of leisure.

The targeting of education as an avenue to social mobility has different consequences under different structural conditions. In a centralized nation such as France, there had until recently been little concern with regional differences. Few concessions have tended to be made to the fact that individuals learn at differing rates of speed. Children who do not learn quickly usually are simply required to repeat classes. The result is that pupils from poorly educated families frequently end up in terminal tracks or too old to gain admittance to any but the most limited postsecondary education.

At the other extreme, the extraordinarily decentralized structures of

American public education, in which local property taxes serve as the basis of school district expenditures, produce a wildly inequitable outcome for its children. This effect is notorious in inner-city public schools in which the "truly disadvantaged" are allowed to fall into increasingly disastrous conditions (Wilson 1987; Wacquant 1989). But even in other areas inequities are rampant. In suburbs with high real estate values, school expenditures are far greater than in the much more numerous lower-middle-class suburbs.[10]

Whereas schools are expected to provide a "practical" cultural capital, potentially applicable to occupational preparation, the art museum's cultural capital is viewed as having no direct payoff and is not considered a legitimate expenditure of public funds. Acknowledged high culture is given only marginal coverage in most public schools, whether in the United States or in France. Even less is given the constantly changing avant-garde art forms, which are unknown in most families. Public school education, therefore, is normally inadequate to compensate for the lack of connoisseurship and easy familiarity of individuals from modest backgrounds. Yet in a world where leisure has expanded considerably and where modern employment is increasingly characterized by work that is not sharply distinguished from play, it is plausible to argue that education for "quality" or "constructive" leisure is a necessity rather than a luxury. This is not a new idea since it has long been the goal of progressive educators who advocate educating the "whole child." But, except in favored educational settings, this project rarely goes beyond the expression of an ideal.

Typically, education for leisure including the arts has been distributed almost exclusively by private schools; when it comes to public schools supported by taxpayers, the arts are viewed not as indispensable but as a frill. Especially in the inner city, the "basics" are favored and the arts and music treated as a stepchild. Even sports programs are granted importance largely if they are competitive occasions that glorify the school and are made available for (mostly male) star talents. Significantly, the latter are increasingly encouraged to view them as professions, not as leisure activities. This tends to be the case as well as for the performance arts (Cookson and Persell 1985). Consistent with his scholarly orientation, Bourdieu has actively pressed for sweeping educational reforms in order to overcome socially based familial culture and its effect on the habitus of children. Among his recommendations is that links be created between the schools and other agencies and institutions, such as museums, to develop a new conception of associational life and civic education. Later, when the minister of national education appointed Bourdieu cochair of a commission to revamp the entire educational program completely, from nursery school to the university, Bourdieu recommended major structural changes to avoid the nearly automatic repeating of grades for slow learners (*Le Monde*, 9 March 1989).[11]

The Art Museum: Barrier, Leveler, or Irrelevant?

Although there have been studies of the effects of educational attainment on subsequent occupation, income, and material conditions generally (DiMaggio and Mohr 1985), little is known about the effect of taste on individual career trajectories. Even though Bourdieu constructs a brilliant portrait of the intertwined nature of cultural, social, and economic capital as the basis of social inequality, he does not go much beyond asserting that the configuration is likely to persist. We need to know more about the precise relations between skills associated with leisure and occupational mobility or social mobility more generally.

Until longitudinal studies are carried out, the social consequences for individuals of being culturally adept remain obscure. Studies that explicitly compare individual career patterns among those born to cultural capital, as opposed to those acquiring it belatedly, would constitute the basis of an important research agenda. Being a museum member or symphony subscriber is not the same as earning a university degree, but just as technical expertise is required at work, cultural competence is also important. In addition, it is important to see the effect of national differences in the degree to which cultural competence is prized, as Michèle Lamont has suggested in comparing France and the United States (Lamont 1989).

Despite the gaps in knowledge, impressionistic observation and convincing anecdotal evidence suggest that, in a domain as central to the economy and the corporation, certain non-job-related skills and tastes seem to be given special attention. Both in the United States and, increasingly, in other countries, corporations encourage managerial personnel and executives to engage in certain leisure pursuits. Traditionally—almost stereotypically—these have included golf, hunting, and tennis. More recently, sports such as squash or racquetball have gained prominence. The entry of corporations into collecting and supporting the arts (special museum exhibits, service on the boards of opera and symphonies, corporate art collecting) suggests that cultural competence may be an advantage when promotions are being considered (Bell 1976; Hirsch 1987; Martorella 1990).

Even though art museums are more affected by the macrotrends of society than responsible for them, they are being called on to play a more active role in preparing the nonelites of society to rise. They are supposed to provide opportunities to acquire the structures of thought and critical faculties that permit them to integrate new information, including how to understand new aesthetic forms. It is clear that, as long as dominated groups depend on the social capital of their parental origins and have little access to the kind of education that teaches them the skills and appropriate demeanor that they have not otherwise acquired, they will be at a disadvantage compared to better-endowed competitors.

It is not clear that, in a "postmodern" world, in which aesthetic relativism seems to obviate "standards," it is still valid to think that there is only *one* elite culture. The art museum, after all, is no stranger to the avant-gardes that have tried to overthrow traditional boundaries between formerly hierarchicalized genres of fine art and low art, academic styles and commercial designs, or to promote the coexistence of art styles and unconventional forms. If there seems to be an "anything goes" ethos in the world of fine art, however, this does not mean that the taste cultures of all social status groups are valued equally. Furthermore, even if much postabstractionist art seems to be visually more accessible to the uneducated (pop art, photorealism, figurative surrealism), understanding and ability to manipulate their meanings, as the Centre Pompidou study suggests, are not less difficult for these works than for the art of the past. Even if the art they prefer is allowed to become part of museum collections, the dominated cannot benefit from its recognition unless they have some familiarity with a discourse of aestheticism congruent with its universalization.

American art museums are justly acclaimed for providing service to a relatively educated public. It is unrealistic to imagine them capable of "providing an elite experience for everyone" (Joshua Taylor, cited in Zolberg 1986, 192). But in the light of the generosity to art museums of the system of public taxation, whether through direct grants to help pay their operating expenses or such indirect tax breaks as exemption from real estate taxes and tax deductions for individual and corporate donors, museums owe a great deal in return (Netzer 1978). Since French art museums depend much more on the state and, ultimately, the *contribuable*, they might seem to have an even greater obligation. In France, the consensus among all elites and political leaders is that the museum represents the state and the nation; access is available to all who choose to use it. The museum is rarely threatened with being cut off completely, as happens occasionally in the United States. Nevertheless, repaying this obligation is complicated by the fact that the art museum is intrinsically *bimorphic*. That is, it caters to individual bearers of taste yet depends on funding from all taxpayers of whatever tastes. It is not surprising that the art museum and democracy make an odd couple.

Notes

I gratefully acknowledge the thoughtful and critical readers of earlier versions of this essay who encouraged me to rethink the ideas and their implications, although not to modify my analysis fundamentally: Daniel Sherman and Irit Rogoff, organizers of the conference on the art museum, Center for European Studies, Harvard University, 1988, where I first presented a version of the essay; Diane Barthel; Paul DiMaggio; Michèle Lamont; and Marcel Fournier. Thanks are due as well to several museum educators who shared their experiences with me.

1. But much of the difference seems to be accounted for by age since museum visitors include many classes of schoolchildren. Even so, as in so many other domains, schools in the poorest neighborhoods were the least likely to be represented. Despite recent change, interviews with museum educators in Chicago, Washington, D.C., and New York (1988–91) continue to support this observation.

2. Museums count their visitors to justify their value to the public, to provide indicators to their administrators of success in fund-raising programs, and to make sure marketing of ancillary products is paying off. The accuracy and validity of such self-studies may be questioned since the claims made from them are not disinterested (DiMaggio, Useem, and Brown 1978).

3. In addition to the development of the tourism industry, equally important is the increasing entry of large corporations into the support of museums. By "advertising" the art museums and their presence in it, they simultaneously present themselves as its patrons and attempt to gain some of its aura (Martorella 1990).

4. This observation is confirmed by data on leisure practices derived from independent surveys. When urban-rural location is considered, Paris turns out to be the only place of whom over 50 percent of the inhabitants say they have visited a museum in the previous twelve months (Mermet 1985, 352).

5. This study of American art museum education commissioned by the Getty Foundation makes no pretense of dealing with a representative sample of art museums. Museum directors and heads of education in twenty museums could not possibly represent the nearly four hundred art museums in all their

variety. Its authors are appropriately modest in their claims, saying that they studied not the actual operations of education programs but rather the goals and perceptions as stated by museum officials. It is worth noting that most of the museums in question were large established institutions in metropolitan centers or at least major cities. The authors have been castigated by some museum officials and curators (although not, to my knowledge, by many educators) for being one sided and hostile to aesthetic values. Their observations converge with those of others studying the relationship of museums to their public, both in the United States and abroad (see, e.g., Hooper-Greenhill 1988; and Bennett 1988).

6. As Bourdieu puts it elsewhere, "The religion of art also has its fundamentalists and its modernists, yet these factions unite in raising the question of cultural salvation in the language of Grace" (Bourdieu and Darbel 1990, 1).

7. Public education efforts are expected to be paid for by the cities and regions and to make use of up-to-date audiovisual technology.

8. Bourdieu defines *habitus* by analogy with Noam Chomsky's generative grammar, as a system of interiorized schemes that permit engendering thoughts, perceptions, and actions (Bourdieu 1967).

9. This is not to imply that those who have access to one kind of capital necessarily are equally at ease with other forms of capital. Rather, economic, cultural, and social capital constitute "usable resources and powers" that are unequally controlled by different classes and class factions in society (Bourdieu [1979] 1984, 114). Although dominant groups in modern societies are most likely to exercise control over economic and political capital (p. 408), they are not necessarily adept in the use of cultural capital. Still others (farm workers or unskilled workers) are usually deficient in both cultural and economic capital (p. 136).

10. A wealthy Dallas suburb spends $6,000 a year to educate each student, whereas in nearby poor towns not even half that amount is allocated (Reich 1991, 45). The inadequacy of programs to which the poor have access has been acknowledged by the U.S. Department of Education and the National Endowment for the Arts. As a result the NEA has established a national research center to promote the study of the performing and fine arts in schools (*New York Times,* 15 October 1987). In the light of increasing budgetary cuts, programs such as these are almost certain to be terminated.

11. Bourdieu was one of the faculty members of the Collège de France called on by the president of France to report on the future of education. The report was published as *Propositions pour l'enseignement de l'avenir* (Collège de France 1985).

References

Bell, Daniel. *The Cultural Contradictions of Capitalism.* New York: Basic, 1976.
Bennett, Tony. "Museums and the People." In *The Museum Time Machine:*

Putting Cultures on Display, ed. R. Lumley. New York: Routledge & Kegan Paul, 1988.

Bernstein, Basil. *Class, Codes and Control.* London: Routledge & Kegan Paul, 1971.

Bloom, Alan. *The Closing of the American Mind.* New York: Simon & Schuster, 1987.

Bourdieu, Pierre. "Postface." In *Architecture gothique et pensée scolastique,* by Erwin Panofsky. Paris: Minuit, 1967.

Bourdieu, Pierre. *Distinction: A Social Critique of the Judgement of Taste.* 1979. Reprint. Cambridge, Mass.: Harvard University Press, 1984.

Bourdieu, Pierre, Alain Darbel, et al. *The Love of Art: European Art Museums and Their Public.* 1969. Translated by C. Beattie and N. Merriman. Stanford, Calif.: Stanford University Press, 1990.

Bourdieu, Pierre, and J.-C. Passeron. *The Inheritors: French Students and Their Relation to Culture.* 1964. Translated by R. Nice. Chicago: University of Chicago Press, 1979.

Coleman, James S. "Social Capital in the Creation of Human Capital." *American Journal of Sociology* 94 (1988): S95–S120.

Collège de France. *Propositions pour l'enseignement de l'avenir.* Paris: Collège de France, 1985.

Cookson, Peter, and Carolyn Hodges Persell. *Preparing for Privilege: The Elite Prep Schools.* Chicago: University of Chicago Press, 1985.

DiMaggio, Paul J. "Cultural Entrepreneurship in Nineteenth Century Boston, Pt. 1." *Media, Culture and Society* 4, no. 1 (1982):33–50.

DiMaggio, Paul, and John Mohr. "Cultural Capital, Educational Attainment, and Marital Selection." *American Journal of Sociology* 90 (1985): 1231–61.

DiMaggio, Paul, Michael Useem, and Paula Brown. *Audience Studies in the Performing Arts and Museums: A Critical Review.* Washington, D.C.: National Endowment for the Arts, 1978.

Eisner, E. W., and S. M. Dobbs. "The Uncertain Profession: Observations on the State of Museum Education in 20 American Art Museums." Report to the J. Paul Getty Center for Education in the Arts. Santa Monica, Calif., 1984.

Freches, José. *Les Musées de France: Gestion et mise en valeur d'un patrimoine.* Paris: La Documentation Française, 1979.

Gans, Herbert J. *Popular Culture and High Culture: An Analysis and Evaluation of Taste.* New York: Basic, 1974.

Gans, Herbert J. "American Popular Culture and High Culture in a Changing Class Structure." In *Prospects: An Annual of American Culture Studies,* vol. 10, ed. Jack Salzman. New York: Cambridge University Press, 1985.

Goblot, Edmond. *La Barrière et le niveau.* Paris: Presses Universitaires de France, 1967.

Halle, David. "The Family Photograph." *Art Journal* 46, no. 3 (1987): 217–25.

Heinich, Nathalie. "The Pompidou Centre and Its Public: The Limits of a Utopian Site." In *The Museum Time Machine: Putting Cultures on Display*, ed. R. Lumley. New York: Routledge & Kegan Paul, 1988.

Hirsch, E. D., Jr. *Cultural Literacy: What Every American Needs to Know*. Boston, Mass.: Houghton Mifflin, 1987.

Hooper-Greenhill, Eilean. "Counting Visitors or Visitors Who Count." In *The Museum Time Machine: Putting Cultures on Display*, ed. R. Lumley. New York: Routledge & Kegan Paul, 1988.

Jencks, Christopher. *Inequality*. New York: Basic, 1972.

Karabel, Jerome, and A. H. Halsey, eds. *Power and Ideology in Education*. New York: Oxford University Press, 1977.

Lamont, Michèle. 1989. "The Power-Culture Link in a Comparative Perspective." *Comparative Social Research* 11 (1989): 131–50.

Lamont, Michèle, and Annette Laureau. "Cultural Capital: Allusions, Gaps and Glissandos in Recent Theoretical Developments." *Sociological Theory* 6 (1988): 153–68.

Lukes, Steven. "Conclusion." In *The Category of the Person: Anthropology, Philosophy, History*, ed. M. Carrithers, S. Collins, and S. Lukes. New York: Cambridge University Press, 1985.

Marshall, T. H. *Class, Citizenship and Social Development*. 1950. Reprint. Garden City, N.Y.: Doubleday Anchor, 1965.

Martorella, Rosanne. *Corporate Art*. New Brunswick, N.J.: Rutgers University Press, 1990.

Mermet, Gérard. *Francoscopie: Les Français: Qui sont-ils? Où vont-ils?* Paris: Larousse, 1985.

Mesnard, André-Hubert. *La Politique culturelle de l'état*. Paris: Presses Universitaires de France, 1974.

Ministry of Culture. *Faire un musée: Comment conduire une opération muséographique?* Paris: La Documentation Française, 1986.

Netzer, Dick. *The Subsidized Muse: Public Support for the Arts in the United States*. New York: Cambridge University Press, 1978.

Pecquet, Claude, and Emmanuel Saulnier. "Le Vide beaubourgeois." *Autrement*, no. 18 (April 1979): 169–78.

Peterson, Richard A. "Patterns of Cultural Choice: A Prolegomenon." *American Behavioral Scientist* 26, no. 4 (1983): 422–38.

Prost, Antoine. *Histoire de l'enseignement en France, 1800–1967*. Paris: Armand Colin, 1968.

Reich, Robert B. "Secession of the Successful." *New York Times Magazine*, 20 January 1991, 16–45.

Robinson, John. *Public Participation in the Arts*. College Park: University of Maryland Survey Research Center, 1985.

Robinson, Robert V., and Maurice A. Garnier. "Class Reproduction among Men and Women in France: Reproduction Theory on Its Home Ground." *American Journal of Sociology* 91, no. 2 (1985): 258–80.

Swartz, David. "Classes, Educational Systems and Labor Markets." *European Journal of Sociology* 22 (1981): 325–53.

Wacquant, Loïc. "The Ghetto, the State, and the New Capitalist Economy." *Dissent* (Fall 1989): 508–20.

Wilson, William J. *The Truly Disadvantaged: The Inner City, the Underclass, and Public Policy.* Chicago: University of Chicago Press, 1987.

Zolberg, Vera L. "Tensions of Mission in American Art Museums." In *Nonprofit Enterprise in the Arts,* ed. P. DiMaggio. New York: Oxford University Press, 1986.

Zolberg, Vera L. *Constructing a Sociology of the Arts.* New York: Cambridge University Press, 1990.

PART THREE

Resources for Boundary Work: The Case of Gender and Ethnicity

NINE

Women and the Production
of Status Cultures

Randall Collins

Gender differences in behavior and culture are producd by differences in the typical patterns by which women and men participate in the vertical class system and in the structures that produce and circulate status symbols. This essay is devoted to discussing the several aspects in which the position of women in the two dimensions of stratification produces female cultures. Although my main focus is on women, I will also comment on the conditions that produce cultures typically found among males. Women's stratification position in these dimensions is generally much more complex than that of men. When women have paid employment, their jobs are frequently in an anomalous, seemingly middle-class sector; but by the criterion of order giving and order taking, most of these women are actually "white-collar working class." The class dimension, however, is usually papered over by a strong admixture of status display—what I call "Goffmanian labor"—within the job itself. That is to say, organizational positions that specialize in the first line of impression management, of depicting the organization's image on the "front stage" analyzed by Goffman, are most typically filled by women; these positions have a significant effect on modifying the working-class culture of women order takers.

I turn then to the dimensions of stratification as they appear in the domestic sphere. At home, the relations of husbands and housewives (as well as of parents and children) can be analyzed also using the class criterion of order givers and order takers; again we see that the "domestic class position" of women is heavily overlaid by work in the area of status production (more than economic reproduction) for the family. Finally, I will consider the organization of cultural production in relation to the economic and occupational structure of the entire society; here we find that women are frequently involved in the production and consumption of culture whereas men are more concentrated in the realm of material production and its power relations.

It is because men and women are located across the grid of class structure in these different ways that they experience life in gender-distinctive patterns. I am taking a materialist view of culture in a broad sense. By *materialist* I do not mean merely the means of economic production or the Weberian material conditions of economic distribution. The material realm of sensuous bodily praxis includes situated activities such as order giving and order taking, rituals of Goffmanian staging display, and rituals of sociable interaction. Of course these have mental components; I stress only that the mental and symbolic aspects are situated in specific occasions in time and space and are produced by the social activities of human bodies oriented toward physical objects. Social materialism here means that culture is not merely given by the cultural order but is produced by the *material means of cultural production*. Our task as sociologists is to understand as a theory the conditions that produce and circulate stratified cultures.

Goffmanian Labor

It would appear that the female white-collar working class is not as alienated from official ideals as the male blue-collar working class. The latter is cynically critical of their superiors and their pretensions (Halle 1984), whereas the white-collar working-class women are more concerned about being respectable. I believe that this can be explained by a Goffmanian twist to the order giving/order taking basis of class cultures. Many white-collar working-class women are in front-stage jobs. Secretaries frequently are the first people whom outsiders meet in an organization; higher-ranking secretaries typically have the job of controlling access to their boss and arranging communications for (usually) him. In other words, they are the first line of Goffmanian organizational self-presentation (Goffman 1959). Within the organizational structure, women tend to be the specialists in initial impression management and in backstage access to the order givers. Salesclerks perform this organizational public presentation for retail stores; nurses do it in a medical setting. The female white-collar working-class thus tends to include a great deal of "Goffmanian labor."

Goffmanian labor results in a tendency to self-indoctrination, self-idealization, and formal manners. The nature of this Goffmanian work prevents the cynicism that is characteristic of the male working class. The latter are typically workers in the ungarnished backstage, and they encounter Goffmanian front staging mainly when it is used against them by order givers, their own hierarchical superiors. The interest of backstage workers is in puncturing idealizations since these are used against them in the operation of organizational power—hence the cynicism typical of the male working class and their ritual defamations such as obscene language. Male blue-collar workers and the female white-collar working class thus share cultural traits on the power dimension (they are both order takers), but they differ typically on the Goffmanian staging dimension. This is a class-anchored source of differences in gender cultures.

Housework and Surplus Domestic Labor

Turn now to female work within the domestic sphere. Housework can be regarded from the Marxist viewpoint as unpaid labor that reproduces the capitalist labor force (Sokoloff 1980). Wives provide services of cooking, cleaning, and clothing, as well as psychological support, for male workers; as mothers, women physically and emotionally care for the next generation of workers. The consequences that can be drawn from this argument, however, are not straightforward. One argument is that capitalism depends on the unpaid labor of women. Although they are not involved in market relations and the direct extraction of surplus value, they provide a necessary input without which the costs to capitalists would be much higher. No one, however, has gone so far as to draw the conclusion that the withdrawal of housework services—a housewives' strike—would bring the downfall of capitalism. The strictly economic interpretation of housework is inadequate. There is evidence that much of household labor is in excess of what is necessary to reproduce the labor force. American full-time housewives report an average of thirty-five to fifty-five hours of housework per week (the higher figure holds if there are children in the household [Davidson and Gordon 1979, 42]). British housewives report even longer hours: seventy-seven hours per week (Oakley 1974).

One might be suspicious of what is being implied here about necessary labor. The latter figure for the British housewives is eleven hours per day, every day of the week. One British housewife reported 105 hours per week, that is, fifteen hours a day, leaving little free time aside from sleep. Housewives who are employed outside the home, however, reduce their housework to about twenty-six hours a week (Davidson and Gordon 1979, 42). Since the hours that husbands help with housework does not increase substantially when wives are employed (Berk

1985, 64; Davidson and Gordon 1979, 43–44), we can infer that the twenty-six hours that employed housewives put in is an approximation to the economically necessary time. The remainder—of fifty-five, seventy-seven, or even 105 hours per week—is surplus domestic labor.

Another piece of evidence comes from historical trends. The amount of time that American housewives spent in housework did not decline during the twentieth century but actually increased (Vanek 1974; Cowan 1983, 3). In the 1920s, American housewives did about fifty-two hours of housework per week; in the 1960s, the figure rose to fifty-five hours. The introduction of household appliances (washing machines to replace hand laundering, automatic dryers to replace hanging clothes on lines, dishwashers, vacuum cleaners, etc.) did not reduce labor time; instead, it seems to have raised standards so that more time was spent on clothes, food, and cleanliness. Again, we see surplus domestic labor being generated as more time and resources become available.

In a Marxist context, the concept of "surplus domestic labor" would suggest that this is labor of wives that is being appropriated by husbands. Whether this is so, however, bears careful consideration. For this extra domestic labor does not appear to be under the control of men, nor does it result in any appropriation of economic capital or of reinvestable labor power. Instead, we have here a siphoning off of female energies into the realm of status and apparently under the strong initiative of women themselves.

An additional piece of evidence concerns class differences. Full-time housewives who are married to working-class men spend more time on housework than their middle- and upper-middle-class counterparts (Rainwater, Coleman, and Handel 1962; Komarovsky 1962; Lopata 1971). This is not merely a matter of higher classes putting off their housework on hired help since there is only one domestic service worker per every eighty-eight American households (*U.S. Statistical Abstract*, 1987, nos. 55 and 657). Rather, it appears that working-class housewives have often been obsessed with the cleanliness of their home and with the housework role generally. This was apparent in studies made during the 1940s and 1950s (Rainwater, Coleman, and Handel 1962; Komarovsky 1962), the period in which the familial ideal was at its highest. The move to the suburbs at that time was primarily a working-class phenomenon (Berger 1960; Gans 1967). Economic growth had reached the level when, for the first time in history, many working-class families could leave urban tenements and acquire single-family dwellings in the country-style settings that had previously been the domain of the middle class (and before that of the upper class with their country estates). In many ways, of course, working-class suburban life continued the traits of working culture generally (Rubin 1976; Gans 1967; Berger 1960). However, suburban residence represented a claim for middle-class status style at least in the realm of consumption: the very possession of a single-family dwelling (Halle 1984).

From the point of view of upper-middle-class observers, including most of the literary elite, this culture appeared only as a dilution of inward-oriented, cultivated aesthetic and moral values of their own class tradition and the ascendancy of gross materialism and conformity. Commentators like Riesman (1950) and Whyte (1956) assumed that it represented change in middle-class culture, a deterioration caused by the surburban mentality, and missed the extent to which what they witnessed was the appearance of working-class culture in ostensibly middle-class settings. Working-class culture in general emphasizes group conformity, localism, and a reified attitude toward cultural objects (Collins 1975, 75–77). I suggest that this "consumerism," moreover, is not so much materialistic and self-centered as a striving to live up to the dominant status ideals of the higher social classes. There is a characteristic irony here, in that the differences in class cultures remain precisely in the structure of this emulation. The working-class outlook fixes on externals, reifies status symbols, and takes them literally, as if they were Durkheimian sacred objects worshiped with primitive faith. The upper middle class, with its more abstract and reflexive consciousness, is concerned largely with the aesthetic dimensions of consumption (Bourdieu 1984). The higher classes, moreover, observing the cultural style of the classes below them, engage in reflexive role distancing, once again re-establishing their superiority to those who have a less sophisticated view of cultural symbols.

It is the working-class housewife, above all, who operates most literally in this realm of symbolic status emulation—that is, who tends to identify status with the appearance of the household itself. For this reason, working-class housewives tend to spend much more time in housework than their middle-class counterparts. There are several complexities here. One is the attitude of women toward paid employment. For upper-middle-class women, a career has recently become an ideal of feminist liberation. For working-class/lower-middle-class women, however, their family tradition has usually meant that women generally worked out of dire necessity, and the standard of middle-class status appeared to be not to be employed but to be a full-time housewife. To some extent this split still exists, in the greater antifeminism and attachment to "traditional" notions of family life found among working-class women.

Such notions of family structure are relatively recent historical developments. Domestic servants composed the largest category of nonfarm workers as late as 1900 in England (Laslett 1977, 35), including men as well as women. At least in England, the typical life-cycle pattern of most families included a period of service in another household, before the possibility might open up of marrying and setting up one's own household. Much of the movement for democratization, from around the French Revolution onward, was couched in terms, not of the demands of factory workers, but of the desire of household servants to escape from the demeaning status of personal service in a patriarchal household (See Tocqueville [1856] 1945, 177–86). The growth of the capitalist market economy was liberating for domestic workers because it opened up employment outside the households of their class superiors. Generally speaking, it liberated virtually all males from domestic service. For women, the change was more complex. In the long run, the middle-class household became defined as one in which a woman did not have to work as a servant elsewhere but presided over her own domestic establishment and did her own housework. This middle-class housewife, in turn, became a status ideal for working-class women. Even if she did housework, she had made a historical shift from being an order taker to being an autonomous worker in the household. Thus, the working class of the mid- and late-twentieth century pursues the status ideals of an earlier epoch, which have come within their means only generations later. But by this time the higher social class has moved on to a new (and often contradictory) status ideal.

The other major source of class differences in housework comes from the fact that nonemployed women of the middle, the upper middle, and above all the upper classes do most of their work in the realm of status production outside the home. The higher the social class, the more likely wives are to belong to clubs and organizations (Lopata 1971). Here again we see the greater cosmopolitanism of the upper classes. The localism of the working class is manifested in the status realm as well as in working-class housewives' focus on housework itself.

Realms of Status Production

My general argument, then, is that housewives' activities are primarily in the realm of status production. An equivalent expression would be "Goffmanian status presentation in the private sphere." In our society, it is largely women who perform the Weberian task of transforming class into status group membership. This status production is done in a number of realms.

Household status presentation itself is the home as Goffmanian product. It includes the cleanliness of the house, the style and orderliness of its furnishings, and the presentation of food. Not surprisingly, there are class differences in the styles in which this is done (Bourdieu 1984; Laumann and House 1970). The working-class emphasis is on orderliness and (when possible) material opulence, and its aesthetics are blatant colors and artistic sentimentality. These are straightforward claims for status attention, whereas the cosmopolitan upper middle classes value more subtly symbolic presentations. This follows from the principle of class culture: cosmopolitanism leads to abstraction and reflectiveness (Collins 1975, 75–76).

Another class difference is that, in the working class, women are more exclusively in charge of status display. Working males are less likely to concern themselves with how the housework is done and with entertaining guests "respectably," preferring the crude and hearty informalities of male carousing as a form of relaxation. This conflict between female "respectability" and male informality or even cynicism is one of the chronic sources of disputes in working-class families (Halle 1984). In upper-middle-class families, on the other hand, males are themselves highly cosmopolitan and oriented toward entertaining their business and professional acquaintances (Kanter 1977). For this reason, upper-middle-class males take more of an interest in the aesthetic display of the home. Certain "female" realms may even become male realms on formal occasions, when high-status males become involved in cooking or at least in the choice and presentation of dishes.

Cooking is the most ceremonial form of household work (Douglas 1982). The presentation of food to outside guests is a Goffmanian ritual par excellence. Any meal eaten collectively has the characteristic of a ritual: it assembles a group, focuses attention on a common activity, and ceremonially marks the boundary between members and nonmembers. Although often taken for granted, the formalities and customs of a meal nevertheless have symbolic significance as signs of "proper" group behavior: this includes the placement of dishes and silverware on the table, the custom of beginning and ending eating together, and such more explicit formalities as saying grace, carving the meat, offering toasts, or presenting a birthday cake. Frequently, ritual praises of the food and compliments to the cook are expected and given.

If rituals create a sense of group solidarity and personal identity, this is particularly so for the person who is in charge of the ritual. This is one reason, I suggest, why housewives tend to identify with their role, and it explains why cooking is their favorite form of housework (Davidson and Gordon 1979, 42). Their least favorites are washing, cleaning house, doing dishes, and ironing: these are Goffmanian back-stage work, which result in front-stage presentations, but ones in which the worker does not get to participate in the front-stage portion of the ritual. It is invisible work, whereas cooking generally culminates with the housewife calling family or guests to the table and presiding there to receive compliments on the results of her stage (or rather table) setting.

An alternative explanation why cooking is the favorite form of household labor is that it is unalienated labor in the Marxist sense. It is craft work; the worker, who controls her own instruments of production, can introduce considerable variety into the process; and its products are for direct consumption. But even here we must depart from a strictly Marxist format since it is not physical consumption of food that is most satisfying, and especially not merely consuming it oneself, but group consumption in a ritual setting producing solidarity within the family. Moreover, I would hypothesize that the most satisfying form of cooking is done for outside guests. There the cook is producing for a market, but it is a symbolic market of status within the community. Conversely, I would hypothesize that, the less ceremonial and collective eating is within a family, the more the cook feels that cooking is merely a burden.

On the other hand, the value of meals as ritual occasions makes them a possible source of conflict. Numerous family disputes break out, usually between mother (sometimes also father) and children, over the issue of getting children to come to the table on time, to eat their food, and generally to "behave themselves properly." These disputes cannot be understood as merely utilitarian matters. There is usually no reason of efficiency why family members have to eat their food at exactly the same time, and the nutritional value of children eating up all their food is probably overrated. Instead, these are ceremonial issues: eating together is a sign of solidarity; not eating is a rejection of ritual participation and hence an affront to the person in charge of the ritual. Housewives are thus engaged in making their children into full ritual members, by requiring them to participate in these mealtime rituals (not always with success, of course).

We see here another aspect of the housewife position. There is a stratification within the home between parents and children. The role of mother is a position of power over children (although also involving labor services for their benefit). The mother is in the order-giving class vis-à-vis her children, especially in regard to ceremonial aspects of the home and of status presentation vis-à-vis outsiders. The latter includes making sure children present a neat, cleaned-up, and even stylish physical appearance, as well as proper moral demeanor, to the outside world. As predicted by the principle that giving orders leads to identifying with one's official role (Collins 1975, 73–74), housewives with children are less alienated from their role and more likely to identify with it than are housewives without children (Lopata, Miller, and Rarnewolt 1984–85; Schoolen et al. 1984). This makes yet another complication in the class position of women. The same individual may be an order taker in her white-collar working-class employment and an order giver as well as a ritual leader within the home in relation to her children and sometimes even in relation to her husband. And even if she does not dominate the domestic ritual sphere without opposition from her children (or husband), she takes part in a domestic "class conflict" as a representative of the ritually official class.

Female Work in the Nonhousehold Status-Production Sector

Women's paid employment is also heavily concentrated within the status-production sector. Let us look analytically at the nature of this sector in relation to class structure (see fig. 1). Class positions directly generate certain attitudes and habits. These are *indigenously produced class cultures,* ways of thinking and behaving that are developed by experiences as order givers and order takers and by being members of cosmopolitan or localistic occupational networks. More elaborate forms of culture are produced by specialized organizations (Collins 1979, 60–71). This *formally produced culture* requires a material input, specialized labor, and sometimes long periods of training on the part of consumers. Culture-producing organizations include all those involved in producing styles, art objects, musical and dramatic entertainments, and literature as well as general training in tastes such as that provided by schools and museums. Bourdieu (1984) tends to subsume both kinds of culture, indigenously and formally produced, into a general category of "cultural capital," although most of his research focuses on the latter kind. This division, however, will enable us to show more clearly the autonomous aspects of the culture-producing system in comparison to the operations of class reproduction.

Class position provides individuals with some of the resources for

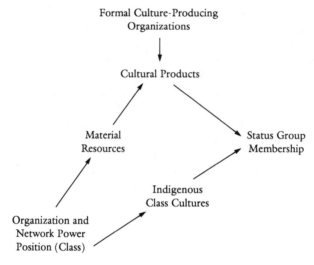

Formal Culture-Producing
Organizations

Cultural Products

Material
Resources

Status Group
Membership

Indigenous
Class Cultures

Organization and
Network Power
Position (Class)

Figure 1. Class, Culture, and Status Production

access to the cultural production sector: above all, the money with which to consume these products but also access to these markets through networks of personal and organizational connection. In addition, indigenous class cultures predispose individuals to consume particular kinds of formally produced culture. Formally produced culture is stratifying, but it does not merely reflect the class hierarchy, for several reasons.

1. Culture is materially produced; hence, money (or similar material resources) is necessary if individuals are to acquire particular kinds of formal culture. But cultural tastes build up over extended periods of time. It is this time lag in the production of cultural tastes that prevents culture from immediately expressing class position. This is the reason why long-standing elites typically look down on the nouveau riche, who do not know how to spend money tastefully. The high arts and sophisticated tastes are not marked by any intrinsic quality, but they are not arbitrary. They are those styles that are produced by the specialized professionals of the formal culture-producing sector. Members of the higher classes can build up their sophisticated tastes and pay attention to subtleties and esoteric references to previous high cultural developments because they have had long years of training as consumers of art, entertainment, and everyday styles and often many years of education devoted to acquiring those tastes. The pattern is redoubled by indirect

transmission of such tastes by personal association with family members and sociable acquaintances who have also undergone years of training.

2. The larger the specialized institutions within the culture-producing sector, the more this sector develops its own internal organizational structure. A specialized class of persons make their occupations as culture producers: artists, teachers, actors, designers, publishers, and all the ancillary personnel connected with them. It is especially easy for people who work in this sector to consume formal culture and to acquire the most "sophisticated" tastes—that is, those that are historically latest, built on the longest accumulation of organizational development within the culture-producing sector. This enables them to short-circuit the loop between class and culture. Their class position may be more modest than their cultural level because they work where the culture is produced and, so to speak, pilfer it for themselves in the process of purveying it to others. This explains why the audiences for the high arts (classical music, serious drama, museum art, etc.) are disproportionately educators and other professionals in these cultural fields (DiMaggio and Useem 1978).

The historical trend in modern societies has been for individuals to place more and more emphasis on status production. Once the basic physical necessities and creature comforts became widely available, most people invest their surplus money and time in cultural goods. These goods cover a wide range. At one end are the physical objects of everyday life (such as clothing, home furnishings, and cuisine) which are permeated with status symbolism; at the other end are activities like experiencing literature and art. But the crucial distinction is not physical versus the nonphysical; there is always a material input into the allegedly etherialized high arts, and the cultural aspect of everyday physical objects is the style of their appearance. As indicated above, the working class tends to reify its status symbols, to take material objects as directly embodying their status value. Members of the cosmopolitan higher classes emphasize the immaterial qualities, the nature of the tastes themselves and the aesthetic qualities for which the material object is a vehicle. It is only an ideology of the higher classes that identifies culture entirely with the immaterial side and that fails to recognize the symbolic aspect of the "materialism" of popular culture.

Women are disproportionately involved in this culture-production sector. As housewives, their role has increasingly shifted from the production of domestic necessities to the consumption of cultural objects for the home: that is, they convert money into and spend time appropriating products from the culture-producing sector. As we have seen, this takes place in different ways in different social classes. Women's paid employment also tends to be concentrated in the culture-production sector itself. This takes place in several ways.

1. Some women are directly involved in the most professional and self-consciously aesthetic levels of culture production: as artists, writers, actresses, and performers. The great desirability of such occupations explains why they attract so many career aspirants, so much so that competition for paying jobs is always high. Hence, only a few top artistic professionals may command great prestige and high incomes; the average economic return may be very low or even negative (Becker 1982). We have no systematic studies of how many individuals have ever trained themselves in acting or music, written literature that remained unpublished, painted, sculpted, or otherwise attempted to enter a "creative" field. I would guess that a considerable proportion of the wives of upper-middle-class men, women who are not employed in some salaried occupation, pursue careers as artists of various sorts. Frequently, the expenditure (e.g., for art supplies) is greater than the professional income, but this material expense is balanced by the subjective status of working in the core sector of cultural production itself.

2. The largest paid employment of women in the professions is in teaching. This too is largely cultural production, in the sense that the main payoffs of education are cultural sensibilities and cultural capital in general (DiMaggio and Mohr 1985). It is true that the mass bureaucratized educational system has resulted in an empty formalization of schooling, where grades and degrees have become a purely external credential (Collins 1979), and that the "inner" cultural meaning of education has diminished for most students. Nevertheless, the social identity of teachers still carries some of the subjective prestige of participating in the culture-production sector, and that prestige motivates teachers themselves to consume the aesthetic rather than the reified material aspects of culture.

3. Aesthetic values are embodied in styles of physical objects, and these are sold in a series of markets specialized by their proximity to the core culture-production sector (cf. Douglas 1979). At the most aesthetic end are contemporary art galleries; at a level closer to "everyday consumption" we find antiques and artistic furnishings as well as clothing associated with high prestige (i.e., professionally esoteric) style. Women are also prominent in this sector. Again, systematic data are lacking, but it appears that women who own businesses are heavily concentrated in little stores that sell art, antiques, and stylish clothes. It also seems that the customers of these stores are largely women. The

main distinctiveness of a boutique's products, what enables it to find a market niche not already filled by large chain and department stores, is the emphasis on ultracurrent styles and tastes nearer to the core of the culture-production sector. A considerable sector of the economy thus consists of women selling the goods of formal culture to other women.

4. Another sector concentrates on producing women's physical demeanor. A considerable proportion of the female manual working class works in this area, the so-called "pink-collar" sector of beauticians and hairdressers. This sector would include contemporary forms of body-image production such as aerobic and other exercise classes. Again, this is a sphere of cultural production and consumption, but it is focused on women's bodies. There is a component of erotic attractiveness in this: women to some extent are making themselves physically attractive in the sexual market in relation to men. But feminine styles are somewhat autonomous of erotic impression management. There are professional networks and trendsetters within the world of "beauty" who generate their own innovations and competitions. The status dynamic of female appearance may well consist largely of women observing and commenting on each other's hairstyles, cosmetics, and clothes, with very little input from male consumers of these female presentations at all. One might say that the realm of cultural status production has different branches, each of which can escalate its own competition as long as material resources keep flowing.

We should note that, in virtually all the sectors of formal culture production and distribution, there are also male professionals. Even though women may predominate numerically, men tend to occupy the top positions: as leading artists and directors, as antique appraisers and connoisseurs, and as famous hair stylists. How and why do men dominate even in female culture sectors? If we leave aside the female fashion industries and ask the question for the arts generally, the answer appears to be that men historically have dominated artistic production, at least since the time when musicians, painters, actors, and other such producers have been organized for extrahousehold production (i.e., since tribal and band societies were superseded by class-stratified agrarian civilizations). This was the historical epoch in which women of the dominant classes were most confined within the household, thus excluding them from professional artistic production. Viewed in this light, the presence of increasingly large numbers of women in the artistic-production sector of the twentieth century seems to indicate that this is a traditionally male sector that is relatively most open to the entrance of women. This in turn is no doubt facilitated by the predominance of women in the consumption of cultural objects.

Volunteer Activities of Middle- and Upper-Class Wives

Finally, we should touch on the cultural activities of wives that do not fall into the realm of either housework or paid employment. A major difference between wives of working-class men and those of men higher in the class hierarchy is the shorter hours spent in housework by the latter and their greater participation in voluntary organizations such as clubs, civic organizations, and charities. Although many of these are often described as "social clubs," their activities are not merely leisure entertainment. These organizations' official self-definitions usually stress their civic or charitable purposes. Upper-class wives in particular spend a great deal of time on boards of charitable organizations, in fund-raising (Ostrander 1984).

There is of course an aspect in which charitable organizations are merely a subterfuge for financial manipulations. The wealthy use charity to claim exemptions from taxes (although from a strictly financial viewpoint the result is still a net loss). More important, control of charitable foundations can be used as a way of maintaining control of blocks of stock, and hence of business corporations, and thus is part of the internal politics of business organizations. Nevertheless, over and above these motivations, there is a realm of charitable ritual that may be regarded as financial investments repaid in a different coin: the coin of status.

The fact that these organizations bring together persons of similar class ranking tends to make them emblems of eliteness, tightening the boundaries of status membership along class lines. Social climbing typically consists in maneuvering to be invited to charity balls and luncheons with members of the upper class. But participation in charities can also be a more direct form of status production rather than merely a reflection of class. Charities are themselves organizations within the cultural status-production sector. Charity is a ritual activity, in the sense described by Mauss ([1925] 1967). Gifts that are not reciprocated on the material level bring a status return to the giver. Since poorer people cannot recompense the gifts of the wealthy, the latter reap a return in prestige. Charity participation, then, is perhaps the purest form of the conversion of wealth into status. There are no physical embodiments at all (such as the objets d'art that exist in the aesthetic side of cultural production). Charity itself cannot be reified into material symbols taken literally as ends in themselves; charity always draws attention to the attitude of the giver rather than the object given. The highest form of the production of status, then, is precisely the nonwork activity that is today most closely identified with the upper class.

Although men tend to dominate the highest positions in charitable organizations, as they dominate elite positions in other formal culture-production sectors, for most families of the higher classes it is the wives who specialize in this charity participation role. There is a family division of labor along Weberian lines. Men tend to specialize in the class sector; their wives specialize in converting these male-generated resources of money and leisure time into status. Women do this through their surplus domestic labor as housewives. In the upper middle class, they frequently do so as aspiring (if unrecognized) artistic culture producers. Often they hold middle-class positions as teachers or as owners of small businesses retailing culture-laden objects. They are consumers (and sometimes producers) of specifically feminine self-presentation. And (especially in the upper class) they are core participants in the rituals of public altruism.

Conclusion

We can see that the position of women in the stratification system is complex. Insofar as women are employed, their most typical positions are in the "white-collar working class." They also work in a wider range of positions, from elite down to manual levels, within the formal culture-production sector itself. All these jobs carry a cultural component that orients them more toward the status hierarchy and its upward emulation rather than toward the class conflicts of order givers versus order takers. The white-collar working class of secretaries and clerks does have a number of the attitudes typical of working-class order takers: a privatized rather than official organizational orientation and a tendency to localism rather than cosmopolitanism. But their activities as secretaries frequently have a Goffmanian front-stage quality that tones down class alienation more than in the male working class. Many women, of course, are in unambiguously manual working-class jobs, especially as factory workers and as cleaning-service workers. A large number of female manual service workers, however, are waitresses—a job that has an important Goffmanian front-stage component. Some of these jobs, cocktail waitresses in particular, have roles that emphasize a female erotic image and hence crosscut the order-taking class role with their sexual marketplace role, another Goffmanian sphere with many complexities of its own.

I have barely touched on this final aspect of male/female gratification: the relations among males and females in the aspect that most explicitly brings them into contact, the erotic sphere. There is no opportunity to go into this topic here at the necessary length. Suffice it to say that, in addition to the class and status differences noted above, males and females are further differentiated socially by their typical styles of operating on the sexual marketplace. These styles have varied historically, including the group-controlled alliance politics of kinship-structured tribes, the "Victorian" marriage market with its dual sexual standards, and modern individually negotiated short-term sexual relationships (Collins 1975, 225–54). Generally, males and females have different motivations and styles of negotiating sexual relationships and emphasize different standards of sexual morality. The greater conservatism of women about the symbolic aspects of sexual communication adds a division of male "macho" and sexual carousing, as opposed to female "respectability," to the other features that distinguish male and female cultures. As Halle (1984) found in his study of working-class men, these differences in emphasis on respectability play a frequent role in male/female conflict within the family.

Altogether, the differences between male and female cultures are likely to be greatest in those families where manual working-class men are married to white-collar working-class women. At the highest class level, strong differences may again appear, with organization-dominating upper-class men inhabiting quite different life spheres than their wives, who specialize in culture-production activities. Probably male/female cultural differences are minimized for upper-middle-class men who themselves work in the culture-production sector; their own class positions are already involved in culture-laden activities that match those of their wives, whether the latter are employed or not.

If we remove the culture-production sector, however, and concentrate on the fundamental organizations of power and property within our society, one basic pattern stands out: the higher reaches of the core class structure are overwhelmingly inhabited by males. It is the culture-production sector, above all, that connects women with the higher reaches of the stratification system. It is the production and consumption of symbols of status that give women virtually all their autonomous success. Women live subjectively—and, in terms of their successes, objectively as well—much more in the realm of status than in the realm of class.

This might make it seem that women are living mainly in a realm of illusion, a cultural fluff floating over the hard material basis of our society. But the capitalist economy of the twentieth century has increasingly derived its dynamism from the permeation of status symbolism into the material objects of everyday consumption. The promotion of new products is done largely by connecting ordinary objects of physical consumption with recent symbols from the culture-production sector. Since there is continuous competition and innovation among culture producers, this gives a dynamic to the material economy, creating symbolically new products and creating demand for them via status consumption. The activities of women, in both the production and the consumption of status culture, may well constitute the feature that keeps modern capitalism alive.

We have seen a number of elements of dynamism in the material aspects of the status realm. The amount of surplus domestic labor—that is, inputs into the production of status-symbolizing objects—has risen as more material resources have become available and as greater material productivity has freed more time for status-producing activities. The dynamic mechanism involves the greater material resources of the higher classes for creating and consuming status-giving objects and their emulation by lower classes as their standard of living also rises. Furthermore, one can argue that capitalism has always depended on new products and new markets (Collins 1991). The consumption of cultural objects in the household (both in finished form and as raw materials transformed by housewives' labor) may thus be the feature that makes contemporary capitalism dynamic and on which its continued expansion rests.

References

Becker, Howard S. *Art Worlds.* Berkeley and Los Angeles: University of California Press, 1982.

Berger, Bennett. *Working-Class Suburb.* Berkeley: University of California Press, 1960.

Berk, Sarah Fenstermaker. *The Gender Factory: The Apportionment of Work in American Households.* New York: Plenum, 1985.

Bourdieu, Pierre. *Distinction: A Social Critique of the Judgment of Taste.* Cambridge, Mass.: Harvard University Press, 1984.

Collins, Randall. *Conflict Sociology: Toward an Explanatory Science.* New York: Academic, 1975.

Collins, Randall. *The Credential Society: An Historical Sociology of Education and Stratification.* New York: Academic, 1979.

Collins, Randall. "Market Dynamics as the Engine of Historical Change." *Sociological Theory* 8 (1991):11–135.

Cowan, Ruth Schwarts. *More Work for Mother: The Ironies of Household Technology from the Open Hearth to the Microwave.* New York: Basic, 1983.

Davidson, Laurie, and Laura Kramer Gordon. 1979. *The Sociology of Gender.* Chicago: Rand McNally, 1979.

DiMaggio, Paul, and John Mohr. "Cultural Capital, Educational Attainment, and Marital Selection." *American Journal of Sociology* 90 (1985): 1231–61.

DiMaggio, Paul, and Michael Useem. 1978. "Cultural Democracy in a Period of Cultural Expansion: The Social Composition of Arts Audiences in the United States." *Social Problems* 26 (1978): 180–97.

Douglas, Mary. *The World of Goods: Toward an Anthropology of Consumption.* London: Allen Lane, 1978.

Douglas, Mary, ed. *Food in the Social Order.* New York: Russell Sage, 1982.

Gans, Herbert J. *The Levittowners.* New York: Random House, 1967.

Goffman, Erving. *The Presentation of Self in Everyday Life.* New York: Doubleday, 1959.

Halle, David. *America's Working Man: Work, Home, and Politics among Blue-Collar Property Owners.* Chicago: University of Chicago Press, 1984.

Kanter, Rosabeth Moss. *Men and Women of the Corporation.* New York: Basic, 1977.

Komarovsky, Mirra. *Blue-Collar Marriage.* New York: Random House, 1962.

Laslett, Peter. *Family Life and Illicit Love in Earlier Generations.* Cambridge: Cambridge University Press, 1977.

Laumann, Edward O., and James S. House. "Living Room Styles and Social Attributes: The Patterning of Material Artifacts in a Modern Urban Community." In *The Logic of Social Hierarchies,* ed. Edward O. Laumann, Paul M. Siegel, and Robert W. Hodge. Chicago: Markham, 1970.

Lopata, Helena Z. *Occupation: Housewife.* New York: Oxford University Press, 1971.

Lopata, Helena Z., Cheryl Allyn Miller, and Debra Rarnewolt. *City Women: Work, Jobs, Occupations, Careers.* 2 vols. New York: Praeger, 1984–85.

Mauss, Marcel. *The Gift.* 1925. Reprint. New York: Norton, 1967.

Oakley, Ann. *The Sociology of Housework.* New York: Pantheon, 1974.

Ostrander, Susan A. *Women of the Upper Class.* Philadelphia: Temple University Press, 1984.

Rainwater, Lee, R. P. Coleman, and G. Handel. *Workingman's Wife.* New York: Macfadden, 1962.

Riesman, David. *The Lonely Crowd.* New Haven, Conn.: Yale University Press, 1950.

Rubin, Lillian. *World of Pain: Life in the Working-Class Family.* New York: Basic, 1976.

Sokoloff, Natalie J. *Between Money and Love: The Dialectics of Women's Home and Market Work.* New York: Praeger, 1980.

Tocqueville, Alexis de. *Democracy in America.* 1856. Reprint. New York: Knopf, 1945.

U.S. Statistical Abstract. Nos. 55 and 657. Washington, D.C.: Government Printing Office, 1987.

Vanek, Joann. 1974. "Time Spent in Housework." *Scientific American* 231 (November 1974): 116–20.

Whyte, William H. *The Organization Man.* New York: Doubleday, 1956.

TEN

Tinkerbells and Pinups: The Construction and Reconstruction of Gender Boundaries at Work

Cynthia Fuchs Epstein

Distinctions between people, groups, and things create the boundaries that separate them physically and symbolically. Among the most pervasive of distinctions are those made between men and women, and these distinctions mark the boundaries of conceptual and actual sex segregation and enunciation. Difference between the sexes is ever present in language, literature, and norms. It is focused on in everyday life, but especially so in times of social change, when boundary distinctions become blurred and mechanisms come into play to reinstate them. Thus, distinction blares out from time to time as a trumpet call to arms, a warning of trouble, or a celebration. Or it lingers below the surface, forming a latent agenda or creating an ideological subtext of discourse. It is infused in the culture, integrated in the social structure, and institutionalized in the patterns and practices of our lives.

The focus on difference spreads out from the narrow acknowledgment of sex differences that make reproduction of the species possible to a set of assumptions about all kinds of capacities and orientations to think and feel. A belief in difference permeates our lives. The belief creates differences or defines that which is the same as different.

Belief in difference invariably results in inequality, in invidious distinctions. Thus, women suffer from the distinctions that proclaim them as different from men; blacks suffer from the distinctions that characterize them as different from whites; youths are regarded as morally deficient compared to adults; and the elderly face contempt for being out of touch with the concerns of those in their middle years. The convergence of attitudes and behaviors is generally not the focus of comparison, only the divergence.

In recent work (Epstein 1988), I have ascertained that, in everyday society and even in science, views about difference mislead us from recognizing how superficial differences between the sexes are for most

232

of life's activities. Research reveals that many of the patterned differences that we note empirically, by statistical methods, or merely by observing the systems in which we are participants may be traced not from the organic qualities of the human body or the deeply rooted attributes of distinct psyches but from the strong arm of the law, of social force or its threat, and from the velvet gloves that provide the subtle restraints and persuasions of social life, keeping men and women in line with social definitions and expectations.

I have explored some of these processes in the workplace, in studies of women lawyers (Epstein 1981, 1990) and, more recently, a study of communications workers conducted with Kai Erikson (forthcoming). In this work, I have seen how boundaries, defining and separating people into classes, communities, working groups, genders, and many other classifications, act as constraints to equality and as constraints on the attempt to institute changes in the workplace. This essay thus focuses on the processes of boundary maintenance at the micro level of interaction, indicating how they intersect with broader institutional structures and cultural values.

How Do Boundaries Get Set?

Social ordering is created and maintained by both conceptual and structural means. Sometimes we can clearly identify who is responsible for social arrangements, but often it seems as if such arrangements are the work of an invisible hand or the collective behavior of individuals acting in patterned responses. According to Gerson and Peiss (1985), boundaries mark the social territories of human relations, signaling who ought to be admitted and who excluded. Moreover, there are rules that guide and regulate traffic, and these rules instruct on the conditions under which boundaries may be crossed.

The boundaries that order individuals, organizing them into categories, are persistent. And those defining gender work roles have been among the most persistent. Of course, there are circumstances in which sex status becomes less salient in work settings and is less a criterion for a boundary distinction. We are noting considerable social changes in the workplace, particularly in the professions where women have "crossed over" into male-dominated work roles and become employed in spheres where there has not been a complete transformation of the sex designation of the job. One example of this is the courtroom, where women practice litigation in the same spheres and according to the same norms as men.

Yet even when the real boundaries of sex, class, or age change, the *conceptual* boundaries remain, as when women take jobs not considered traditional for their sex and the jobs remain labeled as men's or when women are regarded as engaging in behavior or expressing attitudes different from men's—employing different strategies or expressing different degrees of commitment—when, in fact, they are behaving the same as men. Attitudes may remain independent of behavior. After all, individuals and groups develop investments in boundary distinctions. For individuals, boundaries define who they think they are. They set the parameters of what Markus and Nurius (1986) call the "possible selves" that determine motivation, decision making, and behavior in the day-to-day and long-term aspects of our lives.[1] Groups also rely on distinctions to create a "we"-and-"they" boundary to define themselves.

Boundary distinctions that come from the culture, whether from the general ideas and depictions in the mass culture or the ordinary practices of everyday community and family life, are usually regarded as normal, necessary, and just. Ideology accompanies experience. But it may also reflect it, lead it, or contradict it.[2]

Distinctions created by the culture need not logically lead to invidious comparisons, but nearly all inevitably do (Epstein 1985, 1988). They are most often posed as dichotomies and carry evaluations as well as descriptions and prescriptions. Male/female is only one of such designations, but obviously there are many more: black/white; young/old; dirty/clean; skilled/unskilled; informal/formal; workplace/home; upper class/lower class.

From an enlightened perspective, distinctions might be conceived as continual or overlapping phenomena rather than absolute designations, but dichotomous distinctions play a particular role in social categorization. For example, people come in all hues but are sorted dichotomously into black and white (or, more recently, trichotomously into other, also absolute, color designations such as brown). The sorting by color designation and not by actual hue has consequences for education, residence, and social intercourse. In fact, hue may not count at all. The historian Philip Foner (1964, p. 256) writes of the racism of a group of union leaders in testimony submitted to Congress in 1912, "A number of A.F. of L. leaders referred to themselves as 'white men,' lumping the Italians, Poles and Negroes, as 'non-white.'"

Ordinary persons and scientists alike gravitate toward dichotomous classifications in the organization of their thinking (e.g., physical and social sciences, hard and soft data, qualitative and quantitative). Some are attracted by the conceptual economy that dichotomization provides for analytic purposes. Others have a stake in distinctions that have real-world implications. This is, for example, particularly so with those who maximize the interest of one category to the disadvantage of another, as in the distinction upper class/lower class—especially when the distinction goes beyond monetary assets and moves into the sphere of manners and comportment. Michèle Lamont (1992), for example, shows how cultural attributes, such as high culture literacy, and moral attributes create boundaries between middle-class men that have consequences for the acceptability of some for and the exclusion of others from upper-middle-class jobs.

Dichotomous distinctions that delineate personality attributes, such as a capacity to individuate or be relational, as distinctly "male" or "female" have marked the work of such writers as Nancy Chodorow (1978) and Carol Gilligan (1982). These writers have attracted a substantial following of feminist scholars who claim that a female "standpoint" informs their observations. Although not specifically stated, the work of these theorists suggests that women's "caring" as expressed in their relational styles, capacity to nurture, and morality is of greater value than the capacity of an abstract orientation toward individuality and justice that is attributed to men. Today, the feminist scholarly community is at odds, a debate waging between those who claim that differences between men and women are deeply ingrained through early influences (maximalists) and those who believe that differences are social constructions and subject to change by changes in social situation and social intervention (minimalists). Belief in "essentialism" marks a school known as "cultural feminism," which may be found in many disciplines within the academy from the social sciences to the humanities and even in law (marking the work of some scholars doing "feminist jurisprudence") (Epstein 1990). Elsewhere (Epstein 1991), I have analyzed the intellectual underpinning for this debate and the evidence that I believe supports a minimalist perspective.

Clearly, concepts such as "moral" or "immoral," "cultured" or "uncultured," or even "caring" and "aloof" may be translated into real behavior; idea can be turned into reality by means as disparate as the self-fulfilling prophecy and the executive fiat. And, as I shall illustrate further, controls from one sector (e.g., community norms carried into the workplace) may be easily exercised in another.

Yet there is not always consensus on what a boundary encompasses or even on what the designation of a category refers to. Anthony Cohen (1985) notes that, since boundaries are conceptually set, they may be perceived in rather different terms, not only by people on opposite sides of a boundary, but by those on the same side as well. All social categories are variable in meaning, according to Cohen, and often the contents of a category are so unclear that it exists largely in terms of its symbolic boundaries. Such terms as *just* and *unjust* and, perhaps, *masculine* and *feminine* may be impossible to spell out with precision. However, the range of meanings that may be subsumed by these terms (which are, of course, symbols) can be glossed over precisely because they allow their adherents to attach their own meanings to them. Of course, the muddiness may restrict, but it may also allow for, social change.

Interpretations vary depending on the circumstances of interaction and how the interaction is defined in the context in which it occurs. The same behavior may be interpreted differently in different settings. For example, in all-female groups women may act in a bawdy manner without fear of being perceived as unfeminine (Westwood 1985), although bawdiness is usually regarded as male behavior, and in some all-male groups (e.g., in sports and war) men often demonstrate tender and caring behavior (Yarrow 1987) that might be interpreted as unmanly in mixed groups. When such behavior becomes public, however, redefinition or reinterpretation about what is "normal" for a particular category of people may occur.

On the other hand, there are collective agreements about certain connotations that are culturally persistent, and whether or not the definition of a category makes sense, gatekeepers of the traditional view will do all they can to make a boundary intractable. As I shall point out later, they often do so with the compliance of those who may suffer from the distinction or, at most, derive only secondary benefits.

The means of boundary maintenance may be mechanical and physical. But they may also be conceptual and symbolic. They may be engineered with grandiosity by highly visible leaders or, as Ivar Berg (1986) observes, through lower-level tyrannies. And, as Harry Braverman (1974) warned, they may be the intended policies of capitalists optimizing their advantage or, as others have documented, the response of low-level workers trying to find a rationale for their situation. They may be proposed by the most radical advocates of social change as well as by those most in favor of tradition (Epstein 1991). They may also be reinforced in the unnoticed habits and language of everyday life vigilantly attended to by family and friends, business associates and colleagues, or in individual or collective guilt derived from shared values.

Control, then, may be exercised at the micro level, at not always perceptible levels, although it is also true that people may often be clearly aware that words, like symbolic behaviors of other kinds such as rituals and ceremonies, are instruments, tools, and weapons to erect walls or bring them down. At base, language itself creates boundaries by providing the terms by which real or assumed behaviors and things are grouped.

I am suggesting not that cultural designations are more powerful than structural ones or social psychological ones but rather that there is interaction among all three. Perhaps people cling to certain designations because their identities are at risk or because they are embedded in a belief system that convinces them that these distinctions are natural or normal (or God given or devil driven). Such convictions may be held by both those who are served by the distinctions and those who are not.

As individuals have interests in the material conditions of their lives and fight to maintain their advantages and their territory, they also have an interest in preserving their identities. As we shall see, some of the reasons that people become invested in boundaries are because their sense of self, their security, their dignity, all are tied to particular boundary distinctions, and these personal investments are bound up with authority and hierarchy.

In their work on cultural reproduction, Bourdieu (1984) and his associates show the ways in which dominated groups contribute to their own subordination because of class-differentiated mental structures, or *habitus* (i.e., class-differentiated dispositions and categories of perception shaped by conditions of existence). Entrenched in the dominant symbolic system that contributes to its reproduction are binary oppositions (rare/common, interested/disinterested). As I have pointed out elsewhere (Epstein 1970, 1984), dichotomous thinking plays an important part in the definition of women as "others," as deviants, and in their self-definitions. Although they were not the first to do so, the way in which Foucault, Bourdieu, and other European theorists of culture define power—as the ability to impose a specific definition of reality that is disadvantageous to others (e.g., Bourdieu's "symbolic violence") or the capacity to structure the situation of others so as to limit their autonomy and life chances (e.g., Foucault's "regime")—articulates the structure and process relevant to the construction of gender very well. This is "the power to shape alternatives and contain opportunities, to win and shape consent, so that the granting of legitimacy to the dominant classes appears not only spontaneous but natural" (Hall 1984, 38, cited in Lamont and Wuthnow 1990, 295).[3]

These writers are also concerned with the structural effects of culture, that is, how culture, whether cultural signals or ideology, affects people's positioning in the stratification system. Foucault's writings reconstruct how discourse shapes and structures subjectivity and how classification systems structure reality.

The approach shows how power is ubiquitous in social life, operating in micro-level face-to-face relationships and at the macro levels of social reality. This is particularly salient in the case of gender issues since laws and rules segregate men and women in various institutional spheres, and such power also operates in the course of ordinary sociability governed by the latent rules of social interaction.

For Bourdieu, Foucault, and other European cultural theorists, power is not measured by the occurrence of unwilling compliance and is not limited to affecting others' behavior. Influencing their situation or position in the social structure in a disadvantageous way is conceived as a more pervasive and important way of exercising power (Lamont and Wuthnow 1990).[4] This is also true of many social scientists who study these processes and who also become committed to particular distinctions, especially when for methodological reasons they treat statuses as if they were discrete phenomena.

Gender Boundaries

The social ordering of the workplace by sex of worker is a persevering phenomenon, often explained by reference to market forces, personal choices, and so on. But there are distinct social controls that maintain gender distinctions in the workplace. In this section, I shall point to and outline mechanisms that affect gender boundaries in various places of work that I and others have studied in the last decade.[5]

As a result of a 1973 consent decree with the U.S. Government, AT&T instituted an affirmative action program that was to desegregate job categories. As a result, numbers of men and women were placed in jobs not considered traditional for their sex. Thus, men became telephone operators, and women were given opportunities to apply for such jobs as installers and repair personnel.

But long-standing expectations of what men's and women's jobs ought to be, both within the company and outside, among the families of workers as well as in the general culture, were violated by the new policy. Thus, as might be expected, both actual and symbolic behavior was used by both male and female system participants to defend or restore traditional gender boundary distinctions. The following excerpts from interviews Erikson and I conducted with communications workers illustrate the process.

A female telephone operator reported her son's opinion of the male operators she worked with: "I have a 23 year old son and last year he lost his job. I said to him, 'Why don't you fill out an application for the phone company?' [as an operator] . . . He said, 'Ma, I think if they offered me $1,000 a week tax-free, I wouldn't take that job. When I go up with you now [to visit the telephone company] and I see those guys sitting in there I wonder what's wrong with them. Are they pansies or what?'" Some male operators felt the heavy hand of boundary control from outside the workplace, from the customers who called them and got a man on the line instead of the expected woman operator. As a male operator in the same office reported, "I got people calling me a 'tinker bell,' and 'oh, you're one of them gay bastards.' . . . They figure I'm in a female office so I must be queer" (Epstein 1989, 577). Or consider a man's own view about the inappropriateness of being in a "woman's" job: "I would rather be doing manual work if I had to outside instead of sitting in here. I feel like a bull in a china shop. And I don't like it. They have these keyboards and they say use all your fingers. And the ladies are going like, my God. And I'm sitting there—I'll hit a key and I'll hit two keys and then I'll have to erase it." Asked, "The equipment isn't made for a man?" he replied, "It's designed like a typewriter."

Cynthia Cockburn (1983) and, more recently, Patricia Roos (1990) have shown how male printers scorn typesetting by computer, which they regard as women's work. Cockburn found that male compositors' ability to operate a linotype machine under printing-shop conditions was a boon to their sense of manliness. The trauma inflicted by technological change for these men came not only from deskilling but also from the change from a craft workplace with a long tradition to a white-collar environment. In the words of one printer, "I don't know what it is. It just isn't masculine enough to satisfy me." Another commented that automation "may make softies of us. . . . I feel it may make us, I don't know if this is the word, 'effete.' Less manly somehow" (Cockburn 1983, 108).

Entrenched stereotypes that pair sex of worker to job are shared by managers in the telephone company. Even after the 1973 consent decree, they showed resistance to changes in company policy. In one office, charm bracelets were given to the women for perfect attendance. When men worked at the same jobs and scored perfect attendance, they were given the same gift. The lag in developing a more appropriate "male" gift reinforced the definition of the operator's job as woman's work and heightened men's discomfort at doing it.

Women recruited into work formerly reserved entirely for men also faced the ambivalence generated by men's investment in the masculine image of their job as a source of identity and reward and the men's insistence that women were incompetent to deal with the work. Many of the men expressed the view that women would be welcome, but they undermined this receptivity by emphasizing how difficult it would be for them because of the qualities of endurance, strength, and mechanical capacity required to deal with dirty and dangerous work.

Gender Ideology and the Reward System

Male workers in traditionally blue-collar occupations accentuate their manliness by distinguishing their work from women's work. But among men those who regard themselves as most manly derive a sense of identity, and the rewards that go with it, by considering men working in other craft jobs and managers as effeminate, reinforcing a "them/us" boundary. In the telephone company, the most manly jobs were defined as those of the splicers, who derived comfort and affirmation by setting up a boundary between their work and that of installers and repairmen, who were also "outside" craft workers highly regarded in the company. Splicers derisively referred to installers and repairmen as "women" (in the same way as the AFL union leaders referred to Polish and Italian men as nonwhite) to signify their "softer" jobs.

Henry Braverman (1974) has written that lower-level workers subscribe to a logic in boundaries to justify their status and position. They circumscribe their experience from others within the same class to identify those who have even worse situations (Bellows 1991). In her study of factory workers, Barbara Garson (1975) showed that "one way that everyone kept their spirits up . . . was to pity everyone else." The men pity the women because they do the slighter tasks: "The women think it's all right for them but pity a man who has this for his career. The blacks pity any white who'd have to take a job like that. The whites pity the blacks who won't ever get anything better" (Garson 1975, 20).

In the comments from my interviews that follow (Epstein 1989, 581), one can see both how splicers enunciated a sense of pride that

depended on valuing themselves more favorably than men in other jobs
and a high personal investment in splicers' macho qualities:

They're more loyal to each other as opposed to repairmen/installers . . . they're
more loyal to each other in a gang and to their foreman and to the job.
We work outside in all types of weather, down manholes which some repairmen and installers won't come within 25 feet of. . . . I think that they think
of us as animals really.
Yeah, they [installers and repairmen] won't go into basements because it's too
dark and dirty. They'll call for assistance because they don't like the looks of
the neighborhood. I mean, we're allowed to do the same thing but it seems
they'll flag a job a lot faster than that.

This gender ideology and the sense of collectivity experienced by
splicers has fed into their self-definition. Here, occupation and self-
image merge so that the boundaries of the occupation (the job description, as it were) become the boundaries of the self. This is expressed
in the comments of splicers I interviewed (Epstein 1989, 581) that
follow:

There used to be a commercial on television. It was a family decorating a tree
and then it was good night time. The husband and wife had gone to bed, the
children in bed, now the lights are out and the phone rings. The guy answers
the phone and he gets up and gets dressed. He goes out to his car and he
drives to a Telephone garage. He gets in his truck and he clears a failure. He
was a splicer. . . . The idea was that *we, the telephone company* are willing to work
under any conditions at anytime to give *you, the people* service. I appreciated that
commercial. I don't think too many other people really remember it but I do
because that's what we do. *Being a splicer is us.*
I think a splicer is willing to go a little bit further . . . he's willing to go down
into the mud a little quicker than someone else and I think that leads over into
your personal life.
[It makes us] a little more aggressive in our personalities; quicker to make
decisions . . . that's what a splicer does, he makes decisions. A splicer, I think,
has a good sense of balance, a good sense of balance of his job and of his life.

Gender Ideology as a Means of Securing Compliance at Work

Managers may reinforce cultural views about the boundaries between
men's work and women's work because such views seem reasonable,
but they may also manipulate gender ideology because heightening
gender distinctions sometimes provides a means of controlling the

242   Cynthia Fuchs Epstein

workers, of undermining their resistance and maximizing consent on
the job.

A foreman of a group of switchmen interviewed by Steven Vallas
(personal communication) for his study of class consciousness (see
Vallas, forthcoming) among the Communications Workers of America
(CWA) related how he used the culture of manhood among craftsmen
to humiliate them in a grievance over the quality of toilet paper the
company provided (part of a larger group of complaints). The foreman,
resorting to gender ideology, "admitted" to his switchmen that there
had been a mistake. The toilet paper they had received really had been
ordered by the splicers, who naturally were tougher and more manly
than switchmen. As he related it, "The workers knew I was telling
them they couldn't take it. . . . I never heard any more grievances about
toilet paper again."

Gender differentiation may enhance or diminish the ranks and
power of labor. Traditional craft unions used a macho ideology to
organize and retain membership loyalty. Vallas was told by managers
that union militancy was directly related to the physical strength manifested on the job. But unions resisted recruiting women workers, partially because they were women, partially because they were unskilled.
As Brooks (1977) points out, the International Brotherhood of Electri-
cal Workers (IBEW) did not want to unionize women telephone operators because they feared that women's voting rights might require "men
handling the sting of electricity to submit forever to the rule of telephone operators" (Brooks 1977, 11).

The CWA union halls, which I visited in my ethnographic explorations of work settings, were decorated with gun racks and pinups, not
a hospitable environment for women. Language in the slogans and
signs displayed was also coarse—for example, the classic and sociologically astute, "If you've got them by the balls, their hearts and minds
will follow."[6] Women in the construction trades, ship building, and
other male-dominated occupations routinely confront visual assaults
such as pictures of nude women with comments written on them and
sexual teasing.[7] Men also control women by isolating them from the
informal camaraderie of the workplace as well as by using bantering
sexual innuendo. Recent studies have consistently found that about
30 percent of women blue-collar workers report harassment (e.g.,
O'Farrell 1988).

Culturally determined boundaries served male unionists' interests in
the British hosiery company studied by Sallie Westwood. In one conflict, the unions supported large differentials between male and female

wage rates, defending their decision on the grounds that men's work was skilled whereas women's was not. According to Westwood, this illustrates that the fight against low pay is crucially bound up with a struggle against sexist ideologies in the trade union movement (Westwood 1985, 234).

In his work on coal miners in Appalachia, Michael Yarrow has noted that management appeals to the male values of physical strength, competition, and courage as a means of obtaining worker consent to arduous and dangerous work. A coal miner was assigned with two other men to lift heavy steel rails. A miner remarked that it looked like a four-man job. The foreman asked, "What's the matter? Aren't you man enough?" (Yarrow 1987, 9).

Since miners derive psychic rewards from identification with manly work and managers derive economic benefit from appeals to this identity, both groups react hostilely to the intrusion of women in the mines. Foremen fear a loss of productivity and miners a loss of dignity. If women can do men's work, then the prestige accorded male work declines. Although some women have been integrated into these settings, clear demarcations are set up. Women miners may be given especially difficult work to prove that they are incompetent. Or men may go out of their way to help them in order to show that they cannot do the work.

Women who became coal handlers in a power plant studied by Reskin and Padavic (1988) complained that men created bonds among themselves by discussions of sex that excluded women and, further, that they were the butt of pranks such as being tossed back and forth by male workers as if they were children.

Gender boundaries are also maintained by the most sophisticated professionals, even those most dedicated to equality. Today, certain feminist theorists extol a distinctive set of attributes with regard to morality that they ascribe to women. Although women's distinctiveness is placed in a positive light, it nevertheless offers the possibility for sanctioning women who employ a moral stance that differs from the sanctioned view. Mary Douglas's (1966) depiction of the pure and the impure, which are used by groups to stake the boundaries between "us" and "them," is pertinent here. The belief that there is a distinctive "woman's voice" has gained popularity in recent years thanks to the views of the psychologist Carol Gilligan (1982). Gilligan's further views that women are predisposed to a morality based on relationships and caring, unlike men, whose morality tends to abstract notions of justice and fairness, have also influenced many feminists in the legal academy. Most of these scholars assume that women are more moral than men and that, therefore, each has a different orientation to the legal sphere.

These general views are not especially new. However, although the older views about difference have long limited women's opportunities to advance in the legal profession, many feminists (like their turn-of-the-century counterparts in the suffrage movement) make a plea that women ought to have access to the profession because they will make a difference in it (providing, i.e., that they do not "act like men," unnaturally). Bourdieu (1984) suggests that those who have no "real" resources, such as money and cultural contacts, offer their morality and asceticism on the market. This may be a latent strategy of the outspoken advocates of women's "voice." But there is no evidence that, except in a handful of cases (appointments to faculties more than jobs in firms), this strategy is effective. In my *Women in Law* (Epstein 1981), I have documented many cases that attest to the discrimination that flowed from the general cultural beliefs about women's particular nature, but here I will refer briefly to the techniques used in the past and more recently.

Up until the 1970s, discrimination against women entering the law was rampant. For decades, women constituted only 3 percent of the profession because of restrictive quotas against them in the schools and in the legal job market. The few women attorneys who managed to receive law degrees were clustered in a limited number of specialties and types of practice, such as domestic relations, child custody, voluntary legal defense of the poor, and government work. More from the coercion of limited opportunity rather than free choice they devoted themselves to doing good.

With women virtually closed out of corporate work and prosecution and having found a niche as advocates for the betterment and protection of women and children, it is not surprising that the first women to ascend the bench were chosen to serve as judges in the women's juvenile or family courts of inferior jurisdiction (Cook 1986; Epstein 1981). As I found in my studies of women lawyers (Epstein 1968, 1981), employers' assumptions regarding the special personality traits of women led to their assignment to specialties that were usually dead-end and less prestigious, less lucrative, and often less interesting than those of men. Assumptions that they had less motivation and commitment as lawyers than did men made women's prospects for promotion to a partnership poor. Women often found themselves in "no-win" situations, regarded as not tough enough to handle business law and the stress of the courtroom but too tough to be easy collaborators and partners. They were regarded as too pure to make deals, too caring to be tough minded, or too stiff and unyielding to be able to make the kinds of deals and settlements that male lawyers depended on for the easy, informal professional relationships that they regarded as characteristic of professional life. Women who were (and are) tough faced the disapproval of both men and women colleagues and even of feminist attorneys, who faulted them for assuming a "male model" of behavior (or for wearing clothing regarded as "masculine" in style)[8] and otherwise deviating from sex-role-appropriate attitudes. Sometimes the same behavior was characterized by women practitioners as conforming to sex-role designations (e.g., "I am caring") but by their associates as nonconforming (e.g., "She is a barracuda!"). Yet even women who conform to traditional female modes of behavior—such as being demure and deferential—in male-dominated settings are characterized as demonstrating inappropriate behavior. According to a manager in a British study (Fogarty, Rapoport, and Rapoport 1971), they were "nice mice" or "dragons," attesting to the fact that women are in a no-win situation whatever their style of behavior.

Women lawyers have also been faulted for deviating from norms of demeanor and emotion attached to gender roles when they act "straight" and business-like in professional settings. I found (Epstein 1981) that male colleagues find such women stiff and evaluate them as interpersonally incompetent, and women colleagues often agree. Similar stereotypes also attach to women judges. Like those applied to women lawyers, the views are often inconsistent. One stereotype holds that women judges are harsher than male judges; another, closer to the "caring" model, maintains that women judges are apt to be more lenient and empathic than men on the bench. Yet studies that measure the judges' behavior, such as their sentencing practices, show few differences, on average, in their decisions, even those having to do with rape (Epstein 1981).

Only last year, the Supreme Court was split on the issue of whether judgments regarding women's qualities were acceptable under the Civil Rights Act of 1964 or whether they constituted acts of discrimination. *Ann Hopkins v. Price Waterhouse* (1987) is the case of a woman who was passed over for partnership in this large "Big 8" accounting firm because of her alleged aggressive personality and unfeminine appearance and conduct. She was, however, regarded as a good accountant and had obtained a large contract for the firm. The partner responsible for advising Hopkins of the factors that caused her candidacy to be placed on hold indicated that her professional problems would be solved if she would "walk more femininely, talk more femininely, wear make-up, have her hair styled, and wear jewelry." The majority opinion (in a five to four vote) stated, "It takes no special training to discern sex-stereotyping in a description of an aggressive female employee as requiring 'a course at charm school'" (as a partner in the firm had told her). "If an employee's flawed 'interpersonal skills' can be corrected by a soft-hued suit or a new shade of lipstick, perhaps it is the employee's sex and not her interpersonal skills that has drawn criticism."

The newest case to be decided in the partnership assessment process was that of *Nancy O'Mara Ezold v. Wolf Block* (case no. 90-0002, 29 November 1990). Ezold was offered a partnership in the domestic relations department of the firm Wolf Block and denied one in litigation. Her evaluations stated that she was "a good, stand-up effective courtroom lawyer." "She is unafraid," another wrote. "She is one of those people who is here weekends and nights . . . she never complains about the workload. . . . Moreover, she can try cases because of her guts and maturity. That is not true of all of our litigators." However, several male associates who had been evaluated negatively for *lacking* sufficient assertiveness in their demeanor were made partners. Comments about them included, "I doubt that he will ever be anything but a helper who does what he is told adequately but with no spark." "Mr. B is very lazy and when an assignment or case does not interest him, he gives the matter only minimal attention" ("Judge Explains" 1990, 29).

Appraisals of women's attributes and demeanor remain a problem for women lawyers and other professionals who are in a position to assess them. Yet there has been a revolution in the legal workplace. Women are, indeed, a formidable presence because of the number of women obtaining degrees and entering the profession and the fact that, at entry levels, at least, they have been welcomed. Thus, we find women attorneys squared off against each other in the courtroom: defense versus prosecuting attorneys; women lawyers for the public good versus women lawyers for the big corporate interests. Women judges now work at all levels of the judicial system, some appointed by Jimmy Carter manifesting, more or less, the kind of liberal-minded points of view you might expect, and those appointed by Ronald Reagan handing down conservative judgments.

Control over women's conformity to gender-specific norms may also be seen in a traditional woman's occupation, nursing. Attending to the emotional (and physical) needs of others has long been designated as women's work; more recently, caring has been proclaimed as the essence of nursing (Adams 1971; Graham 1983; Laslett and Brenner 1989; Leininger 1984). As Cindy Merkel points out in her recent study of the emotional work of nurses, the assignment of empathic role-taking emotions to women functions as a form of social control in that it ensures the social reproduction of society. It leaves the housekeeping tasks of society to women and the female-dominated professions, and nursing in particular, have enabled society to maintain integrity and continuity (Adams 1971; Merkel 1990). Here, as elsewhere, women are exposed to "feeling rules" as an ideological stance (Hochschild 1979). For nurses, caring is identified as the essence of their practice. In the view of one nurse studied by Merkel, "It's part of our job—holistic care—body, mind, spirit." These nurses attribute their propensity and ability to do emotion work to a range of sources, including learning on the job (professional socialization), society's dictate, and (for some but by no means all) their inherent capabilities as women. Some of the nurses believe that (the mostly male) physicians with whom they work should express caring too, but do not, possibly because they "don't have the time." When asked whether it was also because men were not as good at it, one woman expressed the sentiment of some others: "Well, we're trained to do it." But it is clearly conceptualized as a "duty to care," viewed as an obligation. Yet, because caring behavior is usually invisible to supervisors and not evaluated specifically, as is technical work, and because it is posed against an ideal of the "rational" work of men, nurses do not derive much benefit in terms of advancement or autonomy.[9]

Yet, in certain cases (employing the power of the weak, one might say), some nurses felt that there was some advantage to their assignment of emotion work. Merkel, citing Epstein (1988) and Hochschild (1983), points out that, lacking other resources, women make a resource out of feeling and offer it to men in return for the resources of money, power, and authority. Merkel further observes that this strategy is especially effective since gender stereotypes in our culture largely dictate that men ignore the affective realm. As one of her respondents put it,

It's as if the doctor will say, "you handle that patient and I don't want to hear about it." That's where I get my power base from my role, what the physicians use me for is the patients they can't handle . . . it seems like very subtle power, not direct at all. It's not as if the doctors are saying "Mary handles patients in crisis" at all. It reminds me of the stereotypical 1950's television marriage where the wife is always getting her way by manipulating her husband to think it's his idea.

Merkel found that nurses figured that the doctors still appreciated their intervening to minister to the emotional needs of patients and calculated that they might draw on this when they needed backup to accomplish something they needed to do: "If I had an administrative problem, the Attendings would say, 'who should I talk to and how much money do you need?' . . . Or if I was having trouble with one of the residents, I know they [the resident] would be spoken to immediately. You can use this to *crumble* a resident" (emphasis added).

Men punish women, but women also punish themselves, and each other, for moving over boundary lines. Women engage in brooding or accusations of failure to conform to traditional sex-role behavior that produces guilt. To counteract the negative consequences of violating boundaries, either in the assault to their identity or in response to men's punishing behavior, some women engage in symbolic behavior to highlight gender distinctiveness. In the telephone company, women engaged in both traditional and nontraditional jobs organized celebrations at work with homemade cookies and cakes. Even in the mines, Yarrow (1987) reports, women go into the pits and set the table for a festive occasion.

These women do not want to become "men" and lose their "femininity" because they are punished for it by men's refusal to regard them as "real women"—as dates, for example—outside work, as one divorced woman miner complained to Yarrow. Furthermore, because in the community cleanliness is as much a mark of womanliness as dirt is of manliness, doing dirty work was a threat to women's identity, even as they pursued it for economic reasons. Even in white-collar and professional work such as trial law and financial mergers and takeovers, where coarse and bombastic language is used as a symbolic representation of assertiveness and competence, women also worry about their identities, expressing concern that they have become "men" (Epstein 1981).

Westwood's women hosiery workers engaged in a workplace culture infused with emphasis on traditional priorities for women. Through highly elaborated rituals and ceremonies commemorating engagements and pregnancy, as well as by their choice of workplace attire (slippers and homemade aprons), women's roles as wives and mothers were emphasized over their commitment to the workplace.

The Boundary between Workplace and Home

The boundaries that set the home apart from the workplace in modern society are obvious. Many mechanisms accomplish separation. But it is useful for the analysis of control to consider the overlap and connections that exist between the workplace and the home.

Yarrow points out how miners' dangerous work legitimizes their patriarchal and authoritarian behavior in the home. No one questions their behavior because of the sacrifices they are presumed to make for the family. But when miners are laid off, they can no longer depend on this legitimation, and rising levels of family violence follow, ascribed by Yarrow in part to the miners' attempts to preserve eroding patriarchal positions.

Yet many men exhibit more positive responses. As it becomes more usual for wives to go to work because of economic circumstances, miners take on new family work responsibilities without much resistance. They are, of course, supported by changing ideology and representations in the media that "helping out" at home and with the kids is a reasonable activity for red-blooded American men. Blue-collar telephone company men prefer their wives to stay home (because of the value they place on traditional family life), but nonetheless many of their wives work, and they do not see this as incongruent with the preferred model. Some rationalize it by defining their wife's employment as something she does for her own enjoyment or for "extras" they could otherwise live without. But the men's greater participation in household responsibilities, which may be seen as a change in boundary distinction, may not seriously alter ideological divisions in the household. A number of studies of middle-class managerial and blue-collar men (Yarrow 1987; Weiss 1990) show that a good proportion see themselves as devoted family men. Breadwinning is the linchpin of this model, but "pitching in" is also regarded as the family way and the American way.

Although men may participate more in the home, many are not eager to relinquish their authority by doing so. This is especially the case if they lack authority on the job and can exercise authority only in the home. If men face problems in maintaining authority at home because of an altered situation at work, how does gender ideology affect women who have acquired authority at work?

As a result of the consent decree, the telephone company was forced to promote more women to supervisory roles. Women supervisors interviewed in a commercial representative's office reported that they found it difficult to maintain the home/work boundary; their new selves were activated at home. Yet they found that husbands and male companions tried to reinstate the traditional pattern if they could, and sometimes they did act as a constraint on women's exercise of altered behavior. One woman talked about how the air of authority she had cultivated at work to "get things done" was carried over at home and rebuffed by such comments as, "You're talking to your husband, you're not talking to your employees." Or another, "A guy I was dating . . . said to me . . . 'I don't work for you!'" (Epstein 1989, 587).

The fear of upsetting the authority structure at home affected the way women perceived opportunity. Often, their fears stemmed from past experience and anticipated problems. The rumination of one operator was representative of many others: "I worry about what would happen if I work my way and become a supervisor . . . some women can do that—they figure, well, women's lib: they worked their way up. . . . I don't think I could do that to him [my husband] as a man . . . every week my paycheck is a little more than his because of all the time he takes off. I know it aggravates him—if I make a dollar or two more, he's frustrated that I'm making more than him" (Epstein 1989, 587).

Both separation of home and work and gender ideology are important in defining the goals of work for men and women. Male incomes have long been justified as "family wages." The perspective that men are the breadwinners in the family led, in the past, to defining women's wages at work as "pin money" or second incomes. The definition of work according to gender boundaries leads to some interesting paradoxes and consequences. I found that, among women communications workers, many married women also regard their wages as second incomes. Yet surveying women's contributions to family income in one rural community showed that, typically, they earned more than their husbands, who were often seasonal workers such as fishermen and carpenters (Epstein 1989, 588). Thus, definition of their employment as secondary acted as a control on the women's aspirations because they looked forward to a time (perhaps only in fantasy) when they would leave work and be supported by their husbands. It made the women feel more feminine to feel that they were being supported even when they were providing the most reliable income in the family. Management also accepted this definition, and it figured in their encouragement of men to seek transfers to better jobs and their essentially passive regard for upgrading women.

The specific effects of gender ideology thus may have multiple and even contradictory consequences. Working men may take pride in their ability to withstand harsh and debilitating conditions, and women may accept less pay or advancement because they believe that women deserve less or because it makes life less difficult to manage at home.

Gender Ideology and Worker Resistance

However, gender ideology may stimulate worker resistance as when the development of a woman's work culture reinforces the boundary between women workers and male managers (Costello 1985; Lamphere 1985). Cynthia Costello's (1985) study of clerical workers showed how concerns about family duties (such as being a good mother) provoked a group of women workers to protest collectively the rigid policies of management through a strike. In fact, labor history is replete with examples of women workers' activism in the name of family needs. At Westwood's (1985) factory, the women came together to fight targets and rates. According to Westwood's account, "Solidarity and sisterhood marked the struggles around economic issues on the shop floor."

When Gender Becomes Less Salient

Of course, gender is not always activated, nor is gender ideology always the most powerful determinant of workplace relations. At the telephone company, we found that many women and many men managed to cross over sex-defined and class-defined boundaries to make use of opportunities and often experienced changes in their identities as a result. Many women who were given more responsibility at work became more secure about their competence and exercise of positions of authority. Typically, but not exclusively, these were women who were free from strong community ties and integrated family networks that could act as controls on behavior not considered traditional for women. Men's identity is more at risk taking on nontraditional roles, which were easily assumed when they were stopgaps in an otherwise "male career line." Men's acceptance of a female partner's assumption of a nontraditional role often depended on the security of their own jobs and the nature of the community at work and at home. For both groups, however, economic pressure created both the impetus and the justification for stepping out of line when the opportunity was available, as long as harassment, psychic or physical, was not a real threat.

There are many other types of boundary issues to contemplate in looking at issues of and the force of control in the experience of workers at all levels of the stratification system at home and in the family. This essay represents an attempt to wed cultural and structural factors in the analysis of change and its limits.

Notes

The research on which this essay is based was funded in part by the Russell Sage Foundation and the Research Foundation of the City University of New York. Support of the Institute for Research on Women and Gender at Stanford University is also gratefully acknowledged. I am grateful for comments on sections of this essay by Charles Tilly and Steven Vallas and the editorial hand of Howard M. Epstein. Portions of this analysis and interview material appeared in Epstein (1989).

1. Of course they also serve to limit the possibility of having selves other than those that are assigned.

2. The boundaries of groups, like those of communities, perform the same function as the boundaries of all categories of knowledge. All such categories are marked by symbolism, as Rodney Needham (1979) alerted us. The symbolism may be made explicit through rituals that discriminate between social roles, life and death, the stage of the life cycle, gender, and the pure and the polluted. But much symbolism, as Anthony Cohen (1985) points out, does not have a special vocabulary or idiomatic behavior: it is part of the meaning we ascribe to pragmatic and instrumental things such as words.

Words both denote object and convey attitude. For example, words such as *freedom* and *democracy* do not merely describe forms of government and legal status; they also tell us the attitude to take toward these forms. Similarly, *woman's work* does not merely tell us what women do; it tells us that that work is not for men. And *unskilled work* clearly connotes a form of work inferior to that which is *skilled*. Thus, according to Cranston (1954), words used to make distinctions may be regarded as "hurrah" words to "boo" words.

Mary Douglas (1966) further shows the implicit directives lodged in certain words. For example, she points out that the use of the word *dirt* does more than signify the particles under the fingernails. It also expresses an attitude, "Ugh," and prescribes a remedy, "Scrub!" Thus, a *wimp* is not merely described; he is advised to stand up and be a man.

3. I acknowledge the contribution of Lamont and Wuthnow (1991) for the references to Bourdieu and Foucault and these points. See also Hall (1984) and Epstein (1984, 1988).

4. For further discussion of particular writers on this matter, see Lamont and Wuthnow (1990).

5. Some of the illustrations from communications workers are also cited in Epstein (1989).

6. Yet the CWA faces a diminishing recruitment base because of the reduction in the number of traditionally male craft jobs, and some union officials were becoming more receptive to organizing women. Furthermore, because many of their members were facing job conditions that were similar to or the same as women's, they were learning to appreciate problems formerly dismissed because they were problems of women's work.

7. Recently, a female shipyard welder who accused her employer of sexual harassment won a ground-breaking ruling that posting pictures of nude or partly nude women is a form of sexual harassment. A federal court judge, Howell Melton of the district court in Jacksonville, Florida, held the employer liable for the harassment, claiming that the shipyard maintained a "boys' club atmosphere with an unrelenting assault on the sensibilities of female workers," including calendars and close-ups of women's genitals posted on the walls (Lewin 1991).

8. Or for internalizing "men's dreams," as one popular writer put it. Suzanne Gordon's *Prisoners of Men's Dreams* (1991) criticizes hard-working professional women for not engaging in the care-giving activities that women have traditionally assumed.

9. This is similar to the low value placed on teaching in research universities, where outstanding teaching may be recognized as worthy but not as important as publication when evaluating a person for promotion.

References

Adams, Margaret. "The Compassion Trap." In *Women In Sexist Society*, ed. V. Gornick and B. K. Moran. New York: Basic, 1971.

Ann Hopkins v. Price Waterhouse, 825 F.2d 458, 468 (D.C. Circuit, 1987).

Bellows, Ann. "The New York City Volunteer Corps: An Analysis of Workplace Passages and Boundaries." Department of Sociology, Graduate Center, City University of New York, 1991. Typescript.

Berg, Ivar. "Deregulating the Economy and Reforming Workers: The Eclipse of Industrial Economy." In *Reflections on America 1984: An Orwell Symposium*, ed. R. Mulvihill. Athens: University of Georgia Press, 1986.

Bourdieu, Pierre. *Distinction*. Cambridge, Mass.: Harvard University Press, 1984.

Braverman, Harry. *Labor and Monopoly Capitalism: The Degradation of Work in the Twentieth Century*. New York: Monthly Review Press, 1974.

Brooks, Thomas R. *Communications Workers of America: Story of a Union*. New York: Mason-Charter, 1977.

Chodorow, Nancy. *The Reproduction of Mothering: Psychoanalysis and the Sociology of Gender*. Berkeley and Los Angeles: University of California Press, 1978.

Cockburn, Cynthia. *Brothers: Male Dominance and Technological Change*. London: Pluto, 1983.

Cohen, Anthony. *Symbolic Construction of Community.* London: Tavistock, 1985.

Cook, Beverly. "Legal Institution-Building in the Progressive Era: The Los Angeles Women's Court." Paper presented at the annual meeting of the Southern Political Science Association, 7 November 1986.

Costello, Cynthia. "'WEA're Worth It!' Work, Culture and Conflict at the Wisconsin Education Association Insurance Trust." *Feminist Studies* 11 (Fall 1985): 497–518.

Cranston, M. 1954. *Freedom: A New Analysis.* London: Longman.

Douglas, Mary. *Purity and Danger: An Analysis of Concepts of Pollution and Taboo.* London: Penguin, 1966.

Epstein, Cynthia Fuchs. "Women and Professional Careers: The Case of the Woman Lawyer." Ph.D. diss., Columbia University, Department of Sociology, 1968.

Epstein, Cynthia Fuchs. *Woman's Place: Options and Limits in Professional Careers.* Berkeley: University of California Press, 1970.

Epstein, Cynthia Fuchs. *Women in Law.* New York: Basic, 1981.

Epstein, Cynthia Fuchs. "Ideal Images and Real Roles: The Perpetuation of Gender Inequality." *Dissent* 31, no. 4 (Fall 1984): 441–47.

Epstein, Cynthia Fuchs. "Ideal Roles and Real Roles or the Fallacy of the Misplaced Dichotomy." *Research in Social Stratification and Mobility* 4 (1985): 29–51.

Epstein, Cynthia Fuchs. *Deceptive Distinctions: Sex, Gender and the Social Order.* New York: Russell Sage; New Haven, Conn.: Yale University Press, 1988.

Epstein, Cynthia Fuchs. "Workplace Boundaries: Conceptions and Creations." *Social Research* 56, no. 3 (Autumn 1989).

Epstein, Cynthia Fuchs. "Faulty Framework: Consequences of the Difference Model for Women in the Law." *New York Law School Law Review* 35, no. 2 (1990): 309–335.

Epstein, Cynthia Fuchs. "The Difference Model: Enforcement and Reinforcement of Women's Roles in the Law." In *Social Roles and Social Institutions: Essays in Honor of Rose Laub Coser,* ed. Judith R. Blau and Norman Goodman. Boulder, Colo.: Westview, 1991.

Epstein, Cynthia Fuchs, and Kai T. Erikson. *Workplace Boundaries* (forthcoming).

Fogarty, Michael, Rhona Rapoport, and Robert Rapoport. *Women in Top Jobs: Four Studies in Achievement.* London: Allen & Unwin, 1971.

Foner, Phillip. *The Policies and Practices of the American Federation of Labor, 1900–1909.* New York: International, 1964.

Garson, Barbara. *All the Livelong Day: The Meaning and Demeaning of Work.* 1975. Reprint. New York: Doubleday, 1986.

Gerson, Judith, and Kathy Peiss. "Boundaries, Negotiation and Consciousness: Reconceptualizing Gender Relations." *Social Problems* 32 (April 1985): 317–31.

Gilligan, Carol. *In a Different Voice*. Cambridge, Mass.: Harvard University Press, 1982.

Gordon, Suzanne. *Prisoners of Men's Dreams: Striking Out for a New Feminine Future*. Boston: Little, Brown, 1991.

Graham, Hilary. "Caring: A Labor of Love." In *A Labor of Love: Women, Work and Caring*, ed. J. Finch and D. Groves. London: Routledge & Kegan Paul, 1983.

Hall, S. "Cultural Studies at the Center: Some Problematics and Problems." In *Culture, Media, Language*, ed. S. Hall, Dorothy Hobson, Andrew Lowe, and Paul Willis. London: Hutchison, 1984.

Hochschild, Arlie Russell. "Emotion Work, Feeling Rules, and Social Structure." *American Journal of Sociology* 85, no. 3 (1979): 551–75.

"Judge Explains Wolf Block Decision." *National Law Journal* (10 December 1990).

Lamont, Michèle. *Money, Morals, and Manners: The Culture of the French and the American Upper-Middle Class*. Chicago: University of Chicago Press, 1992.

Lamont, Michèle, and Robert Wuthnow. "Betwixt and Between: Recent Cultural Sociology in Europe and the United States." In *Frontiers of Social Theory: The New Synthesis*, ed. George Ritzer. New York: Columbia University Press, 1990.

Lamphere, Louise. "Bringing the Family to Work: Women's Culture on the Shop Floor." *Feminist Studies* 11 (Fall 1985): 519–40.

Laslett, Barbara, and Johanna Brenner. "Gender and Social Reproduction: Historical Perspectives." *Annual Review of Sociology* 15 (1989): 381–404.

Leininger, Madeline. "Care: The Essence of Nursing and Health." In *Care: The Essence of Nursing and Health*, ed. M. Leininger. Thorofare, N.J.: Slack, 1984.

Lewin, Tamar. "Nude Pictures Are Ruled Sexual Harassment." *New York Times*, 23 January 1991.

Markus, Hazel, and Paul Nurius. "Possible Selves." *American Psychologist* 41 (September 1986): 954–69.

Merkel, Cindy. "The Emotional Labor of Nurses." Department of Sociology, Graduate Center, City University of New York, 1990. Typescript.

Needham, Rodney. *Symbolic Classifications*. Santa Monica, Calif.: Goodyear, 1979.

O'Farrell, Brigid. "Women in Blue-Collar Occupations: Traditional and Nontraditional." In *Women Working: Theories and Facts in Perspective*, ed. Ann Helton Stromberg and Shirley Harkess. Mountain View, Calif.: Mayfield, 1988.

Reskin, Barbara, and Irene Padavic. "Male Plant Supervisors' Resistance to Sex Integration." Paper presented at the annual meeting of the American Sociological Association, Atlanta, 1988.

Roos, Patricia. "Hot-Metal to Electronic Composition: Gender, Technology and Social Change." In *Job Queues, Gender Queues: Explaining Women's Inroads into Male Occupations,* ed. Barbara F. Reskin and Patricia A. Roos. Philadelphia: Temple University Press, 1990.

Vallas, Steven Peter. *Working for Bell: A Study of Technology, Work and Class Consciousness.* Philadelphia: Temple University Press, forthcoming.

Weiss, Robert. *Staying the Course: The Social and Emotional Lives of Men Who Are Successful.* New York: Free Press, 1990.

Westwood, Sallie. *All Day, Every Day: Factory and Family in the Making of Women's Lives.* Champaign: University of Illinois Press, 1985.

Yarrow, Michael. "Class and Gender in the Developing Consciousness of Appalachian Coal Miners." Paper presented to the Fifth UMIST-ASTON annual conference on Organization and Control of the Labor Process, Manchester, England, 22–24 April 1987.

ELEVEN

The Capital(s) of Cultures:
A Nonholistic Approach to
Status Situations, Class,
Gender, and Ethnicity

John R. Hall

Viewed at the surface, the cultural objects of this world have no apparent order to them. They appear everywhere, diverse, often in a jumble. Similarly, to look at how each individual acts is to see cultural practices that form a unique and shifting array. Nevertheless, the dazzling variety and endless differences of culture obtain surprising coherence when we look at them through the lens of social stratification. People prepare and consume food in distinctive ways. Some people are quite concerned with becoming culturally accomplished—learning to quilt, to dance, to ride horses, or to surf. For others, indifference to distinction is itself a badge of honor. Such stances toward culture differ by social position and group, there can be no doubt. Yet how are they to be explained? This question is the fulcrum on which an Archimedes could rearrange core social theory about the connections among social stratification, socialization, group processes of inclusion and exclusion, and cultural meaning.

Pierre Bourdieu can lay a claim to the Archimedean role: his theory of cultural capital provocatively appropriates and synthesizes selected themes from the discipline of sociology's classic triumvirate—Marx, Durkheim, and Weber (Brubaker 1985). Moreover, he has effectively linked issues that too often had become appropriated as the exclusive domains of sociology's subdisciplines.[1] But the power of Bourdieu's vision and the importance of his work should not obscure central difficulties of his theory. By now a number of scholars who generally praise Bourdieu's work nevertheless have voiced criticisms of various aspects of his approach. In this essay, I argue that these criticisms, when consolidated and elaborated, require a retheorization of the basic model of cultural capital. Specifically, I suggest that many of Bourdieu's difficulties noted by critics stem from a single feature, his positing of a holistic and objective field of social distinctions. As an alternative, I propose a theoretical framework of *cultural structuralism* that recognizes heterologous (cf. de Certeau 1986) markets, currencies, and grounds of legitimation of multiple kinds of cultural capital. The alternative framework resolves the difficulties of Bourdieu's approach stemming from its holism, at the same time allowing a more robust theorization of the interplay among diverse forms of cultural capital.

Many of the problems noted by appreciative critics of Bourdieu seem to stem from holism as a general theoretical presupposition, if *holism* is defined as the thesis that a social order has an overall systemic (in this case, cultural) pattern that gives definition to its parts and their interrelations. Essentially, Bourdieu posits cultural capital as a general medium of accumulation and recognition. The array of social distinctions that he describes thus obtains the quality of an objective structure (e.g., Bourdieu 1984; Bourdieu 1985b, 725–26, 730; Bourdieu 1989). This feature of Bourdieu's account of distinction may stem from a residue of French structuralism in his work, from his Durkheimian epistemological objectivism, and from the specific empirical character of the French and especially Parisian social field (Brubaker 1985, 754; Garnham and Williams 1986, 119; Lamont and Lareau 1988, 158, n. 5).[2] True, Bourdieu claimed to have begun from Weber, and his *Outline of a Theory of Practice* ([1972] 1977) offered a phenomenological critique of French structuralist theory, albeit within the comparatively coherent symbolic world of Kabylia, Algeria. But despite these moves, Bourdieu's account remains deeply infused with ideas from the long tradition of French structuralism that emphasizes public culture as socially definitive for individuals subjected to its claims, even if those individuals do not inwardly share its aesthetics or meaningful content.

To be sure, a structuralist approach is well suited to describing the ritual power of culture in the museum, the symphony, the soap opera, the sporting event, and civic symbolic politics (Alexander 1988). As with Emile Durkheim's case of religion (and this as an analogue of "mechanical" solidarity in society), ritual practice establishes boundaries of inclusion and exclusion, thereby forging a group out of diverse individuals, maintaining and sanctifying cultural difference, and, potentially, establishing the outsider as scapegoat (Hall 1987, chap. 12). Yet structuralism is ill prepared to deal with the complexities of multicultural situations tied to complex, market-oriented social formations, except by the holistic device of positing a single matrix or grid of objectively meaningful social location. It is this device that Bourdieu uses to amend the structuralist narrative, defining cultural capital as a medium of cultural affirmation that does not depend on public ritual, by invoking Weber's class-based status groups as the purveyors of the most fundamental distinctions, and by emphasizing the importance of concrete practices of *habitus* in the framing of distinctions.

Whatever its intellectual origins, whatever its validity as a secular theory of France, the positing of an objective field of distinction as a general theoretical model seems problematic, as Lamont and Lareau (1988) have argued. The difficulties manifest themselves on a number of fronts noted by various analysts. In the first place, for Lamont and Lareau, the grounds of high-status distinction are themselves diverse and potentially incommensurate. Second, as Lamont (1992) has shown empirically, the class-fraction source of putatively legitimate standards of distinction may not have the elite provenance that Bourdieu has described. Third, although Bourdieu's *Distinction* (1984) recognizes the existence of divergent standards of distinction among different social classes[3] (see also Bourdieu 1976; cf. Gans 1974), this observation remains theoretically undeveloped in his own work, which primarily addresses the importance of a posited hegemonic, dominant, and legitimate culture (Garnham and Williams 1986, 126–30; Lamont and Lareau 1988, 157). Fourth, the considerable gap between Bourdieu's theoretical claims and his quantitative analyses of empirical evidence (Brubaker 1985, 767) has raised concerns about objectivist measurement realism (Schatzki 1987). Fifth, even if Bourdieu has professed an interest in transcending the subjective/objective binary, both his theory and his statistical studies seem to tilt the analysis in the objectivist direction. Yet Lamont and Lareau (1988, 158, 164–65) have questioned any "zero-sum" model of cultural capital that presumes all specific distinctions to be defined "relationally" within an objective field of distinction. Sixth, Garnham and Williams (1986, 129) have similarly commented on "a functionalist/determinist residue in Bourdieu's concept of reproduction [of class structure] which leads him to place less emphasis on the possibilities of real change and innovation than either his theory or his empirical research makes necessary." Finally, Bourdieu's theory of distinction is an effort to subsume other status distinctions within a class framework or, better put, to enlarge the concept of class to incorporate the entire range of possible distinctions within a single objective field. But there is reason to wonder whether such a move renders analytically inaccessible heterologous and incommensurate processes and interplayings of distinction that obtain on grounds such as ethnicity, gender, religion, and life-style (Brubaker 1985, 763ff.; Lamont and Lareau 1988, 161).

Taken individually, the criticisms seem to require minor emendation of Bourdieu's theory, a more refined methodology, or other remedial practices. Taken together, however, they raise the question of whether a theory of distinction might be formulated on different grounds that could resolve the difficulties *tout à fait*. In the present essay, I explore this possibility in two steps. First, in order to draw out the issues empirically, I review (for purposes of discussion, and not exhaustively) research on processes of distinction *outside* the realm of cultural capital as "institutionalized, i.e., widely shared, high-status culture signals" (Lamont and Lareau 1988, 156). Specifically, I consider distinction processes based on what Lamont and Lareau call "marginal high-status signals," in class, gender, and ethnic (and, more generally, status group) situations.

Second, on the basis of these empirical considerations, I propose a parallel but alternative model of distinction. Whereas Bourdieu has exported Max Weber's theory of status and status groups into a domain of epistemological objectivism and holism, the alternative model—of cultural structuralism—suggests a theory of distinction based on nominalism and methodological individualism. Such a model recognizes the existence of heterologous, relatively coherent cultural objects, texts, and audiences external to any individual whose actions may be structured in terms of them. However, the multiple and overlapping institutionalized cultures described as cultural structures do not have the character of a single, encompassing objective field of distinction, and heterologous "markets" and "currencies" of cultural capital interfigure with one another in ways that do not reduce to a single calculus of distinction.

In an era of postmodern criticism, it will seem unfashionable to assess a theory on the basis of empirical description, for such description is (rightly, in my view) held to be infused with theoretical presuppositions. Even under such a regimen, however, it may be useful to explore the degree of compatibility of various theoretical and empirical discourses, the better to identify the fault lines between them. In this vein, it may be that I have misread Bourdieu completely—as he (1989, 1990) claims about so many others. Perhaps my Bourdieu is only a straw man and his apparent holism of objective social space only an illusion, while the real Bourdieu comes close to approximating the theoretical position I advance. If this is so, then it is my hope that confronting the straw man will help clarify our common understanding of culture and status.

Status Groups, Markets, and Cultural Structures

Theories about culture and stratification cannot be reduce
typology. However, even if nuances remain elusive, we
two main axes of theoretical controversy. One controver
the significance of bounded cultural groups, a second the c
market dynamics. The thought that groups have distinctive cultural
boundaries was classically formulated by Emile Durkheim, in his studies on the division of labor and on religion (1947, [1893] 1964); by
Simmel (1950, 37); and by Weber (1978, 305–7, 932–33), in his
treatment of "status groups."[4] As for the market axis, Weber held that,
in a market-oriented economy, people may claim esteem in ways that
do not depend on group membership (1978, 305–7, 932–33). This
thought was also explored by Thorstein Veblen ([1912] 1953) in his
classic study of "conspicuous consumption" by the "leisure class," and
it was developed further by Gans (1974). Thus, the fact that people of
one class can partake of another class's culture has suggested to Gans
that the boundaries of class-based social groups cannot be very strict.
Classes lack sufficient organization or power to monopolize "their"
culture. Why? They lack sufficient solidarity to maintain their boundaries (i.e., they are ineffective as social groups), and culture is available
through nonclass channels, primarily, the marketplace.

What Bourdieu (e.g., 1984, 165; 1985b, 731) has done is to push
Weber's approach into a new resolution of the relation between market
and group, by treating class as the fundamental and encompassing
basis of status group distinctions and integrating group and market
phenomena through the medium of cultural capital. Like Gans,
Bourdieu has argued for cultural boundaries between classes. Both the
acceptance of these boundaries and the efforts made to cross them
concretize classes as cultural groups, lending legitimacy to the social
order.

As a secular theory of French struggles over legitimate distinction,
Bourdieu's *Distinction* (1984) surely is a tour de force. However, there
are central absences in the French markets of cultural capital described
by Bourdieu—the cultural others who live in the midst of the world
of de facto white, male, elite-class distinction that Bourdieu paints. In
their absence, Bourdieu can offer no account of how their status situations interfigure with the calculus that he paints as publicly legitimate,
and he is reduced to treating them by caveat, noting parenthetically,
"It is in the intermediate positions of social space, especially in the

United States, that the indeterminacy and objective uncertainty of relations between practices and positions is at a maximum, and also, consequently, the intensity of symbolic strategies. It is easy to understand why it is this universe which provides the favorite site of the interactionists and of Goffman in particular" (1989, 20). But Bourdieu has an analytic commitment to a holistic structuralist account that identifies a putatively dominant culture as the source of a hegemonic objective field of distinction. For this reason, Bourdieu's acknowledgment of "intermediate positions" does not become an important theme of his discussions.

The empirical task, then, is to examine how distinctions work in practice both to exclude others and to constitute collective identity within groups. To consider the full range of possibilities would amount to writing a genealogy of status in political and economic terms. My present, more modest purpose is simply to show that the success of such a project depends on specifying a theoretical framework for the analysis of distinction that does not privilege any of its particular historically concrete forms. A brief survey of issues related to class, gender, ethnicity, and status groups can offer reference points by which to assess the utility of Bourdieu's approach as compared to an alternative theorization of "cultural structuralism."

Class

As Lamont and Lareau (1988) observed, Bourdieu wants to assert a single, overarching objective space of distinction. But he also acknowledges that specific groups produce their own distinctive forms of cultural capital, such that different fields exist "that are relatively autonomous, i.e., more or less strongly and directly subordinated" (1985b, 736; cf. Bourdieu 1985a, 43). Similarly, he sometimes discusses the existence of specific markets, and he holds that, under certain conditions, action will be oriented to "the search for culturally pertinent features endowed with value in the field's own economy" (1985a, 19). As Michel Grossetti (1986) has suggested, Bourdieu's work is characterized by an "unfinished" economic metaphor (cf. Honneth 1986, 59).[5] Yet perhaps the metaphor remains unfinished for good reason. If we follow conventional neoclassical economic theory as an analogy, then separate markets exist for particular cultural "commodities," and individuals (and groups) participate in different markets on the basis of diverse values. In neoclassical economics, these diversities do not imply discontinuities. Instead, with money as a generalized medium of exchange, all value can be reduced to a common denominator, and differences in price can in principle be explained on the basis of such calculable considerations as local scarcity and the like. However, neo-classical economics posits a holistic matrix subject to the same difficulties as those of Bourdieu's objective field. A long line of sociological approaches to economics holds that markets are intertwined with culturally structured forms and patterns of social organization (e.g., Parsons 1937; Hamilton and Biggart 1988; Biggart 1989; Hall 1991). The cultural structuration of markets would seem all the more salient for situations where value is measured in distinctions, rather than being expressed in terms of a generalized monetary system.[6]

Even for classes, a putatively objective field of distinction does not yield generally translatable forms of cultural capital. Indeed, Bourdieu's own analysis is predicated on this assumption, for example, in his differentiation of the middle class from higher classes on the basis of the former group's shortfall of panache that results in "pretension." But pretension obtains currency among its practitioners, and this contradicts the idea that cultural capital offers a *general* basis for social ranking and the formulation of distinctions. Simply put, the forms of cultural capital in play in various class situations are likely to be incommensurate with one another. Bourdieu acknowledges this possibility but explains it away because of what amounts to cultural hegemony, in which the lower classes are excluded from the *habitus* of higher distinctions by their lack of access to them in the family and in education. The working class is subjected to a "dominated 'aesthetic,'" defined from the outside, even though that aesthetic may contradict personal preferences: "Yes, it's beautiful, but you have to like it, it's not my cup of tea" (Bourdieu 1984, 41).

The source and signficance of any external aesthetic are key issues, in need of further exploration. Michèle Lamont and Annette Lareau, for example, have suggested that, in the United States, we should look to the upper middle class, rather than the upper class, for the source of the lower middle class's dominated aesthetic (1988). David Halle (1989) questions whether the aesthetics of social classes differ so much as the practices of cultural commodities by which aesthetics are expressed. And Lamont's (1992) research inevitably raises doubts about the significance of high culture distinctions for the upper middle class, the coherence of which is itself undermined by cross-regional and cross-national differences in the relative importance of cultural, moral, and social distinctions.

Even for classes that lack dominant power, aesthetic value may not be defined solely from the outside. In an Italian-American community,

Herbert Gans (1962) found that manual workers can traffic in their own forms of class honor in a positive way and in contradistinction to the standards of higher classes or the mass-produced consumer badges of status. More generally, workers may maintain a respect for craft abilities—for being able to do things with one's hands and to work collectively in physical ways. By these standards, many middle- and upper-class people will seem bumbling, inept, and alienated from the material conditions of their lives. As Bourdieu (1985b) recognizes, the source of aesthetic value of cultural capital is a struggle. Yet quite apart from the struggle to *legitimate* a particular taxonomy, there may coexist multiple and incongruous values and distinctions that cannot be reduced to one another.

The problem deepens for Bourdieu because he knows that not all culture is economically determined: "As the objective distance from necessity grows, life-style increasingly becomes the product of what Weber calls a 'stylization of life,' a systematic commitment which orients and organizes the most diverse practices—the choice of a vintage or a cheese or the decoration of a holiday home in the country" (1984, 55–56). This suggests that other criteria than social class badges come into play in distinctions of pure leisure and consumption, which is to say, in activities tied either to what Tom Wolfe (1968) has called "status spheres" (such as the social worlds of surfing and of foreign-film screenings) or to actual status groups. Much leisure consumption can be located in class differences—of bowling versus handball or horseshoes versus golf. Yet the opposite possibility also warrants consideration: distinctions of life-style may form cultural boundaries that do not depend on social class.

Even if we simply look at the cultures of social class groups whose lives would seem quite likely to be dictated by economic "necessity"—the urban poor and homeless—it is questionable whether the cultural capital approach adequately explains these cultures. The poor will find themselves exposed to the cheapest of petty commercial culture—"dive" restaurants, secondhand stores, tabloids, and cheap movie theaters. And they will be the targets of culturally distinctive state- and religiously organized welfare and charity programs. These realities would suggest that the poor partake of what Bourdieu calls a "dominated" cultural aesthetic. Yet the poor do not engage in commercial consumption in the same way that more monied popular and elite classes do. This means that their culture will lie outside the realm of mass popular culture, and it likely will be considered "deviant" on this basis. Paradoxically, the relatively greater distance of the poor from commercial culture will leave room for the greater importance of "quasi-folk" cultures made in the ongoing practices of the people who live socially marginal lives (Gans 1974). The interplay of such cultures with dominated culture has been described in novels like George Orwell's *Down and Out in Paris and London* (1933), autobiographies by hoboes Jack Black ([1926] 1988) and Boxcar Bertha (Reitman 1988), and ethnographies of the streets such as *Talley's Corner* (Lewis 1967) and *Carnival Strippers* (Meiselas 1976).

Such texts testify to the importance of socially situated distinctions. *Carnival Strippers,* for example, details the lives of women working on the New England girlie show circuit. A good deal of what is known about them can be translated into Bourdieu's terms: the women position themselves in relation to one another by distinguishing their sexual mores and career trajectories, and a sociologists could map an objective field of distinction, both within the occupational world and in relation to the originary worlds of the women and other career opportunities (waitressing, go-go dancing, and prostitution, e.g.). Yet two things are striking about the testimony of the carnival strippers. First, even within the occupational world, different strippers have their own distinctions that they use in affirming their status and dignity in relation to each other. As one of them put it, "Lena thinks she's better than Tami and Tami thinks she's better than Lena. . . . If you're in my dressing room you're as good as me, you're no better than me" (quoted in Meiselas 1976, 48). Incommensurate values yield standards of distinction that are individual, rather than collective. The situation is made only more complex by the quite different distinctions made by the men who work with and often exploit the women and by others who come into their worlds, including the men (and occasionally women) in the audience. The strippers pay a high price of status loss in terms of their interactions with men, but those costs do not figure equally or even have the same basis for all men. Second, the cultural capital that the strippers struggle to maintain in their occupational arena often counts for very little in other domains, certainly, for example, in their (typically small) hometowns as well as in the higher netherworlds of urban nightclubs. Even in an occupational social world, then, the idea of an objective field of distinctions measured in legitimate cultural capital of general tender seems to mask the reality of incommensurate cultural standards. If this is the case in a world organized in terms of market activity, presumably it will be found in other situations, more distant from economic "necessity."

Other ethnographic accounts have underscored what Herbert Gans

(1974, 70) recognized, that class distinctions of culture are mediated by other socially constructed boundaries, for example, those of age, ethnicity, gender, and geographic locale. But these are not simply alternative axes of objective stratification: they are interfigured aspects of concrete status situations. The carnival strippers are women workers in enterprises owned by men. Boxcar Bertha was a woman making it in a predominantly male world of hoboes. The Italian-American workers were predominantly men, perhaps maintaining gender honor as well as class honor. George Orwell described men on the road, who inhabit a different social world than those of us who have a more settled existence—in a city, suburb, town, or farm community. And Talley's Corner is a hangout for black men who form a status group with its own moral code about their relations with the women who live beyond their group boundary.

The possible concatenations of distinctions as they come into play in situations will exceed any attempt to reduce them to logical alternatives or the priority of one analytic dimension over another. Nevertheless, briefly considering the social significance of gender, ethnicity, and status groups more generally can at least bring to light the diverse dynamics of distinction that often interfigure in status situations.

Gender

At the beginning of the twentieth century, Georg Simmel described feminine culture as tied to the specific form of "female nature," and he argued that, "with the exception of a very few areas, our objective [i.e., public] culture is thoroughly male" ([1911] 1984, 67). Feminist theorists may chafe at the assertion of biological difference and at the public/private distinction—both binary oppositions that reinforce essentialist ideologies (cf. Rosaldo 1980). Such binaries deny the many public—yet not "Public"—cultural accomplishments of women artists, novelists, musicians, and others whose work has not been incorporated into the male-defined canon of legitimate cultural accomplishment. But feminists sometimes share Simmel's account of patriarchal society: namely, that the dominant culture—religion, art, music, legal institutions, and so on—is culture created and maintained for the most part by men as the dominant gender. Some feminists have explained cultural patterns of gender relations at the consequence of social differentials of power between male and female that cannot be reduced to class in a patriarchal society (O'Brien 1981; Polatnick 1983).

Because Bourdieu deals in distinctions, his theory might seem well suited to addressing the issue of patriarchy, particularly on the basis of his analyses of struggles over symbolic myths (1985b, 1989). However, Bourdieu has given short shrift to distinctions other than those of class. He tends to see gender in class terms, for example, by pointing to class differences in women's attitudes toward the "working wife" (1984, 178). This approach stems from his argument that other bases of social division—such as age, sex, and ethnicity—are "secondary" to class: "The secondary principles of division . . . indicate potential lines of division along which a group socially perceived as unitary may split, more or less deeply and permanently. . . . groups mobilized on the basis of a secondary criterion (such as age or sex) are likely to be bound together less permanently and less deeply than those mobilized on the basis of the fundamental [i.e., class] determinants of their condition" (1984, 107). In this vein, Bourdieu argued that "there are as many ways of realizing femininity [*sic*] as there are classes and class fractions," and he interpreted statistical data about the photographic tastes of men versus women in class terms (1984, 39–40). Yet even Bourdieu's own data reveal the limits of his approach: neither class nor gender fully explains the range of statistical variation in his survey; some 30 percent of industrial-employee wives fail to regard as ugly what their gendered class sensibilities would dictate as ugly. And so it goes.

Relations between class and gender should not be discounted, but their character suggests a more complex analysis. Historical studies of ongoing industrialization, for example, show changes in gender identities with the emergence of new social classes, and they suggest the subordination of other social classes to the bourgeois classes' public definitions of gender (e.g., Douglas 1977; Peiss 1986; Lynn and Lynn, cited in Bell 1976, 67; Doane and Hodges 1987). Yet various theories of patriarchy turn the tables on the class structuration thesis. Emergent nineteenth-century industrial capitalism can be regarded as a reconstruction of patriarchy under new conditions of production, which maintains patriarchal relations across the entire range of social classes. In such terms, class differences in gender identities and relations become variations on a resilient calculus of patriarchy, in a world where gender always figures in the construction of social difference. This is not to claim gender as the "fundamental" axis of social organization but to reject the reductionist claim of any dominant axis of difference and propose a comparative historical sociology of shifting, multiply configured status situations.[7]

How are we to explain the distinctiveness of male versus female cultures, within and beyond classes? Bourdieu's model might suggest that different sorts of resources and sensibilities—auto mechanics, sewing, nurturing, beauty, authority—would give individuals the cultural capital for maintaining social positions within an overall class system of distinction. For a dominated cultural group—women in a patriarchal society—cultural resources such as a dowry, production of offspring, and the ability to entertain would offer the basis for survival in a "man's world." On these grounds, a woman's cultural capital would be explained by its value to men *within* a particular class fraction. However, women's culture may also establish an *alternative* realm to the world dominated by men. In exploring the social worlds of eighteenth- and nineteenth-century women, Smith-Rosenberg has argued that "women who had little status or power in the larger world of male concerns, possessed status and power in the lives and worlds of other women": "Entire days, even weeks, might be spent almost exclusively with other women. Urban and town women could devote virtually every day to visits, teas, or shopping trips with other women. Rural women developed a pattern of more extended visits that lasted weeks and sometimes months, at times even dislodging husbands from their beds and bedrooms so that dear friends might spend every hour of every day together" (Smith-Rosenberg 1975, 10). Far from concluding that women's cultural capital helped women survive in a man's world, Smith-Rosenberg suggested the opposite—that the extent of sex-segregated life in the nineteenth century may have left both women and men culturally unprepared for the shared world of marriage and thus contributed to the reputed formality of marriages in the Victorian era.

Today, the construction of patriarchal society has shifted ground. Yet the reconstructed gender differences do not function solely to maintain distinctions within class cultures dominated by men. A study of contemporary women and the popular culture of romance novels suggests considerably more complexity. In *Reading the Romance*, Radway (1984) recognizes dual and somewhat contradictory practices at work. Like other genres that construct realistic plots, the romance narratives about women and their love lives unfold with the twists and turns based on protagonists' dilemmas and choices. For women, reading romances may thus suggest that they have the power to shape their lives. Yet the plots are actually "formulaic" in that they follow prescriptions about "the essential ingredients to be included in each new version of the form." In this respect, "each romance is, in fact a mythic account of how women *must* achieve fulfillment in patriarchal society" (Radway 1984, 29, 17). Romance novels thus balance women's freedom to choose with women's conformity to mythic prescription. They thereby perpetuate male dominance by focusing women's exercise of power within constraints of a patriarchically organized society. All the same, the romance readers whom Radway interviewed often reported experiences of empowerment. The novels helped readers establish their own personal realms—separate from their worlds of work, of children, and of husbands. In addition, sorting through the issues confronted by heroines in the romances sharpened readers' skills at negotiating the trials of a patriarchal world.

The women's cultures described by Smith-Rosenberg and Radway differ radically from each other. One suggests that women's culture has value because it sustains an alternative domain altogether; the other sketches a power in the world of men that cannot be reduced to the cultural values of men. In Bourdieu's terms, both cases show that some cultural capital of women is in a currency traded on different markets than one completely defined by women's class situations. There are multiple markets defined by diverse interests of women and men in their situations with others of the same and different gender identities.

Ethnicity

Despite Bourdieu's emphasis on status groups, in *Distinction* (1984) he is strikingly silent on the question of ethnicity. Elsewhere (Bourdieu 1985b, 744, n. 14), he notes in passing that his analysis of the relation of classes "on paper" to real class practices is analogous to his earlier "analysis of the relation between the kinship group 'on paper' and the practical kinship of 'will and representation'" treated in *Outline of a Theory of Practice* ([1972] 1977). Fragmentary comments indicate that he thinks that ethnicity can be reduced to class. Groupings "constructed in terms of capital distribution," he argues, "are more likely to be stable and durable, while other forms of groupings are always threatened by the splits and oppositions linked to distances in social space": "But this never entirely excludes the possibility of organizing agents in accordance with other principles of division—ethnic or national ones, for example—though it has to be remembered that these are generally linked to the fundamental [i.e., capital distribution] principles, with ethnic groups themselves being at least roughly hierarchalized in the social space, in the USA for example (through seniority in immigration)" (1985b, 726). Again, "The most objective differences may be marked by more immediately visible differences (e.g., those between ethnic groups)" (1985b, 730). Empirically, this view is often correct. Caste systems, apartheid, and, in the United States, slavery and "legal" segregation of blacks before the civil rights reforms of the mid-twentieth century are extreme examples of predominantly class-contained ethnic groups.

In addition, members of previously coherent ethnic groups may find themselves distanced from one another across class lines. Thus, William J. Wilson suggests that the expansion of the black middle class after the civil rights movement of the 1960s resulted in a "deepening economic schism," "with the black poor falling further and further behind middle- and upper-income blacks" (1980, 151–52). These changes are underscored culturally by the distinctive leisure pursuits of middle-class blacks, who are likely to engage in activities economically inaccessible to the poor (Woodard 1988). Here, class mobility can foster new status group identity.

As with gender, however, a class analysis of ethnicity seems incomplete. Let us consider a classic study, John Dollard's analysis of a small town in the southern United States during the Great Depression. Dollard detailed an elaborate racist ideology and strict mores of public behavior defined by the dominant white culture. The public culture maintained white solidarity concerning segregation in part by branding any white who deviated as a "nigger lover." Dollard comments, "The tendency among students of culture to consider such acts as tipping the hat, shaking hands, or using 'Mr.' as empty formalisms is rebuked by experience in the South. When we see how severely Negroes may be punished for omitting these signs of deference, we realize that they are anything but petrified customs" ([1937] 1957, 178–79). Long before Wilson's study, Dollard had already found class differences among blacks, with middle-class blacks often going to great lengths to avoid invoking the whites' cultural stereotypes about poor blacks—the "mammy" image, sexual promiscuity, and emotionalistic religion, for example. Here, members of an externally defined caste used class distinction to counteract the negatively privileged ethnicity. Among poorer blacks, Dollard painted a picture of two roles—one to conform to mores enforced ultimately by white violence, the other roles that maintained blacks' own identities beyond the public world dominated by whites. The dualistic posture of blacks in the town, as Dollard saw it, was to accommodate to their inferior position, as defined and maintained by the white caste ([1937] 1957, 255).

A question persists about the potential for political resistance within the world of the black status group hidden from public view. Dollard may have missed the "inside" of southern black culture because he was an outsider. But, whatever the explanation, as with gender, a dominated ethnic group may use one form of cultural capital with a currency in the wider world, while a separate kind of cultural capital establishes status within the group itself. Thus, ethnic cultural capital does not always reduce to class cultural capital by any straightforward "currency exchange."

To be sure, as Bourdieu would expect, there is a "cultural division of labor." But the relations to class are not the hierarchy that he describes. In the now classic view of Fredrik Barth (1969), the internal values and external signals that bound ethnicity may have other bases than economic ones and remain sharper and more fixed than boundaries that derive from distinctions such as those of social class. Analytically, ethnic groups cannot be reduced to occupational niches and social classes. The contrast between relatively sharp ethnic group boundaries and the more graded class distinctions has been explored by Michael Hechter (1978). Analyzing the 1970 U.S. census, he found that certain ethnic groups (e.g., Asians, Yiddish speaking) have a much higher territorial concentration than others. Groups also differ as to their average and diversity of occupational prestige and the degree of occupational specialization of group members (Greek-Americans, e.g., were twice as concentrated into similar occupations as were Irish-Americans). These patterns suggest that some ethnic subcultures (and, by extension, religion, gender, and other subcultural status groups) may have relatively little to do with occupational stratification while others offer bases for attempting to monopolize resources (jobs), sometimes *within* a class level, sometimes cutting *across* class levels in an economic sector (e.g., construction or banking). How might occupational concentration occur?

Given a cultural (as opposed to a biological) definition of ethnicity, a *habitus* infused with an ethnic group's culture may provide an individual with cultural capital that counts within the ethnic group but means very little outside it. Such an ethnic group may become internally stratified, for solidarity and the relative clarity of ethnic membership offer a basis of economic action, and any ethnic group is likely to encompass people with a range of skills and talents. Thus, members of a solidary ethnic group may take collective economic action by "capturing" enterprises that typically will require personnel of different occupational strata. Under such conditions, class distribution within the ethnic group is manifested on other bases than any generalized currency of cultural capital.

Status Groups

Ethnic groups may be construed as special cases of status group phenomena (cf. Molohon, Paton, and Lambert 1979). It would be possible to explore other status axes along which sociologists and people in

general map distinctions and boundaries that offer templates for practical communal and associational life—age, religion, community, social
club memberships, cultural space, and diffuse social categories such as
ski bums, cowboys, and hippies. We would find, it seems likely, a lack
of symmetry in the various ways that cultural associations, boundaries,
and distinctions affect the status situations of individuals. Social classes,
as status groups, are likely to have only graded boundaries, and they
may therefore not be as successful at collective action as more clearly
bounded status groups. Other kinds of status groups may establish
"currencies" of cultural capital that do not align in a simple and direct
way with class distinctions. Such cultural distinctions *cannot* be understood simply as surviving ethnic practices from the old country (used
to rank them within a multicultural society), the class-based practices
of a gendered status group, or the leisure choices of people who are
all seeking distinction within a single class-based system of status hierarchies.

Generalizing in a speculative way, status groups potentially offer
alternative bases of individual identity that are complexly interfigured
with class. As Bendix (1974) argued, prestige and education—among
the very phenomena that interest Bourdieu—are the province of status
groups that operate outside market conditions and in ways that cannot
be traded on some general market of cultural capital. Such groups
sometimes control significant economic resources that make group solidarity an attractive proposition for the individual, even if the group
controls only "poor" resources (lower-level government jobs, e.g.).
Moreover, the relations of status groups to economic markets do not
depend simply on cultural markers of inclusion or exclusion. In addition, the cultural ethos of a group may establish affinities with specific
forms of economic activity. To translate, in Weber's (1958) analysis of
the Protestant ethic, status groups infuse individuals with new forms
of meaningful conduct (cf. Barth 1969, 14). By the opposite token, as
Weber showed for the Protestant ethic, the cultural ethos, the shared
sense of honor, and the group life they inform cannot be reduced to
matters of economic rationality or objective distinction. Status groups
may participate in, but they are not of, the market. To add to the
complexity, in market societies, people typically participate in more
than one status group, and each individual thus works with incommensurate kinds of cultural capital, entering into social relationships with
others whose status situations, and concomitant forms of cultural capital, may be quite different. Even if we assumed, with Bourdieu, that
classes as status groups predominate, the lifeworldly play of distinction

transpires in specific situations subject to diverse forms of cultural capital, such that the dynamics cannot be reduced to the predominant condition. These complexities can be understood only if we maintain an analytic distinction between status group and class and recognize that cultural distinctions may be incommensurate, rather than ordered by an objective hierarchy.

Status Groups and Cultural Structures

Insofar as Bourdieu's theory of classes and cultural capital depends on the holistic assumption of an objective field of distinction, it does not offer a basis to account for divergent and incommensurate forms of cultural capital that interfigure with "legitimate" distinctions; perhaps it is because of this limitation that *Distinction* (1984) gives such short shrift to gender and ethnicity. But there is no reason why an alternative theory cannot incorporate the interplay of multiple forms of cultural capital and group identifications (cf. Bentley 1987). The metaphor of cultural capital offers a way to understand struggles over status group boundaries and prestige. But classes are not the only kinds of status groups that may be understood in these terms. Although Bourdieu (1989) leaves intellectual room for this possibility, he does not pursue it, and with good reason. Such pursuit would undermine any class-based objective field of distinction. The difficulty, then, derives from the core assumption of holism. Without this assumption as a basis for class as the grand field of societal distinction, Bourdieu's theorization of classes as objectively ordered status groups would break down, as would his elaboration of an overarching market in cultural capital. But, as we have seen, the assumption is inadequate to the interplay among multiple class and other bases of cultural capital. Hard as Bourdieu works against its tendency, the holistic assumption gives rise to a class-reductionist analysis that objectifies and hypostatizes the flux of cultural distinctions and obscures the heterologous interplay of various kinds of cultural capital.

The difficulties of this position can be mapped in terms of a dilemma faced by Max Weber. As is well known, Weber analyzed structural features of social formations, including their cultures, in a macro-comparative fashion that still maintained the centrality of subjective meaning. Thus, the dilemma that, because Weber repudiated organicism, he needed to reconcile a methodologically individualist (or non-holistic) ontology with nominalist yet "objective" description.[8] The topic of social stratification raised the dilemma in a particularly acute

274 John R. Hall

way. To discuss "stratification" in systemic terms would seem tanta-
mount to assuming the existence of a whole that structures the orientations of individuals and groups—thus exceeding the bounds of Weber's
antiorganicist ontology. The dilemma is most obvious in Weber's treatment of class. Late in his career, he modified his earlier, more situational conceptualization to include an objective classification.

The earlier approach, contained in part 2 of *Economy and Society,*
hinges class on the joint economic interests of individuals who share
common circumstances in a particular market, whether that market be
concerned with commodities or labor. "Class situation," Weber emphasized, "is ultimately market situation" (1978, 929). This early discussion suggests (1) that a given person may orient action toward more
than one market and hence individually face incongruent class situations; (2) that shared class situation does not translate directly into
common interest, much less action, and thus "to treat 'class' conceptually as being equivalent to 'group' leads to distortion"; and (3) that
cultural conditions rather than objective circumstances alone affect
whether individuals jointly perceive their situations as deriving from a
common external cause (Weber 1978, 927–32).[9]

Toward the end of his life, in what is now part 1 of *Economy and
Society,* Weber undertook a recasting of certain concepts, streamlining
his treatment of classes.[10] He retained "situation" as the basis of class,
and, contra Marx, he refused to theorize a holistic dynamic of class
conflicts and their long-term developmental directions. But Weber did
present a new, objective categorization of property classes, commercial
classes, and social classes. "Social classes" represented the most substantial departure from Weber's earlier formulation, for they effectively
amounted to class-based status groups (Weber 1978, 307). Weber defined a class of this type as "making up the totality of those class
situations within which individual and generational mobility is easy
and typical" (1978, 302).

Essentially, Bourdieu has elaborated Weber's later conceptualization
of *social* classes, inserting the concept of cultural capital as a way of
accounting such class-based status groups' struggles over distinctions
through socialization, education, and cultural practice (Brubaker 1985,
747). Although Bourdieu claimed to "rethink Max Weber's *opposition*
between class and *Stand*" (1984, xii; emphasis added), in fact, he drew
directly on Weber's formulation of *social* classes as status groups, enlarg-
ing their compass and relocating them within an objective field of social
distinctions.

Bourdieu's usage, then, raises the question of how Weber handled the conceptualization of status. Here Weber was even more cautious than with the concept of class: in the earlier text (pt. 2 of *Economy and Society*), he described a status order as "the way in which social honor is distributed in a *community* between typical *groups participating* in this distribution" (1978, 927; emphasis added). His later recasting of definitions, in part 1 of *Economy and Society,* did not revise this approach to status groups even in the direction of listing typical status situations—as he had with class—much less positing any holistic calculus of status (1978, 305–7).[11] Given that Weber did not substantially revise his early formulation, the overall contrast between Weber and Bourdieu on class and status is significant, despite Bourdieu's borrowing. Where Weber refused, Bourdieu is intent on showing that there is an objective field of cultural distinctions and that individuals are left largely to struggle for distinction within the domain as it has been defined and to struggle with and against objectively imposed distinctions.

Bourdieu well recognizes that cultural distinctions do not represent some generalized currency of "legal tender" among all individuals and status groups, yet he builds his account as though they do. He says regarding class, "Because capital is a social relation, i.e., an energy which only exists and only produces its effects in the field in which it is produced and reproduced, each of the properties attached to class is given its value and efficacy by the specific laws of each field" (1984, 113). Such incomplete interchangeability is even more pronounced for culture than for money. A corporate executive cannot expect her art collection to impress a butcher, any more than a factory worker wears clothes to gain distinction with people beyond a certain social circle. Similarly, wearing diamonds will carry different currencies at a debutante's ball than in a truckstop café. Cultural capital, after all, is good only (if at all) in the social worlds where a person lives and acts, and the value that it has depends on sometimes ephemeral distinctions of currency in those particular social worlds.

Bourdieu emphasizes the importance of action in his depiction of the social struggle to impose a collective definition of the world, yet he presupposes the actor confronting an objective social field. This "symbolic system" or "space of life-styles," however, derives from a form of measurement realism: having measured cultural variation in a way that shows coherent patterns, and his own claims to the contrary, Bourdieu takes the patterns discerned through the measurement to illustrate an objective reality. Postmodernist theorists would question the validity of such a demonstration. Another measurement perspective presumably would yield another set of patterns, equally coherent. As

Schatzki (1987) has argued, if Bourdieu's ([1972] 1977) basic thesis about subjective strategic use of symbols is correct, then the objective intelligibility of an array of symbols cannot be mistaken for the subjective structures of intelligibility that give rise to action (cf. de Certeau [1974] 1984, 58). In short, there is a contradiction between Bourdieu's objectivist holism and his emphasis on concrete practices in matters of distinction. Bourdieu (1989) would prefer to characterize this contradiction as a dialectical relation, in which any social action to construct meaningful categories and distinctions takes place within an actor's objective position, and succeeds to the extent that the actor's worldview aligns with objective reality. This claim is revealing of Bourdieu's problem: even if he emphasizes that practices establish and sustain distinctions, his secular theory of elite domination through legitimation of its cultural standards requires the positing of a socially objective "symbolic system," and his survey research methodology gives the appearance of mapping one, whether it is real or not.

The difficulties of reconciling holistic structuralism and measurement realism with cultural heterogeneity and the actual practices of distinction disappear if we formulate a theory of distinction on the basis of a different presupposition. Let us assume that there is no socially constructed objective reality and offer a treatment of status that mirrors Weber's treatment of class defined on the basis of potentially multiple situations. This is not to deny that there are socially constructed real conditions and distinctions, but these conditions and distinctions are manifold and situational and cannot necessarily be reduced to a single, ordered objective matrix. Under this assumption, a "social order" may exist empirically and define "the way in which social honor is distributed in a community between typical groups participating in this distribution" (Weber 1978, 927). Two points about any such social order seem relevant. First, within a given community, not all groups or individuals necessarily participate in any socially legitimated distribution of honor. Second, the boundaries of any community and the effective range of any ordered distribution of honor have empirical limits, not only in relation to a larger population, but also for community participants. This is especially the case in societies organized by markets, as opposed to Weber's "status societies." In market societies, communities interpenetrate one another (or, put differently, individuals typically participate in more than one community and with varying degrees of commitment).[12] Compared to status societies, in market societies the enforcement of an overarching status order becomes both more problematic and less relevant to the issue of societal order. As

Durkheim worried in *The Division of Labor* ([1893] 1964); in an "organic" social formation no inherent societal community can establish its moral boundaries in a *conscience collective*. For much the same reasons that Durkheim identified, societies integrated via markets inherently operate in ways that undercut any overall hierarchicalization of status, instead producing a multiplicity of sometimes parallel, sometimes autonomous, sometimes conflicting plays of distinction.

Of course, the difference between a market society and a status society is an ideal typical one, and, empirically, any given contemporary social formation is likely to have both group boundaries and market accumulation of cultural capital at work. The question then becomes, What is the interaction between markets and groups, between class and status, beween economic formations and cultural formations? There is no simple theoretical answer to this puzzle: it represents perhaps the key issue of post-Marxist sociology today. Any answer seemingly will amount to a political economy of class, status, and culture. Empirically, there are multiple economic markets and, by analogy, multiple cultural markets of distinction as well as interpenetrating communities with varying degrees of integration and status groups of all descriptions. For issues of economic class, specific coalitions and oppositions of interest will depend on concrete market situations in relation to commodities, real property, capital, services, and labor. But the people in any specific class situation are not a random sample of the population. Rather, their market situations are structured in part by their associations with various social groups. Among these groups, what Weber called *social* classes (i.e., class status groups) figure prominently, as considerable research (e.g., Blau and Duncan 1967; Aldrich 1988) shows. However, because social classes are subject to the vicissitudes of market society, their memberships are not very homogeneous in terms of social origins, and their badges of difference, as described by Bourdieu, for example, do not preclude status mobility. Especially beyond the boundaries of any putative aristocracy—in the American *moyen bourgeoisie,* for example—the distinctions of membership may be fairly easy for newcomers to assimilate.

By contrast to class distinctions, other cultural distinctions, although hardly immutable, are often somewhat more fixed in their social construction, and the boundaries of inclusion/exclusion may thus be comparatively more effectively maintained. At the least, the nuances of how *habitus* may be figured by gender, by ethnicity, by religious identity, are as strongly formed as class distinctions. If schooling may partially compensate for class traits gained in a *habitus,* it probably can do less in the way of changing certain of an individual's gender, ethnic, or religious cultural dispositions. Perhaps most important, such traits do not vary independently; they form configurations of individual and group life-styles.

In the postindustrial/postmodern/post–Cold War era, we have to be struck by the salience of multiple boundaries, many of them based on nonclass axes of difference. Enduring and even multiplying cleavages have awakened us from both the liberal dream of a universalistic social order and the Marxist account of a class society, much less the dream of a classless society. The obvious complexity of contemporary social conflict means that putative objective standards of cultural judgment are the sites of public contention in and of themselves and from diverse sources (witness the parallel struggles along different lines of cleavage over collegiate literary canons, children's textbooks, abortion, pornography, art, and freedom of speech). But the public struggles described by French structuralist approaches (e.g., in Alexander 1988) do not exhaust the play of difference. They are only the visible, which fails to represent the iceberg below. Beyond public discourse, in nonsocietal communities—both subcultural and countercultural—individuals deal in admixtures of ethos and the most divergent badges of honor. In everyday life, distinctions are invoked within particular social situations and by individuals and groups who draw culture and conditions into conjunctive relevance (cf. de Certeau [1974] 1984; Swidler 1986).

How are such empirical processes to be theorized? Whereas Bourdieu (1989, p. 14) would "speak of *constructivist structuralism* or of *structuralist constructivism*" (and by *structures* he means objectively real symbolic ones), I propose a model of *cultural structuralism,* in which social "structural" arrangements of power and of practices are infused with cultural bases, if culture is understood, not as necessarily holistic, but as diverse configurations of institutionalized meanings, recipes, and material objects that may be differently drawn on by various actors within the same social arena or society (Hall 1988, 1990).

A theory of cultural structuralism does not specify a homology between cultural structures, groups, and social action, nor does it portray a grid of binary distinctions along which action becomes ordered in its significance. Instead, it opens up exploration of the dynamics among these phenomena amid concrete cultural struggles. Conventionally, stratification is mapped by sociologists with concepts like class, gender, ethnicity, and status group. However, an approach of cultural structuralism suggests that institutionalized social situations are concatenations of these and diverse other characteristics in unique meaningful configurations that exist only as the array of practices, not as objective "stratification." Significant cultural struggles—for example, the Protestant Reformation and subsequent revivals (Weber 1958; Thompson 1963) or the hippie counterculture (Hall 1978)—reorganize the webs of interaction and group affiliation and promote distinctive ethics of action. Within historically dynamic societies, a multiplicity of overlapping and sometimes contradictory distinctions and boundaries persist as the residues of previous struggles to order the world culturally as a meaningful totality. In diverse, sometimes purely situational, and potentially conflicting ways, these cultural structures may find their ways both into any individual's *habitus* and into the criteria of distinction used by individuals and groups. But *stratification* in the typical objectivist sense is a misnomer that obscures the concrete practices of status situations, just as it obscures the dynamics of economic class situations.

This means that Bourdieu's approach to cultural capital must be reversed. Instead of reducing status to class, social classes must be recognized as one among myriad kinds of status groups. Sometimes status groups are based on class, sometimes on other cultural criteria. Their kinds of cultural capital sometimes interpenetrate, sometimes conflict, sometimes subsume other marketable distinctions. Thus, people may face objective conditions in their lives—conditions that they cannot simply will away—but any attempt to construct an objective space of social relations either represents an interpretive sociological act or is an attempt at symbolic domination by a social group bent on imposing its meaningful interpretation of the world. To accept the sociological account as real is to engage in a misplaced concreteness; to describe any one social group's calculus as the effective one is to confer legitimacy to a calculus that, as Bourdieu recognizes, remains in play with others.

A holistic assumption about an objective social space obscures the potentially polymorphous character of status group dynamics that may be relatively autonomous from one another and that may gear into or conflict with one another in ways that cannot be reduced to class dynamics of cultural capital. The holistic assumption of an objective social space adds nothing to the explanation of distinction. Worse, it distorts the capacity of a cultural capital model to theorize the diverse formations where cultural distinctions come into play. If the holistic assumption is abandoned, sociological analysis need not be concerned with offering an objective realism; instead, it can pursue a "sociological realism" by trying to understand the cultural structures of meaning that actors take to be real, act out, and attempt to enforce as real in the play of everyday life.

Notes

This essay is based on a talk presented at the Twelfth World Congress of Sociology, Madrid, 10 July 1990. I wish to thank Michèle Lamont, Guenther Roth, and Judith Stacey for their comments on earlier drafts and to take responsibility myself for what is written.

1. For example, Bourdieu has examined the relation between the maintenance of class distinctions and the restricted vs. large-scale character of cultural production (1985a), and he has applied his model to topics such as religion (1982).

2. It would be interesting to explore how Bourdieu came to his approach. A strategic methodological resource and secular theory for such an investigation would be Michèle Lamont's (1987) account of Derrida's ascendancy to fame. Interestingly, Bourdieu's overall account of distinction, transfigured for intellectual matters, well describes the French academic world dominated by the Paris scene out of which he operates. It is a world where formal theorizing often counts less than rhetorical performance and where scholars seem predisposed to found their own schools—ignoring the work of their closest intellectual adversaries—as the route to prestige. Thus, Bourdieu's model may work well for the milieu of his own intellectual community and for the view from there to the rest of France. Indeed, Bourdieu necessarily is in the business of amassing cultural capital within this milieu, and his model thus has a reflexive existence both as a sociological theory and as the strategy for advancing this theory in the intellectual world. Not only is Bourdieu intellectually brilliant, but he is also adept at intellectual combat, so much so that his rhetorical postures—such as the denial of formal theory and the indifference to ambiguity and contradiction—become conflated with his actual argument in ways that both make it difficult to evaluate his argument and concurrently "protect" his academic prestige against pretenders to the throne of French intellectual life.

3. I use *social class* in both Weber's and Bourdieu's sense and in a way conceptually distinct from Weber's (1978, 302–5) various *economic* classes.

4. For a discussion of the general problem of boundaries and distinctions, see Zerubavel (1991).

5. A better metaphor might be that of language, which—unlike capital—cannot be saved but can be used again and again and not exhausted. Neither saved nor spent, language nevertheless is a resource that individuals may possess and bring into play. It therefore amounts to more than simply a badge, yet it also operates as a badge, for in its usage it offers the listener instant clues to the speaker's cultural facility. But even if it might seem a more appropriate metaphor, language would not work well for Bourdieu's approach. Unlike the

concept of capital and the economic metaphor, which assume a single objective matrix or value, a poststructuralist approach would eschew the claim of a single, objective language in favor of recognizing *representations* of language in organs of legitimation such as dictionaries and a wide range of dialects and personal usages among communities of speakers who may themselves speak more than one language. These are the characteristics of a nonholistic model, not of one that posits an objective field of distinction.

6. For much the same reason, efforts to push Bourdieu's schema into a conventional Marxist analysis (namely, of the circulation of capital) are theoretically problematic, despite their interesting substantive insights. For an example of such an effort, see Zukin (1990). For a valuable Marxist reading and appreciation of Bourdieu (which, for all its virtues, is undercut by the use of an economic metaphor pushed in a reductionist direction toward treating culture as "investment" and "return"), see Garnham and Williams (1986).

7. For a discussion of approaches, see Scott (1988).

8. One of Weber's solutions to this dilemma was the ideal type, or socio-historical model (Roth 1971, 1976), used to depict salient features of a social reality, without claiming to represent, or otherwise wholly capture, that reality. By this device, Weber could discuss cultural objects (called *cultural structures* here) and social complexes without acceding either to holism or to a correspondence approach to concept formation.

9. Weber was ready to grant that the distribution of property is the central defining fact of class situations, but he argued that the kind of property (or service)—e.g., commodity, capital, factory, livestock, land, slaves, labor, etc.—distinguishes heterogeneous class situations that might arise in distinct markets (cf. Giddens 1971, 165). Thus, the long-term historical shifts in predominant forms of class struggle (in Weber's day, "toward wage disputes on the labor market") could be discussed only "at a cost of some precision" (1978, 930). For concrete analyses, Weber saw as indispensable the consideration of specific market situations.

10. The reasons for this shift are open to debate. Wolfgang Schluchter argues that the two parts of *Economy and Society* represent "stages in the realization of one project. One could characterize them as two mutually independent drafts" (1989, 462). Yet Schluchter does not discuss Weber's reasons for making significant emendations. Roth (1988–89, 145) has argued that the shift represented a turn to the "new objectivity" popular at the time but that, for Weber, it was a "continuation of his political war with other means."

11. Indeed, in my opinion, Weber references his earlier discussion of status groups for the problem of status groups and markets when he promises, "More on that separately" (1978, 307). But cf. Schluchter (1989, 449–51).

12. It is worth remembering that Weber originated his concept of community (*Gemeinde*) in the analysis of religion and later borrowed the formulation for political analysis (Roth 1979). Within close-knit religious communities, the question of a status order would amount to an issue of legitimation for the

group as a whole, and the character of group solidarity may be affected by the specific character of the status order (Hall 1988). If, on the other hand, a community is to define a status order among more diffuse groups effectively, it must operate through the auspices of the state, a mediated or public culture such as television, or the panoptic gaze described by Michel Foucault ([1975] 1977).

References

Aldrich, Nelson W., Jr. *Old Money: The Mythology of America's Upper Class.* New York: Knopf, 1988.
Alexander, Jeffrey, ed. *Durkheimian Sociology: Cultural Studies.* New York: Cambridge University Press, 1988.
Barth, Fredrik. "Introduction." In *Ethnic Groups and Boundaries,* ed. Fredrik Barth. Boston: Little, Brown, 1969.
Bell, Daniel. *The Cultural Contradictions of Capitalism.* New York: Basic, 1976.
Bendix, Reinhard. "Inequality and Social Structure: A Comparison of Marx and Weber." *American Sociological Review* 39 (1974): 149–61.
Bentley, G. Carter. "Ethnicity and Practice." *Comparative Studies in Society and History* 29 (1987): 24–55.
Biggart, Nicole W. *Charismatic Capitalism: Direct Selling Organizations in America.* Chicago: University of Chicago Press, 1989.
Black, Jack. *You Can't Win.* 1926. Reprint. With a foreword by William S. Burroughs. New York: Amok, 1988.
Blau, Peter M., and Otis D. Duncan. *The American Occupational Structure.* New York: Wiley, 1967.
Bourdieu, Pierre. *Outline of a Theory of Practice.* 1972. Reprint. New York: Cambridge University Press, 1977.
Bourdieu, Pierre. "Anatomie de goût." *Actes de la recherche en sciences sociales* 2 (1976): 5–81.
Bourdieu, Pierre. "La Sainte Famille: L'Épiscopat français dans le champ du pouvoir." *Actes de la recherche en sciences sociales* 44–45 (1982): 2–53.
Bourdieu, Pierre. *Distinction.* Cambridge, Mass.: Harvard University Press, 1984.
Bourdieu, Pierre. "The Market of Symbolic Goods." *Poetics* 14 (1985a): 13–44.
Bourdieu, Pierre. "The Social Space and the Genesis of Groups." *Theory and Society* 14 (1985b): 723–44.
Bourdieu, Pierre. "Social Space and Symbolic Power." *Sociological Theory* 7 (1989): 14–25.
Bourdieu, Pierre. "A Reply to Some Objections." In *In Other Words,* by Pierre Bourdieu. Stanford, Calif.: Stanford University Press, 1990.
Brubaker, Roger. "Rethinking Classical Theory: The Sociological Vision of Pierre Bourdieu." *Theory and Society* 14 (1985): 745–75.

de Certeau, Michel. *The Practice of Everyday Life.* 1974. Reprint. Berkeley and Los Angeles: University of California Press, 1984.

de Certeau, Michel. *Heterologies: Discourse on the Other.* Minneapolis: University of Minnesota Press, 1986.

Doane, Janice, and Devon Hodges. *Nostalgia and Sexual Difference: The Resistance to Contemporary Feminism.* New York: Methuen, 1987.

Dollard, John. *Caste and Class in a Southern Town.* 1937. Reprint. New York: Doubleday, 1957.

Douglas, Ann. *The Feminization of American Culture.* New York: Knopf, 1977.

Durkheim, Emile. *The Division of Labor in Society.* 1893. Reprint. New York: Free Press, 1964.

Durkheim, Emile. *The Elementary Forms of Religious Life.* Glencoe, Ill.: Free Press, 1947.

Foucault, Michel. *Discipline and Punish: The Birth of the Prison.* 1975. Reprint. New York: Random House, 1977.

Gans, Herbert. *The Urban Villagers: Group and Class in the Life of Italian-Americans.* New York: Free Press, 1962.

Gans, Herbert. *Popular Culture and High Culture.* New York: Basic, 1974.

Garnham, Nicholas, and Raymond Williams. "Pierre Bourdieu and the Sociology of Culture: An Introduction." In *Media, Culture, and Society,* ed. Richard Collins et al. London: Sage, 1986.

Giddens, Anthony. *Capitalism and Modern Social Theory.* New York: Cambridge University Press, 1971.

Grossetti, Michel. "Metaphore economique et economie des pratiques." *Recherches sociologiques* 17 (1986): 233–46.

Hall, John R. *The Ways Out: Utopian Communal Groups in an Age of Babylon.* Boston: Routledge & Kegan Paul, 1978.

Hall, John R. *Gone from the Promised Land: Jonestown in American Cultural History.* New Brunswick, N.J.: Transaction, 1987.

Hall, John R. "Social Organization and Pathways of Commitment: Types of Communal Groups, Rational Choice Theory, and the Kanter Thesis." *American Sociological Review* 53 (1988): 679–92.

Hall, John R. "Social Interaction and Cultural History." In *Symbolic Interaction and Cultural Studies,* ed. Howard S. Becker and Michal McCall. Chicago: University of Chicago Press, 1990.

Hall, John R. "The Patrimonial Dynamic in Colonial Brazil." In *Brazil and the World-System,* ed. Richard Graham. Austin: University of Texas Press, 1991.

Halle, David. "Class and Culture in Modern America: The Vision of the Landscape in the Residences of Contemporary Americans." *Prospects* 14 (1989): 373–406.

Hamilton, Gary G., and Nicole Woolsey Biggart. "Market, Culture and Authority: A Comparative Analysis of Management and Organization in the Far East." *American Journal of Sociology* 94 (1988): S52–S94.

Hechter, Michael. "Group Formation and the Cultural Division of Labor." *American Journal of Sociology* 84 (1978): 293–318.

Honneth, Axel. "The Fragmented World of Symbolic Forms: Reflections on Pierre Bourdieu's Sociology of Culture." *Theory, Culture, and Society* 3 (1986): 55–66.

Lamont, Michèle. "How to Become a Dominant French Philosopher: The Case of Jacques Derrida." *American Journal of Sociology* 93 (1987): 584–622.

Lamont, Michèle. *Money, Morals, and Manners: The Culture of the French and the American Upper-Middle Class.* Chicago: University of Chicago Press, 1992.

Lamont, Michèle, and Annette Lareau. "Cultural Capital: Allusions, Gaps and Glissandos in Recent Theoretical Developments." *Sociological Theory* 6 (1988): 153–68.

Lewis, Hylan. *Talley's Corner.* Boston: Little, Brown, 1967.

Meiselas, Susan. *Carnival Strippers.* New York: Farrar, Straus, & Giroux, 1976.

Molohon, Kathryn T., Richard Paton, and Michael Lambert. "An Extension of Barth's Concept of Ethnic Boundaries to Include Both Other Groups and Developmental Stage of Ethnic Groups." *Human Relations* 32 (1979): 1–17.

O'Brien, Mary. *The Politics of Reproduction.* Boston: Routledge & Kegan Paul, 1981.

Orwell, George. *Down and Out in Paris and London.* New York: Harper & Bros., 1933.

Parsons, Talcott. *The Structure of Social Action.* New York: Free Press, 1937.

Peiss, Kathy. *Cheap Amusements: Working Women and Leisure in Turn-of-the-Century New York.* Philadelphia: Temple University Press, 1986.

Polatnick, M. Rivka. "Why Men Don't Rear Children: A Power Analysis." In *Mothering: Essays in Feminist Theory,* ed. Joyce Trebilcot. Totowa, N.J.: Rowman & Allanheld, 1983.

Radway, Jane. *Reading the Romance: Women, Patriarchy, and Popular Literature.* Chapel Hill: University of North Carolina Press, 1984.

Reitman, Ben L. *Boxcar Bertha: An Autobiography, as Told to Dr. Ben L. Reitman.* New York: Amok, 1988.

Rosaldo, M. Z. "The Use and Abuse of Anthropology: Reflections on Feminism and Cross-cultural Understanding." *Signs* 5 (1980): 389–417.

Roth, Guenther. "Sociological Typology and Historical Explanation." In *Scholarship and Partisanship: Essays on Max Weber,* ed. Reinhard Bendix and Guenther Roth. Berkeley: University of California Press, 1971.

Roth, Guenther. History and Sociology in the Work of Max Weber. *British Journal of Sociology* 27 (1971): 306–18.

Roth, Guenther. "Charisma and the Counterculture." In *Max Weber's Vision of History: Ethics and Methods,* ed. Guenther Roth and Wolfgang Schluchter. Berkeley and Los Angeles: University of California Press, 1979.

Roth, Guenther. "Max Weber's Political Failure." *Telos,* no. 78 (Winter 1988–89): 136–49.

Schatzki, Theodore R. "Overdue Analysis of Bourdieu's Theory of Practice." *Inquiry* 30 (1987): 113–35.

Schluchter, Wolfgang. *Rationalism, Religion, and Domination: A Weberian Perspective.* Berkeley and Los Angeles: University of California Press, 1989.

Scott, Joan Wallach. "Gender: A Useful Category of Historical Analysis." In *Gender and the Politics of History,* ed. Joan Wallach Scott. New York: Columbia University Press, 1988.

Simmel, Georg. "Female Culture." 1911. Reprinted in *Georg Simmel: On Women, Sexuality, and Love,* ed. Guy Oakes. New Haven, Conn.: Yale University Press, 1984.

Simmel, Georg. *The Sociology of Georg Simmel.* New York. Free Press, 1950.

Smith-Rosenberg, Carroll. "The Female World of Love and Ritual: Relations between Women in Nineteenth-Century America." *Signs* 1 (1975): 1–29.

Swidler, Ann. "Culture in Action: Symbols and Strategies." *American Sociological Review* 51 (1986): 273–86.

Thompson, E. P. *The Making of the English Working Class.* New York: Random House, 1963.

Veblen, Thorstein. *The Theory of the Leisure Class.* 1912. Reprint. New York: Macmillan, 1953.

Weber, Max. *The Protestant Ethic and the Spirit of Capitalism.* New York: Scribner's, 1958.

Weber, Max. *Economy and Society,* ed. Guenther Roth and Claus Wittich. Berkeley and Los Angeles: University of California Press, 1978.

Wilson, William J. *The Declining Significance of Race.* 2d ed. Chicago: University of Chicago Press, 1980.

Wolfe, Tom. *The Pump House Gang.* New York: Farrar, Straus, & Giroux, 1968.

Woodard, Michael D. "Class, Regionality, and Leisure among Urban Black Americans." *Journal of Leisure Research* 20 (1988): 87–105.

Zerubavel, Eviatar. *The Fine Line: Making Distinctions in Everyday Life.* New York: Free Press, 1991.

Zukin, Sharon. "Socio-spatial Prototypes of a New Organization of Consumption: The Role of Real Cultural Capital." *Sociology* 24 (1990): 37–56.

PART FOUR Exclusion and
the Polity

TWELVE   Citizen and Enemy as Symbolic Classification: On the Polarizing Discourse of Civil Society

Jeffrey C. Alexander

Sociologists have written much about the social forces that create conflict and polarize society, about interests and structures of political, economic, racial, ethnic, religious, and gender groups. But they have said very little about the construction, destruction, and deconstruction of civic solidarity itself. They are generally silent about the sphere of fellow feeling that makes society into society and about the processes that fragment it.[1]

I would like to approach this sphere of fellow feeling from the concept of "civil society." Civil society, of course, has been a topic of enormous discussion and dispute throughout the history of social thought. Marx and critical theory have employed the concept to theorize the very lack of community, the world of egoistic, self-regulating individuals produced by capitalist production. I am relying for my understanding of the term on a different tradition, on the line of democratic, liberal thought that extended from the seventeenth century to the early nineteenth, an age of democratic theorizing that was supplanted by industrial capitalism and the concern with "the social question" (cf. Keane 1988a, 1988b; and Cohen 1982).

I will define *civil society* as a sphere or subsystem of society that is analytically and, to various degrees, empirically separated from the spheres of political, economic, and religious life. Civil society is a sphere of solidarity in which abstract universalism and particularistic versions of community are tensely intertwined. It is both a normative and a real concept. It allows the relation between universal individual rights and particularistic restrictions on these rights to be studied empirically, as the conditions that determine the status of civil society itself.

Civil society depends on resources, or inputs, from these other spheres, from political life, from economic institutions, from broad cultural discussion, from territorial organization, and from primordiality. In a causal sense, civil society is dependent on these spheres, but only by what Parsons called a "combinatorial logic." Civil society—and the groups, individuals, and actors who represent their interests in this system's terms—pulls together these inputs according to the logic and demands of its particular situation. This is to say that the solidary sphere that we call civil society has relative autonomy and can be studied in its own right (cf. Durkheim [1893] 1933; Parsons 1967, 1977).

Against the new utilitarianism (e.g., Coleman 1990; cf. Alexander, in press) and critical theory (Habermas 1988) alike, therefore, I wish to defend the position that there is, indeed, a *society* that can be defined in moral terms. The stipulations of this moral community articulate with (not determine) organizations and the exercise of power via institutions like constitutions and legal codes, on the one hand, and "office," on the other. Civil society also has organizations of its own: the courts, institutions of mass communication, and public opinion polls are all significant examples. Civil society is constituted by its own distinctive structure of elites, not only by functional oligarchies that control the legal and communications systems, but by those that exercise power and identity through voluntary organizations ("dignitaries" or "public servants") and social movements ("movement intellectuals" [Eyerman and Jamison 1991]).

But civil society is not merely an institutional realm. It is also a realm of structured, socially established consciousness, a network of understandings that operates beneath and above explicit institutions and the self-conscious interests of elites. To study this subjective dimension of civil society we must recognize and focus on the distinctive symbolic codes that are critically important in constituting the very sense of society for those who are within and without it. These codes are so sociologically important, I would argue, that every study of social/sectional/subsystem conflict must be complemented by reference to this civil symbolic sphere.

The codes supply the structured categories of pure and impure into which every member, or potential member, of civil society is made to fit. It is in terms of symbolic purity and impurity that centrality is defined, that marginal demographic status is made meaningful and high position understood as deserved or illegitimate. Pollution is a threat to any allocative system; its sources must either be kept at bay or transformed by communicative actions, like rituals and social movements, into a pure form.

Despite their enormous behavioral impact, however, pure and impure categories do not develop merely as generalizations or inductions from structural position or individual behavior. They are imputations that are induced, via analogy and metaphor, from the internal logic of the symbolic code. For this reason, the internal structure of the civil code must become an object of study in itself. Just as there is no developed religion that does not divide the world into the saved and the damned, there is no civil discourse that does not conceptualize the world into those who deserve inclusion and those who do not.[2] Members of national communities firmly believe that "the world," and this notably includes their own nation, is filled with people who either do not deserve freedom and communal support or are not capable of sustaining them (in part because they are immoral egoists). Members of national communities do not want to "save" such persons. They do not wish to include them, protect them, or offer them rights because they conceive them as being unworthy and amoral, as in some sense "uncivilized."[3]

This distinction is not "real." Actors are not intrinsically either worthy or moral: they are determined to be so by being placed in certain positions on the grid of civil culture. When citizens make judgments about who should be included in civil society and who should not, about who is a friend and who is an enemy, they draw on a systematic, highly elaborated symbolic code. This symbolic structure was already clearly implied in the very first philosophical thinking about democratic societies that emerged in ancient Greece. Since the Renaissance it has permeated popular thinking and behavior, even while its centrality in philosophical thinking has continued to be sustained. The symbolic structure takes different forms in different nations, and it is the historical residue of diverse movements in social, intellectual, and religious life—of classical ideas, republicanism and Protestantism, Enlightenment and liberal thought, of the revolutionary and common law traditions. The cultural implications of these variegated movements, however, have been drawn into a highly generalized symbolic system that divides civic virtue from civic vice in a remarkably stable and consistent way. It is for this reason that, despite divergent historical roots and variations in national elaborations, the language that forms the cultural core of civil society can be isolated as a general structure and studied as a relatively autonomous symbolic form.[4]

The basic elements of this structure can be understood semiotically—they are sets of homologies, which create likenesses between various terms of social description and prescription, and antipathies, which establish antagonisms between these terms and other sets of symbols. Those who consider themselves worthy members of a national community (as most persons do, of course) define themselves in terms of the positive side of this symbolic set; they define those who are not deemed worthy in terms of the bad. It is fair to say, indeed, that members of a community "believe in" both the positive and the negative sides, that they employ both as viable normative evaluations of political communities. For the members of every democratic society, both the positive and the negative symbolic sets are thought to be realistic descriptions of individual and social life.[5]

The binary discourse occurs at three levels: motives, relations, and institutions. The motives of political actors are clearly conceptualized (What kind of people are they?) along with the social relations and institutions they are capable of sustaining.[6]

Let us first discuss motives. Code and countercode posit human nature in diametrically opposed ways. Because democracy depends on self-control and individual initiatives, the people who compose it are described as being capable of activism and autonomy rather than as being passive and dependent. They are seen as rational and reasonable rather than as irrational and hysterical, as calm rather than excited, as controlled rather than passionate, as sane and realistic, not as given to fantasy or as mad. Democratic discourse, then, posits the following qualities as axiomatic: activism, autonomy, rationality, reasonableness, calm, control, realism, and sanity. The nature of the countercode, the discourse that justifies the restriction of civil society, is already clearly implied. If actors are passive and dependent, irrational and hysterical, excitable, passionate, unrealistic, or mad, they cannot be allowed the freedom that democracy allows. On the contrary, these persons deserve to be repressed, not only for the sake of civil society, but for their own sakes as well. (These qualities are schematized in table 1).

On the basis of such contradictory codes about human motives, distinctive representations of social relationships can be built. Democratically motivated persons—persons who are active, autonomous, rational, reasonable, calm, and realistic—will be capable of forming open social relationships rather than secretive ones; they will be trusting rather than suspicious, straightforward rather than calculating, truthful rather than deceitful. Their decisions will be based on open deliberation rather than conspiracy, and their attitude toward authority will be critical rather than deferential. In their behavior toward other community members they will be bound by conscience and honor rather than by greed and self-interest, and they will treat their fellows as friends rather than enemies.

Table 1. The Discursive Structure of Social Motives

Democratic Code	Counterdemocratic Code
Activism	Passivity
Autonomy	Dependence
Rationality	Irrationality
Reasonableness	Hysteria
Calm	Excitable
Self-control	Passionate
Realistic	Unrealistic
Sane	Mad

Table 2. The Discursive Structure of Social Relationships

Democratic Code	Counterdemocratic Code
Open	Secret
Trusting	Suspicious
Critical	Deferential
Honorable	Self-interested
Conscience	Greed
Truthful	Deceitful
Straightforward	Calculating
Deliberative	Conspiratorial
Friend	Enemy

If actors are irrational, dependent, passive, passionate, and unrealistic, on the other hand, the social relationships they form will be characterized by the second side of these fateful dichotomies. Rather than open and trusting relationships, they will form secret societies that are premised on their suspicion of other human beings. To the authority within these secret societies they will be deferential, but to those outside their tiny group they will behave in a greedy and self-interested way. They will be conspiratorial, deceitful toward others, and calculating in their behavior, conceiving of those outside their group as enemies. If the positive side of this second discourse set describes the symbolic qualities necessary to sustain civil society, the negative side describes a solidary structure in which mutual respect and expansive social integration has been broken down (see table 2).

Given the discursive structure of motives and civic relationships, it should not be surprising that this set of homologies and antipathies extends to the social understanding of political and legal institutions themselves. If members of a national community are irrational in motive and distrusting in social relationships, they will naturally create institutions that are arbitrary rather than rule regulated, that emphasize brute power rather than law and hierarchy rather than equality, that are exclusive rather than inclusive and promote personal loyalty over impersonal and contractual obligation, that are regulated by personalities rather than by office obligations, and that are organized by faction rather than by groups that are responsible to the needs of the community as a whole (see table 3).

These three sets of discursive structures are tied together. Indeed, every element in any one of the sets can be linked via anological relations—homologous relations of likeness—to any element in another set on the same side. "Rule regulated," for example, a key element in the symbolic understanding of democratic social institutions, is considered homologous—synonymous or mutually reinforcing in a cultural sense—with "truthful" and "open," terms that define social relationships, and with "reasonable" and "autonomous," elements from the symbolic set that stipulates democratic motives. In the same manner, any element from any set on one side is taken to be antithetical to any element from any set on the other. According to the rules of this broader cultural formation, for example, "hierarchy" is thought to be inimical to "critical" and "open" and also to "activistic" and "self-controlled."

When they are presented in their simple binary forms, these cultural codes appear merely schematic. In fact, however, they reveal the skeletal structures on which social communities build the familiar stories, the rich narrative forms, that guide their everyday, taken-for-granted political life.[7] The positive side of these structured sets provides the elements for the comforting and inspiring story of a democratic, free, and spontaneously integrated social order, a civil society in an ideal-typical sense. People are rational, can process information intelligently and independently, know the truth when they see it, do not need strong leaders, can engage in criticism, and easily coordinate their own society. Law is not an external mechanism that coerces people but an expression of their innate rationality, mediating between truth and mundane events. Office is an institutional mechanism that mediates between law and action. It is a calling, a vocation to which persons adhere because of their trust and reason. Those who know the truth do not defer to authorities, nor are they loyal to particular persons. They obey their conscience rather than follow their vulgar interest; they speak plainly

Table 3. The Discursive Structure of Social Institutions

Democratic Code	Counterdemocratic Code
Rule regulated	Arbitrary
Law	Power
Equality	Hierarchy
Inclusive	Exclusive
Impersonal	Personal
Contractual	Ascriptive loyalty
Social groups	Factions
Office	Personality

rather than conceal their ideas; they are open, idealistic, and friendly toward their fellow human beings.

The structure and narrative of political virtue form the discourse of liberty. This discourse is embodied in the founding documents of democratic societies. In America, for example, the Bill of Rights postulates "the right of people to be secure against unreasonable searches" and guarantees that "no person shall be deprived of liberty without due process of law." In so doing it ties rights to reasons and liberty to law. The discourse is also embodied in the great and the little stories that democratic nations tell about themselves, for example, in the American story about George Washington and the cherry tree, which highlights honesty and virtue, or in English accounts of the Battle of Britain, which reveal the courage, self-sufficiency, and spontaneous cooperation of the British in contrast to the villainous forces of Hitlerian Germany.

Whatever institutional or narrative form it assumes, the discourse of liberty centers on the capacity for voluntarism. Action is voluntary if it is intended by rational actors who are in full control of body and mind. If action is not voluntary, it is deemed to be worthless. If laws do not facilitate the achievement of freely intended action, they are discriminatory. If confessions of guilt are coerced rather than freely given, they are polluted.[8] If a social group is constituted under the discourse of liberty, it must be given social rights because the members of this group are conceived of as possessing the capacity for voluntary action. Political struggles over the status of lower-class groups, racial and ethnic minorities, women, children, criminals, and the mentally, emotionally, and physically handicapped have always involved discursive struggles over whether the discourse of liberty can be extended and applied. Insofar as the founding constitutional documents of democratic societies are universalistic, they implicitly stipulate that the discourse can and must be.

The elements on the negative side of these symbolic sets are also tightly intertwined. They provide the elements for the plethora of taken-for-granted stories that permeate democratic understanding of the negative and repugnant sides of community life. Taken together, these negative structures and narratives form the "discourse of repression." If people do not have the capacity for reason, if they cannot rationally process information and cannot tell truth from falseness, then they will be loyal to leaders for purely personal reasons and will be easily manipulated by them in turn. Because such persons are ruled by calculation rather than by conscience, they are without the honor that is critical in democratic affairs. Since they have no honor, they do not have the capacity to regulate their own affairs. It is because of this situation that such persons subject themselves to hierarchical authority. These anticivil qualities make it necessary to deny such persons access to rights and the protection of law.[9] Indeed, because they lack the capacity for both voluntary and responsible behavior, these marginal members of the national community—those who are unfortunate enough to be constructed under the counterdemocratic code—must ultimately be repressed. They cannot be regulated by law, nor will they accept the discipline of office. Their loyalties can be only familial and particularistic. The institutional and legal boundaries of civil society, it is widely believed, can provide no bulwark against their lust for personal power.

The positive side of this discursive formation is viewed by the members of democratic communities as a source not only of purity but also of purification. The discourse of liberty is taken to sum up "the best" in a civil community, and its tenets are considered to be sacred. The objects that the discourse creates seem to possess an awesome power that places them at the "center" of society, a location—sometimes geographic, often stratificational, always symbolic—that compels their defense at almost any cost. The negative side of this symbolic formation is viewed as profane. Representing the "worst" in the national community, it embodies evil. The objects it identifies threaten the core community from somewhere outside it. From this marginal position, they present a powerful source of pollution.[10] To be close to these polluted objects—the actors, structures, and processes that are constituted by this repressive discourse—is dangerous. Not only can one's reputation be sullied and one's status endangered, but one's very security can be threatened as well. To have one's self or movement be identified in terms of these objects causes anguish, disgust, and alarm. This code is taken to be a threat to the very center of civil society itself.

Public figures and events must be categorized in terms of one side of this discursive formation or the other, although, when politics functions routinely, such classifications are neither explicit nor subject to extended public debate.[11] Even in routine periods, however, it is their specification within the codes of this underlying discourse that gives political things meaning and allows them to assume the role they seem "naturally" to have.[12] Even when they are aware that they are struggling over these classifications, moreover, most political actors do not recognize that it is they who are creating them. Such knowledge would relativize reality, creating an uncertainty that could undermine not only the cultural core but also the institutional boundaries and solidarity of civil society itself. Social events and actors seem to "be" these qualities, not to be labeled by them.

The discourse of civil society, in other words, is concrete, not abstract. It is elaborated by narrative accounts that are believed to describe not only the present but also the past faithfully. Every nation has a myth of origin, for example, that anchors this discourse in an account of the historical events involved in its early formation.[13] Like their English compatriots, early Americans believed their rights to have emerged from the ancient constitution of eleventh-century Anglo-Saxons.[14] The specifically American discourse of liberty was first elaborated in accounts of Puritan saints and later in stories about revolutionary heroes. It was woven into the myth of the yeoman farmer and then into tales about cowboys and still later into pulp stories about detectives and the malcontents they hoped to ferret out. The discourse of repression was made palpable through early religious accounts of miscreants and stories about loyalists and aristocrats in the Revolutionary War. Later it was elaborated in accounts of wild Indians and "popist" immigrants and then in regional myths about treason during the Civil War.[15]

For contemporary Americans, the categories of the pure and the polluted discourses seem to exist in just as natural and fully historical a way. Democratic law and procedures are seen as having been won by the voluntary struggles of the founding fathers and guaranteed by historical documents like the Bill of Rights and the Constitution. The qualities of the repressive code are embodied in the dark visions of tyranny and lawlessness, whether those of eighteenth-century British monarchs or Soviet Communists. Pulp fiction and highbrow drama seek to counterpose these dangers with compelling images of the good.[16] When works of the imagination represent the discursive formation in a paradigmatic way, they become contemporary classics. For the generation that matured during World War II, for example, George Orwell's *1984* made the discourse of repression emblematic of the struggles of their time.

Within the confines of a particular national community, the binary codes and concrete representations that make up the discourse of civil society are not usually divided up between different social groups. To the contrary, even in societies that are wrent by intensive social conflict, the constructions of both civic virtue and civic vice are in most cases widely accepted.[17] What is contested in the course of civic life, what is not at all consensual, is how the antithetical sides of this discourse, its two symbolic sets, will be applied to particular actors and groups. If most of the members of democratic society accepted the "validity" and "reality" of *1984,* they disagreed fundamentally over its relevant social application. Radicals and liberals were inclined to see the book as describing the already repressive or at least imminent tendencies of their own capitalist societies; conservatives understood the work as referring to Communism alone.

Of course, some events are so gross or so sublime that they generate almost immediate consensus about how the symbolic sets should be applied. For most members of a national community, great national wars clearly demarcate the good and the bad. The nation's soldiers are taken to be courageous embodiments of the discourse of liberty; the foreign nations and soldiers who oppose them are deemed to represent some potent combination of the counterdemocratic code.[18] In the course of American history, this negative code has, in fact, been extended to a vast and variegated group, to the British, native peoples, pirates, the South and the North, Africans, old European nations, fascists, Communists, Germans, and Japanese. Identification in terms of the discourse of repression is essential if vengeful combat is to be pursued. Once this polluting discourse is applied, it becomes impossible for good people to treat and reason with those on the other side. If one's opponents are beyond reason, deceived by leaders who operate in secret, the only option is to read them out of the human race. When great wars are successful, they provide powerful narratives that dominate the nation's postwar life. Hitler and Nazism formed the backbone of a huge array of Western myth and stories, providing master metaphors for everything from profound discussions about the "final solution" to the good guy/bad guy plots of television dramas and situation comedies.

For most events, however, discursive identity is contested. Political fights are, in part, about how to distribute actors across the structure of discourse, for there is no determined relation between any event or group and either side of the cultural scheme. Actors struggle to taint one another with the brush of repression and to wrap themselves in the rhetoric of liberty. In periods of tension and crisis, political struggle becomes a matter of how far and to whom the discourses of liberty and repression apply. The effective cause of victory and defeat, imprisonment and freedom, sometimes even of life and death, is often discursive domination, which depends on just how popular narratives about good and evil are extended. Is it protesting students who are like Nazis or the conservatives who are pursuing them? Are members of the Communist party to be understood as fascistic or the members of the House Un-American Activities Committee who interrogate them? When Watergate began, only the actual burglars were called conspirators and polluted by the discourse of repression. George McGovern and his fellow Democrats were unsuccessful in their efforts to apply this discourse to the White House, executive staff, and Republican party, elements of civil society that succeeded in maintaining their identity in liberal terms. At a later point in the crisis, such a reassuring relation to the culture structure no longer held.

The general discursive structure, in other words, is used to legitimate friends and delegitimate opponents in the course of real historical time. If an independent civil society were to be fully maintained, of course, the discourse of repression would be applied only in highly circumscribed ways, to groups like children and criminals who are not usually taken to be in sufficient possession of their rational or moral faculties. It is often the case, indeed, that individuals and groups within civil society will be able to sustain the discourse of liberty over a significant period of time. They will be able to understand their opponents as other rational individuals without indulging in moral annihilation.

Over an extended historical period, however, it is impossible for the discourse of repression not to be brought into significant play and for opponents to be understood as enemies of the most threatened kind. It may be the case, of course, that the opponents are, in fact, ruthless enemies of the public good. The Nazis were moral idiots, and it was wrong to deal with them as potential civic participants, as Chamberlain and the other appeasers did. The discourse of repression is applied, however, whether its objects are really evil or not, eventually creating an objective reality where none had existed before. The symbolism of evil that had been applied by the Allies in an overzealous way to the

German nation in World War I was extended indiscriminately to the German people and governments of the postwar period. It produced the debilitating reparations policy that helped establish the economic and social receptiveness to Nazism.

This points to the fact that the social application of polarizing symbolic identifications must also be understood in terms of the internal structure of the discourse itself. Rational, individualistic, and self-critical societies are vulnerable because these very qualities make them open and trusting, and if the other side is devoid of redeeming social qualities, then trust will be abused in the most merciless terms. The potential for dependent and irrational behavior, moreover, can be found even in good citizens themselves, for deceptive information can be provided that might lead them, on what would seem to be rational grounds, to turn away from the structures or processes of democratic society itself. In other words, the very qualities that allow civil societies to be internally democratic—qualities that include the symbolic oppositions that allow liberty to be defined in any meaningful way—mean that the members of civil society do not feel confident that they can deal effectively with their opponents, from either within or without. The discourse of repression is inherent in the discourse of liberty. This is the irony at the heart of the discourse of civil society.

Notes

This essay is drawn from a work in progress on democracy, civil society, and discourse. Sections have earlier appeared in Italian (Alexander 1990b).

1. For a general discussion of the poverty of recent social scientific treatments of politics and democracy in particular, from a perspective that emphasizes the importance of the civil sphere, see Alexander (1990a).

2. In this sense (cf. Barthes 1977), there is a "structure" and a "narrative" to the discourse of civil society. The first, the binary discourse that describes those who are in and those who are out, should be theorized in terms of the legacy of the Durkheimian tradition. As I have argued elsewhere (Alexander 1982, 1988a), Durkheim's ambition was to create a theory of "religious society," not a social theory of religion, and his major contribution in this regard was his conceptualization of the sacred and the profane as the primitive elements of social classification. The narrative element of contemporary discourse can be taken from Weber's historical investigations into what Eisenstadt (1986) has called the religions of the Axial Age. Weber's principle insight in this regard (cf. Alexander 1989b) was that these religions introduced a fateful tension between this world and the next that could be resolved only through salvation and that, henceforth, a focus on eschatology and theodicy dominated the reli-

gious consciousness of the age. It is a relatively simple thing to see how Durkheim's structural categories provide the reference points for the journey of salvation that Weber describes. (For the prominence in historical religions of the devil imagery, see Russell [1988].)

The central challenge for developing a useful symbolic approach to politics is to translate the understanding and relevance of this classical sociological work on the centrality of religion in traditional society into a framework that is relevant for contemporary secular societies. This means going beyond the overly cognitive emphasis of semiotic and poststructuralist analysis—from Lévi-Strauss to Michel Foucault—that typically highlights "discourse" in a manner that removes it from ethical and moral concerns and from affectivity as well. This removal is one problem with the recent "linguistics turn" in history, which in so many other respects is vital and important.

3. Rogin's (1987) is the only body of social scientific work of which I am aware that seeks to place this concern with the projection of unworthiness at the center of the political process. He describes his work as the study of "demonology." From my perspective, there remain several problems with this serious investigation. (1) Because Rogin's conception of motive is psychological—he does look at social structure—he provides no independent analysis of symbolic patterns. (2) Because he focuses exclusively on overt practices of violent domination—particularly of American whites over Native Americans—he fails to tie demonology to either the theory or the practice of civil society, which can and does allow the inclusion as well as the exclusion of social groups. (3) Because Rogin studies exclusively oppressed groups, he locates his terminology in terms of the aberrant behavior of conservatives, whereas it is just as common among left-wing and centralist forces.

4. This broad argument, of course, cannot even begin to be supported in the present essay. The focus on particular strands of culture that actually have caused or underlain the specific democratic traditions and structures of particular nations has generated a vast field of scholarship for most of this century, singling out specific religious, social, and intellectual movements, influential thinkers, and great books. In American political historiography, e.g., one can trace the debate between those who emphasize Locke, like Louis Hart, those who emphasize Puritanism, like Perry Miller, and those who emphasize republicanism, like Bernard Bailyn and J. G. A. Pocock.

When one surveys even a small part of this enormous historiographic field, the dangers of examining only particular causal studies at the expense of broader hermeneutic constructions soon become apparent. It seems clear that many different historical movements contributed to the emergence of democratic discourse and practice and that, indeed, each is responsible for the particular emphasis, constructions, and metaphors that make every national and even regional configuration of democracy unique. At the same time, it is also clear that there is an overarching "structure" of democratic discourse that is more general and inclusive than any of these particular parts. In one sense, this structure actually preceded these early modern and modern movements because it was already formed in its broad outlines in ancient Greece. More important, this structure is more general because its broader range is implied by the "silences," the "what is not said," of each particular positive formulation of freedom and civility. This is the advantage of the dualistic approach recommended here.

5. It is precisely this dualistic, or, in Hegel's sense, dialectical, quality of symbolic systems that discussions of culture in modern society have generally overlooked. Whether framed as "values," "orientations," or "ideologies," culture has been treated in a one-sided and often highly idealized way. Not only has such an approach made culture less relevant to the study of social conflict, but it has also produced an atomistic and ultimately fragmented understanding of culture itself. Whether in the writings of Parsons, Bellah, and Kluckhohn, on the one hand, or Marx, Althusser, and Gramsci, on the other, culture is identified in terms of discrete normative ideals about the right and the good. Certainly, political culture is normative and evaluative. What is vital to recognize, however, is that this quality does not mean that it is either one sided or idealized. To the contrary, as structuralists from Saussure to Barthes and Lévi-Strauss would insist, political culture has a binary structure, a structure that I view as establishing the categories of sacred and profane of civic life. Indeed, it is only within the contradictory pull of these oppositional forces that the cultural dynamics of the political world emerge. From the perspective offered here, it is precisely this dualistic or "dialectical" quality of symbolic systems that discussions of culture in modern society have generally overlooked.

From the perspective offered here, all cultural systems involve an inherent strain, or tension, as each side of the duality that is culture gives rise—indeed, necessitates—its moral, cognitive, and affective antithesis. Because this internal dynamism is overlooked, cultural analysis is too often taken to imply a static approach to society, in contrast to social structural analysis, which typically focuses on conflicts between institutions and groups. When those who acknowledge the importance of culture do focus on dynamics, they typically do so by analyzing the tension between internally integrated cultural patterns and a society that fails to supply the resources necessary to fulfill (institutionalize) them. This leads to discussions about the failure of socialization and the breakdown of social control, which focus primarily on the social rather than cultural sources of conflict and strain and give an unrealistically utopian, or reformist, picture of the opportunities for creating an integrated and nonconflictual society. Of course, there have been a number of students of culture who have recognized internal strains, but they have done so in a manner that portrays these divisions as historically contingent and reflecting social conflict and, therefore, as associated only with particular cultural systems of passing phases of development (e.g., the work of Raymond, Gramsci, and Bourdieu).

6. The following discussion can only appear schematic. It summarizes an ongoing exploration into the elementary structures that inform the complex

and messy mixture of meaning and motives that form the basis for civic cultural life. I want to stress that, despite their schematic form, these models of structure have not been deduced from some overarching theory of action, culture, or democratic societies. Rather, they have been induced from three different sources: (1) American popular magazines, newspapers, and television news reports during the period 1960–80 (see, e.g., Alexander 1989a); (2) an examination of popular discourse, as recorded in secondary and primary material, during crisis periods of American history from the Revolution through Contragate (Alexander and Smith, 1992); and (3) an examination of some of the principal themes and symbolic structures of Western political philosophy.

One qualification that must be registered at this point concerns the boundary at which these codes cease to compel and the codes that inform other kinds of (presumably noncivil) societies begin. For example, many modernizing but nondemocratic theories and movements employ much the same set of binary oppositions while placing their emphasis on a different side. Fascist and Nazi societies and capitalist and Communist dictatorships employ related types of codes, although they differ in strategic ways (Lefort 1988). What all these societies have in common with democratic societies is some degree of what must very awkwardly be called "modernity," a social-cum-cultural complex that emphasizes rationality and self-control, two elements of what I will describe as the discourse of liberty. Communist and fascist dictatorships combine these elements with a collectivist, or corporeal, emphasis that belies the individualistic emphasis of the civil society code; both, in their revolutionary emphases, also exalt a vitalistic, and irrational, approach to action.

7. To translate fully into an understanding of the discursive nature of everyday life, in other words, semiotic or structural analysis must give way to narrative analysis. Narrative transforms the static dualities of structure into patterns that can account for the chronological ordering of lived experience that has always been an essential element in human history (see Ricoeur 1984; and Entrikin 1990).

8. Until the twentieth century, confession was apparently a uniquely Western phenomenon, one that emerged in tandem with the gradual social recognition of the centrality of individual rights and self-control for the organization of political and religious societies. At least from the Middle Ages on, criminal punishment was not considered to be fully successful until the accused had confessed his or her crimes since only this confession demonstrated that rationality had been achieved and individual responsibility assumed. The discourse of civil society is, therefore, inextricably tied to public confession of crimes against the individuals that compose the collectivity and, indeed, of crimes against the collectivity itself. This is demonstrated by the great effort that is expended on extorting fraudulent confessions in those situations where coercive force has obliterated civility, as in instances of political brutality in democratic societies and show trials in dictatorships (see Hepworth and Turner 1982).

9. In discussing this process, Aristotle (1962, 109) combined different references from different levels of civil discourse: "The name of citizen is particularly applicable to those who share in the offices and honours of the state. Homer accordingly speaks in the *Iliad* of a man being treated 'like an alien man, *without honor*,' and it is true that those who do not share in the offices and honours of the state are just like resident aliens. To deny men a share [may sometimes be justified, but] when it is done by subterfuge; its only object is merely that of hoodwinking others." Aristotle's translator, Ernest Barker, footnotes this discussion with a comment that illustrates the rule of homology I am suggesting here, according to which concepts like honor, citizenship, and office are effectively interchangeable: "The Greek word *time* which is here used means, like the Latin *honos*, both 'office' and 'honor.' The passage in the *Iliad* refers to honour in the latter sense: Aristotle himself is using it in the former; but it is natural to slide from one into the other."

10. The role of the sacred and profane in structuring primitive consciousness, action, and cosmology is widely understood. See, e.g., the classic exposition by Durkheim ([1912] 1963) in *The Elementary Forms* and its important reformulation in Caillois (1959), the provocative treatment of archaic religion by Eliade (1959), and the powerful overview provided by Franz Steiner (1956). The challenge, again, is to find a way to translate these understandings of religious processes into a secular frame of reference.

11. "In an existing ethical order in which a complete system of ethical relations has been developed and actualized, virtue in the strict sense of the word is in place and actually appears only in exceptional circumstances when one obligation clashes with another" (Hegel 1952, 108).

12. The omnipresence of cultural frames within even the most mundane political process is powerfully argued by Bennett (1979). The "naturalness" of cultural codes is argued here from the macroscopic perspective. From the perspective of individual interaction, the argument can be made in terms of phenomenology.

Certainly, Bourdieu's (1984) work represents an important contribution to the "secularization" of the Durkheimian tradition and its instantiation in a social structural and micro-sociological frame. Bourdieu's concentration on vertical rather than horizontal social divisions, however, and his insistence that symbolic boundaries are modeled on and derive from social, primarily economic, distinctions detract from the cultural interest of his writing. Bourdieu conceives of the social codes not as a differentiated, representational system of society but as a hegemonic code tied directly to the interest of the powerful. How liberating conflict and democracy are possible in this model is not at all clear.

13. For a discussion of the role of the myth of origin in archaic societies, which has clear implications for the organization of mythical thought in secular societies, see Eliade (1959). For a contemporary discussion of secular society that employs the notion or origin myth to great advantage, see Apter (1987).

14. For this belief in the existence of an ancient constitution and the role it played in the ideological discourse of the American Revolution, see Bailyn (1963). For background, see Pocock (1974).

15. For Puritans and revolutionaries as figures in the discourse of liberty, see, e.g., Middlekauff (1972) and, more systematically, Bailyn (1963). Bailyn, and the many who have followed him, have argued that the ideology that inspired Americans during the revolutionary period was mainly a negative and conspiratorial one, that it was the fear of being overtaken and of being manipulated by the revengeful and evil British, with their royalty and their empire, that primarily inspired the American nation. In fact, however, even on the basis of the material that Bailyn himself provides, it is clear that the American Revolution rested on the bifurcation and interconnection of two discourses and that each could be defined only in terms of order.

For the myth of the yeoman farmers and its intrinsic connection to the discourse of liberty, see the brilliant and still compelling work by Henry Nash Smith (1950, esp. pt. 3). For the relation between this mythical discourse and narratives about cowboys, mountain men, and detectives, see Smith (1950, pt. 2, esp. 90–122). In his work on the manner in which Hollywood's stories about "G-men" fit into these archetypes, Powers emphasizes the manner in which these central characters embodied the contrasts of the overarching discourse. The "mystery" that provides the focus of the detective story rests on the circumstances that allow "a startlingly intelligent hero" to finally pick "a devious murderer out of a crowd of equally likely suspects" (Powers 1983, 74). See also Curti's (1937, 765) argument that the mystical exploits of these early dime store heros "confirmed Americans in the traditional belief that obstacles were to be overcome by the courageous, virile, and determined stand of the individual as an individual."

For mythical constructions of religious miscreants in terms of the discourse of repression, see early Puritan discussions of antinomianism, particularly Anne Hutchinson's (Erikson 1965). For stories about the evils of the Loyalists and aristocrats in the Revolution, see Bailyn (1974). For the mythical reconstruction of the Native American in terms of the discourse of repression, see Slotkin (1973). Higham's work (1965, e.g., 55, 138, 200) is filled with examples of how earlier core groups in American society constructed southern and central European immigrants under this repressive discourse. These immigrants were often involved in the radical labor politics of the day. Higham displays the antinomian character of the discourse that was used to understand these struggles, and their immigrant participants, in a particularly sharp way.

16. The counterpositioning of heroic enactors of liberty with criminals who act out of uncontrolled passion seems to have been the major point of the "action detective" genre that emerged in pulp fiction in the late nineteenth century, whose popularity has continued unabated in the present day (see Cawelti 1976; and Noel 1954). This genre provided the symbolic framework for J. Edgar Hoover's highly successful manipulation of the popular image of

the FBI, as Powers (1983) demonstrates. Thus, when Americans looked at Hoover, Powers writes, they "saw . . . not a spokesman for a partisan political philosophy, but a suprapolitical national hero" (p. xii) modeled on the action genre. Powers emphasizes the binary nature of the discourse that hallowed Hoover's actions, arguing that, "for the mythological process to produce a Hoover-style hero, there had to be a universally understood formula within the culture for dealing with the sort of villain who had come to represent the public's fears" (p. xiv). In the popular culture/political culture hybrid of the twentieth century, the criminals pursued by "officials" were persistently portrayed as subject to "gang rule," which posed the danger that this form of repressive social organization would spread to "still wider areas of life" (p. 7). For their part, the G-men pursuing these criminals were portrayed both as "rebelliously individualistic" (p. 94) and as the upholders of rational law, as involved in "an epochal struggle between lawful society and an organized underworld."

17. This suggests a modification of my earlier, more traditionally functionalist model of the relations between codes and conflict groups (Alexander 1988b). Rather than neatly separating refracted value conflicts from columnized ones, I would note the possibility that there may be a more general discourse from which even columnized, fundamentally conflictual cultural groupings derive their ideologies. The issue is one of level of generality.

18. Philip Smith (1991) has documented the bifurcated discourse of war in this insightful investigation of the cultural underpinnings of the British war with Argentina over the Falkland Islands. For a more impressionistic but still fascinating account of the powerful role that semiotic codes play in producing and enabling war, see Fussell (1975).

References

Alexander, Jeffrey C. *The Antinomies of Classical Thought: Marx and Durkheim.* Vol. 2 of *Theoretical Logic in Sociology.* Berkeley and Los Angeles: University of California Press, 1982.

Alexander, Jeffrey C., ed. *Durkheimian Sociology: Cultural Studies.* New York: Cambridge University Press, 1988a.

Alexander, Jeffrey C. "Three Models of Culture/Society Relations: Toward an Analysis of Watergate." In *Action and Its Environments,* ed. Jeffrey C. Alexander. Berkeley and Los Angeles: University of California Press, 1988b.

Alexander, Jeffrey C. "Culture and Political Crisis." In *Structure and Meaning: Relinking Classical Sociology,* ed. Jeffrey C. Alexander. New York: Columbia University Press, 1989a.

Alexander, Jeffrey C. "The Dialectic of Individuation and Domination: Weber's Rationalization Theory and Beyond." In *Structure and Meaning: Relinking Classical Sociology,* ed. Jeffrey C. Alexander. New York: Columbia University Press, 1989b.

Alexander, Jeffrey C. "Bringing Democracy Back In: Universalistic Solidarity and the Civil Sphere." In *Intellectuals and Politics: Social Theory Beyond the Academy,* ed. Charles Lemert. Newbury Park, Calif.: Sage, 1990a.

Alexander, Jeffrey C. "Morale e Repressione." *MondOperaio* (Rome) no. 12 (December 1990b): 127–30.

Alexander, Jeffrey C. "Shaky Foundations: The Presuppositions and Internal Contradictions of James Coleman's *Foundations of Social Theory.*" *Theory and Society* (in press).

Alexander, Jeffrey C., and Philip Smith. "The Discourse of American Civil Society: A New Proposal for Culture Society." Typescript, 1992.

Apter, David. "Mao's Republic." *Social Research* 54 (1987): 691–729.

Aristotle. *The Politics of Aristotle.* Translated by Ernest Barker. New York: Oxford University Press, 1962.

Bailyn, Bernard. *The Ideological Origins of the American Revolution.* Cambridge, Mass.: Harvard University Press, 1963.

Bailyn, Bernard. *The Ordeal of Thomas Hutchinson.* Cambridge, Mass.: Harvard University Press, 1974.

Barthes, Roland. "Introduction to the Structural Analysis of Narratives." In *Image, Music, Text.* New York: Hill & Wang, 1977.

Bennett, W. Lance. "Imitation, Ambiguity, and Drama in Political Life: Civil Religion and the Dilemmas of Public Morality." *Journal of Politics* 41 (1979): 106–33.

Bourdieu, Pierre. *Distinction.* Cambridge, Mass.: Harvard University Press, 1984.

Caillois, Roger. *Man and the Sacred.* New York: Free Press, 1959.

Cawelti, John. *Adventure, Mystery and Romance: Formula Stories as Art and Popular Culture.* Chicago: University of Chicago Press, 1976.

Cohen, Jean. *Class and Civil Society: The Limits of Marxian Critical Theory.* Amherst: University of Massachusetts Press, 1982.

Coleman, James. *Foundations of Social Theory.* Cambridge, Mass.: Belknap, 1990.

Curti, Merle. "Dime Store Novels and the American Tradition." *Yale Review* 26 (1937): 765.

Durkheim, Emile. *The Division of Labor in Society.* 1893. New York: Free Press, 1933.

Durkheim, Emile. *The Elementary Forms of Religious Life.* 1912. New York: Free Press, 1963.

Eisenstadt, S. N., ed. *The Origins and Diversity of Axial Age Civilizations.* Albany: State University of New York Press, 1986.

Eliade, Mircea. *The Sacred and the Profane.* New York: Harcourt, 1959.

Entrikin, Nicholas. *The Betweeness of Place.* Baltimore: Johns Hopkins University Press, 1990.

Erikson, Kai. *Wayward Puritans.* New Haven, Conn.: Yale University Press, 1965.

Eyerman, Ron, and Andrew Jamison. *Social Movements: A Cognitive Approach.* Cambridge: Polity, 1991.

Fussell, Paul. *The Great War in Modern Memory.* New York: Oxford University Press, 1975.

Habermas, Jurgen. *Critique of Functionalist Reason.* Vol. 2 of *Theory of Communicative Action.* Boston: Beacon, 1988.

Hegel, G. H. W. *Philosophy of Right.* New York: Oxford, 1952.

Hepworth, Mike, and Bryan S. Turner. *Confession: Studies in Deviance and Religion.* London: Routledge & Kegan Paul, 1982.

Higham, John. *Strangers in a Strange Land.* New York: Atheneum, 1965.

Keane, John, ed. "Despotism and Democracy: The Origins and Development of the Distinction between Civil Society and the State, 1750–1850." In *Civil Society and the State.* London: Verso, 1988a.

Keane, John. "Remembering the Dead: Civil Society and the State from Hobbes to Marx and Beyond." In *Democracy and Civil Society.* London: Verso, 1988b.

Lefort, Claude. *Democracy and Political Theory.* Cambridge: Polity, 1988.

Middlekauff, Robert. "The Ritualization of the American Revolution." In *The National Temper,* ed. Lawrence Levine and Robert Middlekauff. 2d ed. New York: Harcourt Brace, 1972.

Noel, Mary. *Villains Galore.* New York: Macmillan, 1954.

Parsons, Talcott. "Durkheim's Contribution to the Theory of Integration of Social Systems." 1960. Reprinted in *Sociological Theory and Modern Society.* New York: Free Press, 1967.

Parsons, Talcott. *The Evolution of Societies,* Edited by Jackson Toby. Englewood Cliffs, N.J.: Prentice-Hall, 1977.

Pocock, J. G. A. *The Ancient Constitution and the Feudal Law.* Bath: Chivers, 1974.

Powers, Richard. *G-Men: Hoover's FBI in American Popular Culture.* Carbondale: Southern Illinois University Press, 1983.

Ricoeur, Paul. *Time and Narrative,* vol. 1. Chicago: University of Chicago Press, 1984.

Rogin, Michael. *Ronald Reagan: The Movie and Other Essays in American Demonology.* Berkeley and Los Angeles: University of California Press, 1987.

Russell, Jeffrey Burton. *The Prince of Darkness.* Ithaca, N.Y.: Cornell University Press, 1988.

Slotkin, Richard. *Regeneration through Violence: The Mythology of the American Frontier, 1600–1860.* Middletown, Conn.: Wesleyan University Press, 1973.

Smith, Henry Nash. *Virgin Land: The American Western as Symbol and Myth.* Cambridge, Mass.: Harvard University Press, 1950.

Smith, Philip. "Codes and Conflict: Toward a Theory of War as Ritual." *Theory and Society* 20 (1991): 103–38.

Steiner, Franz. *Taboo.* London: Cohen & West, 1956.

THIRTEEN

Democracy versus Sociology: Boundaries and Their Political Consequences

Alan Wolfe

The public stories that modern liberal democracies tell and retell emphasize the gradual triumph of inclusion. Once upon a time, it is said, such societies were ruled by privileged elites. Governing circles were restricted to those of the correct gender, breeding, education, and social exclusiveness (Cannadine 1990). All this changed as a result of those multiple forces usually identified by the term *democracy*. First the middle classes, then working men, then women, then racial minorities all won not only economic rights but political and social rights as well (Marshall 1964). While the process is by no means complete—and while there are those who argue for the extension of such rights beyond the human species to nature (Nash 1989)—the history of modern democracy is understood as a process of taking in rather than of keeping out.

There is much truth in this story. Moreover, it is a good story, one that can, and does, make us feel that history has a purpose that in some way corresponds with a more positive understanding of human potential. In this essay I have no intention of suggesting that the story is either incorrect in its basic features or unfortunate in its consequences. My point is simply that it contains a potential conflict with another account, which I will call a sociological, rather than a democratic, understanding of the dialectic of inclusion and exclusion.

A sociological understanding is one that recognizes humans as best fulfilled when living in groups rather than as isolated atoms. But groups by their very nature are exclusive rather than inclusive. They function best only by keeping others out (Coser 1956). A richly textured social life requires boundaries, membership rituals, privileged space, and other demarcations designed to ensure that the group will constitute itself at some point lower than the universality of all humankind (Cohen 1985, 1986). The study of society, from either a sociological or an anthropological perspective, is therefore inevitably tied up with an appreciation of classifications and distinctions (Needham 1979; Douglas 1970). Modernity, to be welcomed enthusiastically from the democratic standpoint of inclusion, is usually welcomed skeptically from the sociological standpoint of exclusion.

There need not necessarily exist strong tension between a democratic and a sociological account of individual versus group obligations. A large portion of the history of liberal thought is an effort to reconcile these tendencies; Tocqueville, Constant, Durkheim, Laski, Bradley, T. H. Green, and John Dewey could all be cited as engaged in such a project. For a variety of reasons, however, there is something of a polarization in contemporary thought between those who find exclusion inexcusable and those who find inclusion omnipresent.

The former development is best illustrated by those tendencies generally labeled *postmodernist* or *poststructuralist*. Although, there is often considerable debate about what these philosophical tendencies are actually trying to say, the essence of the approach is to question the presumed boundaries between groups: of signifiers, people, species, or texts. What appears at first glance to be a difference is reinterpreted, discovered to be little more than a distinction rooted in power or a move in a rhetorical game. Differences, in other words, never have a fixed status in and of themselves; there are no *either/ors* (nor are there no *not either/ors*): "Deconstruction is both, it is neither, and it reveals the way in which both construction and deconstruction are themselves not what they appear to be" (Johnson 1987, 12–13; see also Derrida 1981). An artful deconstruction of a text—or a social institution—will reveal the strategies by which artificial boundaries have been preserved and protected.

There is some debate over whether postmodernism is a critique or an extension of modernism, but from the perspective of one particular feature of modern society, democracy, postmodern theories are unquestionably hypermodern. Because they are skeptical of presumed boundaries, postmodern theories imagine a world of near perfect equality. Not only do race, class, and gender differences become less important, but even such distinctions as impairment/normalcy, sick/healthy, and victim/victimizer would also be minimized (Minow 1990). Yet precisely because their political implications are so democratic, postmodern theories tend to have little appreciation for the sociological. If all differences are transient, then no firm basis for group life—short of some universal group that we share with all other species—is possible. Any effort by any group of people to protect and assign privilege to the particularities of their group will be understood as a futile and self-defeating strategy of protecting difference. No wonder that a quite overt hostility toward sociology can be found in so many postmodernist thinkers or that sociology is one of the few academic fields in the United States that has not been especially susceptible to postmodern inclinations (Rosenau 1991). If social groups have a precarious life in modern society, they would, in postmodern society, have no life at all.

A second major turn in contemporary thought, consequently, takes us away from a universalist move toward inclusion in favor of a particularism that, explicitly or not, implies exclusion. This trend, in contrast to the hyperdemocratic aspects of postmodern thought, can be called *hypersociological* in its rediscovery of groups, traditions, and the claims of the particular. "Communitarians" (Bellah et al. 1985; Sandel 1982), who worry about the consequences of rules premised on universal categorical imperatives, are perhaps the best example. They tend to focus on the weakness of what has been called "civil society," those aspects of social life that refer to the informal, the local, and the intimate (see, e.g., Alexander, this volume; and Wolfe 1989). But because they concentrate on the family, the neighborhood, friendship, ethnic groups, voluntary associations, and personal networks, theories of civil society can easily become exclusionary: defending the needs of specific groups against the general claims of strangers unrestrictedly is a recipe for parochialism and privilege (Benhabib 1988; Ignatieff 1985). Communitarians have a healthy respect for boundaries, but this can lead to a distrust of democracy, at least those features of modern society emphasizing equality and the abolition of unearned privilege.

Although they would seem to work to some degree at cross-purposes, both inclusive democracy and exclusive group centeredness are necessary for a rich but just social life. Without particular groups with sharply defined boundaries, life in modern society would be unbearable. We would be constant pawns in power struggles taking place over our heads. Our identity as residents of a particular place would have no currency in the face of national and international needs. In the absence of social boundaries, in short, we could never belong to anything with texture and character. Yet if the boundaries between particular groups are too rigid, we would have no general obligations. Our lives would be characterized by what Durkheim called *mechanical solidarity*. We would live together with people exactly like ourselves, unexposed to the challenges of strangers, the lure of cosmopolitanism, and the expansion of moral possibility that comes with responsiveness to the generalized other. Living sociologically we can never be Kohlbergians. Living democratically, at least in its modern form, we can never be Jeffersonians.

Because we live in societies where democracy has greater popular legitimacy than sociology, it is more difficult to make a case for exclusion rather than inclusion. As Cynthia Fuchs Epstein (this volume) writes, claims of fairness and justice inevitably demand skepticism toward distinctions. Yet if there were no distinctions, there would be no Bourdieu—or Durkheim, Weber, Marx, and Veblen. To the degree that sociologists imagine a society without exclusion, they imagine themselves out of business. Exclusion, however difficult to justify, is what makes diversity possible, societies interesting, institutions necessary, practices creative, customs variable, and ambiguity important. If a totally inclusive society were possible, which it most likely is not, it would hardly be desirable, at least to those fascinated with the unpredictability of human choices. Hence even those committed to the notion that difference all too often presupposes hierarchy generally attempt a reformulation that would still permit difference to exist, but this time without invidious discrimination. For example, Minow, who worries "that a difference assigned by someone with power over another will become endowed with an apparent reality," nonetheless concludes that "boundaries and categories of some form are inevitable" (1990, 374, 390). As good liberals we must worry about inclusion and do our best to ensure that no person is treated unjustly because of the group into which she or he was born. But as good sociologists we also must think about exclusion, for only in so doing can we help imagine and protect a society in which groups will continue to enrich the identities that make social existence meaningful.

Solutions to the problem of boundaries that either reify their existence or deny their importance, it would seem, are not especially helpful. Just as a postmodern distaste for boundaries, taken to its logical conclusion, produces a society imperfect in its perfection, the communitarian preference for boundaries, if taken to its logical conclusion, results in a society fundamentally at odds with modernity. In the futile and self-defeating debate over boundaries, one point often gets lost: not all boundaries are the same. Despite all postmodern efforts to displace them, boundaries will continue to reinforce differences. But despite all communitarian efforts to protect them, boundaries, in a modern society, will always be permeable. We are more likely to negotiate the discussions over boundaries that will continue to confront us if we have a better sense of how different kinds of boundaries differ.

Temporary and Permanent Boundaries

One way to approach differences among boundaries is to ask whether such boundaries are permanent or a temporary response to a particular condition. The importance of the permanence of a condition of difference is illustrated by an example provided by Martha Minow (1990). She contrasts the way we think about the situation of the handicapped in the schools compared to the situation of children whose primary language is not English. In the former case, the demands of fairness and respect for difference urge that the handicapped be brought into the regular classroom to mix with all other children; indeed, in her most graphic thought experiment, Minow asks us to think about teaching all children, even "normal" ones, with sign language if there is a partially deaf child in the room. (Some might consider Minow's account [1990, 96] of how some hospitals treat all patients as having AIDS so that those who do will not perceive discrimination equally thought provoking.) But in the latter case the same demand of fairness seems to suggest that children be taken out of the classroom and be given special attention. They need at least some time in which the language of instruction ought to be their own native language to that they can better compete with those children whose native language is English.

Minow argues that, while the responses in each case are different, the basic dilemma of difference is the same. From her perspective, it is important not to take a difference between groups and, by giving it a name, reinforce unfair and hierarchical relations between groups. The power of Minow's argument stems from the importance she places on empathy. By abolishing the boundary between the handicapped and others, children who have good hearing will learn what it is like to be hearing impaired. They will, consequently, be more sympathetic to those on the other side of the boundary. On the other hand, native non-English speakers need to feel a sense of competence, one they can best develop by being allowed to speak with each other before entering the wider world with a foreign tongue. Since her goal is empowerment more than consistency in policy, it makes perfect sense to respond differently in these two cases.

Minow's democratic sympathies, present everywhere throughout her analysis, force us to recognize that every boundary presupposes a point of view, that there are no neutral boundaries, that every distinction we make is to some degree arbitrary. Yet there remains one distinction between those who have hearing loss and those who speak a language other than English at home that is relevant to the question of empathy. We do not expect that the deaf will develop perfect hearing. But we do expect that children whose first language is not English will learn English; indeed, the point of bilingual education, at least in theory, is to help them learn English as fast as possible (Porter 1990). We have, therefore, two kinds of boundaries, one that is more or less temporary, the other more or less permanent.

Does it make sense to ask people to emphathize with those on the other side of a boundary when that boundary cannot really be crossed? In a perfect world, it does. If everyone were altruistic, or if we lived in a society that made altruism its highest priority, we might all be required to pretend that we were hard of hearing for a certain number of hours per day in order to demonstrate our empathy with those on the other side of this boundary. The same might be true with AIDS or with homelessness. But it is also clear that there are any number of boundaries between some who are more fortunate than others. We might therefore spend all our time learning empathy and very little time learning how to use the hearing abilities that those of us who are not disabled have. Most parents would likely object to too much experimentation in forced empathy. They would likely be understanding toward those struggling to overcome impairments, but they would also ask some common-sense questions. What is to be gained by participating in a form of difference that, being permanent, is one from which those who possess it would escape if they had the chance? Why universalize the condition of being handicapped when being handicapped is not a universal state of fulfillment toward which people want to strive?

Boundaries, in short, may always represent someone's point of view and in that sense will always be unfair. But boundaries are also only to some degree a factor of the way we name differences between people. Despite the often dramatic and enlightening ways by which those who have AIDS or are hearing impaired try to show that there is no essential difference between themselves and everyone else, differences exist. When such differences are permanent, it may make more sense not to pretend that the difference does not exist but instead to educate people around differences—which presupposes that we acknowledge that the differences are there. Treating everyone as if they have AIDS is much kinder to those with the condition, but also more problematic to those who do not. Indeed, in denying the difference between those with the condition and those without it, we make the kind of empathy that is the product of learning about the other more difficult.

On the other hand, the condition of not speaking English is a temporary rather than a permanent condition. It may therefore make far more sense not to take other than English-speaking students out of the classroom. Language is the crucial mechanism by which ethnic groups become assimilated. By shedding (or adopting) the old language that was determined for them, children become part of the new world to which they belong. Linguistic identity, therefore, changes depending on context; bilingual speakers can choose the appropriate language for the situation. (The same is not true for the handicapped; sign language is a substitute for the spoken language that cannot be used and in that sense must be used. If there were no deaf or hard of hearing, there would be no sign language. If there were no Latin speakers, there would still be Latin.) Because English represents the universal condition toward which all other than English-speaking immigrants in the United States aspire, there is reason, at least with respect to official policy, to encourage students to make their move away from the particular to the universal. Bilingualism is a valuable property, but the argument against making it an official policy of a public institution like the schools is that it reinforces a difference that, being only temporary, is going to disappear in any case. Just as it makes little sense to universalize a permanent particularity, it makes little sense to particularize a universal end result.

To include all people in a category when that category reflects a permanent difference seems to represent excessive democratic zeal; it is never easy to justify exclusion, but one boundary that ought to be acknowledged is a boundary that can never be crossed. To exclude people, by contrast, when the boundary that makes them different is one that we expect (and actively encourage) to disappear also seems like an excessive concern for sociological particularities. This is not meant as a formula for deciding when boundaries are to be overriden or protected. One could easily imagine a permanent distinction, such as race, that ought not to be reified at the cost of excluding one particular racial group from full membership in the national community. My only point is that we have to begin to look at the many factors that make up the character of boundaries and that one such factor is the degree to which the boundary is expected to disappear in time anyway or whether, for whatever reason, the boundary is one that cannot.

The Givenness of Boundaries

If those who are influenced by postmodernist thought tend to deny boundaries that are undeniable, those influenced by communitarianism are likely to reinforce boundaries that might best be crossed. A common charge made against communitarian (sometimes called *republican*) thought is that it is insufficiently appreciative of difference, including the kinds of differences, such as between those who are handicapped and those who are not, that have just been discussed (Hirsch 1986). Yet Americans especially, but other liberal democrats as well, live in societies increasingly composed of extremely diverse social groups. A commitment to community so strong that it denies the possibility of movement between such groups is too strong.

Race is a boundary that is often uncrossable but also one that, in the best versions of liberal democratic theory, demands to be crossed. Yet it is often not the barrier itself that constitutes the problem. If a group of whites chooses to live together in one neighborhood and a group of blacks to live together in another, one might not, from the perspective of pluralism, like the result, but one would have at least to respect that each community is trying, by constructing boundaries, to strengthen its own racial identity. But that is rarely what happens in real life. In real life most blacks live in segregated communities not of their own choosing but determined by the racial preferences of whites. The boundary between a housing project and the close-knit white ethnic neighborhood nearby is in that sense determined by the racial identity of those living on either side and is not the result of a mutual decision to put up barriers. To impose a boundary to prevent someone from walking from the one to the other is to treat a boundary that was not freely chosen as if it were freely chosen. Americans believe that people should be free to choose and should then be responsible for the choices they freely made. To the degree that people choose their identity, and not just their cars or their politicians, there is good wisdom in this belief. But it applies only when people have in fact chosen. If someone chooses to be a parent, he or she should be expected to act like a parent. But in cities like New York decisions about where to live are often givens, having little to do with individual preferences.

Ethnic boundaries, in contrast to racial ones, offer a somewhat more complex illustration of the conflict between democratic inclusion and sociological exclusion. The idea of people living in segregated ethnic communities—Jews here, Italians there—seems somehow less invidious than living in racially segregated communities. Indeed, the term *communitarian* seems often to imply an ethnic community, for the images of ethnicity conjure up old worlds, traditions, hierarchies, superstitions, informal networks, kinship, trust, hatred, differentiations—in short, just about every characteristic or practice that modernity is presumably in the process of abolishing. Because of its focus on exclusivity, sociology has long been fascinated by ethnicity. When sociologists find the coldness and impersonality of the modern world a problem, the ethnic group becomes the foil; one of the major characters in *Habits of the Heart* is Massachusetts Irish—the ethnic group that defines the standard for ethnic groups (Bellah et al. 1985, 8–13).

But if ethnicity appears as the last gasp of a sociological concern with exclusion, it also stands in violation of a democratic principle of inclusion. This appears to be the case even though ethnicity—in an inclusive and democratic culture such as America's—has been in decline (Alba 1990). Yet it does not follow that, because of the "thinness" of ethnicity in America, exclusion has been transcended. For Alba also discovered that what gives ethnicity its identity is the existence of something he calls *European-Americans*. White Americans define themselves on the basis of where their ancestors came from, knowing full well that at least one visible group of Americans—blacks—came from somewhere else. If Alba is correct, then no matter how inclusive ethnic identity has become, it is still, among whites, exclusive with respect to one extremely important aspect of American pluralism. It is precisely for this reason that ethnicity tends to be distrusted by those whose commitment to liberal democracy is more determinant than their commitment to sociological particularity. Karst (1989), for example, defines belongingness as membership in a national community, not as participation in the rituals of ethnic subcultures that may be exclusionary, even though a national community of abstract citizens cannot have the same kind of binding ties as the particular traditions and folk ways associated with ethnic origins.

Ought we then to welcome the weakening of ethnicity because our commitment to democracy is strong or to lament it because our commitment to community takes priority? Phrased in this "strong" form, the question begs a third alternative. One has been offered by Mary Waters, who argues that "one can have a strong sense of ethnic identity without a specific idea that ethnicity means anything." In her account, Americans have options: "Ethnicity is increasingly a personal choice of whether to be ethnic at all, and, for an increasing majority of people, of which ethnicity to be" (1990, 145, 147). Since ethnic choice reinforces ethnic identity, Americans can solve the problem posed by the choice between predemocratic communitarian longings and postdemocratic individualistic desires. We can choose something to which we can belong while at the same time being free to choose. These are attractive ways to try and reconcile democratic inclusion and sociological exclusion, but in the final analysis they do not work. If people can pick and choose their ethnic group, then the group can no longer serve the function of particularity. Ethnicity would become simply one more option among the many options offered by a liberal and capitalist democracy. But although she has not found a third alternative between democracy and sociology, Waters hits on the crucial point: how we think of a boundary like ethnicity is connected to how we understand the "givenness" of the boundary. For Waters is arguing that the boundaries between ethnic groups are no longer given; they have become socially constructed, in ways similar to the boundaries between genders or between those with different sexual preferences (Eisenstein and Jardine 1980; Epstein 1988; Greenberg 1988). Any discussion of ethnicity, indeed any discussion of difference, has to focus on the kind of difference, on the nature of the boundary itself.

This is not the time or the place to argue whether ethnic boundaries are in fact essentially determined or constructed by the activities of those whose lives are organized by them. I wish instead to make the point that there are legal, moral, and social implications involved in the ways in which one takes a position on this issue. If boundaries are given by forces that antedate the individual choices of those who live around them, such boundaries ought to be understood as crossable. If, on the other hand, the boundaries between groups are understood as socially constructed, there are grounds for concluding that we ought to respect them. For what we do, in respecting the constructed boundaries, is to respect the human and social potentials that enable people to make their own boundaries, just as what we do, in looking beyond given boundaries, is to search for ways that people ought not to be classified against their will.

This is not the conclusion that many of those who argue for social construction may want to reach. They are more likely to suggest that, since boundaries have been put up, they can also be taken down. Indeed, the whole point of those who are fascinated by social construction arguments is usually to "deconstruct" the justifications for difference implied by any boundaries on the grounds that all boundaries are put up by power holders to reinforce their power over those unable to define boundaries themselves. In that sense, boundaries are chosen not by "us" but by "them." There is much truth in such a position; clearly, some definitions of the boundary between men and women reflected little more than a dominant male ideology, and the same could be said for race, ethnicity, and other distinctions. The vibrancy with which feminists and scholars of race and ethnicity have demonstrated the alien character of boundaries constructed by others has clearly altered the way everyone has to think about distinction.

Yet the matter cannot be put to rest. For to view boundaries as invariably created by "their" power over "us" is to denigrate the capacity of people to change the definitions of the boundaries around them. For every boundary that is ascribed, others can be achieved. But to think this way means, not to reject all boundaries, but instead to give special recognition to those boundaries that are the products of human action. If we do not, we are more likely to find them replaced, not with the absence of any boundaries at all, but with boundaries that cannot be altered because we lack the conceptual skills to recognize and understand them.

The Thoughtfulness of Boundaries

A third way to distinguish between boundaries is to evaluate whether the cognitive skills that went into putting them into place are more rational and justifiable. If we value human rational faculties the way, for example, that Habermas (1987) does, then we would naturally be inclined to value boundaries that make use of them. The most justifiable boundaries would be those that were the product of some model of communicative action that called on the skills of the members of society.

One way to illustrate this concern with the thoughtfulness of boundaries is to examine concrete conflicts between democratic inclusion and sociological exclusion. Consider, for example, what are commonly called NIMBY (for "not in my backyard") movements. Americans are now predisposed to question the placement of nearly all public facilities in their neighborhoods. From the perspective of sociological exclusion, NIMBY movements seem worth celebrating. They speak to the needs of neighborhood and community. They develop without official leadership in spontaneous, organic form and constitute an example of people taking responsibility for their own lives, especially for the lives of those with whom they are in close contact. Yet, from the perspective of democratic inclusion, there is also much that ought to cause concern. It is not only the dirty and the dangerous that are rejected; in some cases, neighborhood organizations have protested the placement of playgrounds, old age homes, and other seemingly more benign activities. But even the dirty and the dangerous raise troubling moral issues: if not here, then where? Do local communities have obligations to strangers? Can we as a collectivity make rational decisions about how to dispose of our wastes? Do NIMBY movements shift the location of the dirty and the dangerous to places whose residents have neither the means nor the time to protest? Do we not all have a stake in helping those with AIDS? Is there any fundamental difference between the selfishness of the invididual ego and the selfishness of the group, especially when life in modern society has become as interdependent as it has?

The kinds of questions raised by NIMBY movements are often impossible to answer satisfactorily, but in thinking about them the least we can do is to raise the issue of the thoughtfulness of public response to them. When a community seeks to protect itself against "outsiders" and "strangers," are its wishes a kind of ignorant reaction against the unknown or instead a thoughtful response to a difficult dilemma of public policy? Ask people, especially in their local settings, whether they want prisons in their neighborhoods, taxes raised to pay for the homeless, or an AIDS facility nearby, and their answers are likely to be negative. But ask them if society does indeed have an obligation to the unfortunate, and their answers may well be positive.

Americans, it would seem, often speak in two languages as a way of reconciling the tension between democratic inclusion and sociological exclusion (Bellah et al. 1985, 152–62). Philosophers have expressed a similar idea by talking of first-order and second-order preferences as a way of distinguishing between choices and choices about choices (Frankfurt 1988). Both ways of thinking reflect a general reluctance to accept as a true statement of a group's preferences points of view that appear to be the product of unthoughtful, emotion-laden prejudice. By not taking the first response of a group as its final response, such a way of thinking causes us to look further for more thoughtfulness. While there is a danger in so doing—the Marxist theory of false consciousness still serves as a warning against dismissing what people say about themselves too readily—it does seem as if people do speak in both a sociological and a democratic language at the same time. In thinking about the boundaries that people want to draw between themselves and strangers, the trick is to discover which language ought to have the greater currency.

One way to approach this problem is to use the concept of a moral passage. Moral passages are those special moments of clarity imposed by a break with the routines of daily life. We are, at all moments of our lives, moral creatures in the sense that what we do has implications for what others can and cannot do. But much of our moral agency is carried out without forethought; well-functioning social institutions enable individuals to act "normally" in the sense that they do not have to think at every waking moment about the implications of what they do. Despite the flow of ordinary life, however, there come, for most people, special moments that seem to stop the flow of time and demand special moral thoughtfulness. These moments of moral passage are often marked off by rituals, such as marriage, which, at one level, is about a relationship with another person but, at another level, is about a very special relationship with a very special person. Moral passages can be anticipated, but they can also come on us unexpectedly. As Kathryn Pyne Addelson has pointed out, the decision to have or not to have an abortion constitutes a moment of moral passage, bringing with it inevitable reflections about how one leads one's life in relation to others, including others not yet born. (For the concept of moral passages, used here in a different way than she intended, see Addelson 1991.)

Boundaries that are the product of a moral passage ought to have more benefit of the doubt than those that are the products of unreflective considerations. To illustrate some of the issues involved in the "thoughtfulness" that goes into boundaries, we can turn to the issue of busing for public school students in order to achieve the objective of racial equality. Here is a classic dilemma between respecting the sociological particular, in this case the desires of white parents to have their children attend school in their neighborhood, and respecting universal democratic principles, in this case the belief that integrated schools will improve the life chances of children from minority racial backgrounds. There are, clearly, opinions on both sides of the matter: those who would override local objections as well as those who would defend "turf" and the primacy of neighborhood. (For an excellent statement of the dilemma, see Hochschild 1984.) The concept of a moral passage in this context is offered to shift the discussion from the abstract qualities of particulars and locals to the specifics of particular situations.

Although one could disagree with my assessment, the accounts of the Boston school wars indicate enough controversy and moments of reflection outside the normalities of everyday life to have constituted a moment of moral passage. (For treatments that are fair to all sides, see Formisano 1991 and Lukas 1985.) White parents opposed to the judicial enforcement of busing requirements did not just make their opinion known in the relatively cost-free form of an answer to a survey. They maintained their opinion in the face of newspapers that accused them of racism, judges who dismissed their concerns, and a series of confrontations that took them out of their local worlds into the national news. In general, people who become exposed to the world outside their local communities tend to grow in the process. When people are exposed to ideas other than those associated with their local community and then still insist on their original ideas, those ideas ought to be accorded more respect than when expressed in their particular form. Because the white parents of Boston experienced such a moment of moral passage, we should be careful in overriding the particular in favor of the universal.

There are situations in New York City that seem to stand in sharp contrast to the Boston events. The emotional rage that led to the killing of an innocent black who happened to walk into a neighborhood whose residents consider it white illustrates the problem. (For a journalistic account, see Sleeper 1990.) Here was something close to tribalism, a withdrawal of whites from the larger world into a defense of turf with little exposure to national issues. In that sense the whites of Bensonhurst did not experience a moment of moral passage. Their defense of their locality was, like many tribal situations, based on implicit coercion, the primacy of blood, and an us/them mentality that dismissed any possibility of worth in their antagonists. Because the expression of support for locality and neighborhood in this context was premised on reinforcement of primary sentiments as opposed to exposure to new sentiments, there are grounds for believing that the particular should give way to the universal.

The concept of a moral passage is meant as one way to approach the thoughtfulness that goes into the construction of a boundary. It is an attempt that does not necessarily ask for perfectly rational communication but instead requires a more minimal indication that members of a group have at some point had to consider the position of an other. Before we tear down all boundaries, this way of thinking asks, we must first at least try to understand why it is that people may want a boundary. We may find that they are not sure, that their desire for the boundary is simply a projection of fears about the world outside their sociological group, that the boundary, in that sense, is meant to prevent them from ever coming into contact with a more inclusive and pluralistic world. But we might also discover that they are aware of the world outside their sociological particulars, that they recognize and understand the competing claims of others, but that, having been exposed to all that, they still want to protect the boundary that distinguishes their neighborhood from others. Discovering that the latter is in the fact the case does not necessarily mean that the boundary is justified;

all these matters are too complex to be reduced to any simple formulas. But it does offer us one more way of thinking about the nature of the boundary itself before making judgments about its legitimacy.

Conclusion

The debate over boundaries cannot really be a debate over the question of whether they ought to exist. It is as impossible to imagine a society without boundaries as it is inconceivable for modern liberal democracies to return to a feudalism in which boundaries are everything. Boundaries are both here to stay but also here to be crossed.

Those who share both a sociological respect for the group lives of real people and a democratic commitment to the universal rights of abstract agents have little choice but to concern themselves with the rules that both protect and violate social boundaries. If we become too carried away by the invidious consequences of difference, we will extend equality, but at the price of homogeneity. At some point we ought to ask ourselves if the harm done by difference—and there will usually always be harm done by difference—ought to be tolerated as the cost of a more variegated and rich world of meaning. But if we become too carried away by difference rather than its abolition, we will protect the group life of civil society, but at the cost of unfairness and discrimination. At some point we will have to ask ourselves whether the harm done by such discrimination is not so great that we ought to pay the cost in a little more uniformity.

How, then, do we know when we ought to respect sociological exclusion or democratic inclusion? This is a meta-question of universals and particulars that itself can have neither a universal nor a particular answer. Those who seek to preserve and protect social groups in civil society may be tempted to argue for the primacy of the particular. But to argue that the particular must always triumph is to use universal language to justify particular claims, thereby slipping an unwanted moral absolutism into a defense of contingency and circumstance. Those who want to abolish difference, or at least to limit its effects, apply a universalistic formula to achieve universalistic results, which is never going to convince advocates of particularism. For these reasons it makes far more sense to argue that there ought not to be universal answers—of either the particular or the universal type—to the meta-question of the moral principles by which our moral principles ought to be guided. Whether the universal or the particular ought to guide us can be determined only by the specific kinds of moral controversies with which we are confronted. The resulting uncertainty may be a difficult thing with which to live, but those who want to be good sociologists and good democrats simultaneously ought to make the effort.

References

Addelson, Kathryn Pyne. "Moral Passages." In *Impure Thoughts: Essays on Philosophy, Feminism, and Ethics*. Philadelphia: Temple University Press, 1991.

Alba, Richard. *Ethnic Identity: The Transformation of White America*. New Haven, Conn.: Yale University Press, 1990.

Bellah, Robert, Richard Madsen, William M. Sullivan, Ann Swidler, and Steven M. Tipton. *Habits of the Heart: Individualism and Commitment in American Life*. Berkeley and Los Angeles: University of California Press, 1985.

Benhabib, Seyla. "The Generalized and Concrete Other." In *Women and Moral Theory*, ed. Eva Kittay and Diane Meyers. Totowa, N.J.: Rowman & Littlefield, 1988.

Cannadine, David. *The Decline and Fall of the British Aristocracy*. New Haven, Conn.: Yale University Press, 1990.

Cohen, Anthony P. *The Symbolic Construction of Communities*. London: Tavistock, 1985.

Cohen, Anthony P. "Of Symbols and Boundaries, or, Does Ertie's Greatcoat Hold the Key?" In *Symbolising Boundaries: Identity and Diversity in British Cultures*, ed. Anthony P. Cohen. Manchester: University of Manchester Press, 1986.

Coser, Lewis. *The Functions of Social Conflict*. Glencoe, Ill.: Free Press, 1956.

Derrida, Jacques. *Disseminations*. Chicago: University of Chicago Press, 1981.

Douglas, Mary. *Natural Symbols: Explorations in Cosmology*. New York: Pantheon, 1970.

Eisenstein, Hester, and Alice Jardine. *The Future of Difference*. Boston: Hall, 1980.

Epstein, Cynthia. *Deceptive Distinctions: Sex, Gender and the Social Order*. New Haven, Conn.: Yale University Press, 1988.

Formisano, Ronald P. *Boston against Busing: Race, Class and Ethnicity in the 1960s and 1970s*. Chapel Hill: University of North Carolina Press, 1991.

Frankfurt, Harry. "Freedom of the Will and the Concept of the Person." In *The Importance of What We Care About: Philosophical Essays*. Cambridge: Cambridge University Press, 1988.

Greenberg, David. *The Construction of Homosexuality*. Chicago: University of Chicago Press, 1988.

Habermas, Jurgen. *Lifeworld and System: A Critique of Functionalist Reason*. Vol. 2 of *The Theory of Communicative Action*. Translated by Thomas McCarthy. Boston: Beacon, 1987.

Hirsch, H. N. "The Threnody of Constitutional Liberty and the Renewal of Community." *Political Theory* 14 (August 1986): 423–89.

Hochschild, Jennifer. *The New American Dilemma: Liberal Democracy and School Desegregation*. New Haven, Conn.: Yale University Press, 1984.

Ignatieff, Michael. *The Needs of Strangers: An Essay on Privacy, Solidarity, and the Politics of Being Human*. New York: Penguin, 1985.

Johnson, Barbara. *A World of Difference*. Baltimore: Johns Hopkins University Press, 1987.

Karst, Kenneth L. *Belonging to America: Equal Citizenship and the Constitution*. New Haven, Conn.: Yale University Press, 1989.

Lukas, J. Anthony. *Common Ground: A Turbulent Decade in the Lives of Three American Families*. New York: Knopf, 1985.

Marshall, T. H. "Citizenship and Social Class." In *Class, Citizenship, and Social Development*, ed. S. M. Lipset. Garden City, N.Y.: Anchor, 1964.

Minow, Martha. *Making All the Difference: Inclusion, Exclusion and American Law*. Ithaca, N.Y.: Cornell University Press, 1990.

Nash, Roderick Frazier. *The Rights of Nature: A History of Environmental Ethics*. Madison: University of Wisconsin Press, 1989.

Needham, Rodney. *Symbolic Classification*. Santa Monica, Calif.: Goodyear, 1979.

Porter, Rosemary Pedalino. *Forked Tongue: The Politics of Bilingual Education*. New York: Basic, 1990.

Rosenau, Pauline Marie. *Post-Modernism and the Social Sciences: Insights, Inroads, and Intrusions*. Princeton, N.J.: Princeton University Press, 1991.

Sandel, Michael J. *Liberalism and the Limits of Justice*. Cambridge: Cambridge University Press, 1982.

Sleeper, Jim. *The Closest of Strangers: Liberalism and the Politics of Race in New York*. New York: Norton, 1990.

Waters, Mary C. *Ethnic Options: Choosing Identities in America*. Berkeley and Los Angeles: University of California Press, 1990.

Wolfe, Alan. *Whose Keeper? Social Science and Moral Obligation*. Berkeley and Los Angeles: University of California Press, 1989.

CONTRIBUTORS

Jeffrey C. Alexander is professor in and chair of the Department of Sociology at the University of California, Los Angeles. His most recent books are *Rethinking Progress: Movements, Forces, and Ideas at the End of the 20th Century* and *Postpositivist Sociology: Essays on Rationality, Relativism, and the Problem of Progress.*

Nicola Beisel is assistant professor of sociology at Northwestern University. Her research focuses on the roles of family and culture in class formation. She is currently completing a book manuscript entitled *Morality and Class Formation: Censorship and the Upper Class in America, 1870–1900.*

Randall Collins is professor of sociology at the University of California, Riverside. His books include *Weberian Sociological Theory* (1986), *Theoretical Sociology* (1988), and *Sociology of Marriage and the Family: Gender, Love and Property* (3d ed. coauthored with Scott Coltrane, 1990).

Diana Crane is professor of sociology at the University of Pennsylvania. She is the author of several books on the sociology of culture, including *The Transformation of the Avant-Garde* and *The Production of Culture: Media Industries and Urban Arts.*

Paul DiMaggio is professor of sociology at Princeton University. He has written widely on organizations and culture and is editor of *Nonprofit Enterprise in the Arts* (1986), *Structures of Capital: The Social Organization of Economic Life* (with Sharon Zukin, 1989), and *The New Institutionalism in Organizational Analysis* (with Walter W. Powell, 1991). He is also the author of *Managers of the Arts* (1986) and *Race, Ethnicity and Participation in the Arts* (with Francie Ostrower, 1992). A recipient of a fellowship from the Center for Advanced Studies in the Behavioral Sciences and the John Simon Guggenheim Memorial

Foundation, he is completing a book on the social organization of the arts in the United States.

Cynthia Fuchs Epstein is Distinguished Professor of Sociology at the Graduate Center of the City University of New York. Her work has focused on the interplay between structure and culture in the professions, occupations, and political spheres and on the analyses of theoretical and methodological problems in gender research. Her books include *Woman's Place, Women in Law,* and *Deceptive Distinctions: Sex, Gender and the Social Order.*

Marcel Fournier is professor in and chair of the Department of Sociology at the Université de Montréal. His published work has focused on the history of sociology, sociological theory, the sociology of culture and higher education, and the sociology of science and intellectual life. Author of several books, he is currently working on *Marcel Mauss: Le Savant et le militant.*

Herbert J. Gans is the Robert S. Lund Professor of Sociology at Columbia University. He is the author of eight books, including *The Urban Villagers, The Levittowners, Popular Culture and High Culture, Deciding What's News, Middle American Individualism,* and, most recently, *People, Plans and Policies.* He is currently studying the effect of the conception of the underclass and the undeserving poor on antipoverty policy. He is past president of the Eastern Sociological Society and the American Sociological Association.

Joseph R. Gusfield is professor emeritus of sociology at the University of California, San Diego. Among his major work are *Symbolic Crusade: Status Politics and the American Temperance Movement* and *The Culture of Public Problems: Drinking-Driving and the Symbolic Order.* His current interests are in social ritual and symbol, sociology of law, social movements, and the rhetoric of social science.

John R. Hall is professor of sociology at the University of California, Davis. He is the author of *The Ways Out: Utopian Communal Groups in an Age of Babylon* and *Gone from the Promised Land: Jonestown in American Cultural History.* His most recent book is *Culture: Sociological Perspective* (with coauthor Mary Jo Neitz). Currently, he is using hermeneutics and discourse analysis to elaborate sociohistorical inquiry as an enterprise that transcends conventional disciplinary boundaries. This project in postpositivist epistemology is the subject of a book with the working title *History and Society: On Discourse and Sociohistorical Inquiry.*

David Halle was born and educated in England. He is associate professor of sociology at the State University of New York at Stony Brook and the University of California, Los Angeles. He is the author of *America's Working Man* (1984). His chapter on abstract art is part of a forthcoming study of the meaning of art and culture as displayed in the homes of a cross section of social classes in the New York region.

Michèle Lamont teaches sociology at Princeton University. Her published work has focused on comparative stratification, contemporary social theory, and the sociology of culture and knowledge. She is the author of *Money, Morals, and Manners: The Culture of the French and the American Upper-Middle Class* (1992). She is currently working on a book on French and American working-class culture that analyzes the symbolic boundaries typically drawn by white and African-American men who live in the New York suburbs and by white and Algerian men who live in the Paris suburbs.

Richard A. Peterson is professor of sociology at Vanderbilt University. He is the coeditor (with Melton McLaurin) of *Singing Stories: Lyrical Themes in Country Music* (in press). He is currently working on a monograph titled *The Fabrication of Authenticity*, which deals with the creation of country music genres in the second quarter of the twentieth century.

Albert Simkus is an assistant professor at the University of North Carolina at Charlotte. His primary work involves studies of objective measures of social distances between classes in formerly socialist Eastern Europe. He is also doing studies of comparative differences in attitudes toward egalitarianism.

Alan Wolfe is the Michael E. Gellert Professor of Sociology and Political Science and dean of the Graduate Faculty, New School for Social Research. His books include *The Limits of Legitimacy, Whose Keeper?* and *America at Century's End*. A frequent reviewer and essayist for popular publications, Wolfe has recently finished a manuscript on sociology and the human subject.

Vera Zolberg is a senior lecturer in the Department of Sociology of the Graduate Faculty, New School for Social Research, in New York City. Acting director of the Committee on Liberal Studies, she works on aspects of the sociology of culture, the arts, education, race, and gender. Her book *Constructing a Sociology of Art* was published in 1990. Currently, she is writing a book on the avant-garde art movements of the turn of the century as an international phenomenon related to rising new status communities. In addition, she is completing a book on the American art museum.

INDEX

Abbey, Henry, 33
Abbey Theatre, 49n.17
Aborn, Milton, 50n.22
Abortion, 278
Abrams, M. H., 76
Abstract art, x, 10, 63, 131–51, 199;
  audience for, 131–51; definition of,
  136–37
Academy Opera, 33
Acting, 223–26. *See also* Theater; Occupations
Adams, Margaret, 247
Addelson, Kathryn Pyne, 321
Adelphi College, 53n.34
Aesthetic dance. *See* Dance
Aesthetics, viii, x–xii, 21–57 passim, 58,
  61–62, 152, 154, 188, 197, 204, 223,
  263–64; and middle class culture,
  217; and musical taste, 154; as an aspect of culture production, 224; as criteria for gatekeeping, 61, 62; as a human right, 197; internal and external
  sources of, 263–64; in legitimating ideologies of the high culture model, 21–
  57 passim; of art objects, 131, 134–
  35; in household styles, 219–21
A.F.L. (American Federation of Labor),
  234, 240
African-American minstrelsy, 51n.28
African-Americans, 65, 164–65, 167. *See
  also* Race; Racism
Age, 12, 14, 105, 106, 108–11, 118–
  19, 232, 234, 319; and class distinctions in culture, 266; and musical
  taste, 164; old age homes and NIMBY
  movements, 319; perception of chil-

dren in Western history, 76; youth and
  obscenity, 105, 108, 109–11, 118–
  19; youthful attraction to new styles,
  61
AIDS, 313–14, 320
Alba, Richard, 317
Alcott, William, 88
Aldrich, Nelson W. Jr., 277
Alexander, Jeffrey C., 12, 14, 258, 278,
  311
Allan, Maud (dancer), 39, 51n.20,
  52n.32
Allentown, Pa., 37
Allies, 299
Althusser, Louis, 3, 302n.5
American Ballet, 41–42
American Drama League, 24
American Opera Company, 35–36
American Southwest, 72n.4
American Temperance Society, 82
Amon Duul II, 67
Anomie, 89
Antiques, 224–25
Appalachia, 243
Archimedes, 257
Aristotle, 304n.9
Armelagos, George, 80, 81
Art, 10, 21–57, 60, 61, 131–51, 152–
  86, 187–209, 223–25, 266, 278;
  and conflicts over cultural standards,
  278; and male dominance of culture,
  266; fine art, as a model for opera,
  38; literature and obscenity, 104–
  27; paintings and obscenity, 121,
  123; performing arts, 21–57;
  visual arts, abstract, 131–51;

Art (*continued*)
visual arts, in museums, 187–209;
women as sellers of, 224–25. *See also*
Dance; Music; Opera; Theater
Art collecting, x, 63, 131–51, 199, 275
Art criticism, 61, 144
Art forms, 10, 21–57 passim, 67, 76,
187–209, 221; as cultural boundaries,
22; avant-garde, education about, 202;
in museums, 192
Art galleries, 9, 62, 63, 64
Artists. *See* Art; Occupations
Art museums, 22, 39–40, 62, 70, 140,
141, 187–209, 223; Art Institute of
Chicago, 27; Boston Museum of
Fine Art, 53n.35; Centre Beaubourg
(Paris), 194, 200; Centre Beaubourg,
criticism of, 191, 200; Centre Pompi-
dou (Paris), 193–94, 204; Guggen-
heim Museum (New York), 14; Hart-
ford, Conn. (art museum in), 41;
Metropolitan Museum of Art (New
York), 141; Museum of Modern Art
(New York), 14, 41, 46–47, 70; Museum of Modern Art, as national institution, 46–47; Whitney Museum
(New York), 141. *See also* Museums
Art organizations, 22–57; nonprofit, in
urban centers, 22. *See also* Museums;
Drama clubs and guilds
AT&T, 238
Audiences, 10, 22–57 passim, 59, 60–
61, 67–68, 71, 88, 131–51, 152, 154,
170–71, 190, 223; and recognition of
cultural products, 60–61; culture producers in, 223; diversity of, 71; female, for dance, 39, 40; for antimasturbation lectures, 88; for music concerts,
152, 154, 170–71; for theater, 25–26,
28; manipulation of, 68
Avant-garde in art and culture, 62, 63,
64, 66, 70, 71, 199, 202, 204; and
overthrow of art establishments, 199

Balanchine, George, 41, 42, 50n.23,
54n.37; and dance as an art form, 42;
and Russian ballet tradition, 41
Ballet. *See* Dance
Ballet Caravan, 41–42

Ballet Russe de Monte Carlo, 39, 42,
50n.23
Baltimore, 53n.34
Baltzell, E. Digby, 116
Balzac, Honoré de, 63, 122; censorship
of, 122; literary works of, as canons of
classic high culture, 63
Barrows, Mr., 122
Barth, Fredrik, 272
Barthes, Roland, on food symbolism, 80,
81, 97, 302n.5
Battle of Britain, 293
Becker, Howard, 3, 60, 61, 72n.2, 224
Beethoven, Ludwig von, 40, 42, 47n.1,
52n.31, 54n.37
Beisel, Nicola, 9
Belasco, Warren, 91, 95
Bell, Daniel, 203, 267
Bellah, Robert, 311, 317, 320
Bellows, Ann, 240
Bendix, Reinhard, 272
Benhabib, Seyla, 311
Bennett, D. M., 125n.2
Bensman, Joseph, 153
Bentley, G. Carter, 273
Berg, Ivar, 236
Berger, Bennett, 216, 217
Berger, Peter, 5
Berlin, Irving, 36
Bernstein, Basil, 200
Bichat, Xavier (French physiologist), 82
Biggart, Nicole W., 263
Bilingualism in schools, 313–15
Bill of Rights, 295, 297
Birmingham School (sociology), 5
Black, Jack (writer), 265
Blacks. *See* African-Americans; Race;
Racism
Blatchford, Judge, 125n.2
Blatt, Martin Henry, 108
Blau, Peter M., 277
Blodgett, Geoffrey, 114
Bloom, Alan, 195
Blue collar. *See* Working class; Class
Boas, George, 76
Boccaccio, censorship of, 105, 117,
119–20, 122
Body, human, 9, 75–103 passim, 214,
223, 225; and cultural status produc-

CWA (Communications Workers of America), 242, 253n.6

Dallas, Texas, 206n.10
Damrosch, Leonard, 33
Dance, 21, 23, 24, 38–43, 44; aesthetic dance, 23–43; and morality, 24; ballet, 38, 39, 41–43, 134
Dante, 52n.31
Darbel, Alain, 188, 190, 194
Davidson, Laurie, 215–16, 220
Davis, Adelle, and contemporary health foods movement, 93, 94, 97
Davis, James A., 153, 155
de Certeau, Michel, 278
Deeter, Jaspar, 47n.4
Delaunay, Sonia, 143
Delsarte, François, 39, 51n.29
Delsartianism, influences on modern dance and women's health movement, 39, 51n.29, 52–53n.33, 53n.35
DeMille, Agnes (stage dancer and choreographer), 51n.25, 53n.34
DeMille, Cecil B., and dance, 40, 51n.25
Democracy, xiv, 10, 12, 218, 289, 291–300, 309–25; and art, 10, 187–209; and discourse of liberty, 12, 297; and symbolic classification of members, 291–300; vs. sociology, 309–25
Democratization, and art museums, 189, 192–94, 200, 201
Democrats, 299
Denishawn (school and dance company), 40
DeNora, Tia, 22
Depew, Chauncey, 48n.8
Derrida, Jacques, 6, 310
Detroit (Mich.), 26, 148n.3; survey of cultural practices in, 148n.3
Detroit Arts and Crafts Guild, patron of little theater, 27
Deviance, 3
Dewey, John, 310
Diaghilev, 39
Dickens, Charles, 63
Dickinson, Thomas H., 24, 26, 27
Dilthey, Wilhelm, 6, 16n.25
DiMaggio, Paul, xi, 8, 9, 64, 69, 132, 159, 165, 188, 190, 203, 223, 224

Doane, Janice, 267
Dobbs, S. M., 194, 195–96
Dodge, William, and NYSSV, 104
Dodworth, Allen, 38
Dollard, John, 270
Douglas, Ann, 267
Douglas, Mary, 3, 80, 81, 106–7, 124–25, 152, 219, 224, 243, 252n2, 310; and the anthropology of food symbolism, 80; on divisions in society and bodily metaphors, 106–7
Dows, David, 104
Drama, 8, 21, 23–30, 44, 221, 223, 297–98; and categories of pure and polluted discourse, 297–98. See also Theater
Drama clubs and guilds: Drama Committee of Boston's Twentieth Century Club, 23; Little Theatre Society of Indiana, 27; National Federation of Theatre Clubs, 26; National Theatre Conference, 45; New York Theatre Guild, 26; Plays and Players' Club (Philadelphia), 47n.5; Drama League of America, 25, 26
Duchamp, Marcel, 63–64
Duffus, R. L., 27, 43
Dufy, Raoul, 141
Duncan, Elizabeth, 52n.31
Duncan, Isadora, 40, 52n.31, 53nn.35 and 36, 54n.37; and dance as high culture, 52n.31
Duncan, Otis D., 277
Durkheim, Emile, 2, 6, 89, 152, 198, 217, 257, 258, 261, 277, 290, 300n.2, 304nn.10 and 12, 310, 311, 312; Durkheimian perspective, 6, 217, 256, 304n.12; notions of social solidarity of, 2, 311, 312; relations with work of Bourdieu, 257, 258, 261, 277
Dwight, T. S., and legitimacy of classical music standards, 29, 54n.37

Eastman School and dance, 41
Eaton, Quaintance, 32, 33, 34, 35, 36, 37
Ecole Sociologique Française, 2. See also Durkheim; Mauss